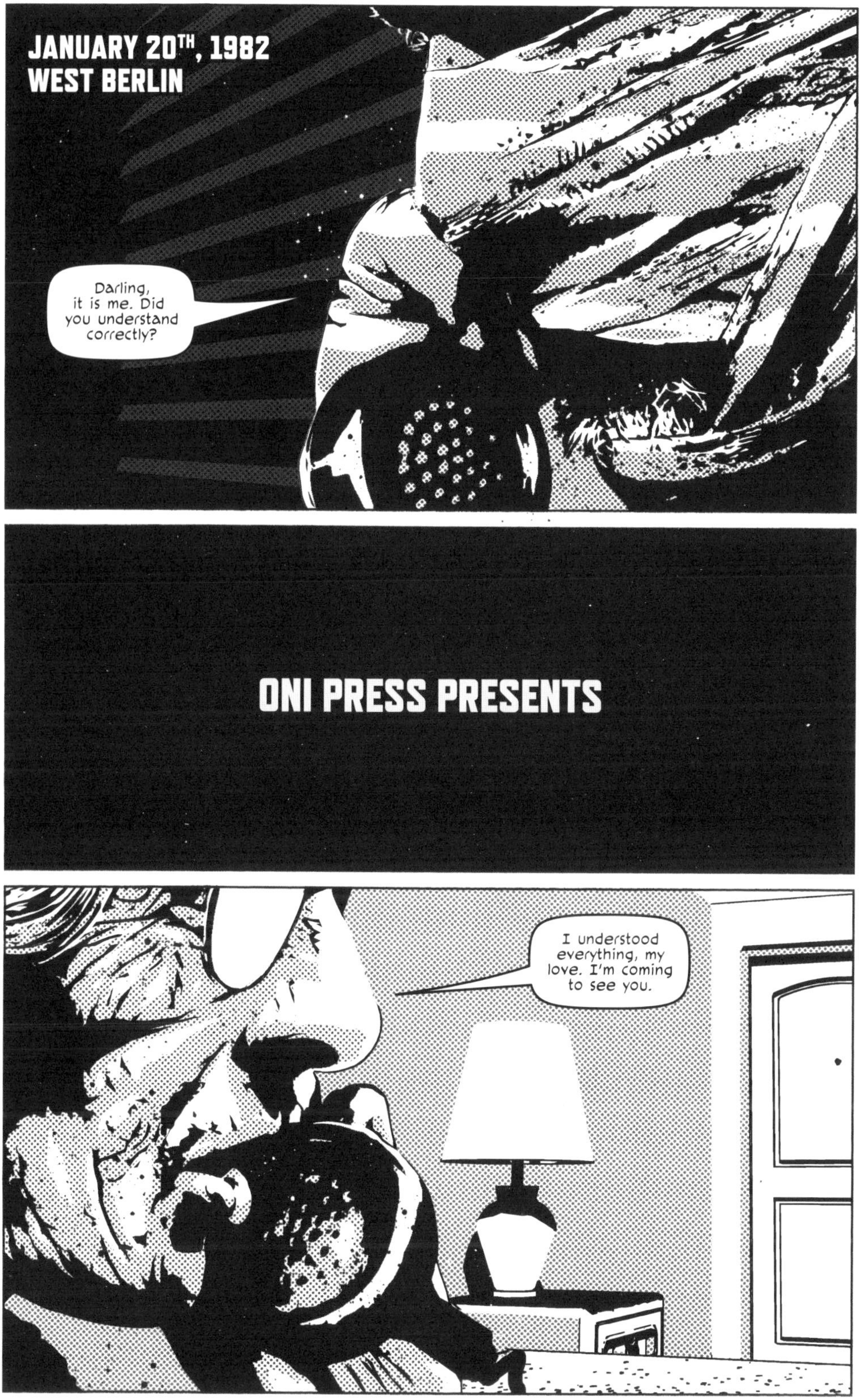
JANUARY 20TH, 1982
WEST BERLIN
Darling, it is me. Did you understand correctly?
ONI PRESS PRESENTS
I understood everything, my love. I'm coming to see you.

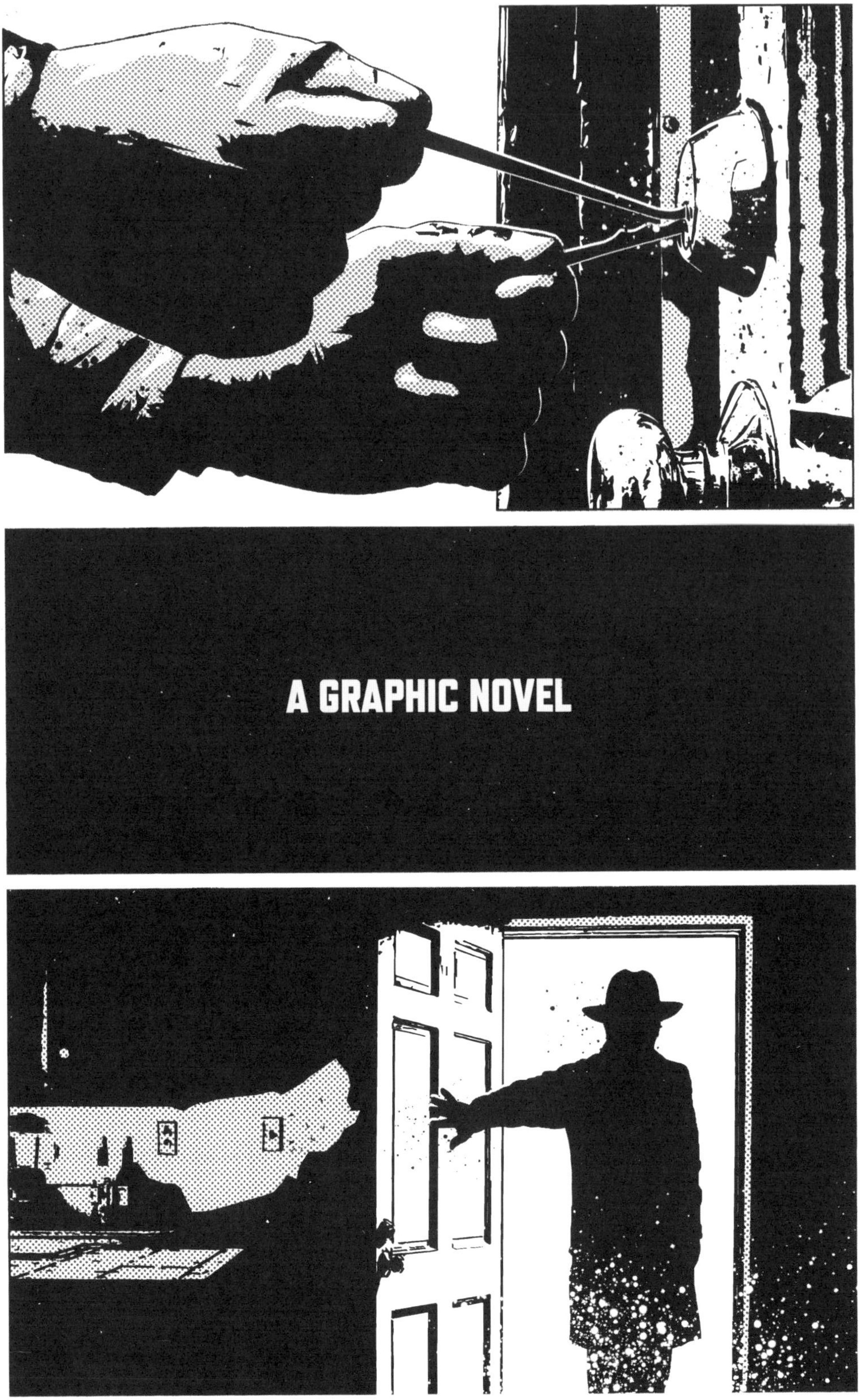
A GRAPHIC NOVEL

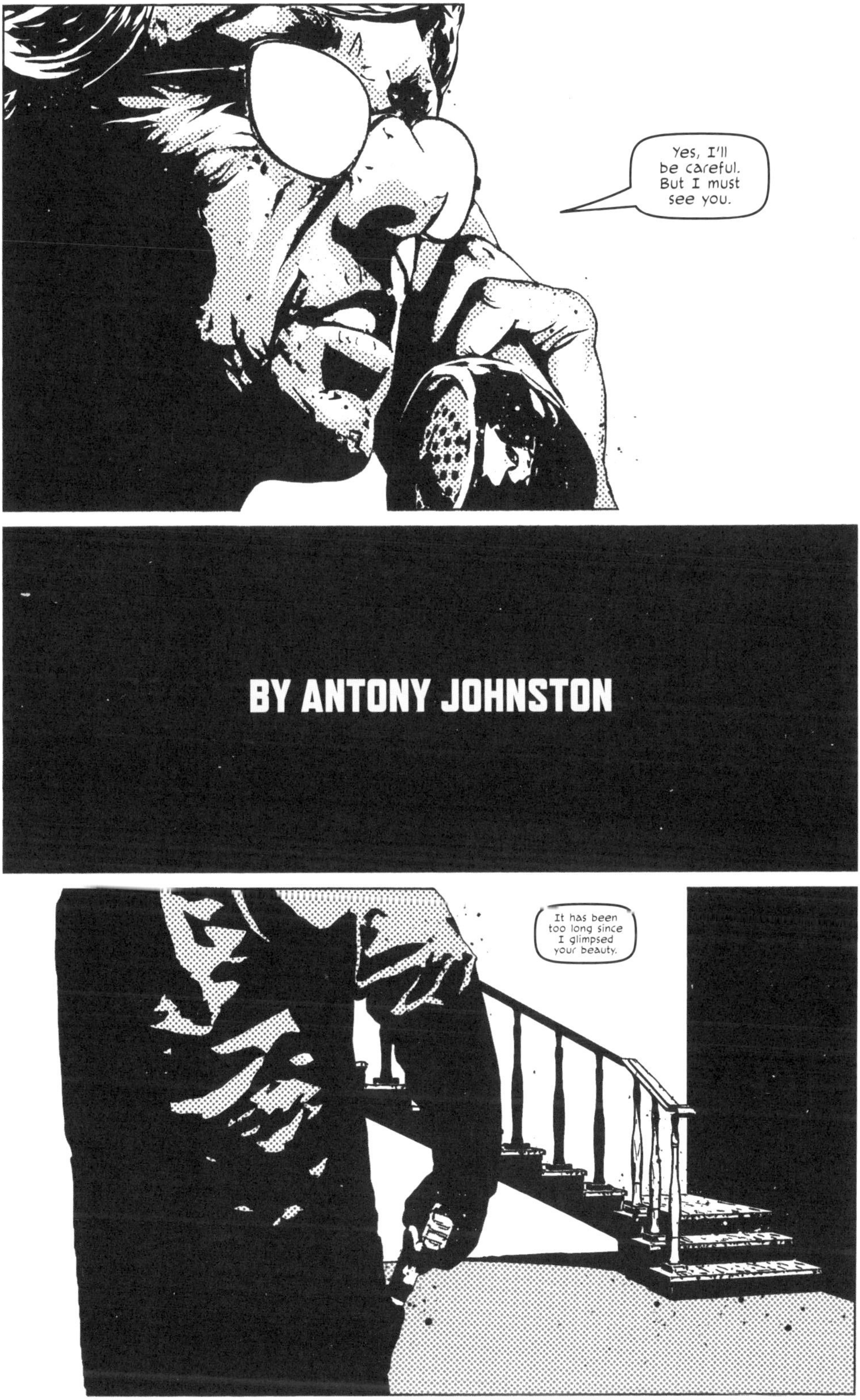
Yes, I'll be careful. But I must see you.
BY ANTONY JOHNSTON
It has been too long since I glimpsed your beauty.

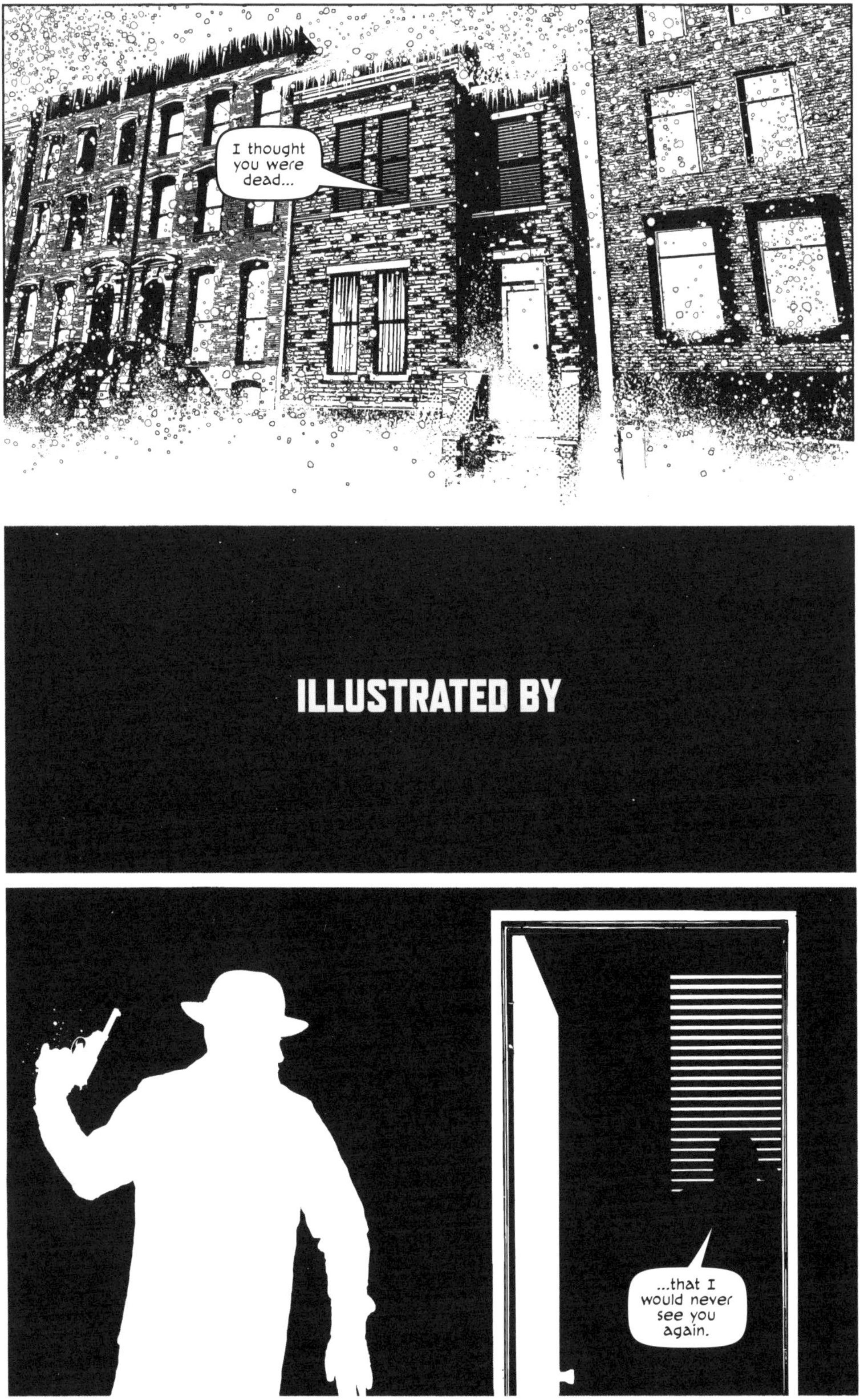
I thought you were dead...
ILLUSTRATED BY
...that I would never see you again.

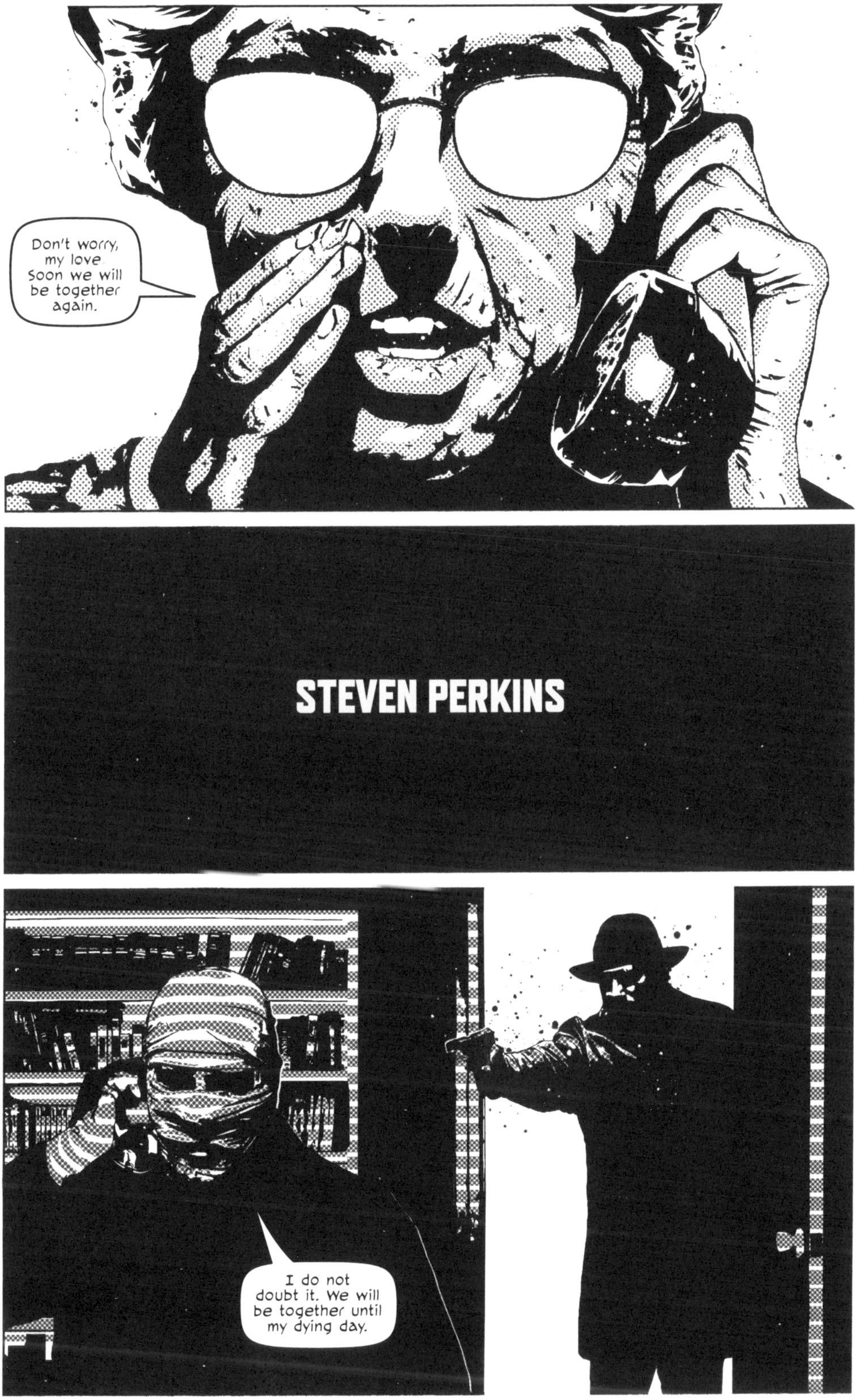
Don't worry, my love. Soon we will be together again.
STEVEN PERKINS
I do not doubt it. We will be together until my dying day.

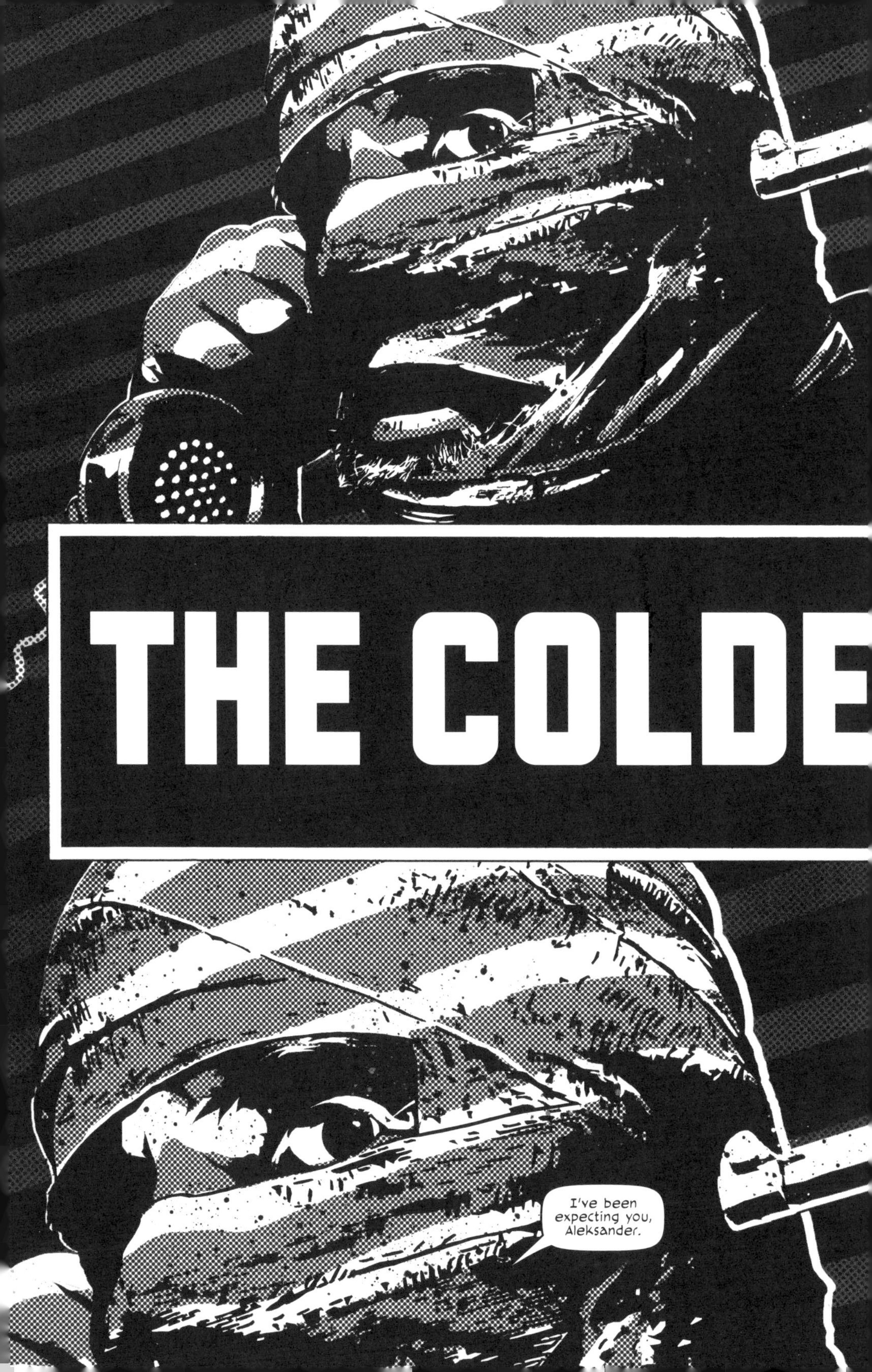
THE COLDE
I've been expecting you, Aleksander.

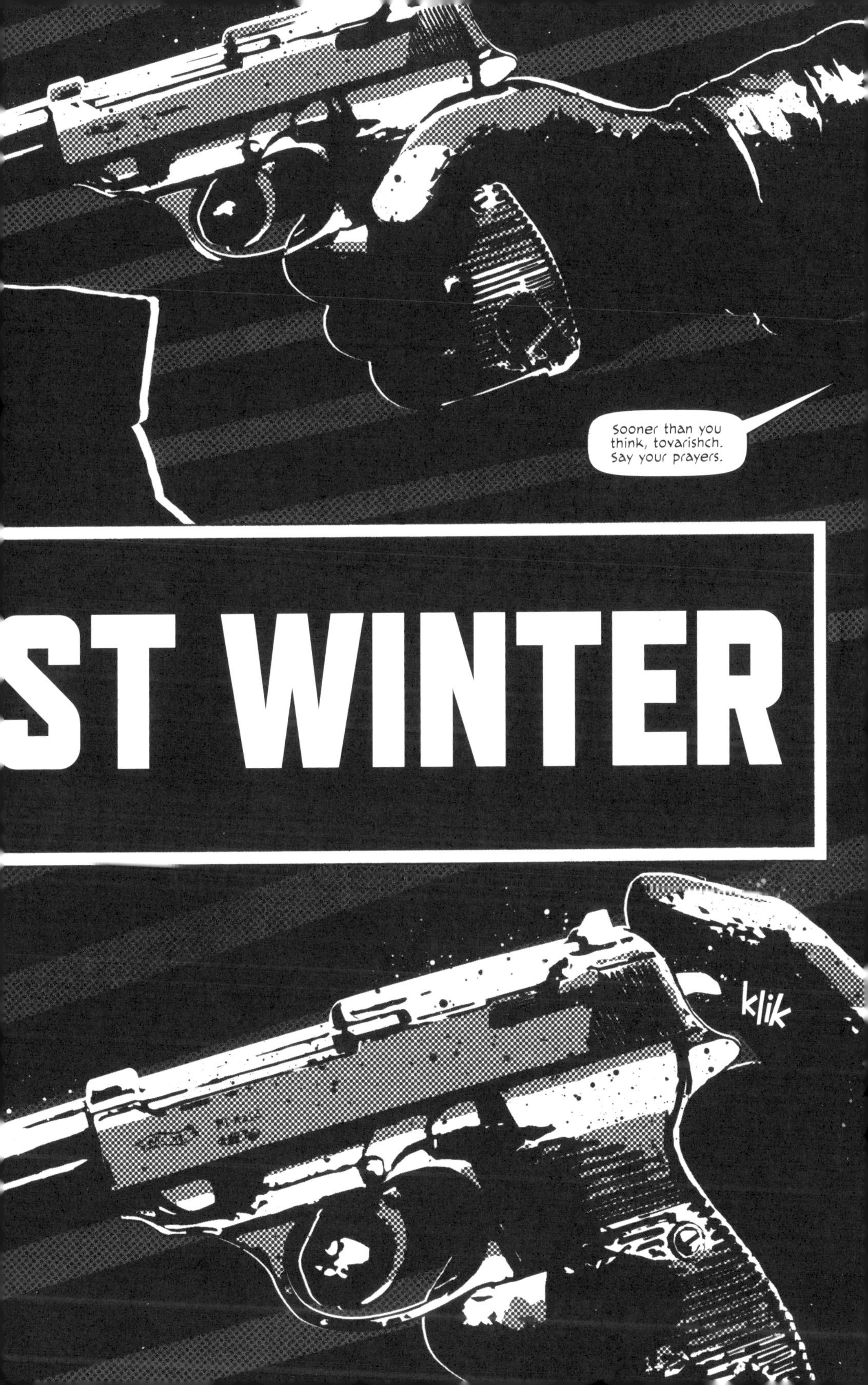
Sooner than you think, tovarishch. Say your prayers.
ST WINTER
klik

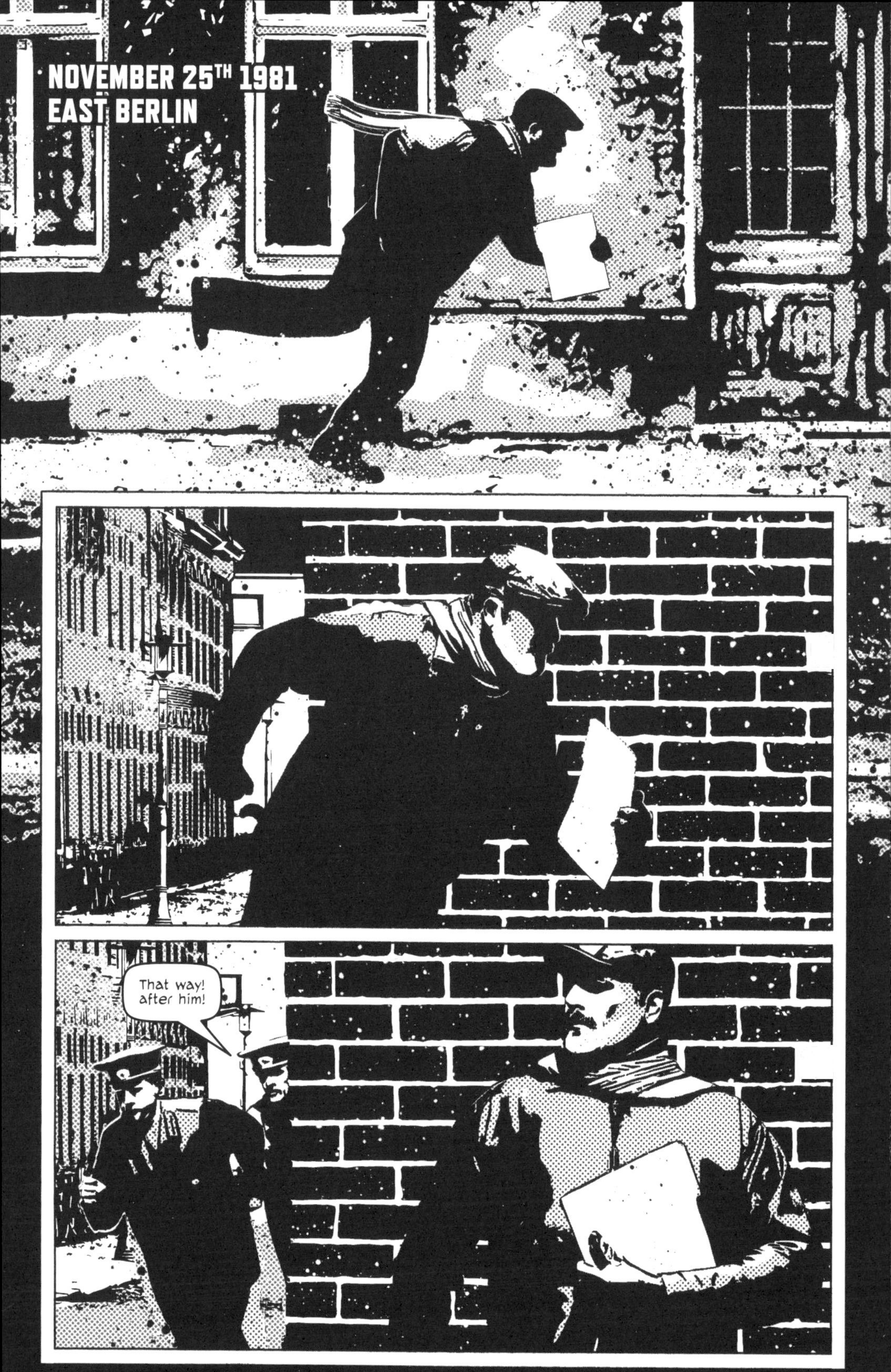
NOVEMBER 25TH 1981
EAST BERLIN
That way! after him!

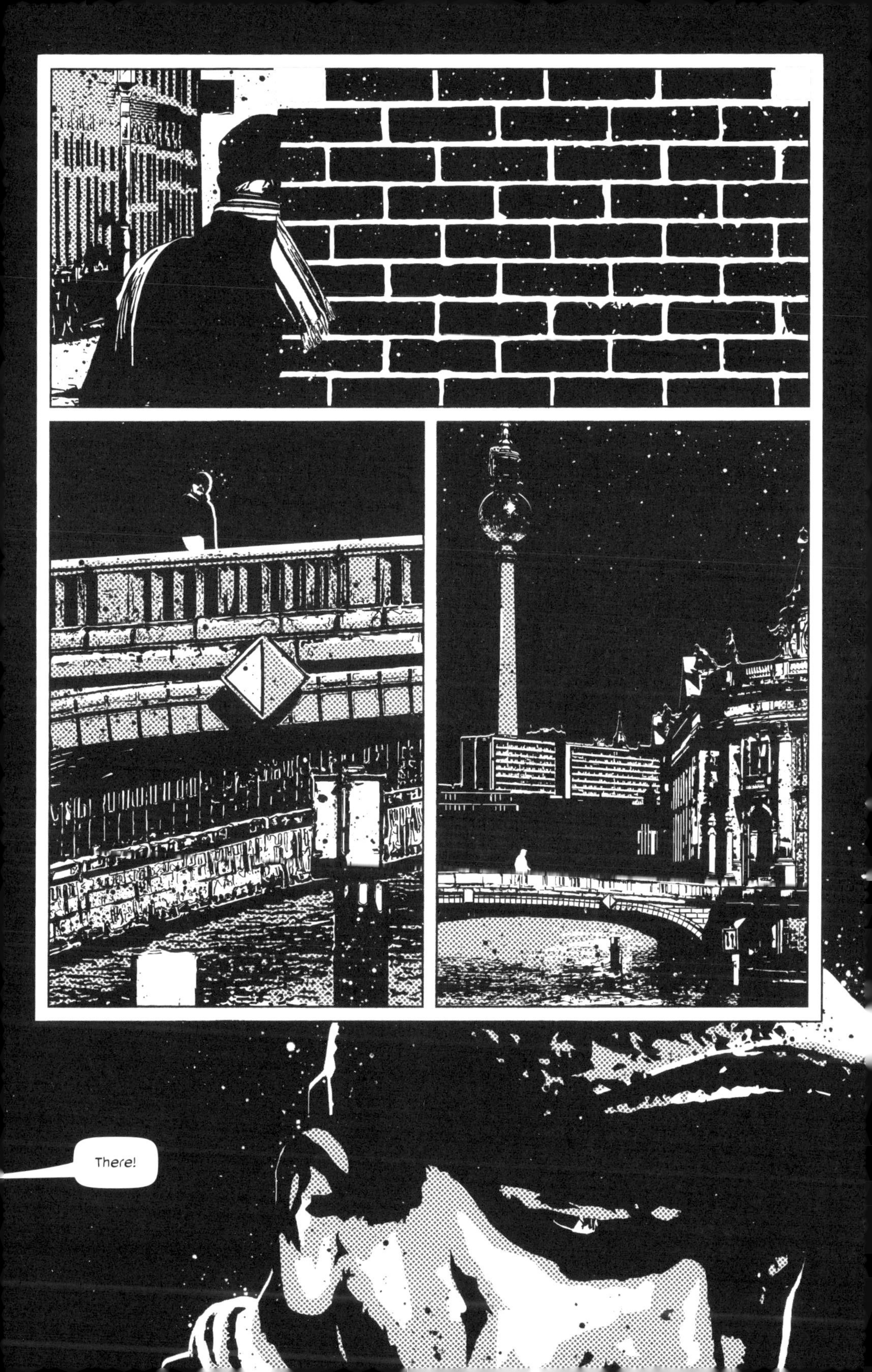
There!

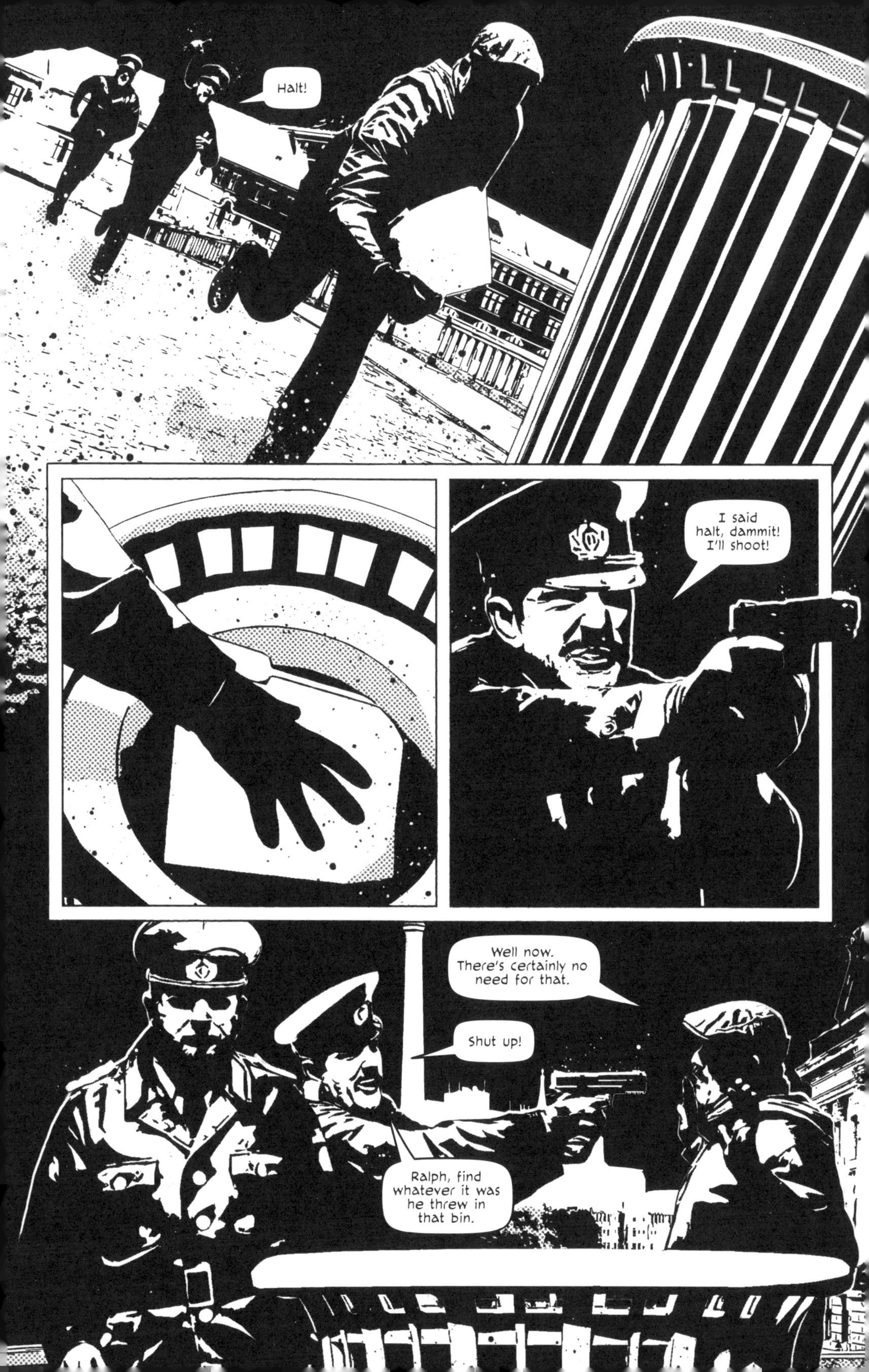
Halt!
I said halt, dammit! I'll shoot!
Well now. There's certainly no need for that.
Shut up!
Ralph, find whatever it was he threw in that bin.

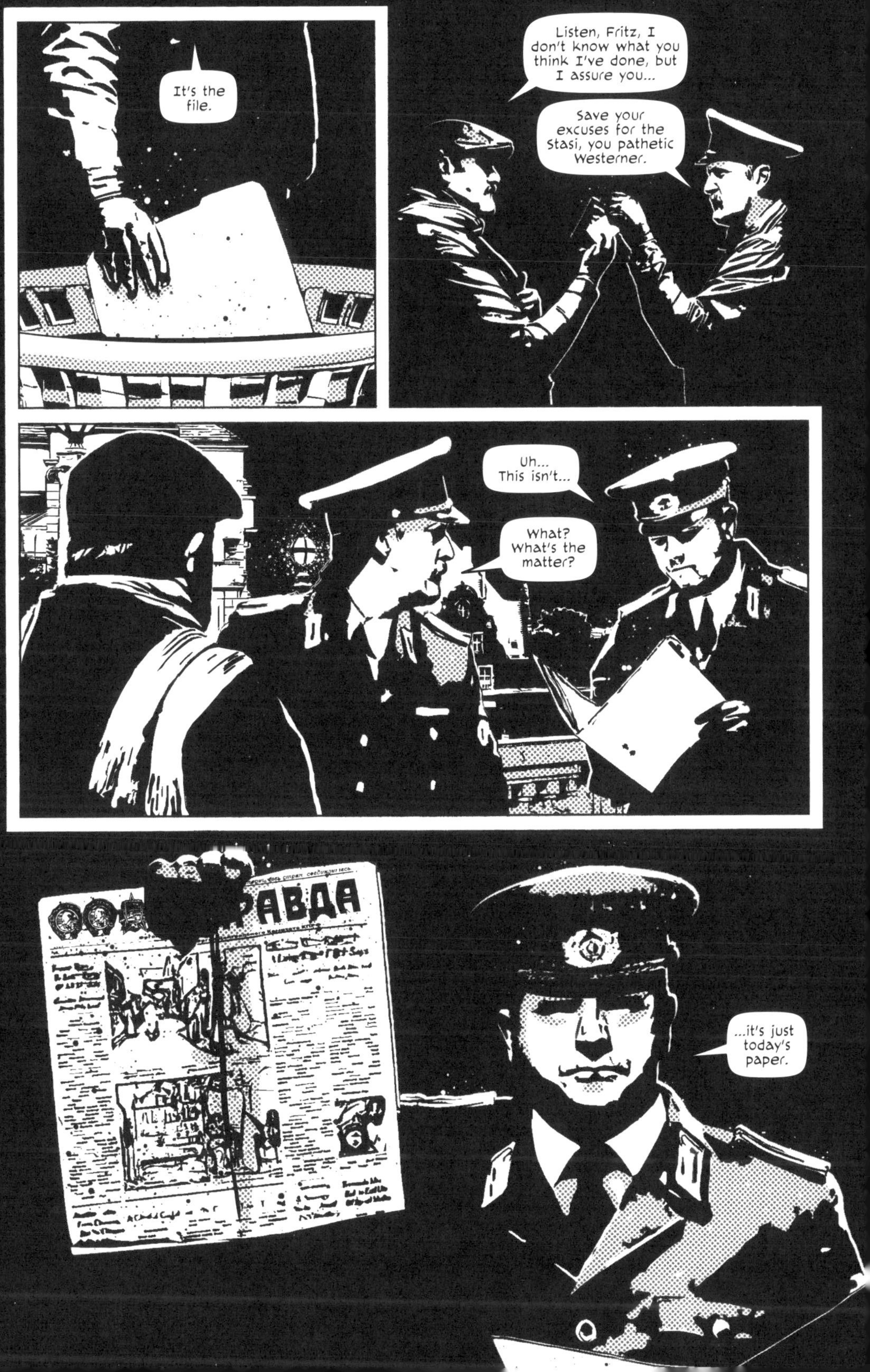
It's the file.
Listen, Fritz, I don't know what you think I've done, but I assure you...
Save your excuses for the Stasi, you pathetic Westerner.
Uh... This isn't...
What? What's the matter?
ПРАВДА
...it's just today's paper.

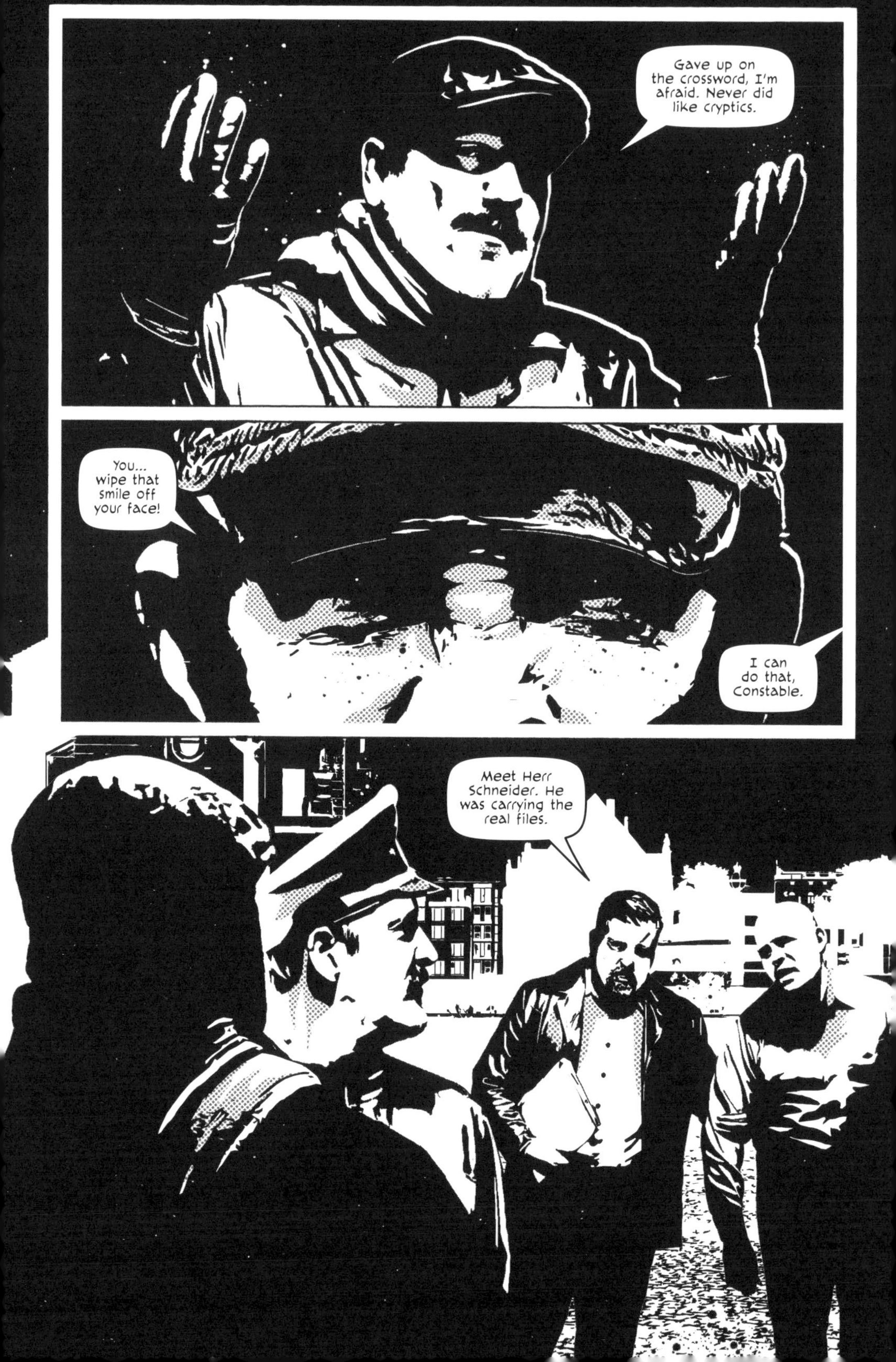
Gave up on the crossword, I'm afraid. Never did like cryptics.
You... wipe that smile off your face!
I can do that, Constable.
Meet Herr Schneider. He was carrying the real files.

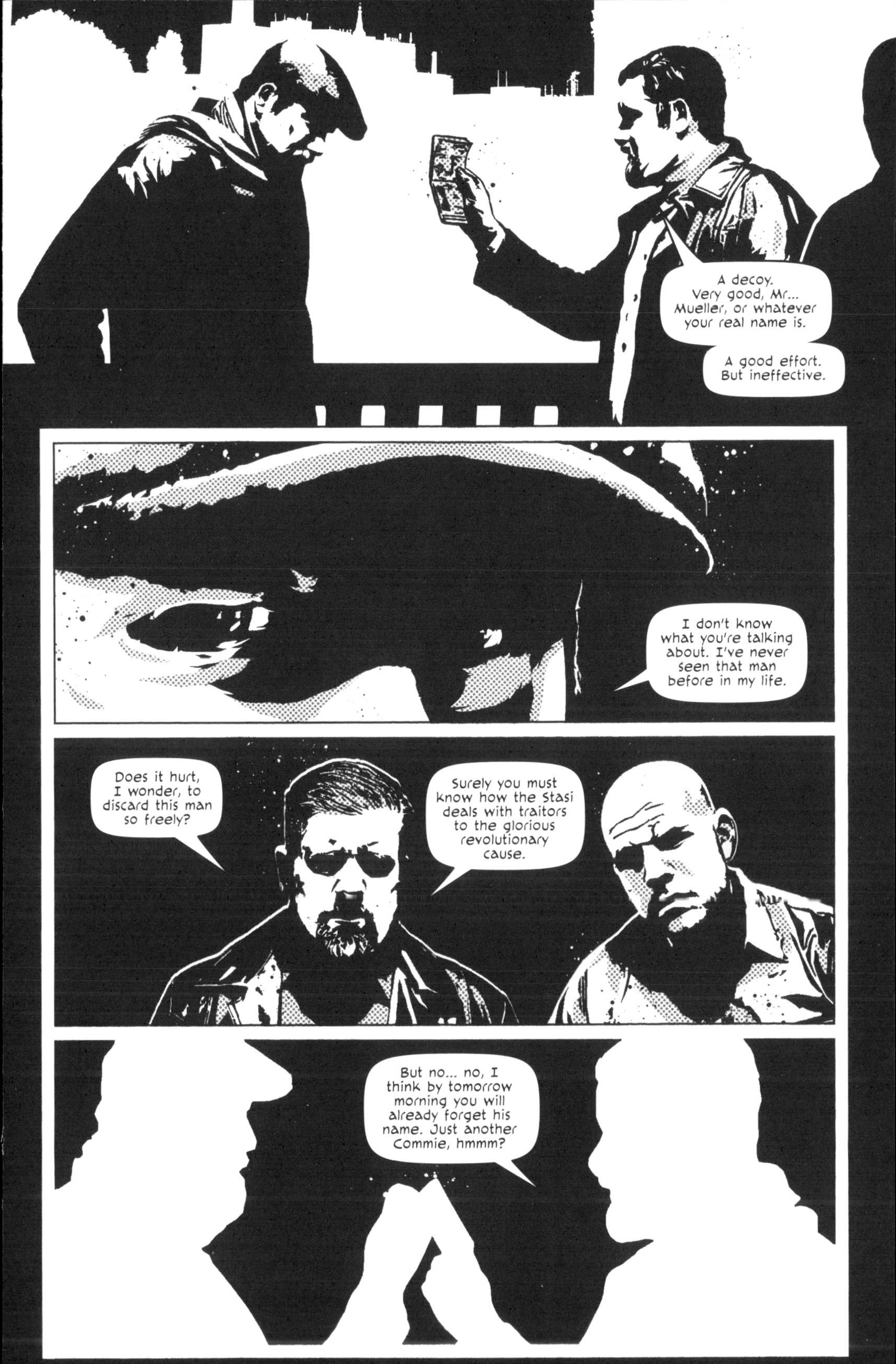
A decoy. Very good, Mr... Mueller, or whatever your real name is.
A good effort. But ineffective.
I don't know what you're talking about. I've never seen that man before in my life.
Does it hurt, I wonder, to discard this man so freely?
Surely you must know how the Stasi deals with traitors to the glorious revolutionary cause.
But no... no, I think by tomorrow morning you will already forget his name. Just another Commie, hmmm?

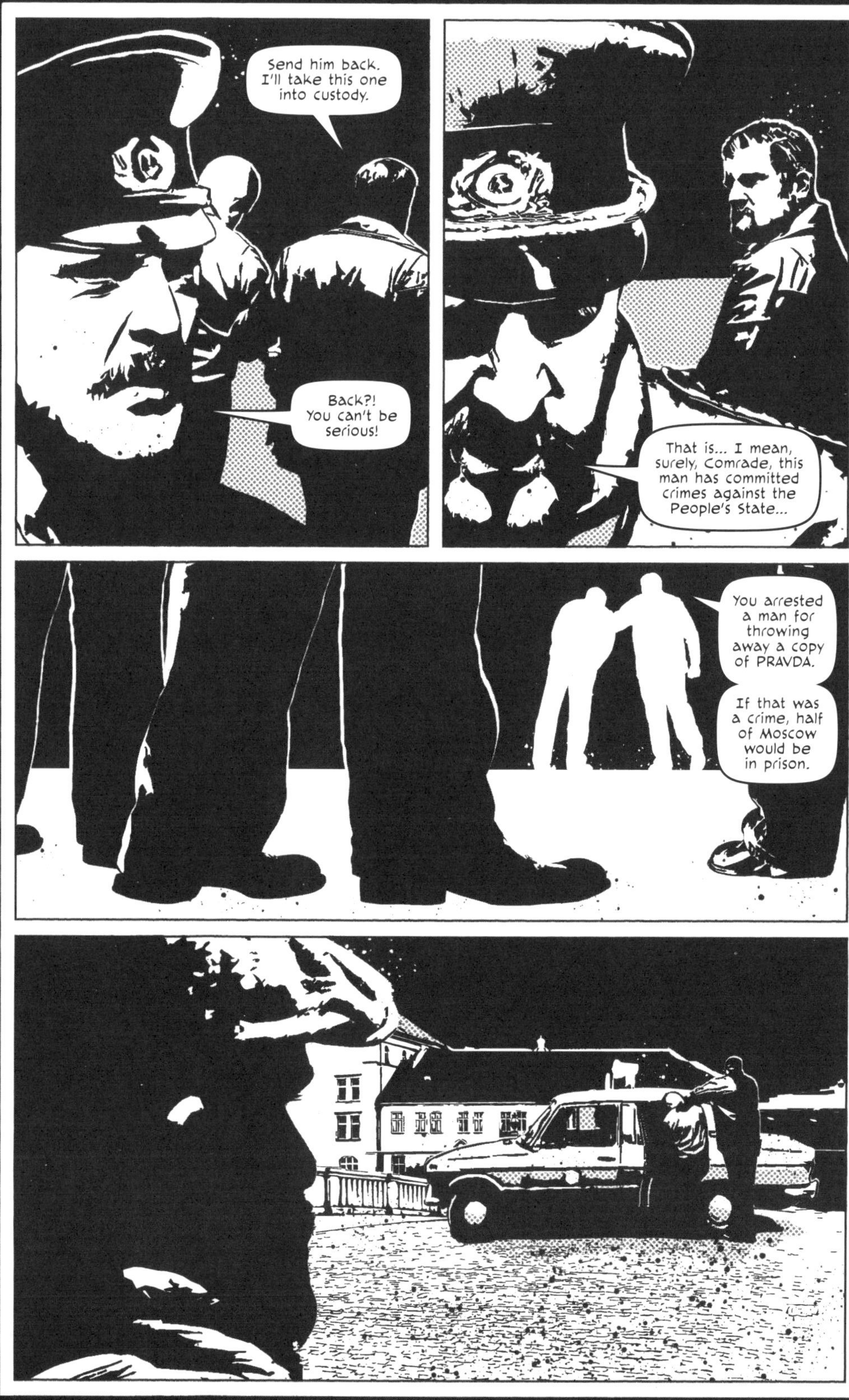
Send him back. I'll take this one into custody.
Back?! You can't be serious!
That is... I mean, surely, Comrade, this man has committed crimes against the People's State...
You arrested a man for throwing away a copy of PRAVDA.
If that was a crime, half of Moscow would be in prison.

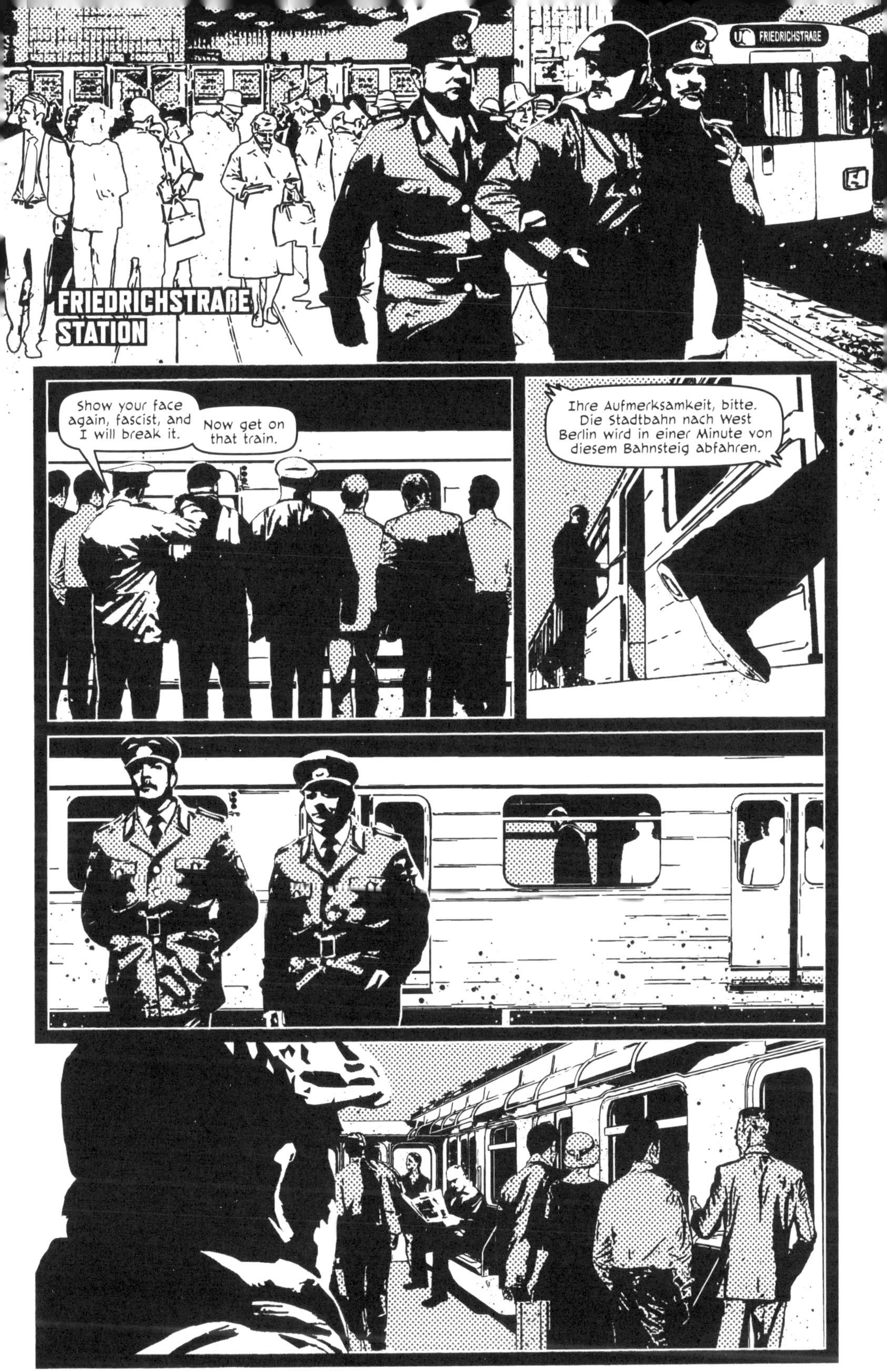
FRIEDRICHSTRAßE STATION
FRIEDRICHSTRAßE
Show your face again, fascist, and I will break it.
Now get on that train.
Ihre Aufmerksamkeit, bitte. Die Stadtbahn nach West Berlin wird in einer Minute von diesem Bahnsteig abfahren.

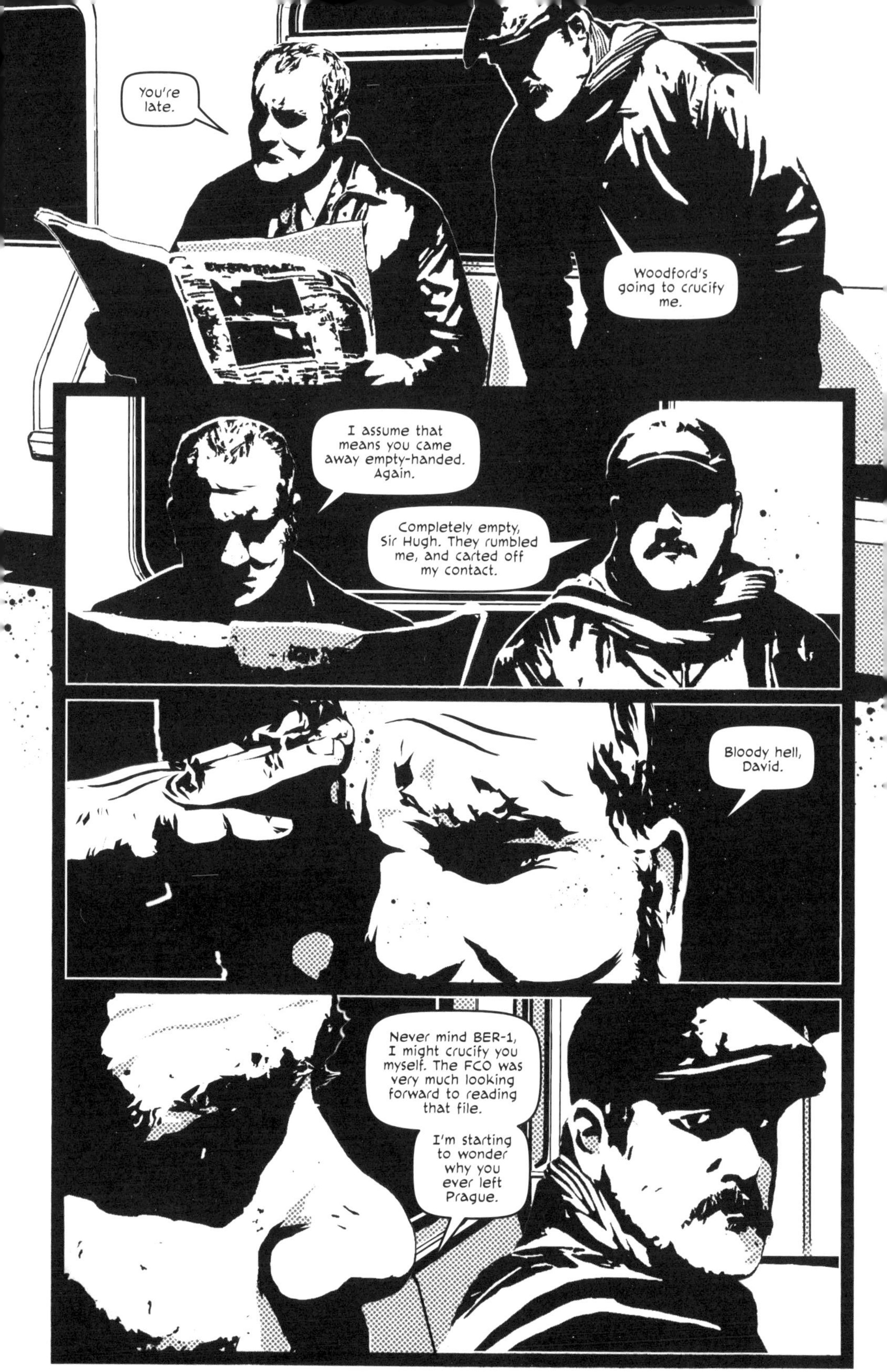
You're late.
Woodford's going to crucify me.
I assume that means you came away empty-handed. Again.
Completely empty, Sir Hugh. They rumbled me, and carted off my contact.
Bloody hell, David.
Never mind BER-1, I might crucify you myself. The FCO was very much looking forward to reading that file.
I'm starting to wonder why you ever left Prague.

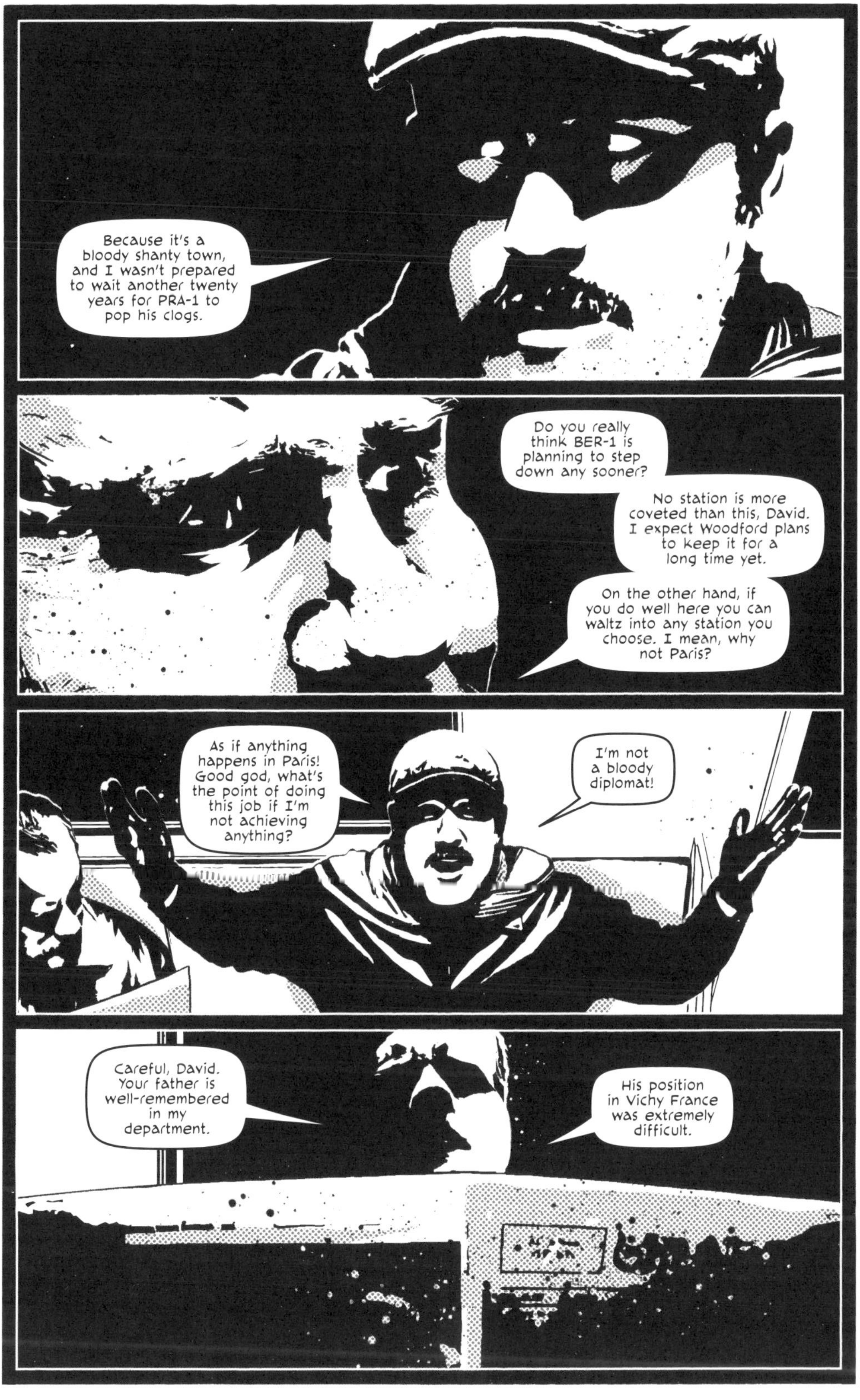

Because it's a bloody shanty town, and I wasn't prepared to wait another twenty years for PRA-1 to pop his clogs.
Do you really think BER-1 is planning to step down any sooner?
No station is more coveted than this, David. I expect Woodford plans to keep it for a long time yet.
On the other hand, if you do well here you can waltz into any station you choose. I mean, why not Paris?
As if anything happens in Paris! Good god, what's the point of doing this job if I'm not achieving anything?
I'm not a bloody diplomat!
Careful, David. Your father is well-remembered in my department.
His position in Vichy France was extremely difficult.

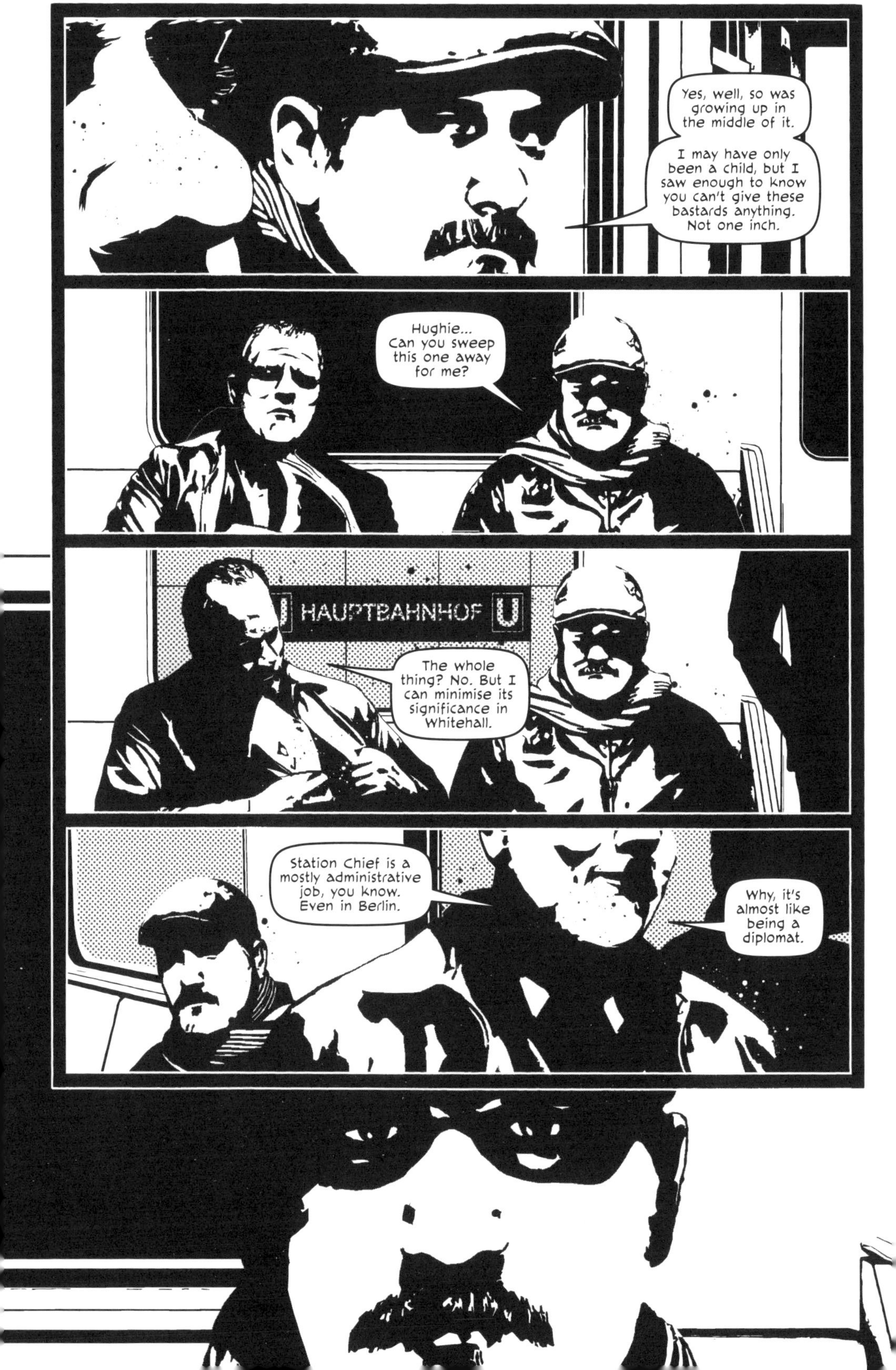
Yes, well, so was growing up in the middle of it.
I may have only been a child, but I saw enough to know you can't give these bastards anything. Not one inch.
Hughie... Can you sweep this one away for me?
HAUPTBAHNHOF
The whole thing? No. But I can minimise its significance in Whitehall.
Station Chief is a mostly administrative job, you know. Even in Berlin.
Why, it's almost like being a diplomat.

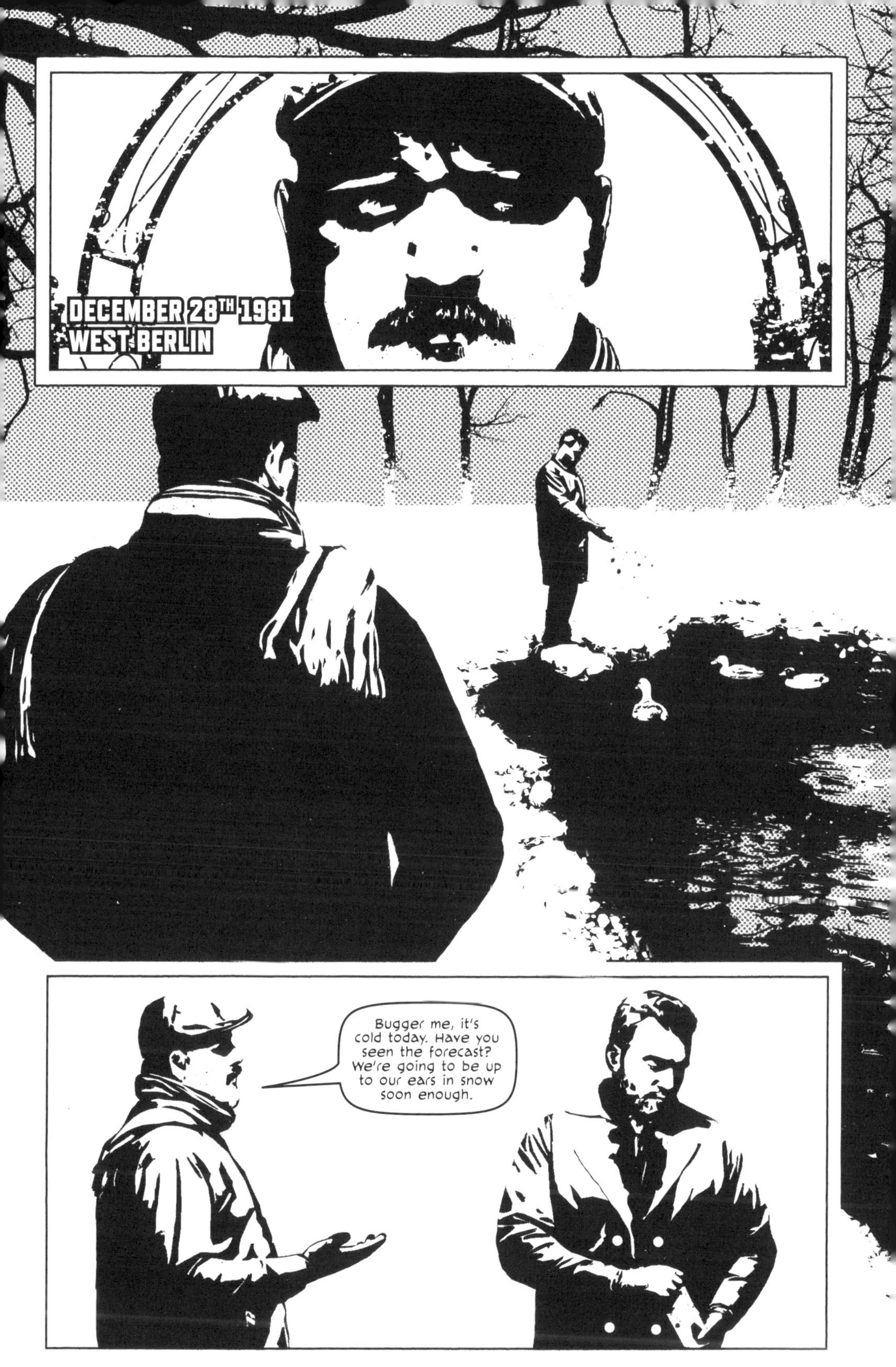
DECEMBER 28TH 1981
WEST BERLIN
Bugger me, it's cold today. Have you seen the forecast? We're going to be up to our ears in snow soon enough.

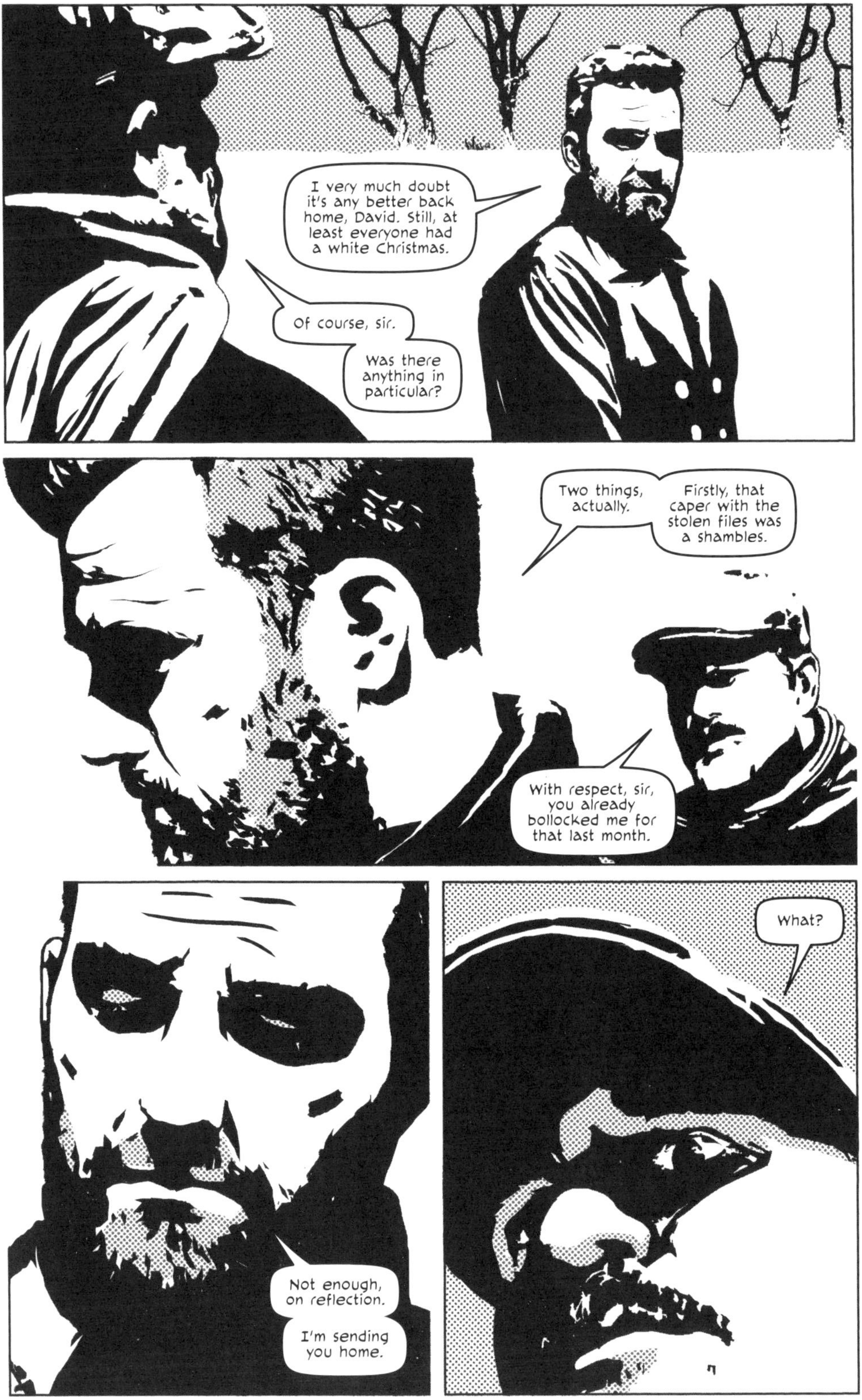

I very much doubt it's any better back home, David. Still, at least everyone had a white Christmas.
Of course, sir.
Was there anything in particular?
Two things, actually.
Firstly, that caper with the stolen files was a shambles.
With respect, sir, you already bollocked me for that last month.
Not enough, on reflection.
I'm sending you home.
What?

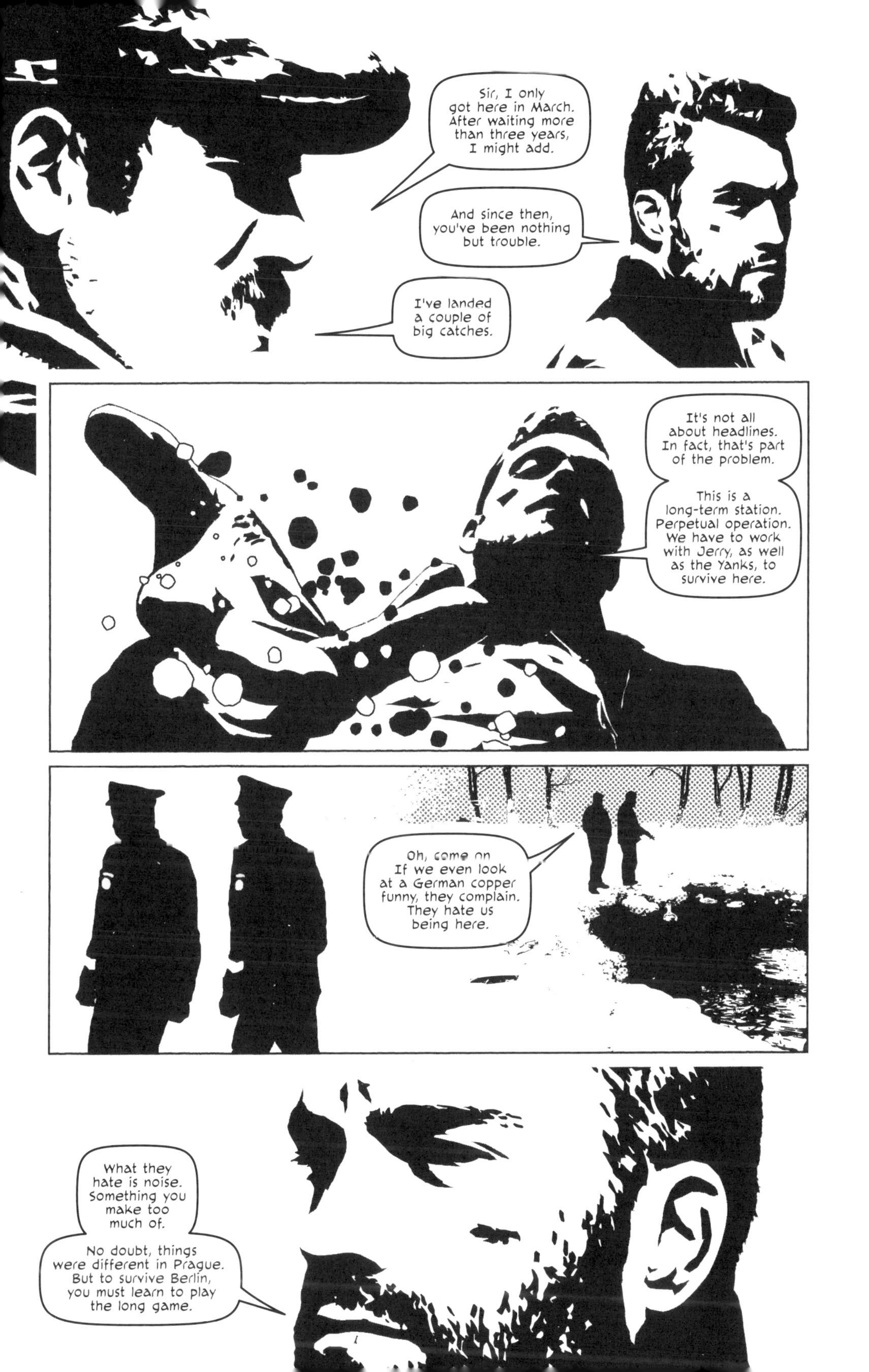
Sir, I only got here in March. After waiting more than three years, I might add.
And since then, you've been nothing but trouble.
I've landed a couple of big catches.
It's not all about headlines. In fact, that's part of the problem.
This is a long-term station. Perpetual operation. We have to work with Jerry, as well as the Yanks, to survive here.
Oh, come on If we even look at a German copper funny, they complain. They hate us being here.
What they hate is noise. Something you make too much of.
No doubt, things were different in Prague. But to survive Berlin, you must learn to play the long game.

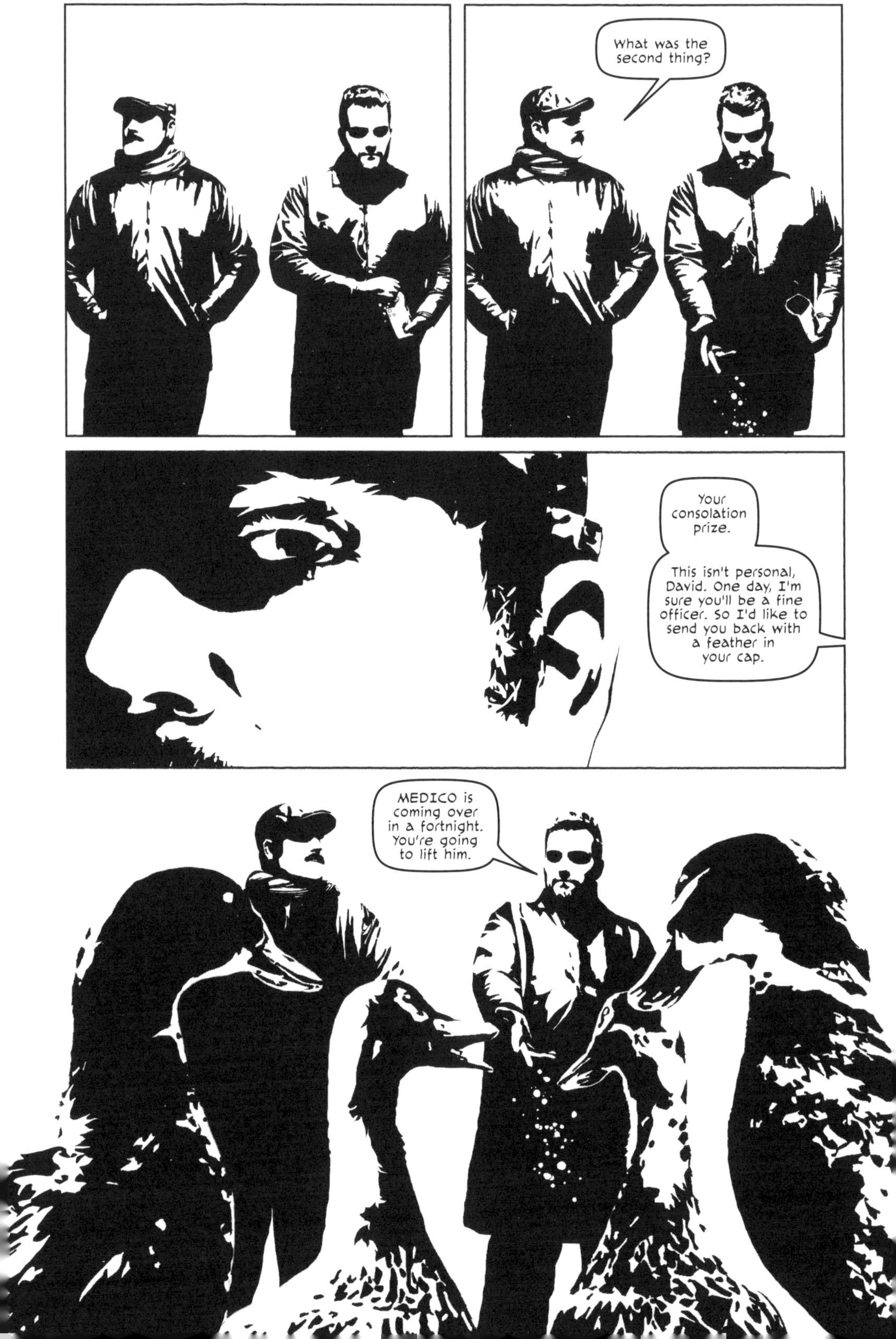
What was the second thing?
Your consolation prize.
This isn't personal, David. One day, I'm sure you'll be a fine officer. So I'd like to send you back with a feather in your cap.
MEDICO is coming over in a fortnight. You're going to lift him.

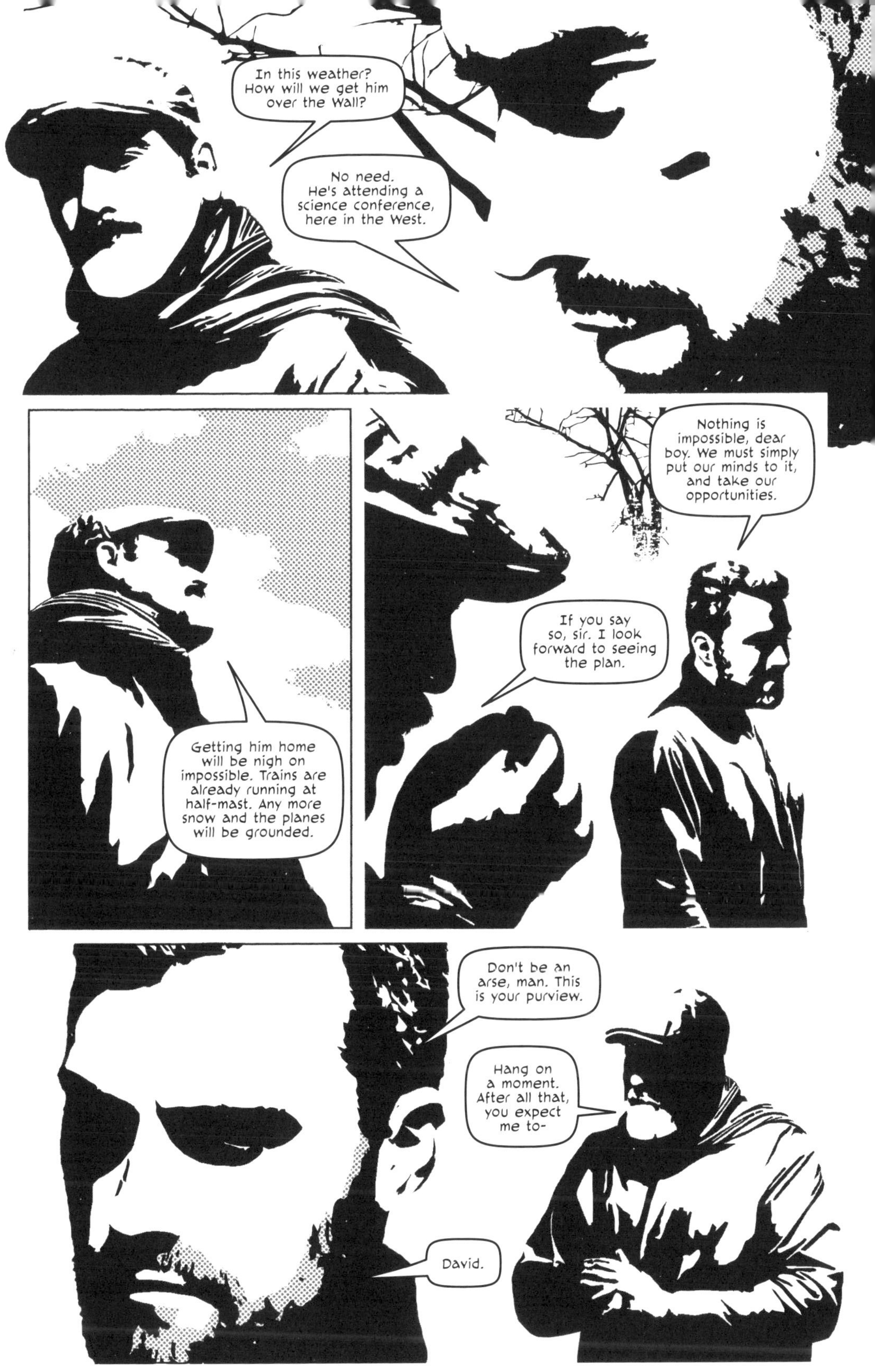
In this weather? How will we get him over the Wall?
No need. He's attending a science conference, here in the West.
Getting him home will be nigh on impossible. Trains are already running at half-mast. Any more snow and the planes will be grounded.
Nothing is impossible, dear boy. We must simply put our minds to it, and take our opportunities.
If you say so, sir. I look forward to seeing the plan.
Don't be an arse, man. This is your purview.
Hang on a moment. After all that, you expect me to-
David.

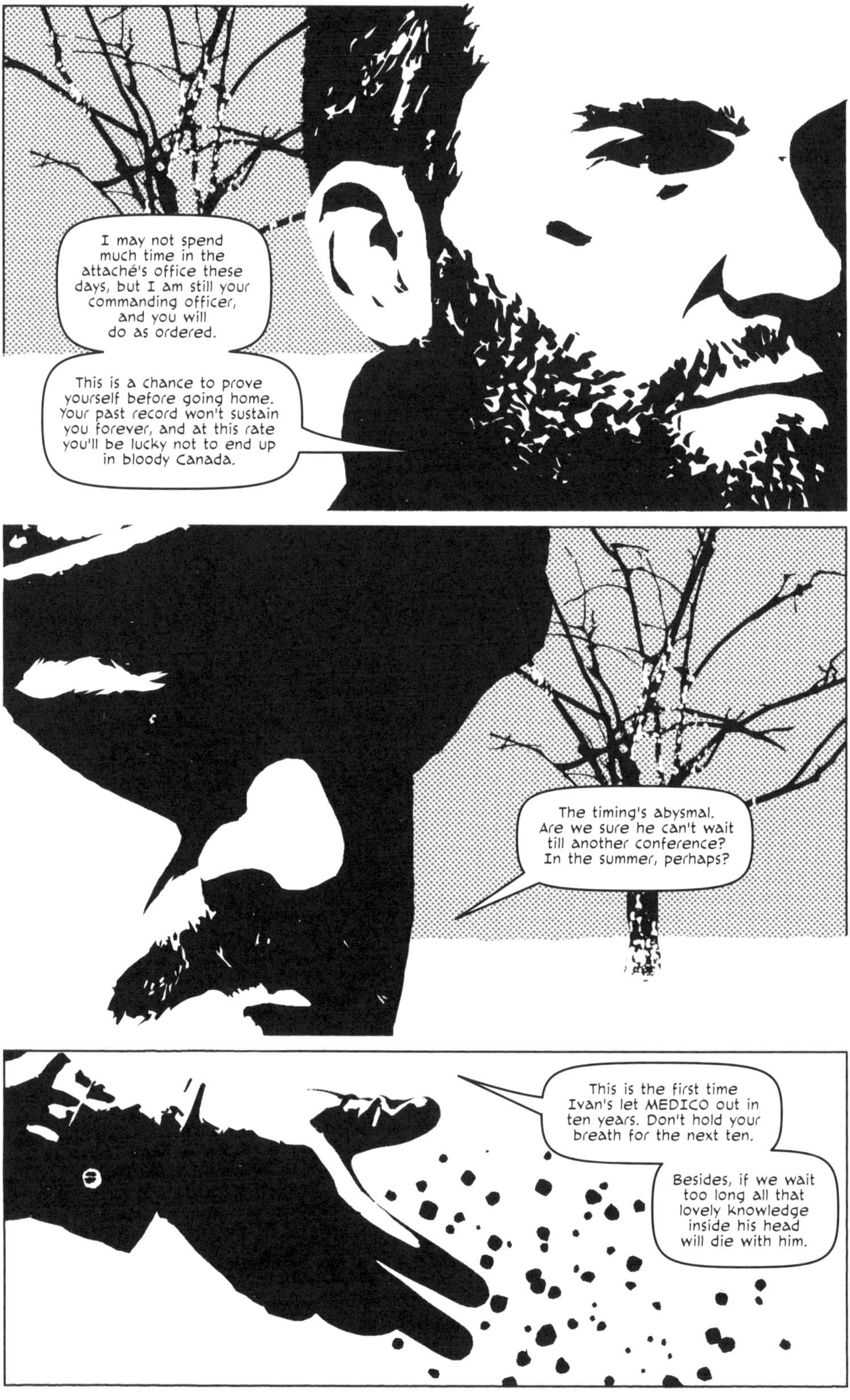
I may not spend much time in the attaché's office these days, but I am still your commanding officer, and you will do as ordered.
This is a chance to prove yourself before going home. Your past record won't sustain you forever, and at this rate you'll be lucky not to end up in bloody Canada.
The timing's abysmal. Are we sure he can't wait till another conference? In the summer, perhaps?
This is the first time Ivan's let MEDICO out in ten years. Don't hold your breath for the next ten.
Besides, if we wait too long all that lovely knowledge inside his head will die with him.

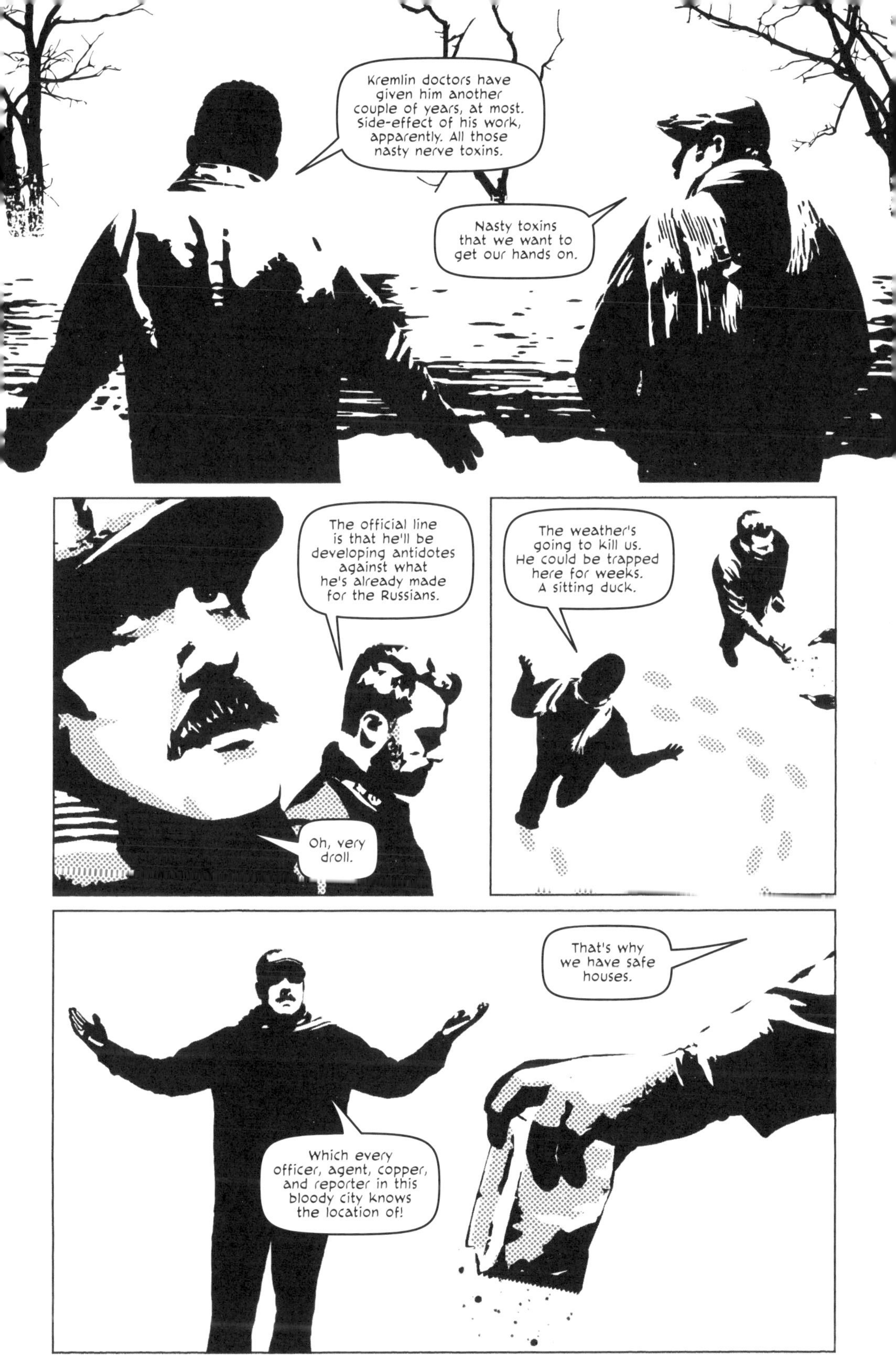
Kremlin doctors have given him another couple of years, at most. Side-effect of his work, apparently. All those nasty nerve toxins.
Nasty toxins that we want to get our hands on.
The official line is that he'll be developing antidotes against what he's already made for the Russians.
Oh, very droll.
The weather's going to kill us. He could be trapped here for weeks. A sitting duck.
That's why we have safe houses.
Which every officer, agent, copper, and reporter in this bloody city knows the location of!

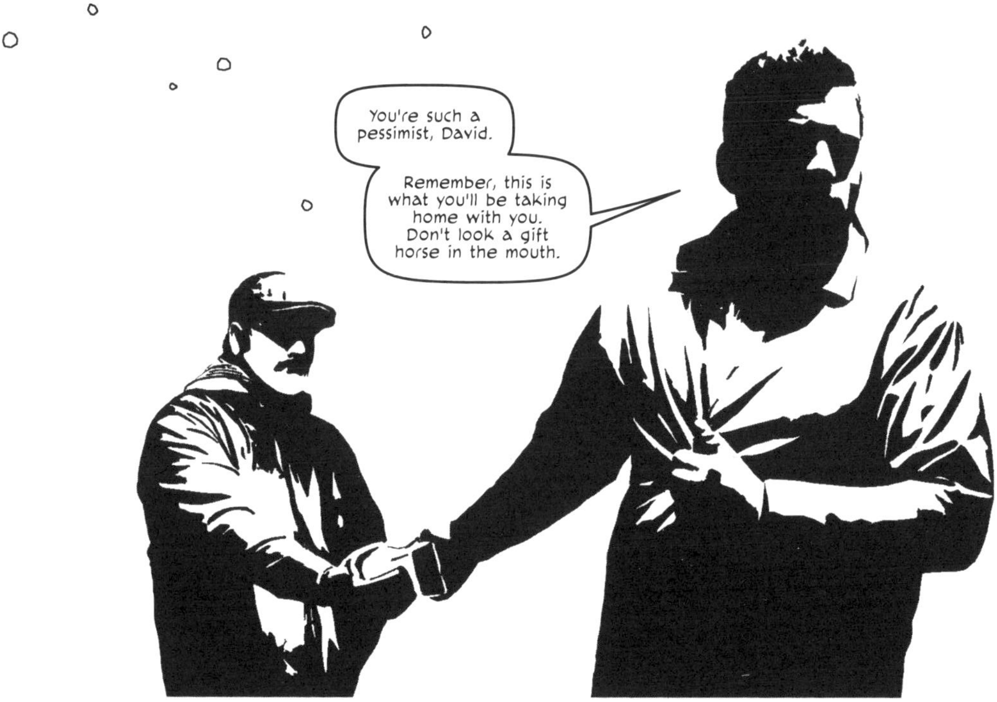
You're such a pessimist, David.
Remember, this is what you'll be taking home with you. Don't look a gift horse in the mouth.

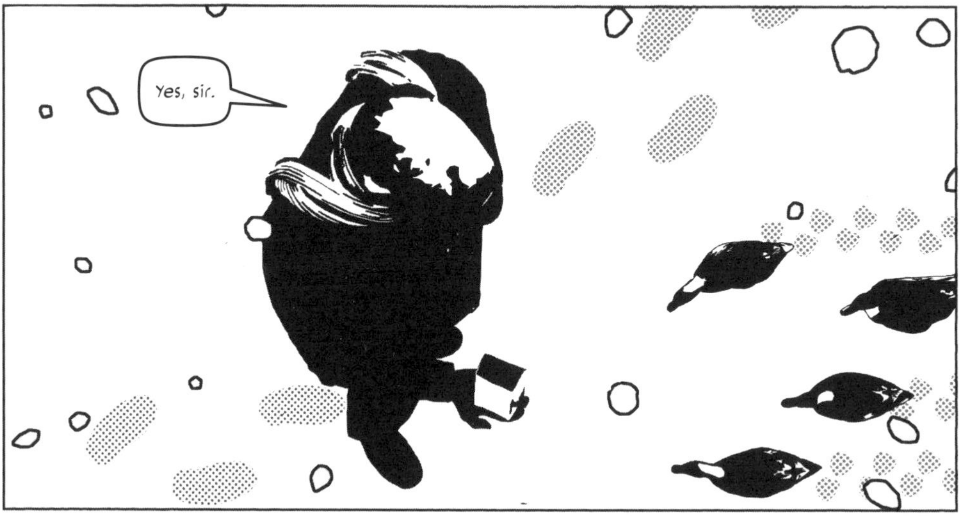
Yes, sir.

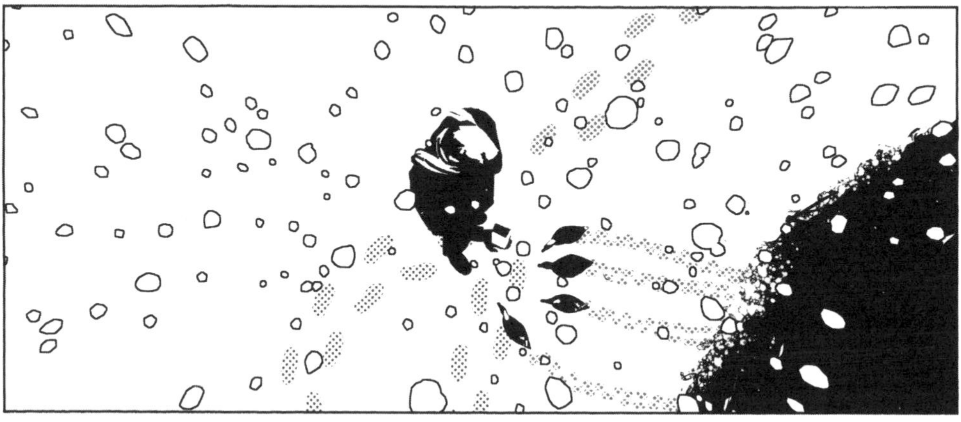

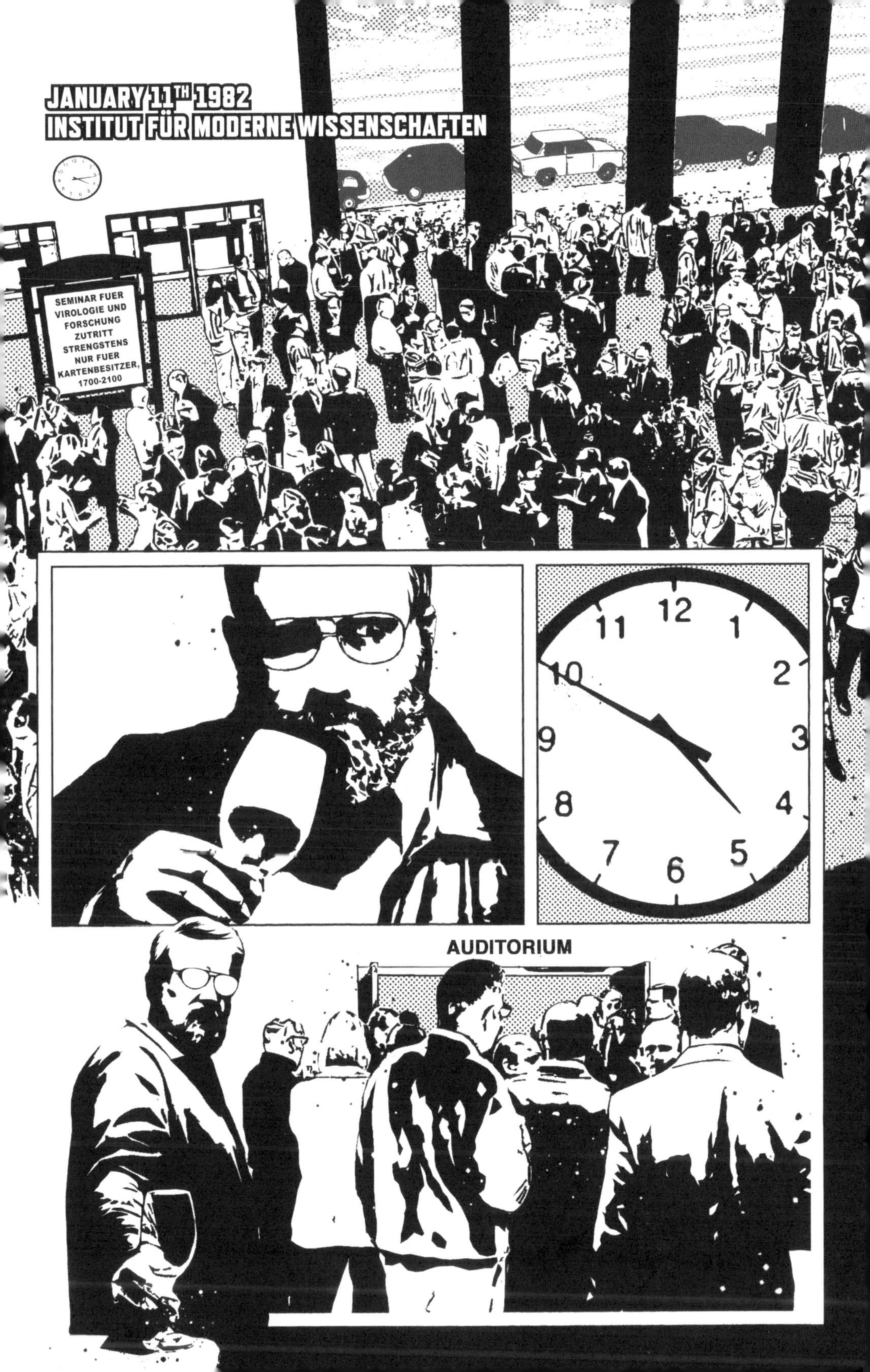
JANUARY 11TH 1982
INSTITUT FÜR MODERNE WISSENSCHAFTEN
SEMINAR FUER VIROLOGIE UND FORSCHUNG ZUTRITT STRENGSTENS NUR FUER KARTENBESITZER, 1700-2100
AUDITORIUM

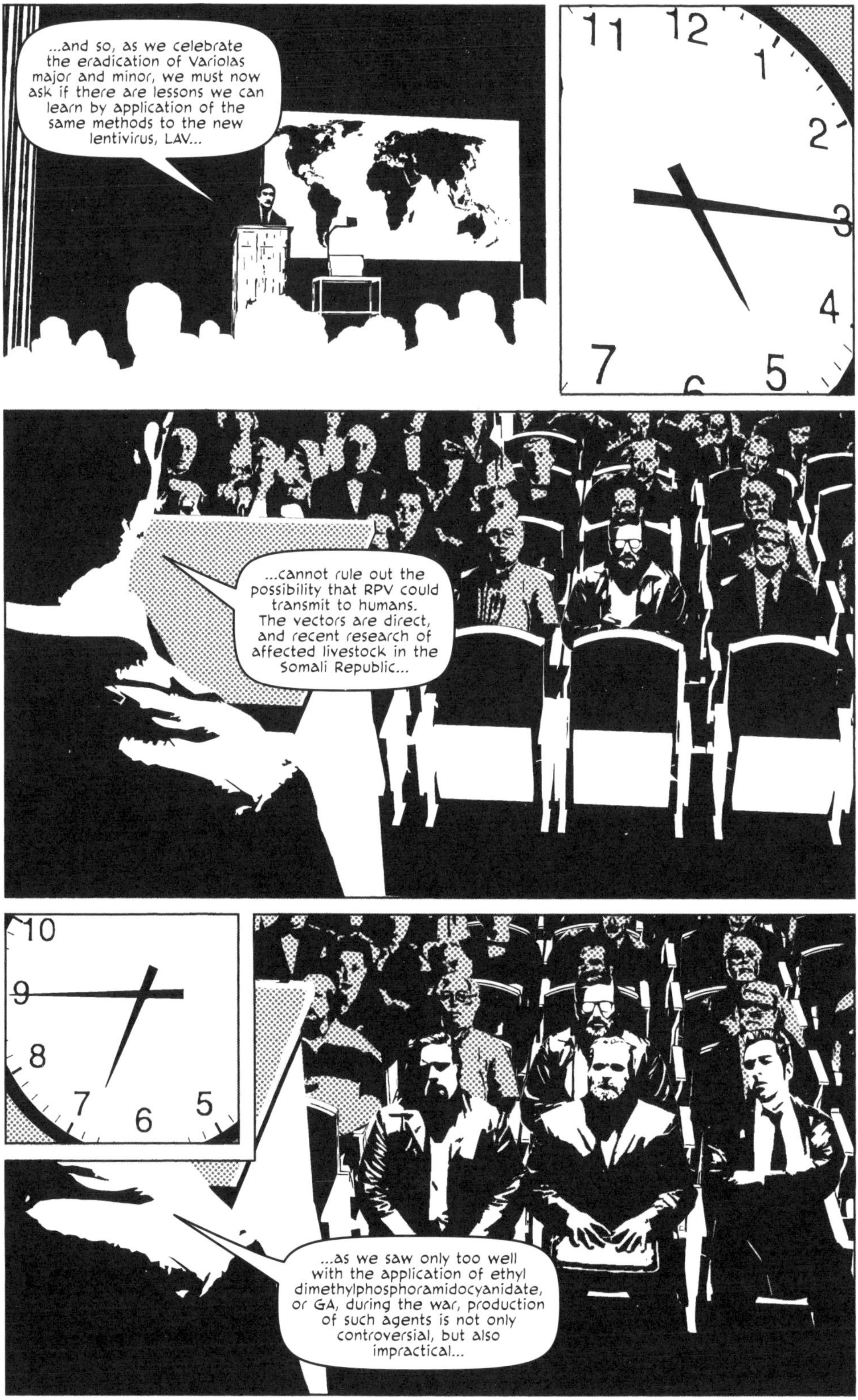
...and so, as we celebrate the eradication of Variolas major and minor, we must now ask if there are lessons we can learn by application of the same methods to the new lentivirus, LAV...
...cannot rule out the possibility that RPV could transmit to humans. The vectors are direct, and recent research of affected livestock in the Somali Republic...
...as we saw only too well with the application of ethyl dimethylphosphoramidocyanidate, or GA, during the war, production of such agents is not only controversial, but also impractical...

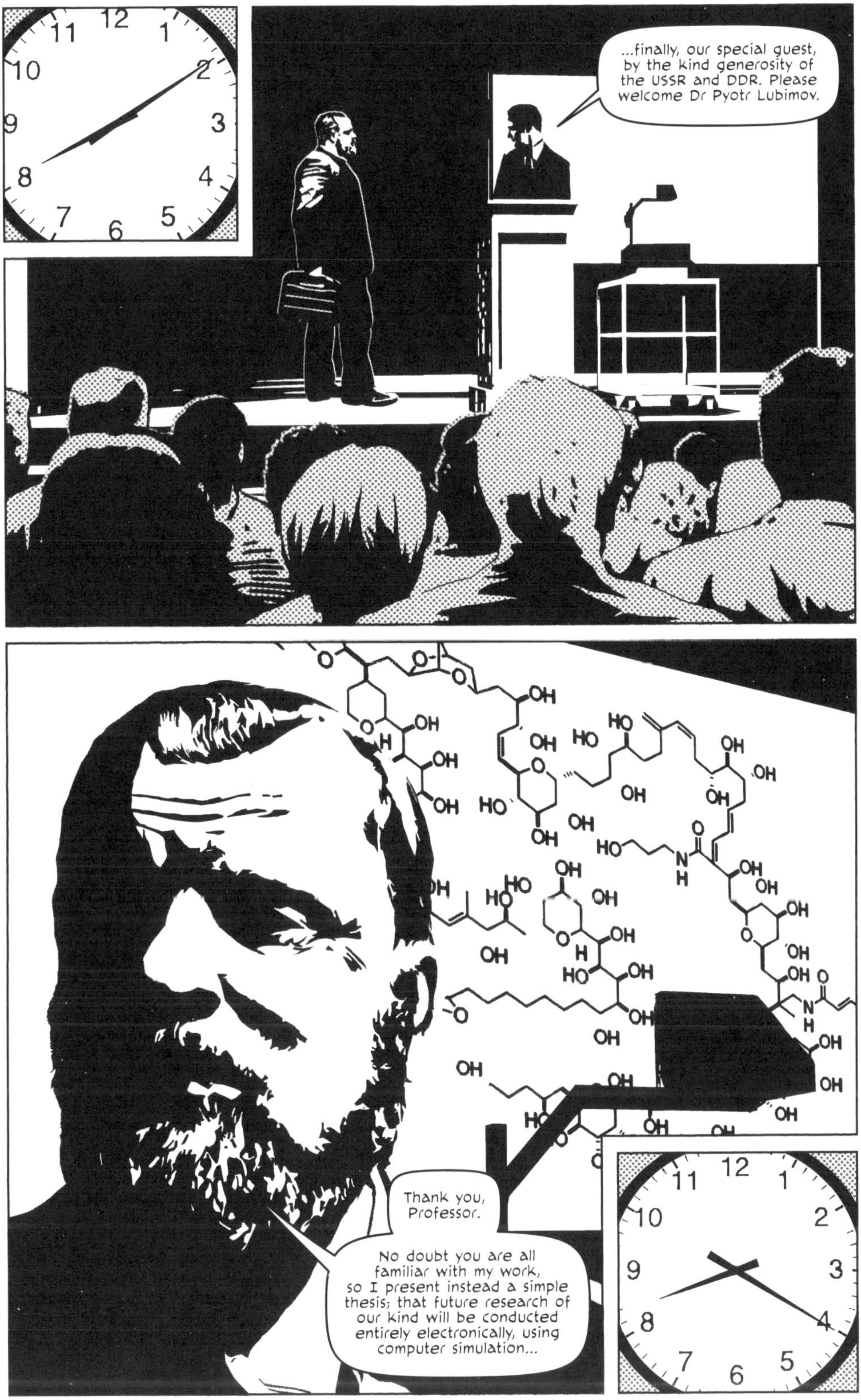
...finally, our special guest, by the kind generosity of the USSR and DDR. Please welcome Dr Pyotr Lubimov.
Thank you, Professor.
No doubt you are all familiar with my work, so I present instead a simple thesis; that future research of our kind will be conducted entirely electronically, using computer simulation...

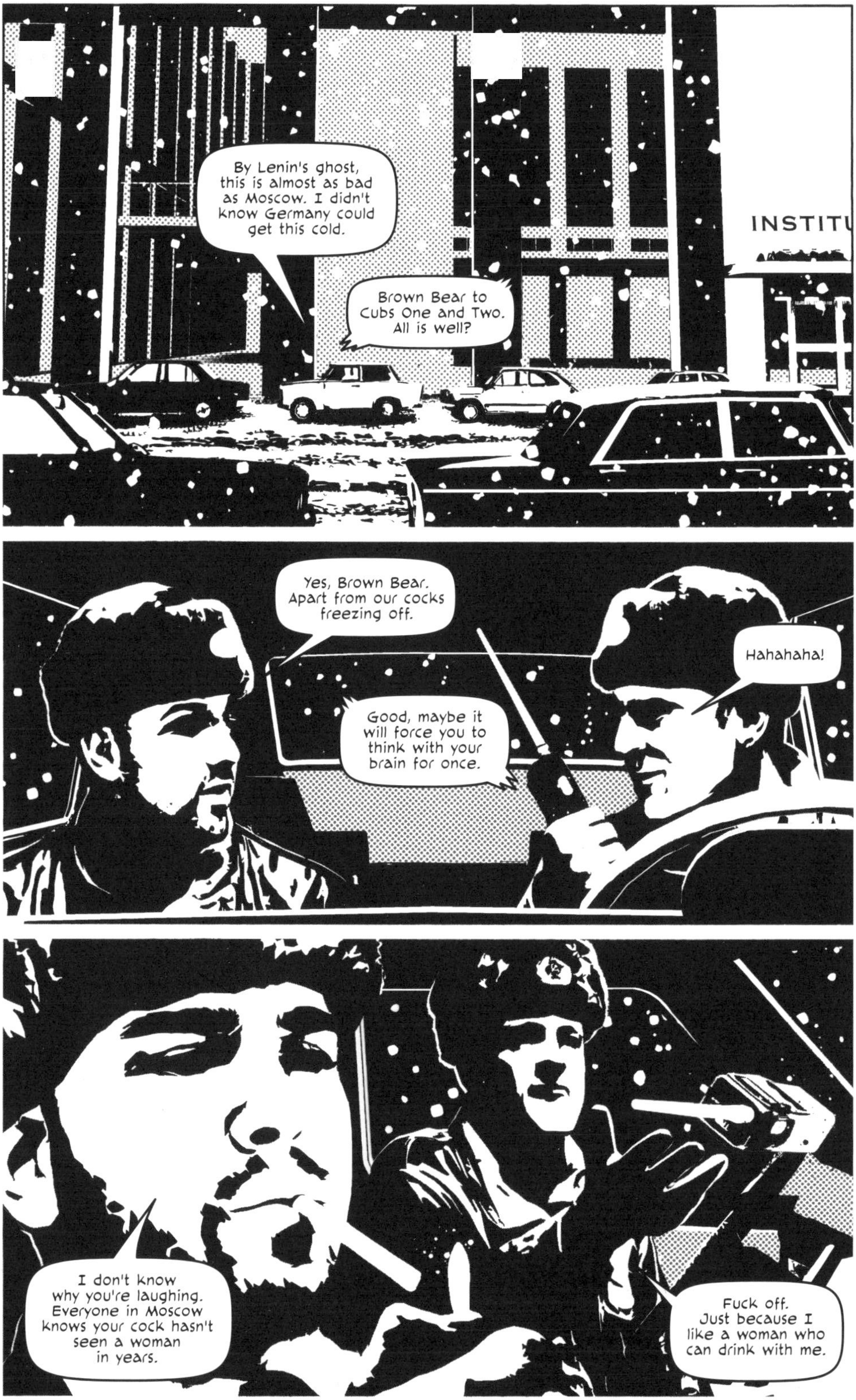
By Lenin's ghost, this is almost as bad as Moscow. I didn't know Germany could get this cold.
Brown Bear to Cubs One and Two. All is well?
INSTIT
Yes, Brown Bear. Apart from our cocks freezing off.
Hahahaha!
Good, maybe it will force you to think with your brain for once.
I don't know why you're laughing. Everyone in Moscow knows your cock hasn't seen a woman in years.
Fuck off. Just because I like a woman who can drink with me.

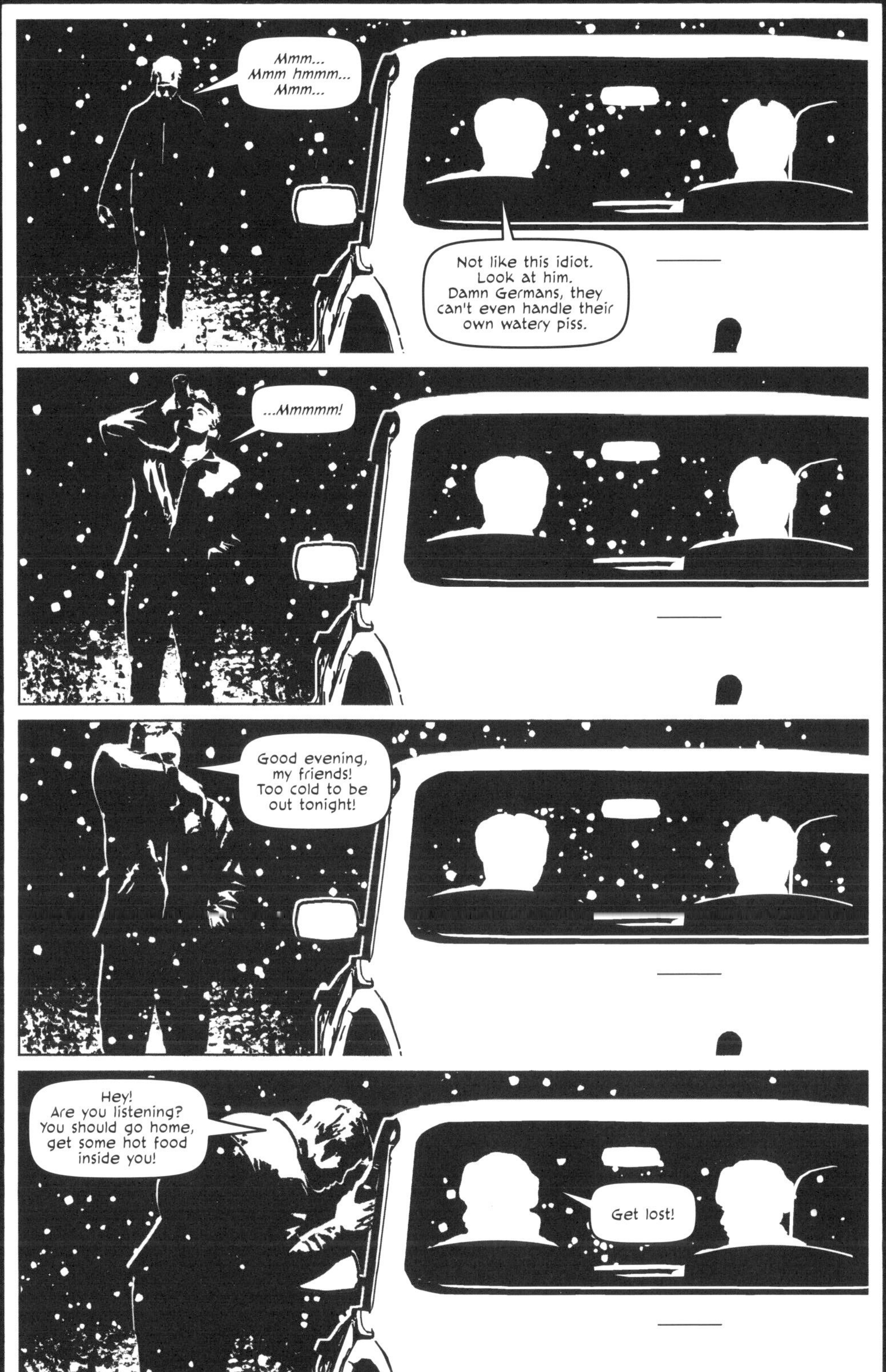
Mmm...
Mmm hmmm...
Mmm...
Not like this idiot. Look at him. Damn Germans, they can't even handle their own watery piss.
...Mmmmm!
Good evening, my friends! Too cold to be out tonight!
Hey! Are you listening? You should go home, get some hot food inside you!
Get lost!

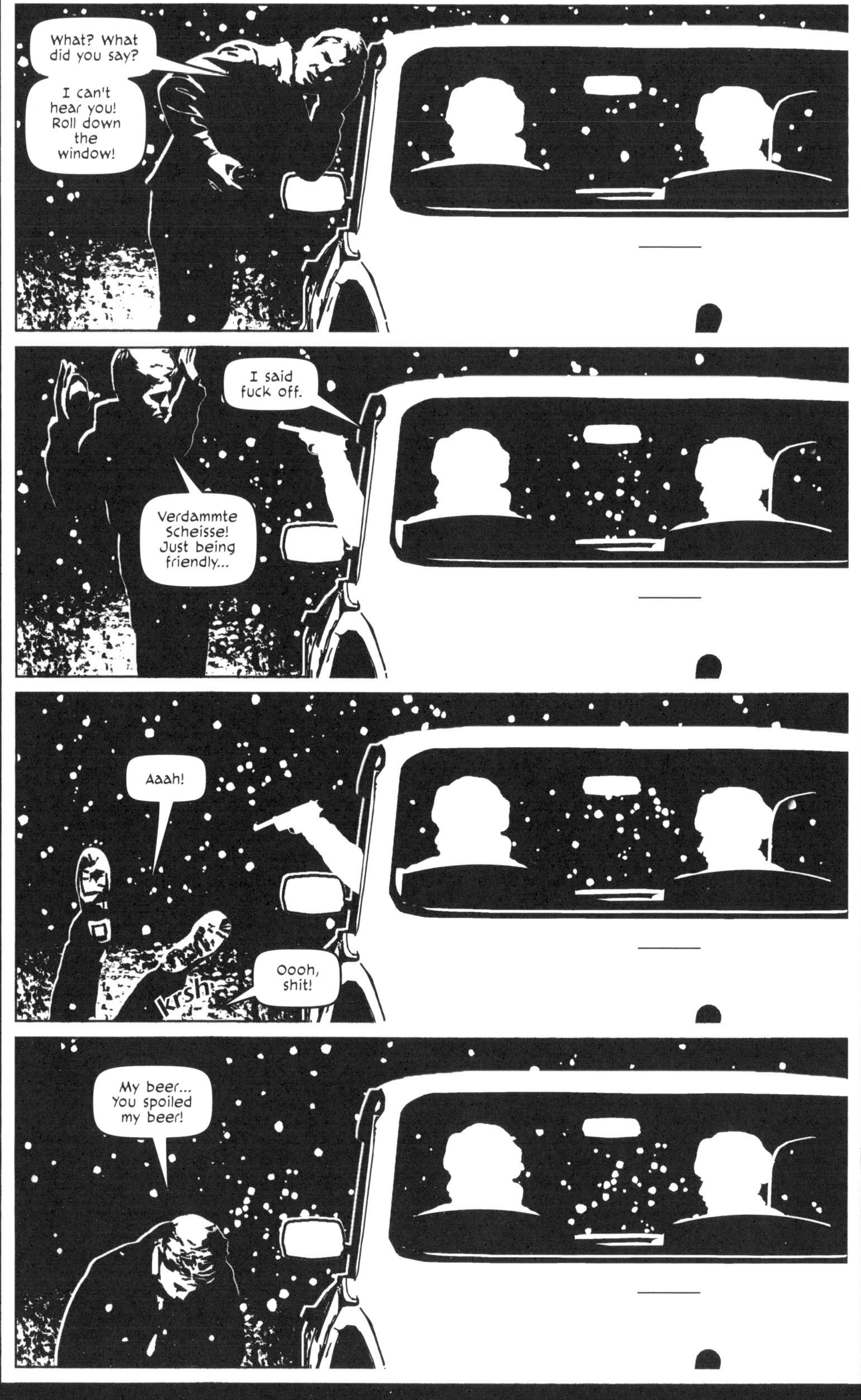
What? What did you say?
I can't hear you! Roll down the window!
I said fuck off.
Verdammte Scheisse! Just being friendly...
Aaah!
krsh
Oooh, shit!
My beer... You spoiled my beer!

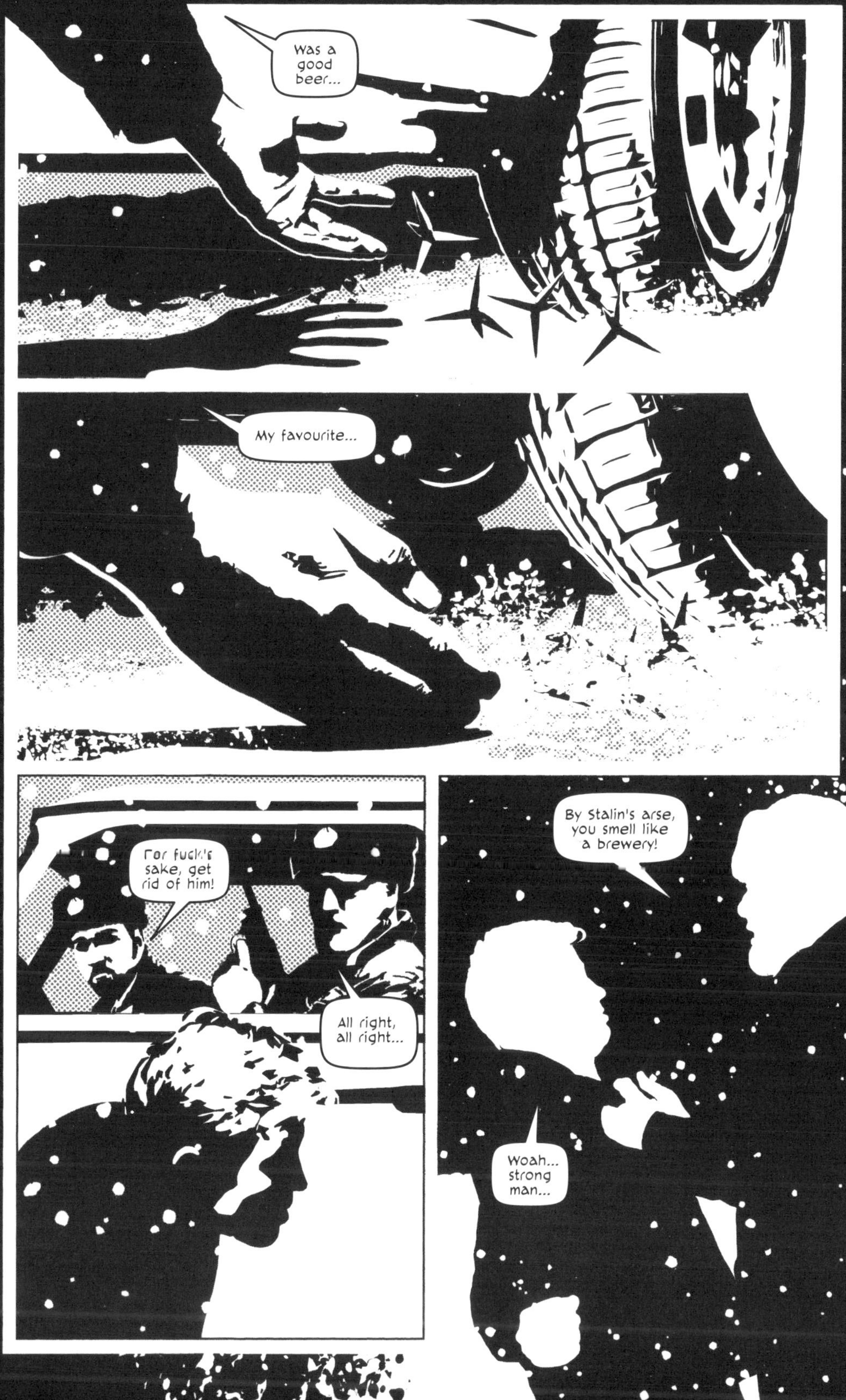
Was a good beer...
My favourite...
For fuck's sake, get rid of him!
All right, all right...
By Stalin's arse, you smell like a brewery!
Woah... strong man...

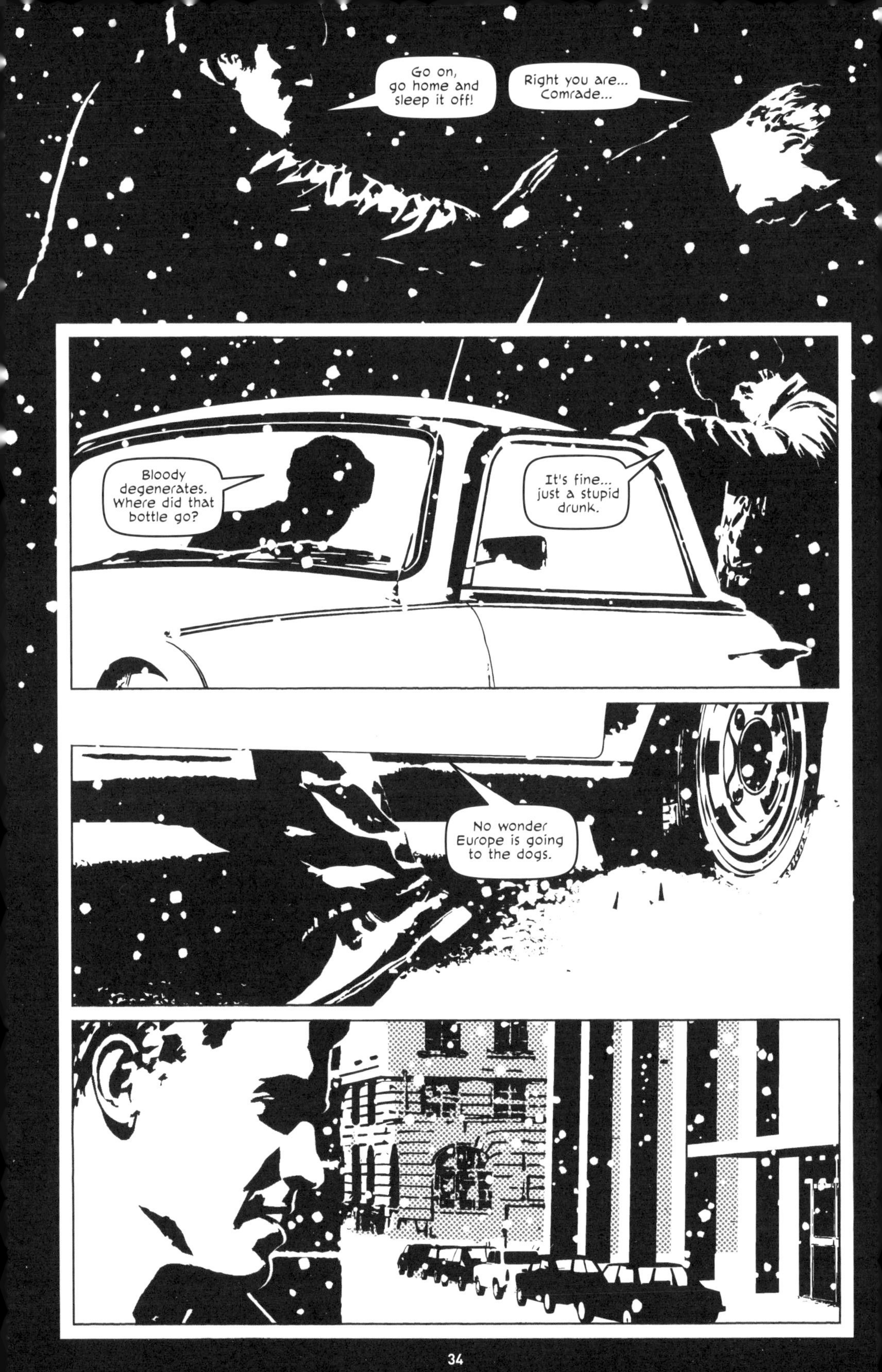
Go on, go home and sleep it off!
Right you are... Comrade...
Bloody degenerates. Where did that bottle go?
It's fine... just a stupid drunk.
No wonder Europe is going to the dogs.

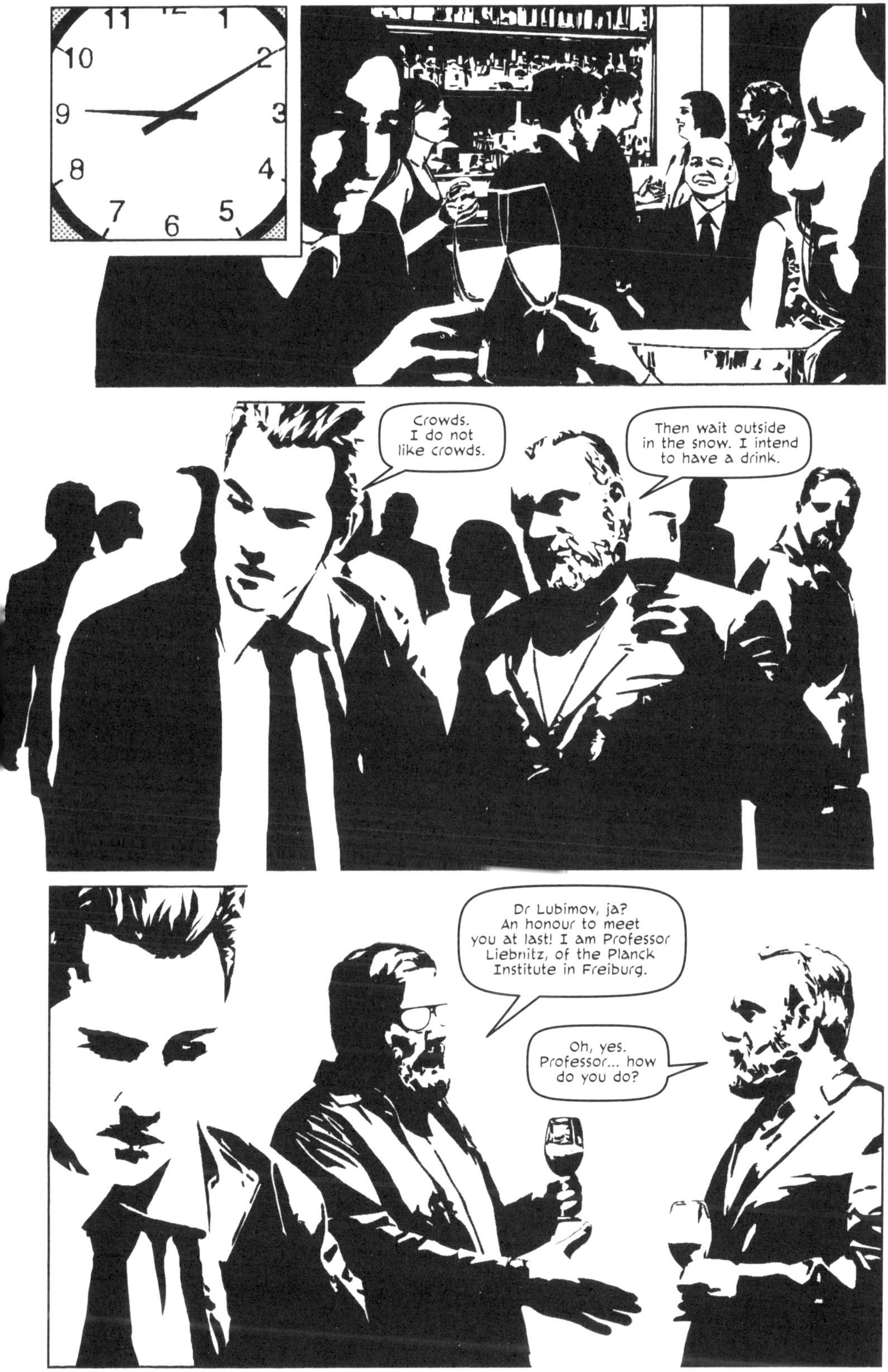
Crowds. I do not like crowds.
Then wait outside in the snow. I intend to have a drink.
Dr Lubimov, ja? An honour to meet you at last! I am Professor Liebnitz, of the Planck Institute in Freiburg.
Oh, yes. Professor... how do you do?

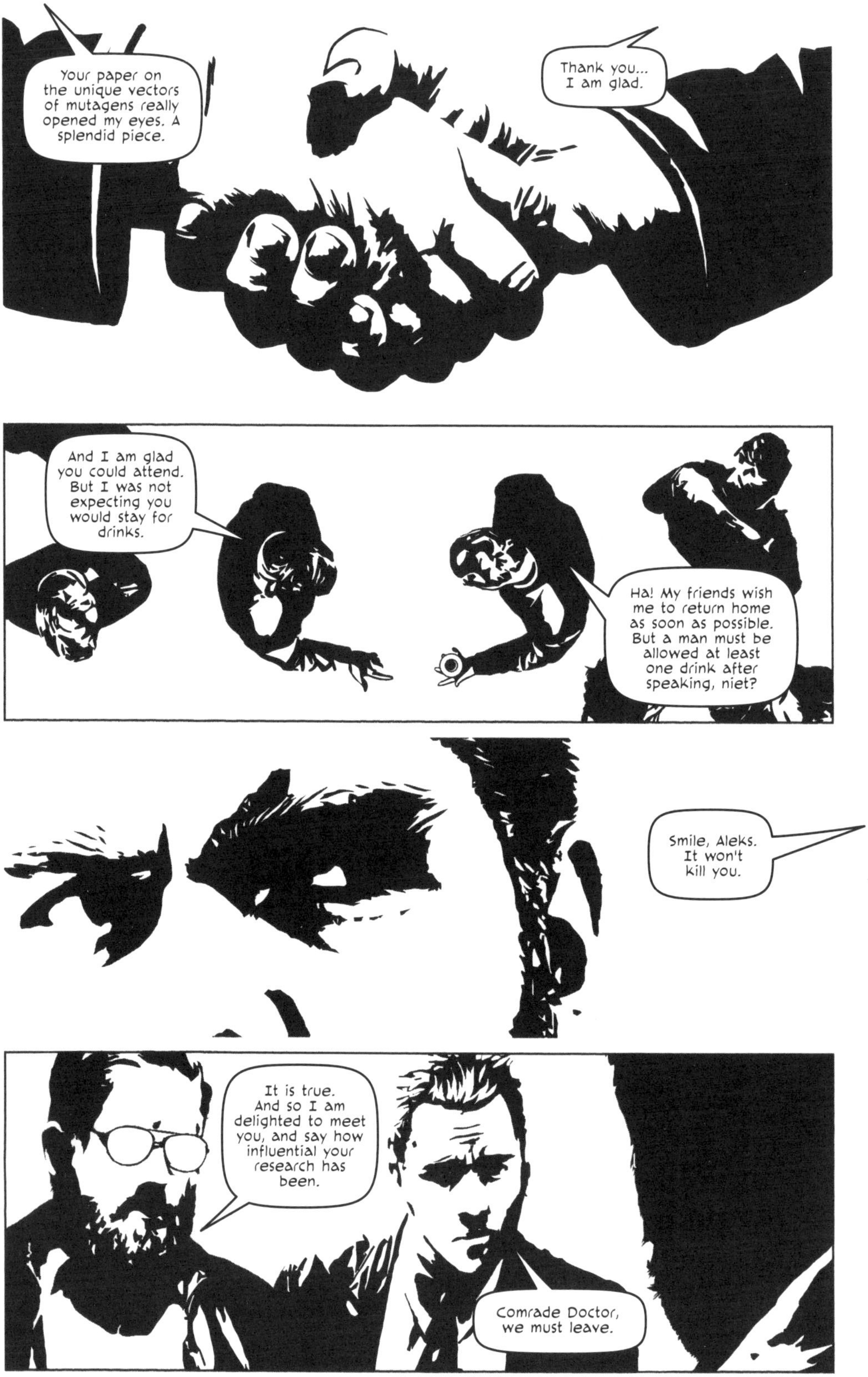
Your paper on the unique vectors of mutagens really opened my eyes. A splendid piece.
Thank you... I am glad.
And I am glad you could attend. But I was not expecting you would stay for drinks.
Ha! My friends wish me to return home as soon as possible. But a man must be allowed at least one drink after speaking, niet?
Smile, Aleks. It won't kill you.
It is true. And so I am delighted to meet you, and say how influential your research has been.
Comrade Doctor, we must leave.

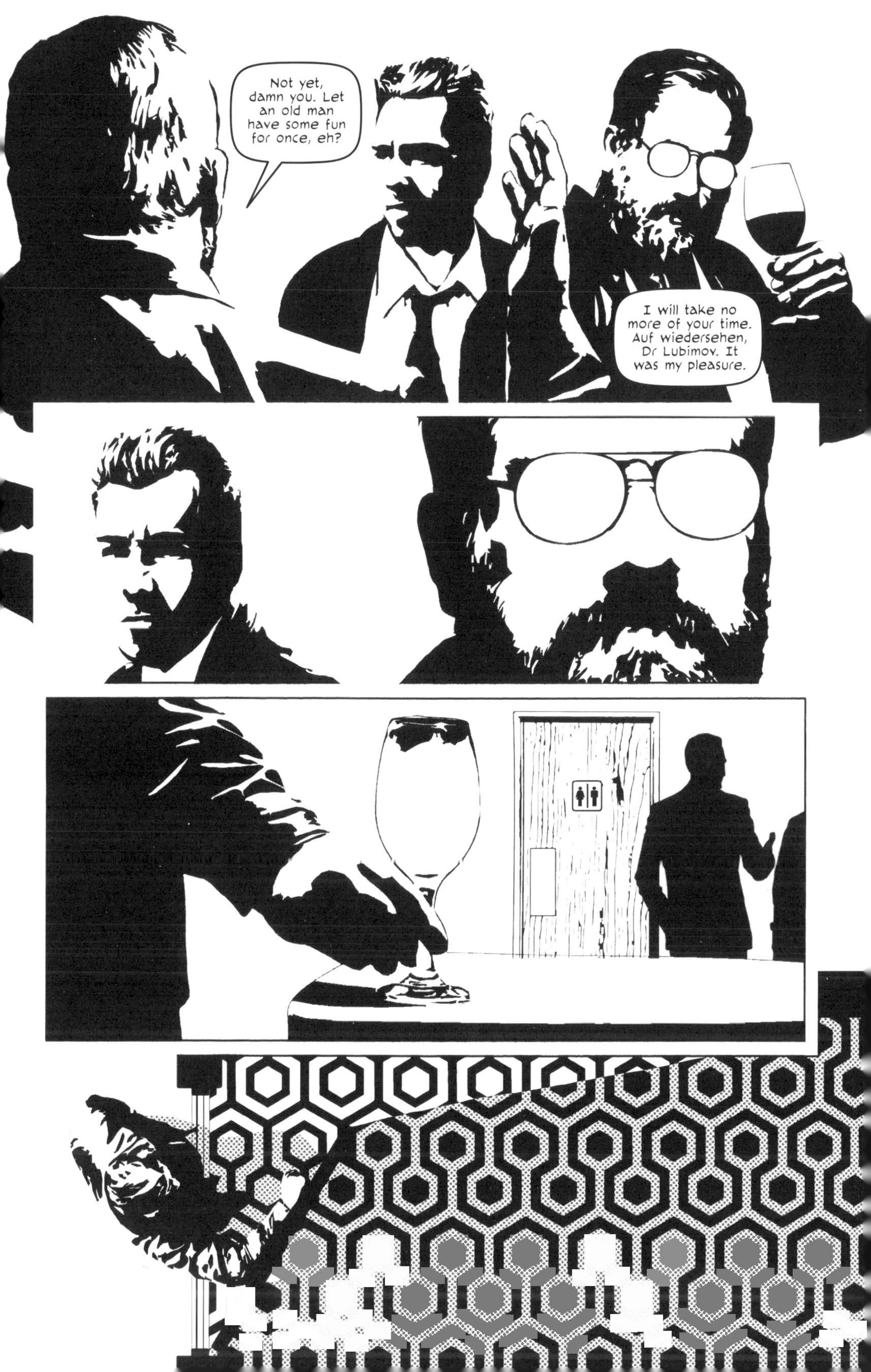
Not yet, damn you. Let an old man have some fun for once, eh?
I will take no more of your time. Auf wiedersehen, Dr Lubimov. It was my pleasure.

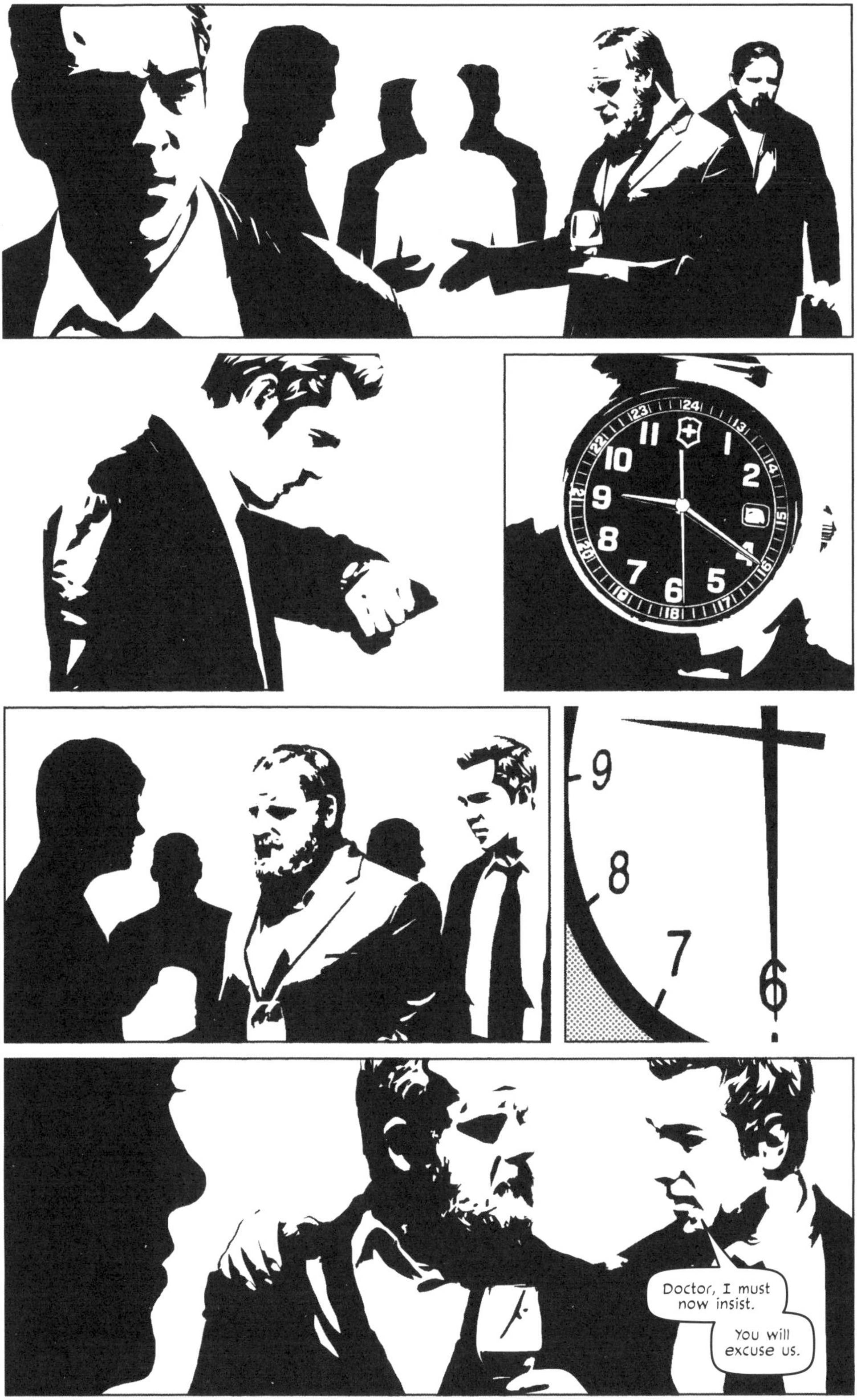
Doctor, I must now insist.
You will excuse us.

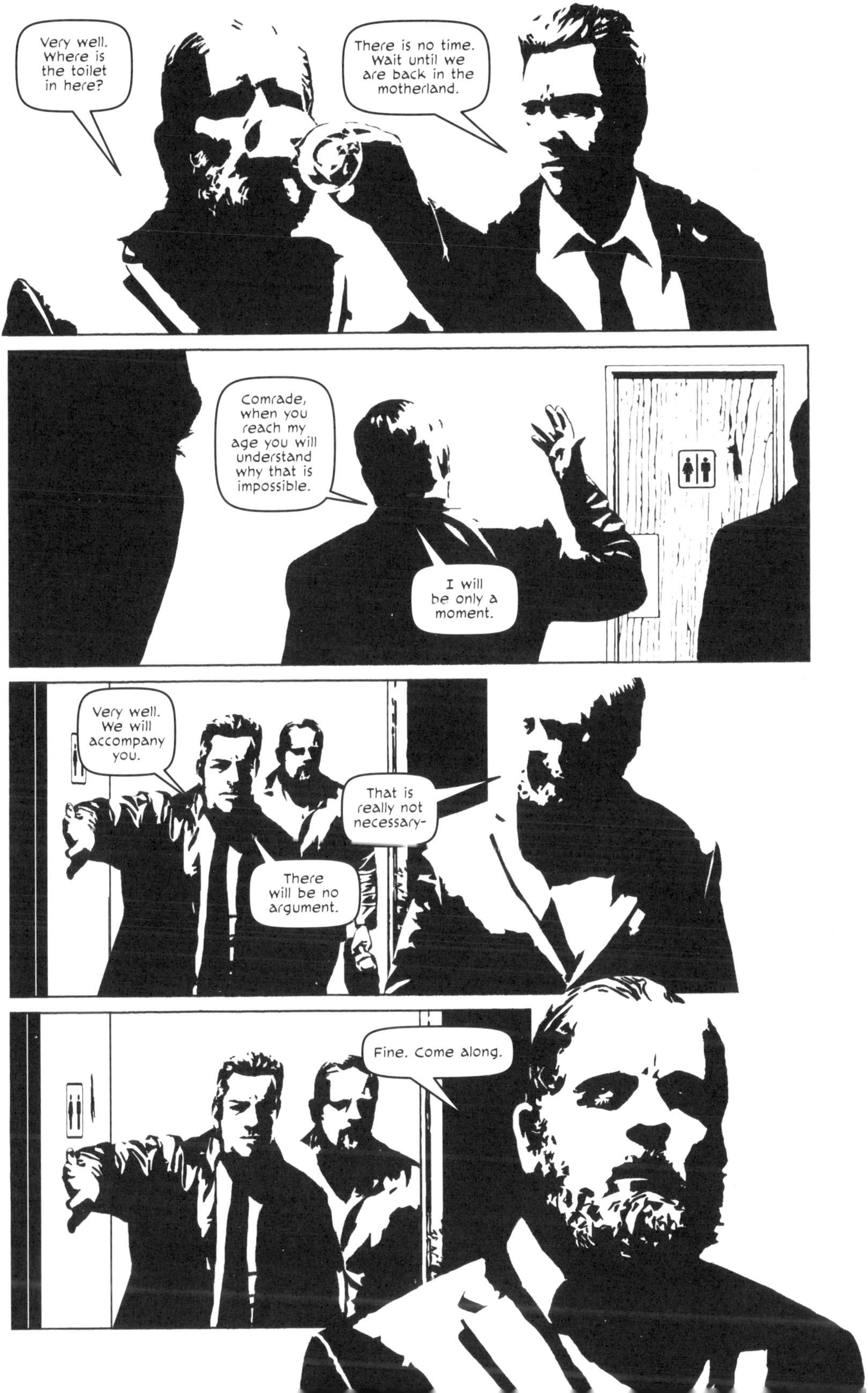
Very well. Where is the toilet in here?
There is no time. Wait until we are back in the motherland.
Comrade, when you reach my age you will understand why that is impossible.
I will be only a moment.
Very well. We will accompany you.
That is really not necessary-
There will be no argument.
Fine. Come along.

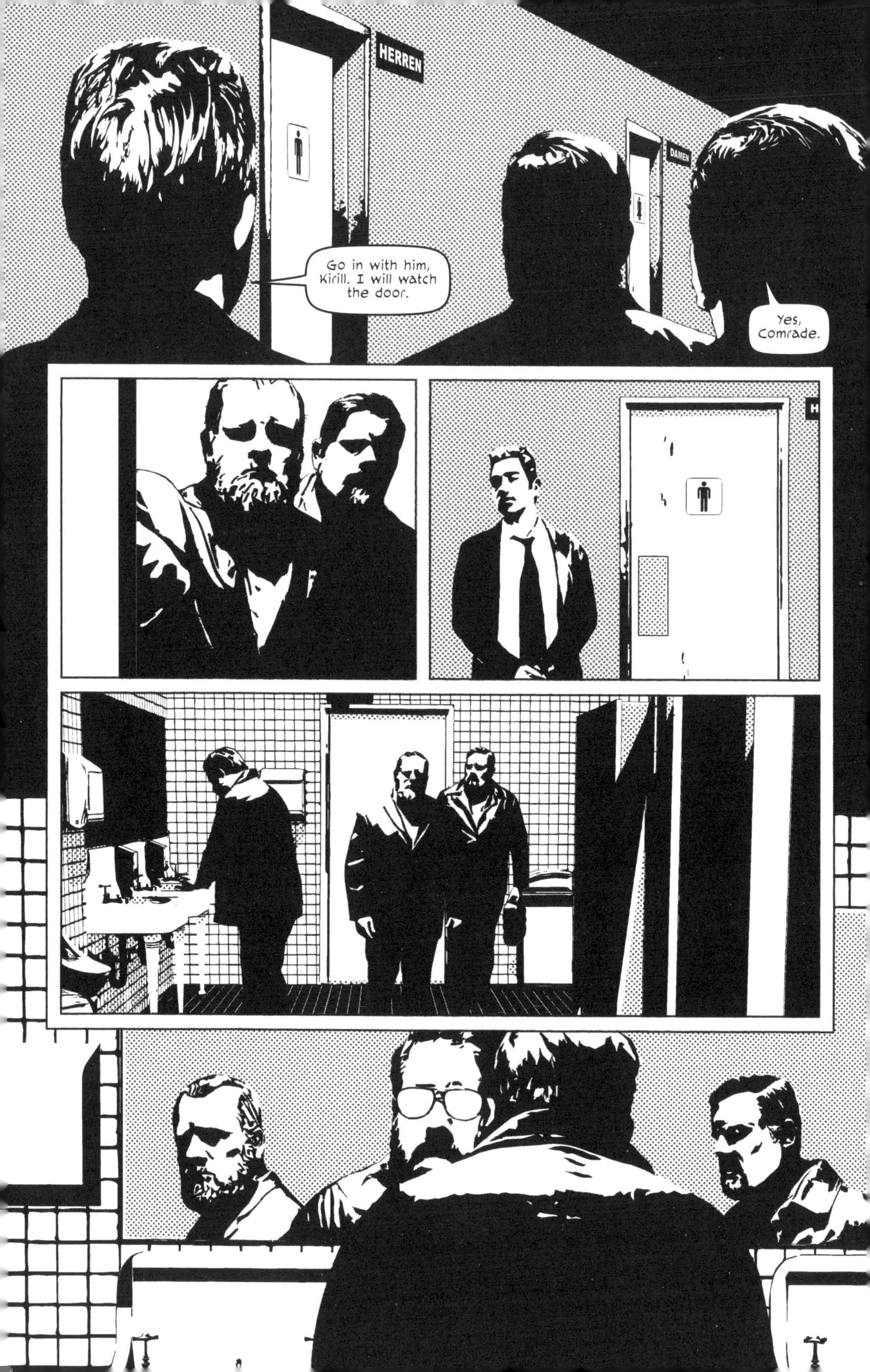
HERREN
DAMEN
Go in with him, Kirill. I will watch the door.
Yes, Comrade.
H

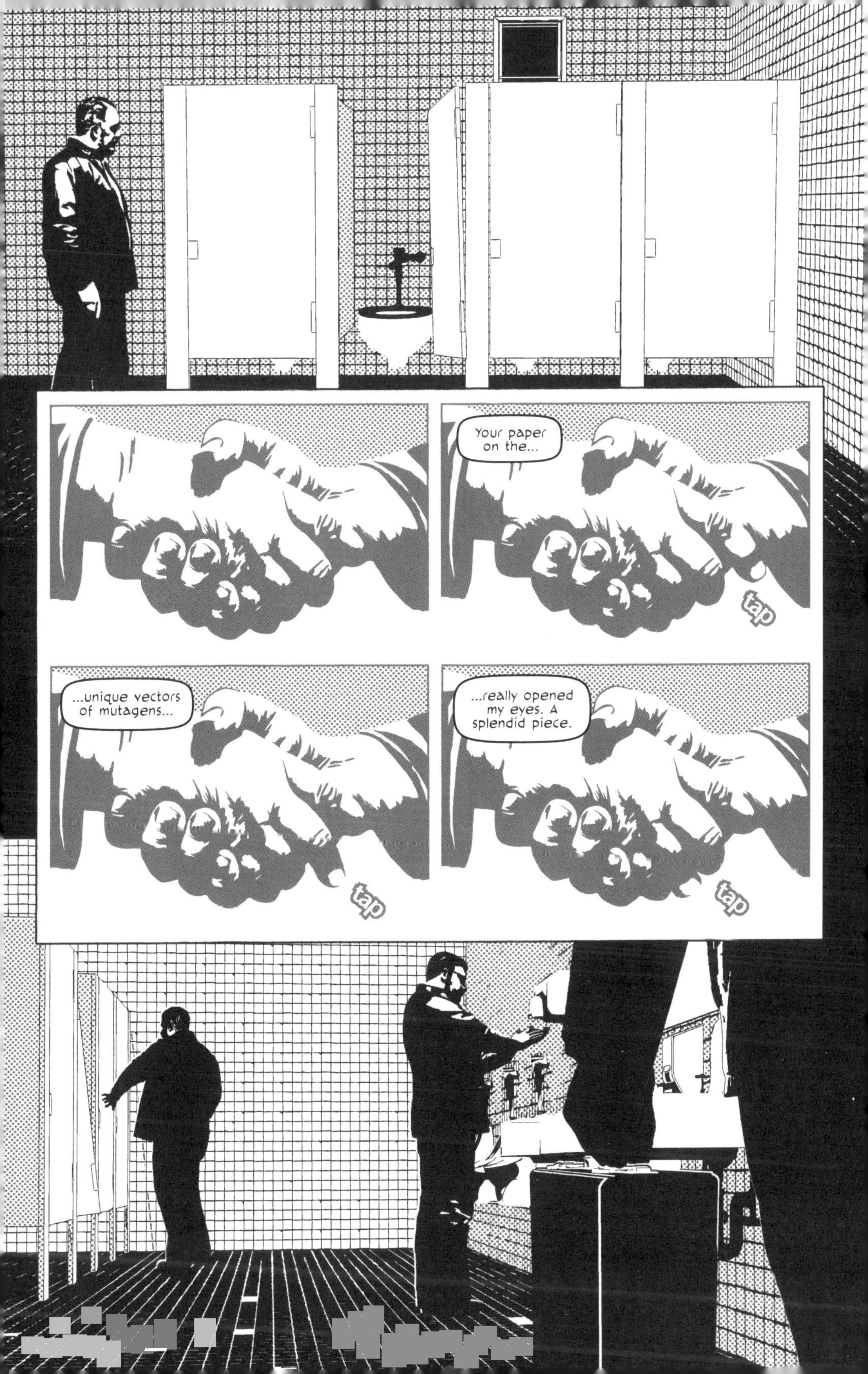
Your paper on the...
tap
...unique vectors of mutagens...
tap
...really opened my eyes. A splendid piece.
tap

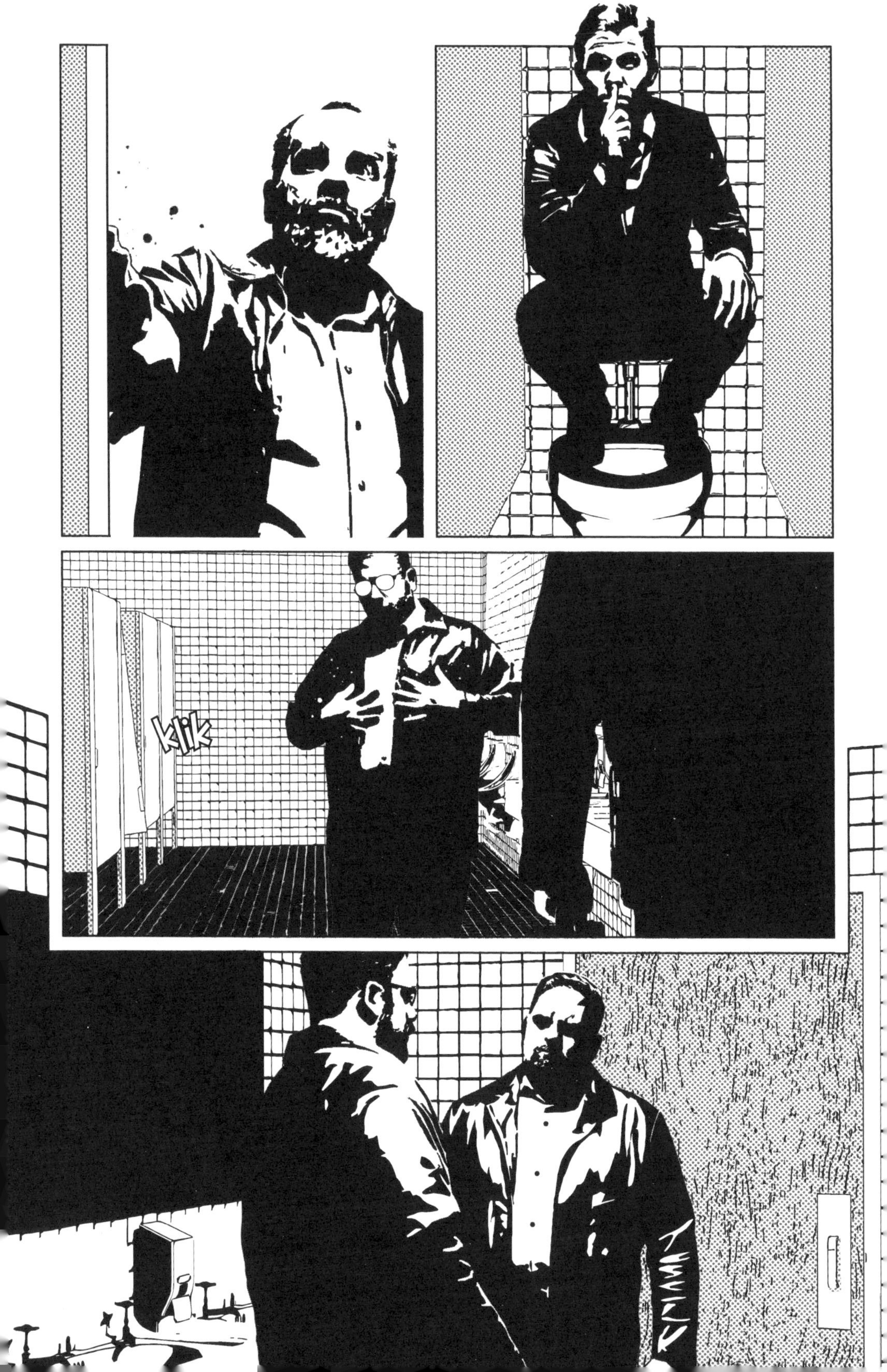
klik

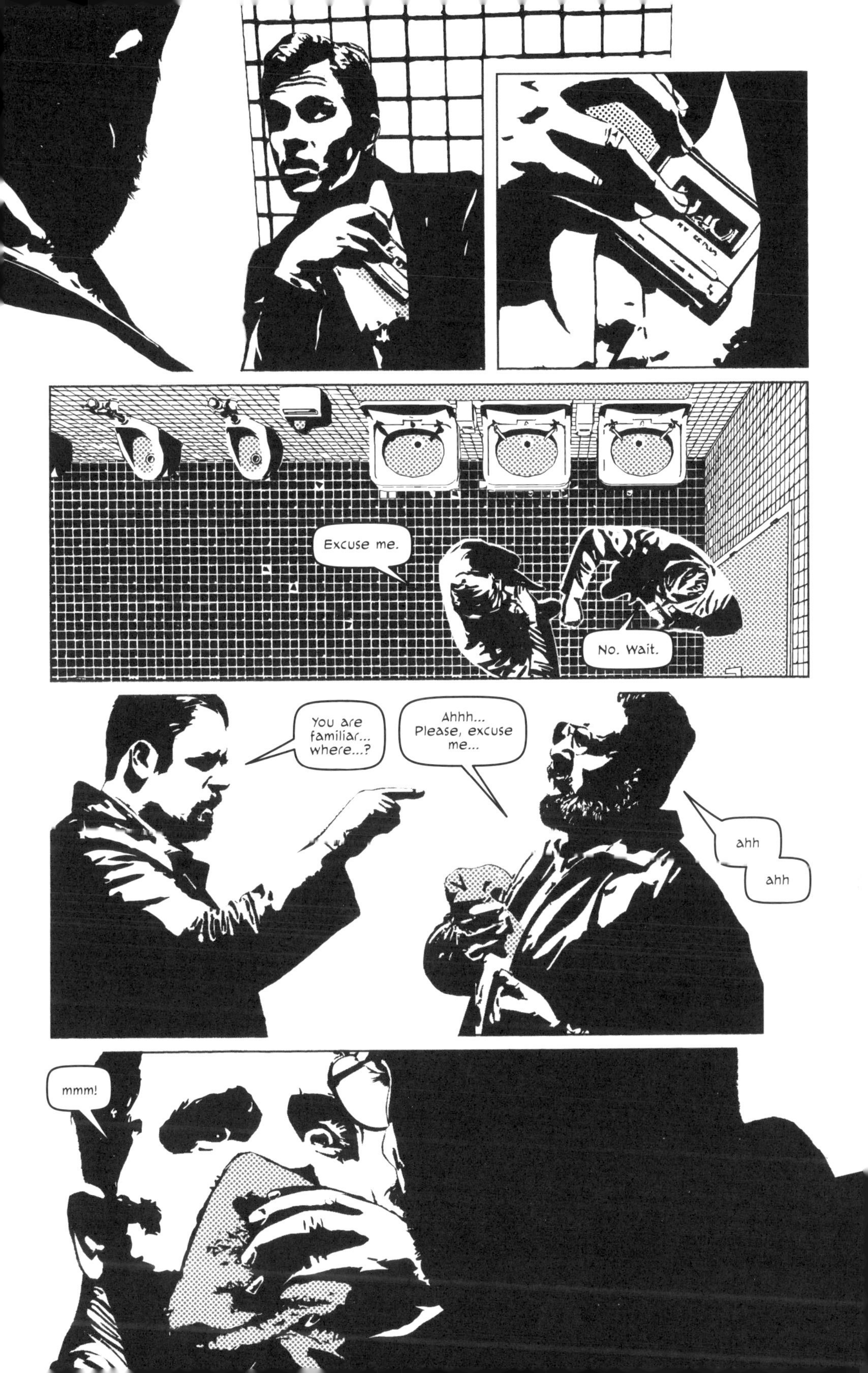
Excuse me.
No. Wait.
You are familiar... where...?
Ahhh... Please, excuse me...
ahh
ahh
mmm!

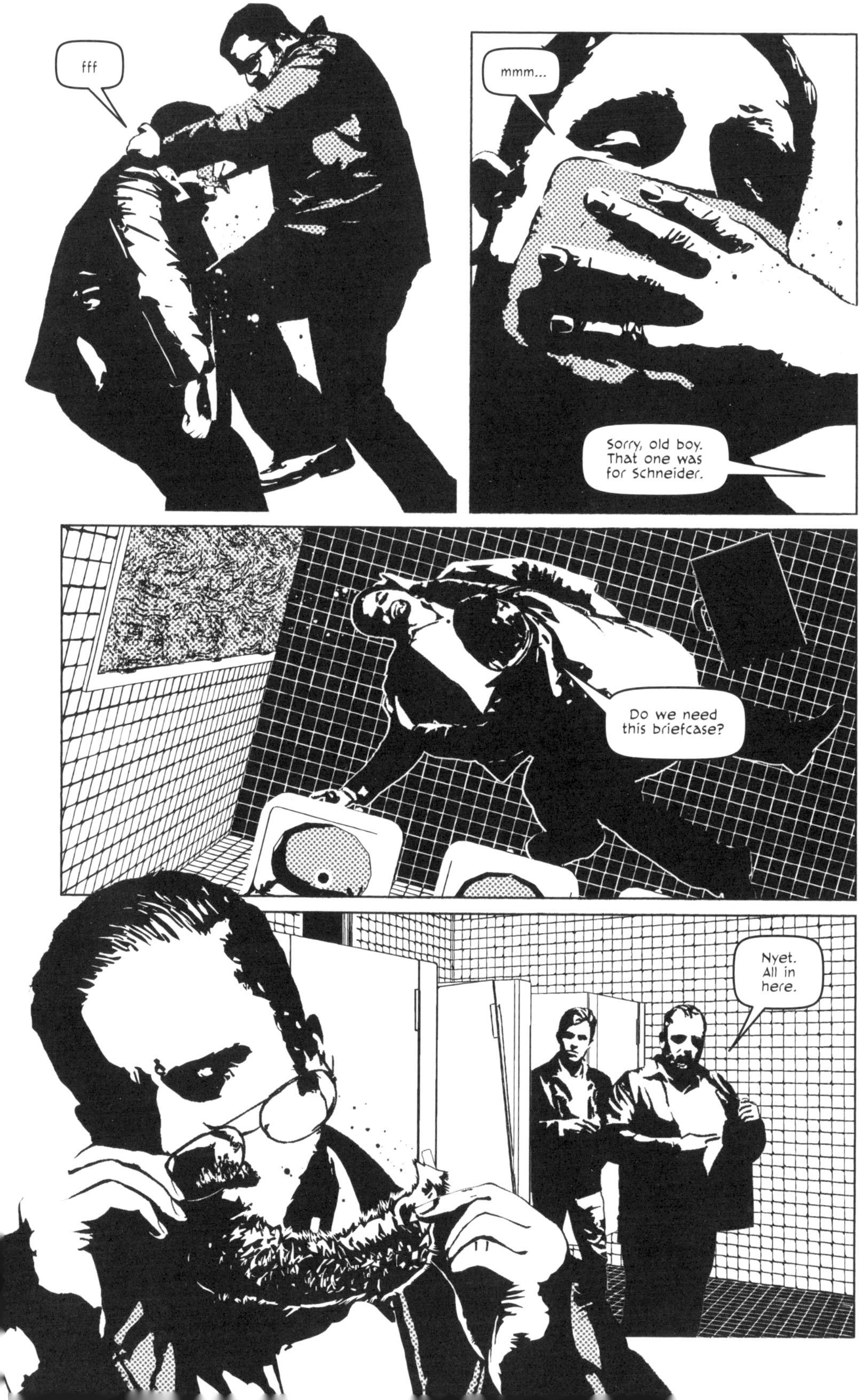
fff
mmm...
Sorry, old boy. That one was for Schneider.
Do we need this briefcase?
Nyet. All in here.

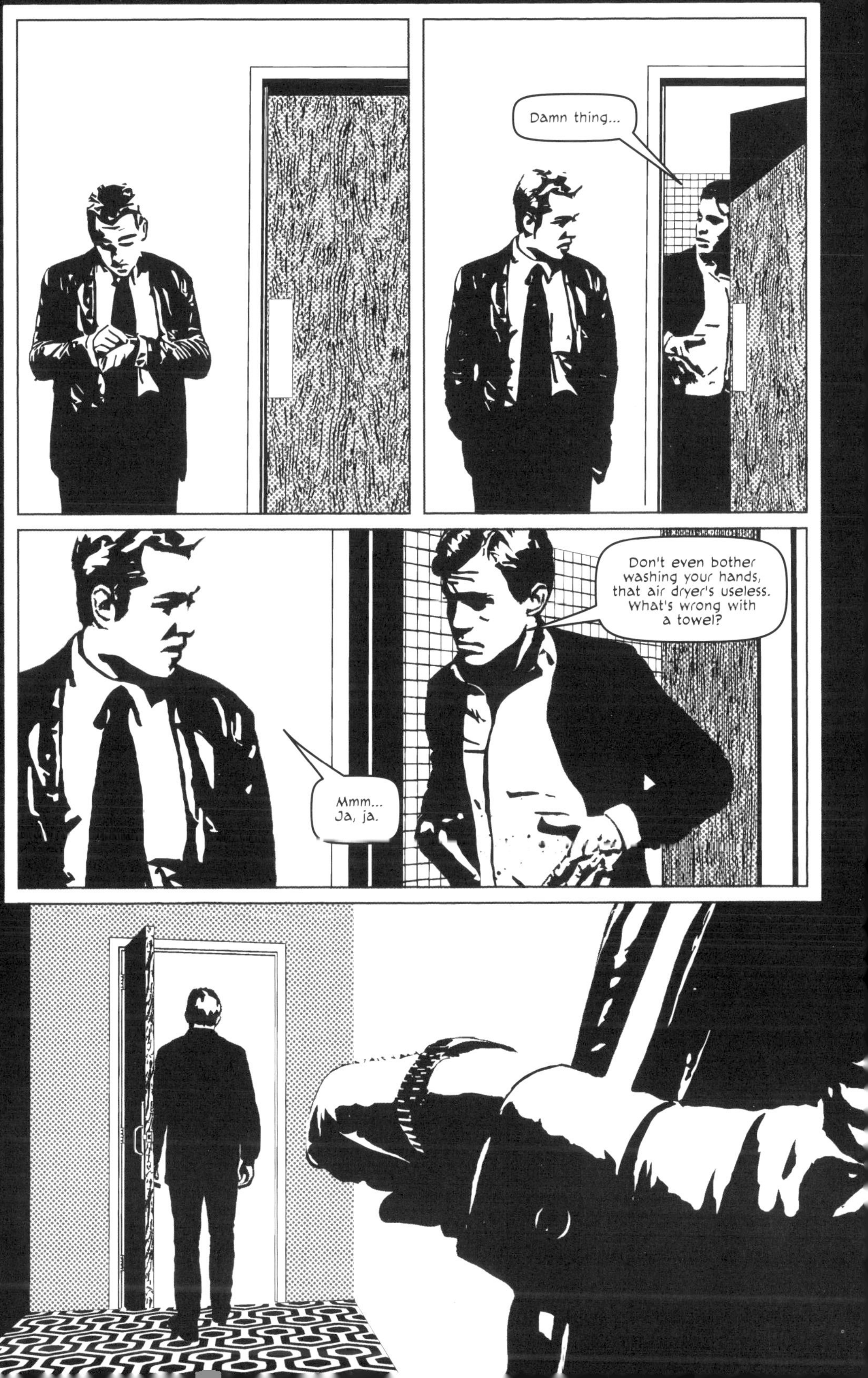
Damn thing...
Don't even bother washing your hands, that air dryer's useless. What's wrong with a towel?
Mmm... Ja, ja.

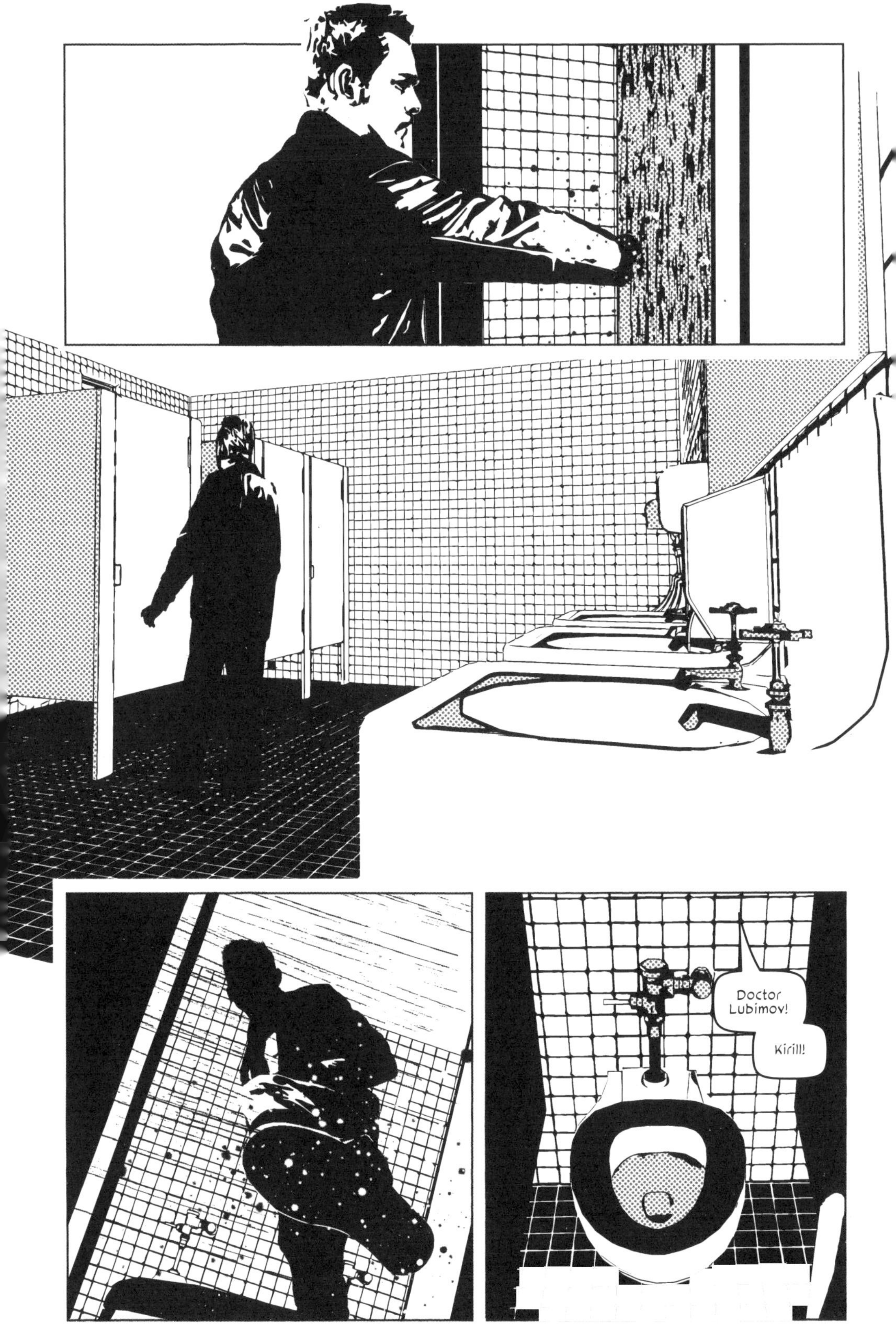
Doctor Lubimov!
Kirill!

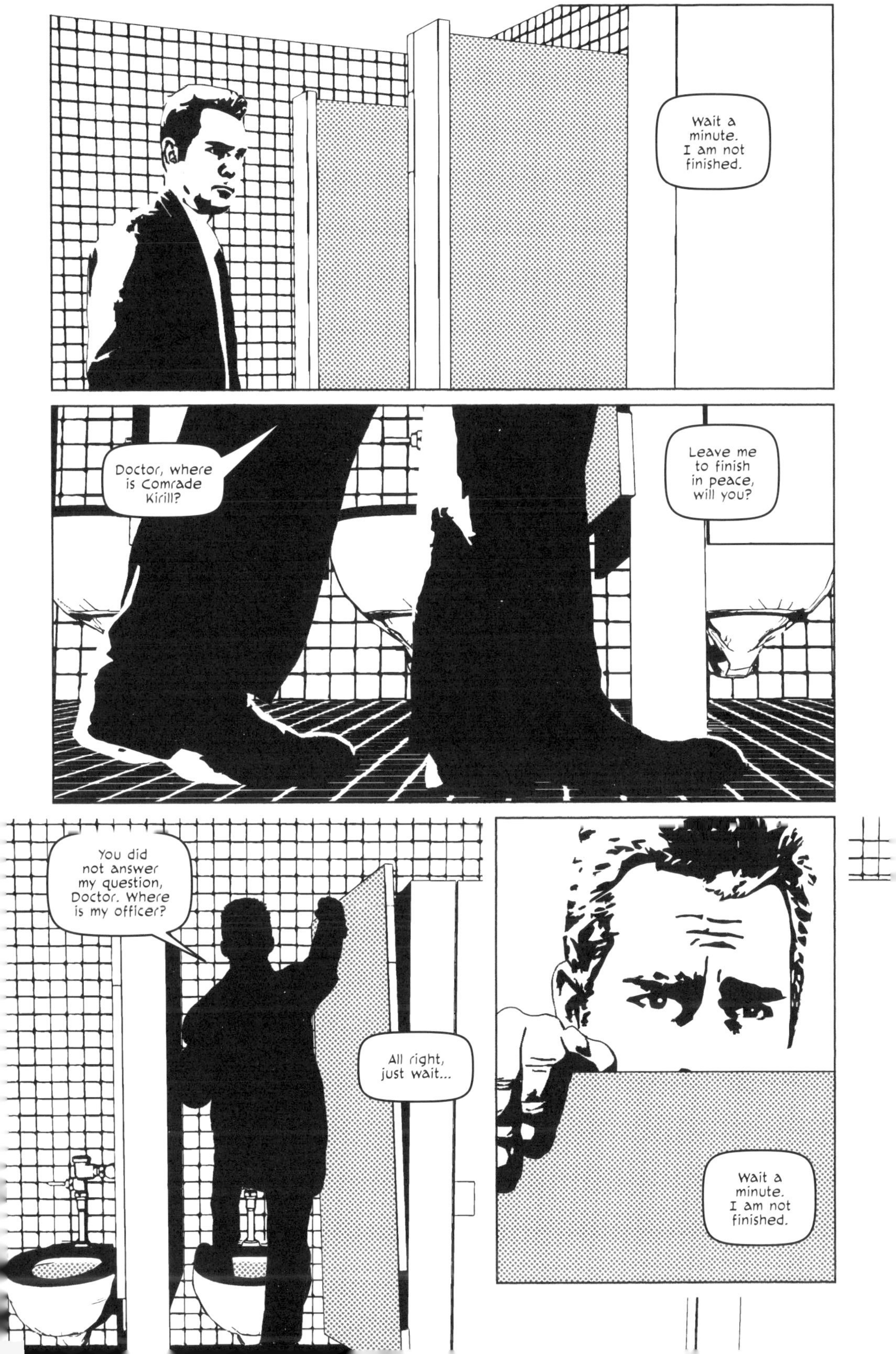
Wait a minute. I am not finished.
Doctor, where is Comrade Kirill?
Leave me to finish in peace, will you?
You did not answer my question, Doctor. Where is my officer?
All right, just wait...
Wait a minute. I am not finished.

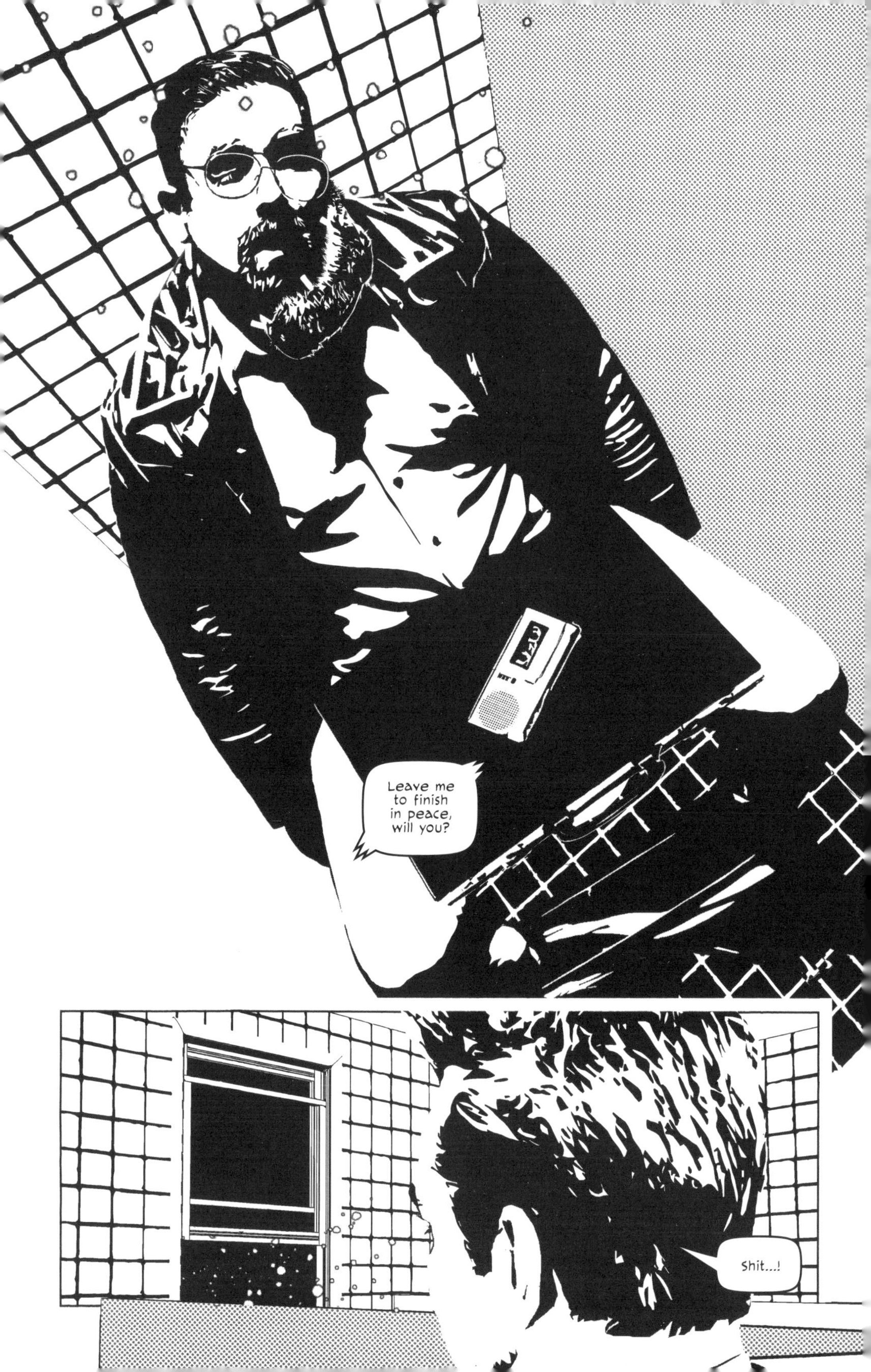
Leave me to finish in peace, will you?
Shit...!

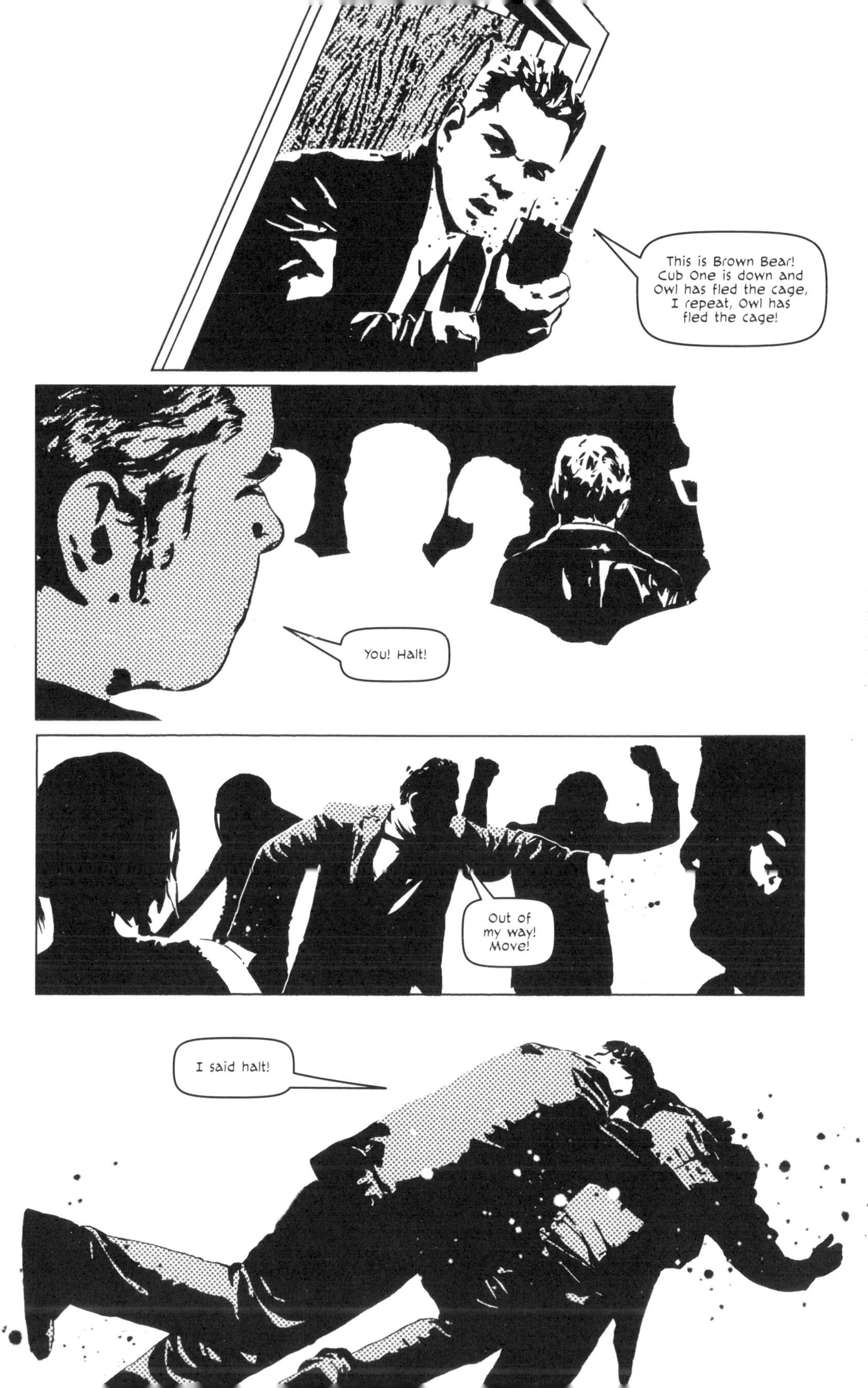
This is Brown Bear! Cub One is down and Owl has fled the cage, I repeat, Owl has fled the cage!
You! Halt!
Out of my way! Move!
I said halt!

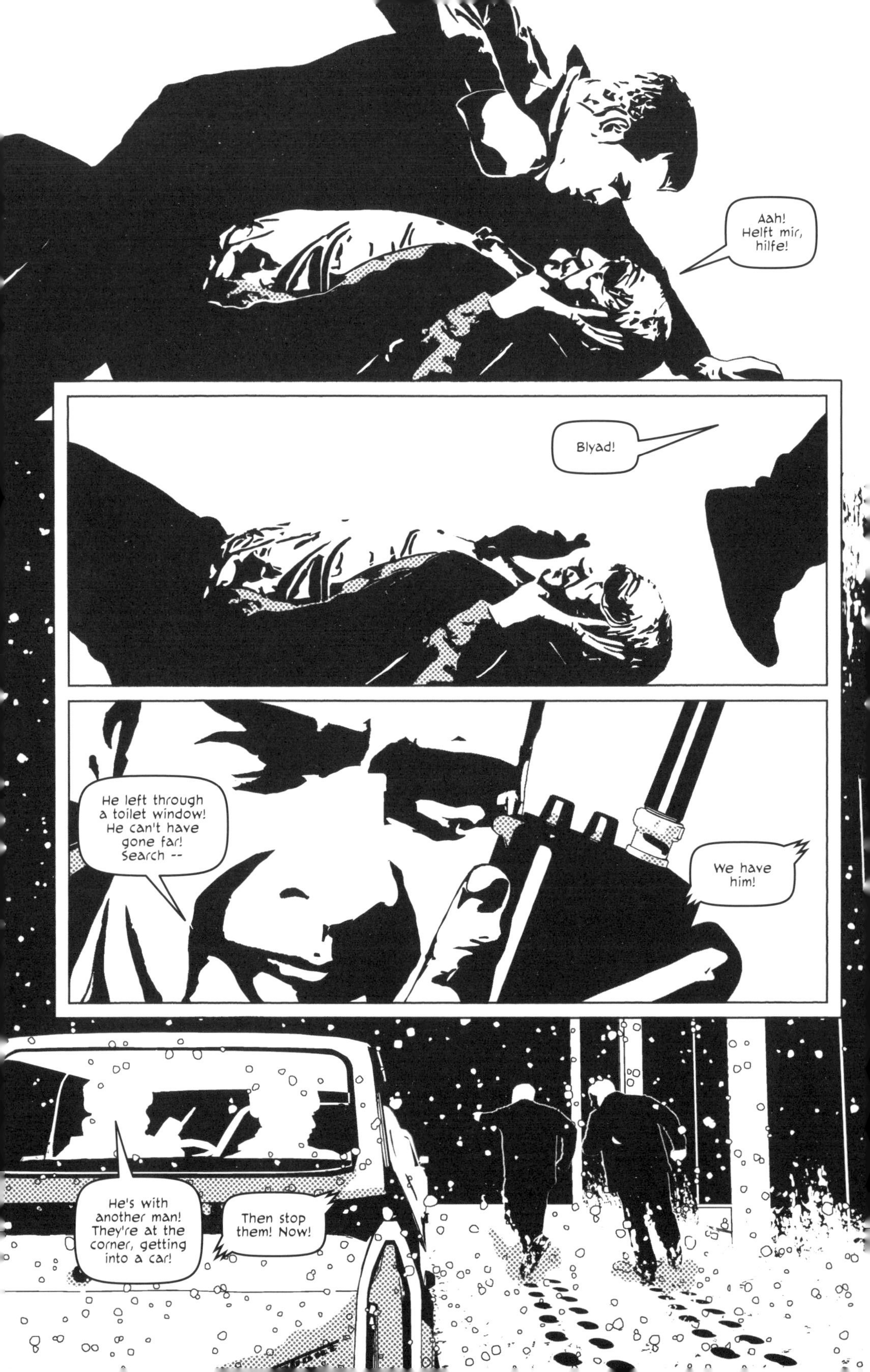
Aah! Helft mir, hilfe!
Blyad!
He left through a toilet window! He can't have gone far! Search --
We have him!
He's with another man! They're at the corner, getting into a car!
Then stop them! Now!

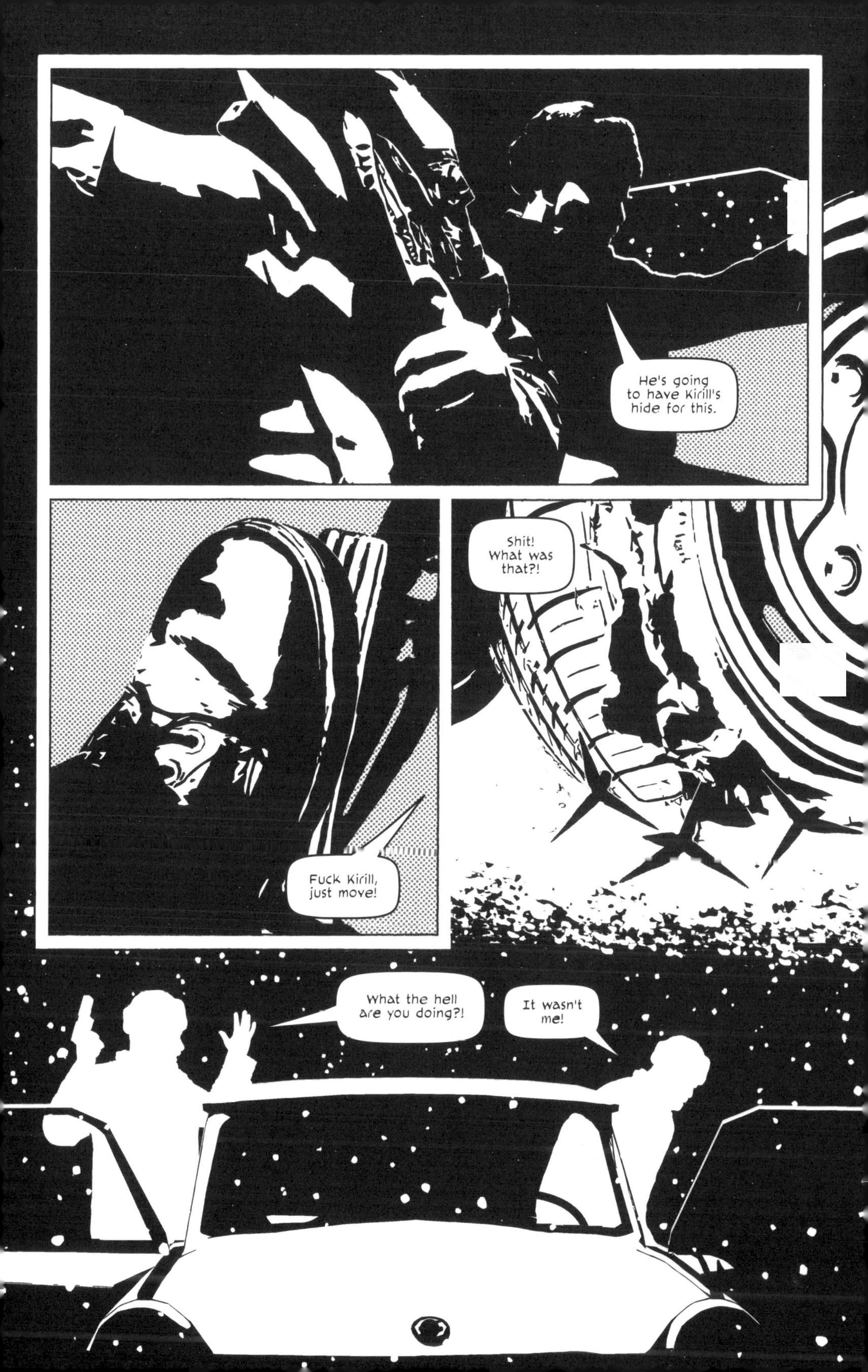
He's going to have Kirill's hide for this.
Fuck Kirill, just move!
Shit! What was that?!
What the hell are you doing?!
It wasn't me!

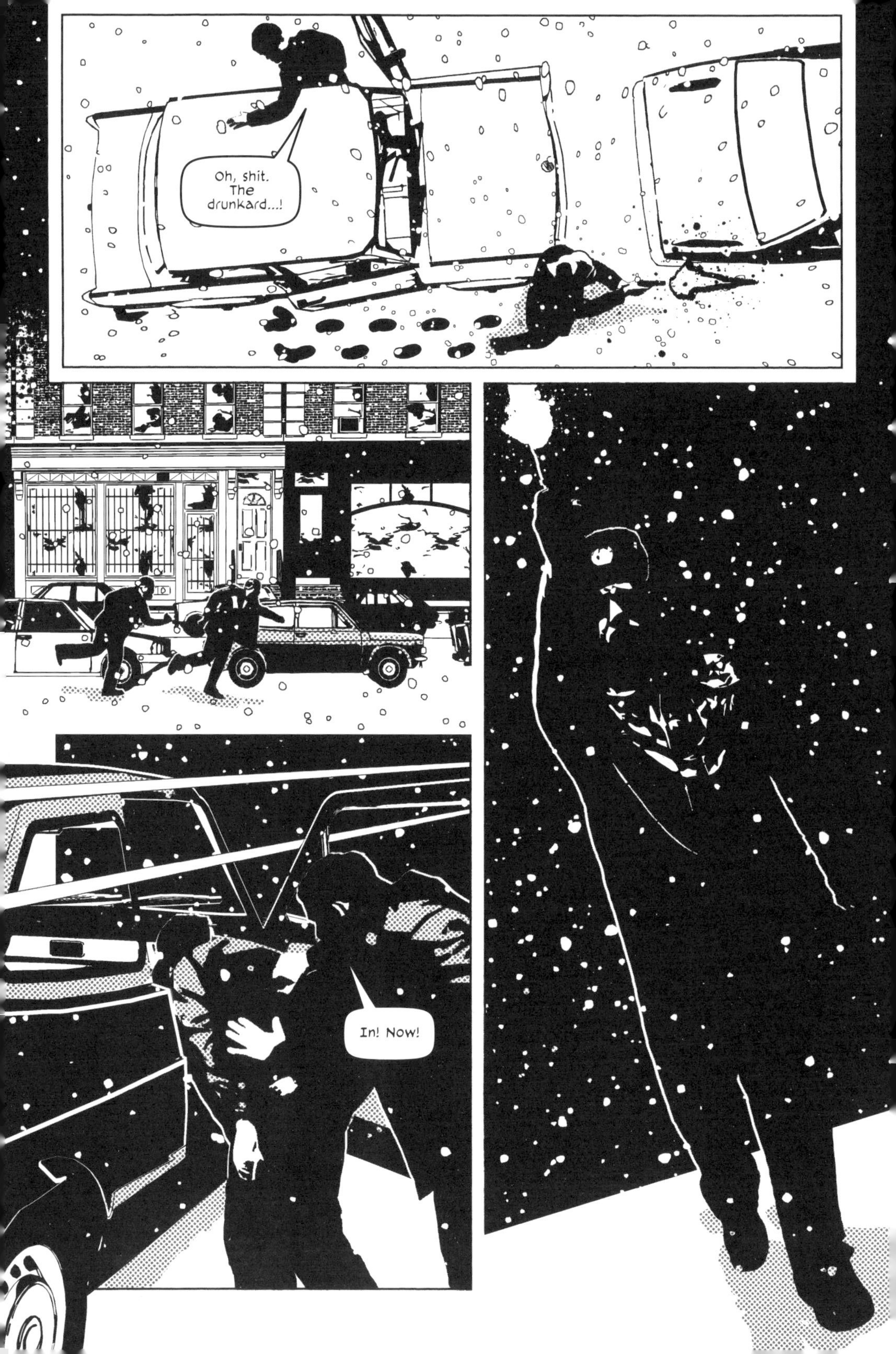
Oh, shit. The drunkard...!
In! Now!

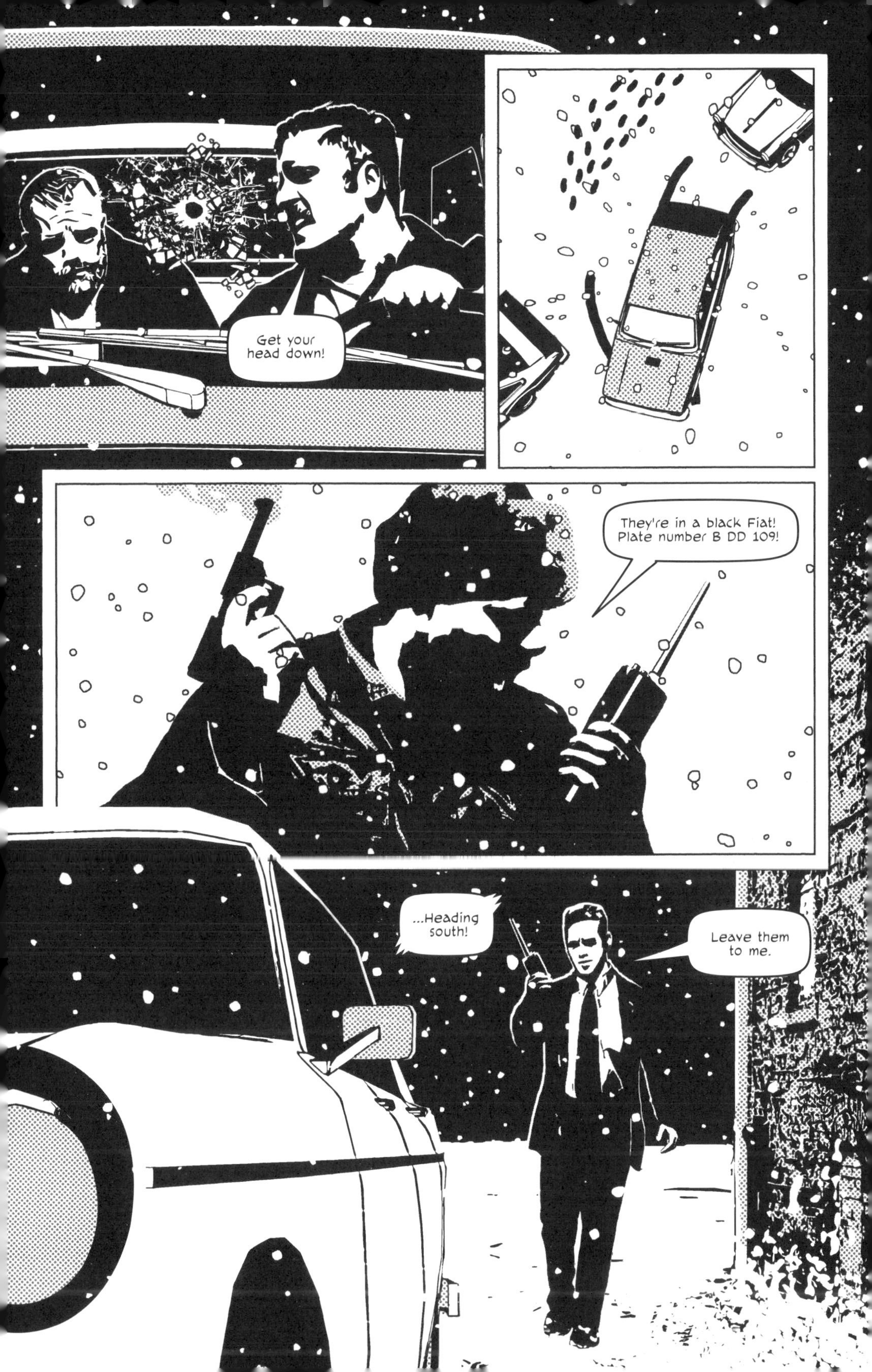
Get your head down!
They're in a black Fiat! Plate number B DD 109!
...Heading south!
Leave them to me.

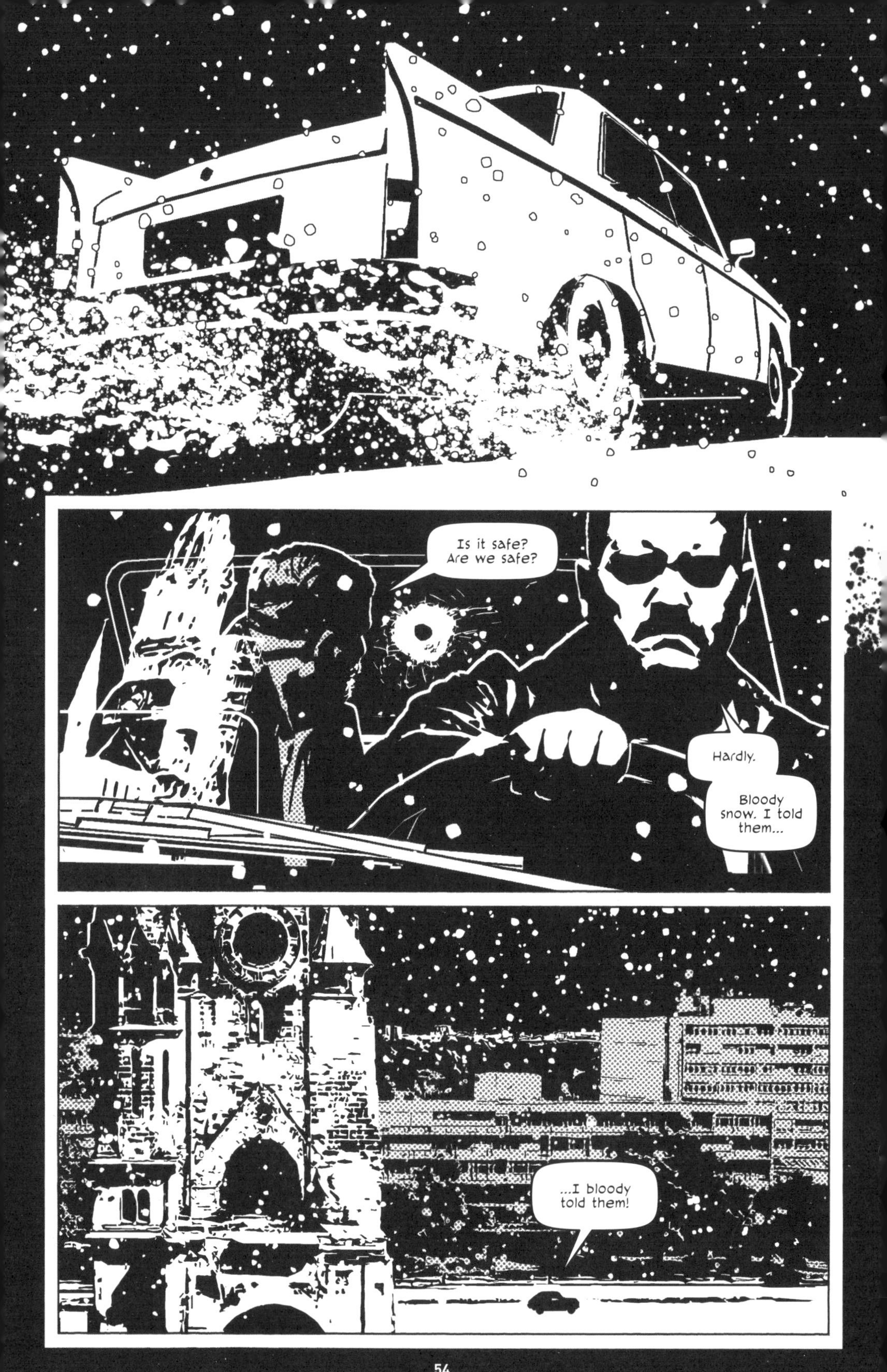
Is it safe? Are we safe?
Hardly.
Bloody snow. I told them...
...I bloody told them!

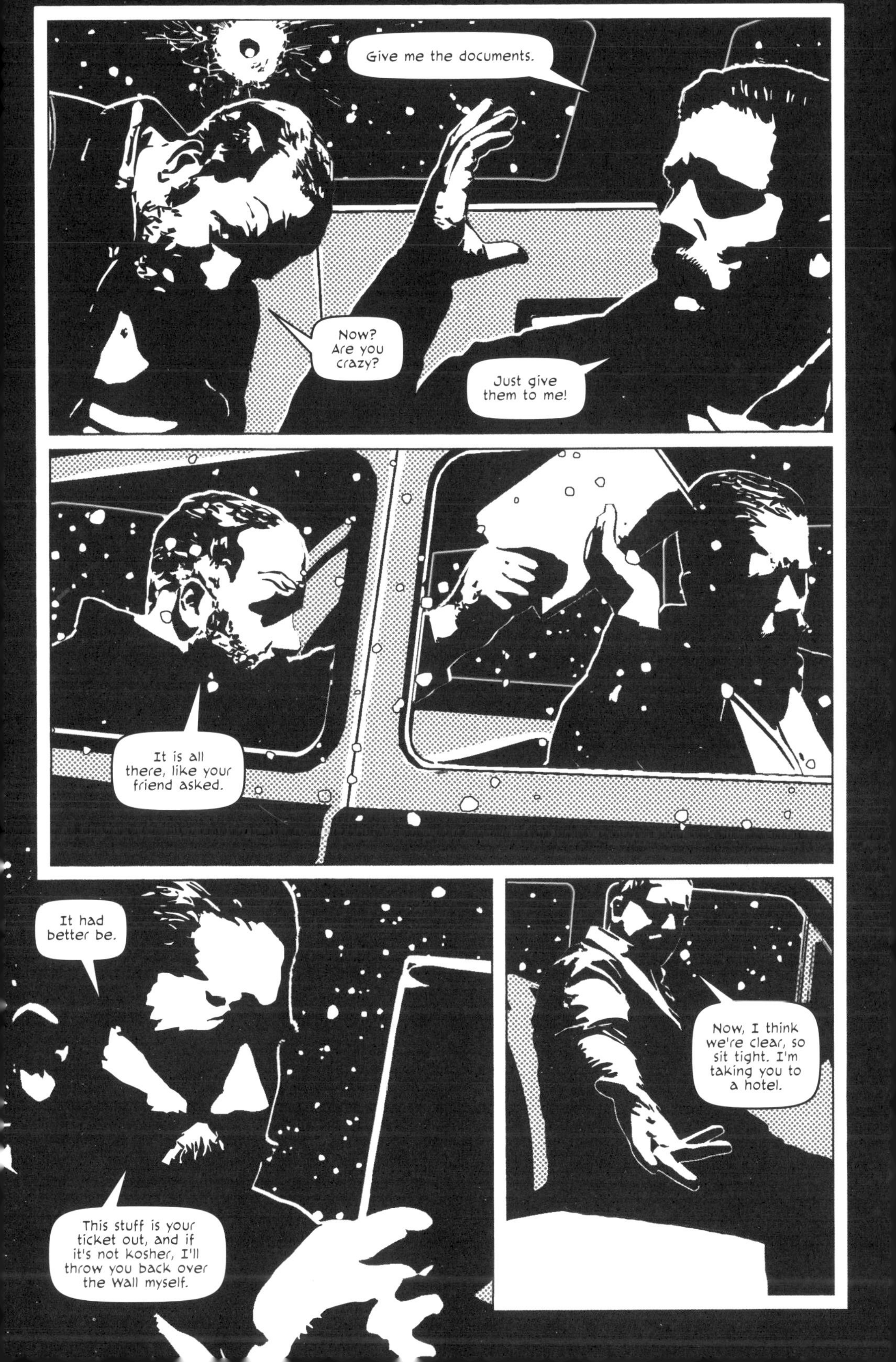
Give me the documents.
Now? Are you crazy?
Just give them to me!
It is all there, like your friend asked.
It had better be.
This stuff is your ticket out, and if it's not kosher, I'll throw you back over the Wall myself.
Now, I think we're clear, so sit tight. I'm taking you to a hotel.

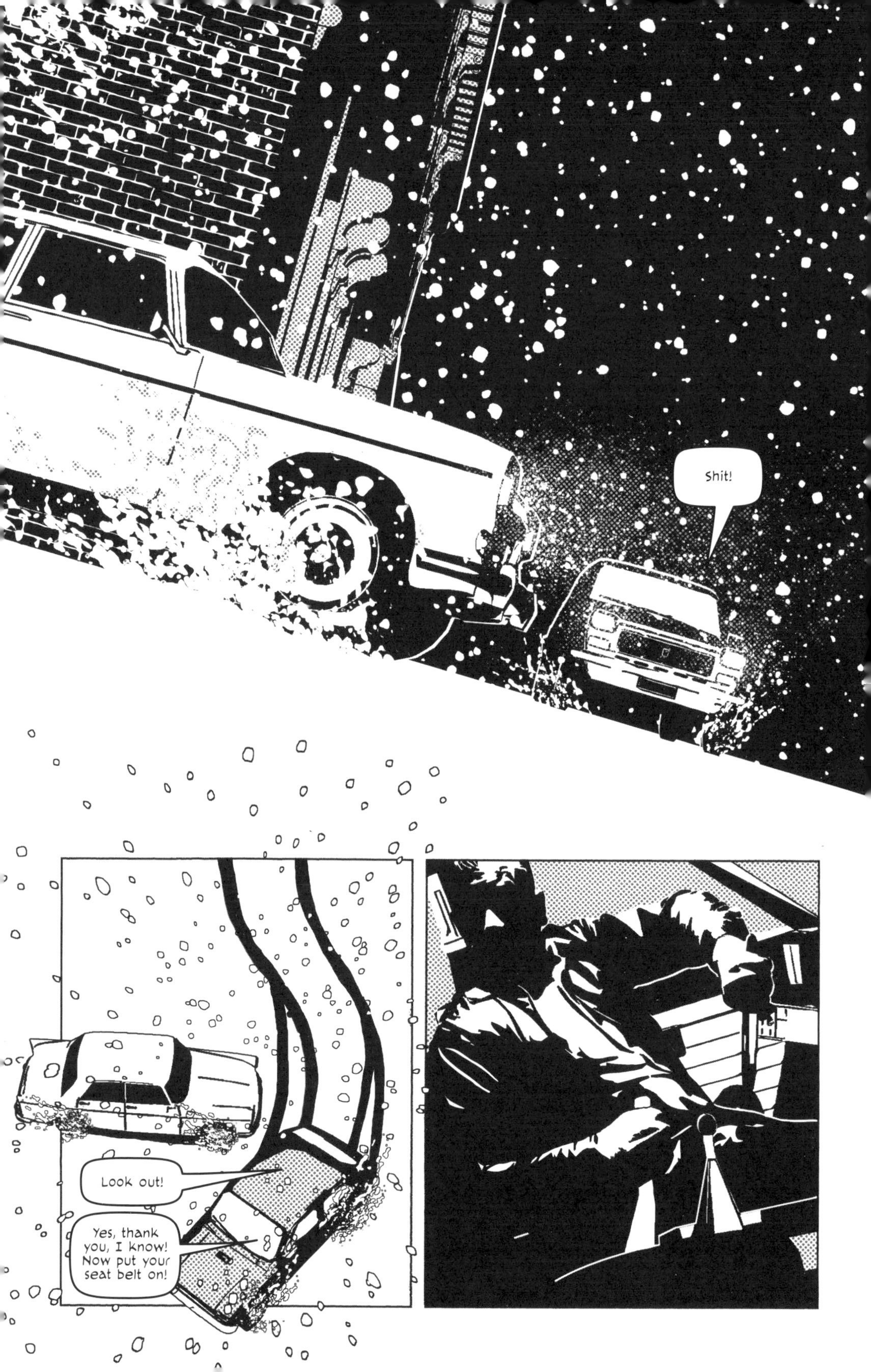
Shit!
Look out!
Yes, thank you, I know! Now put your seat belt on!

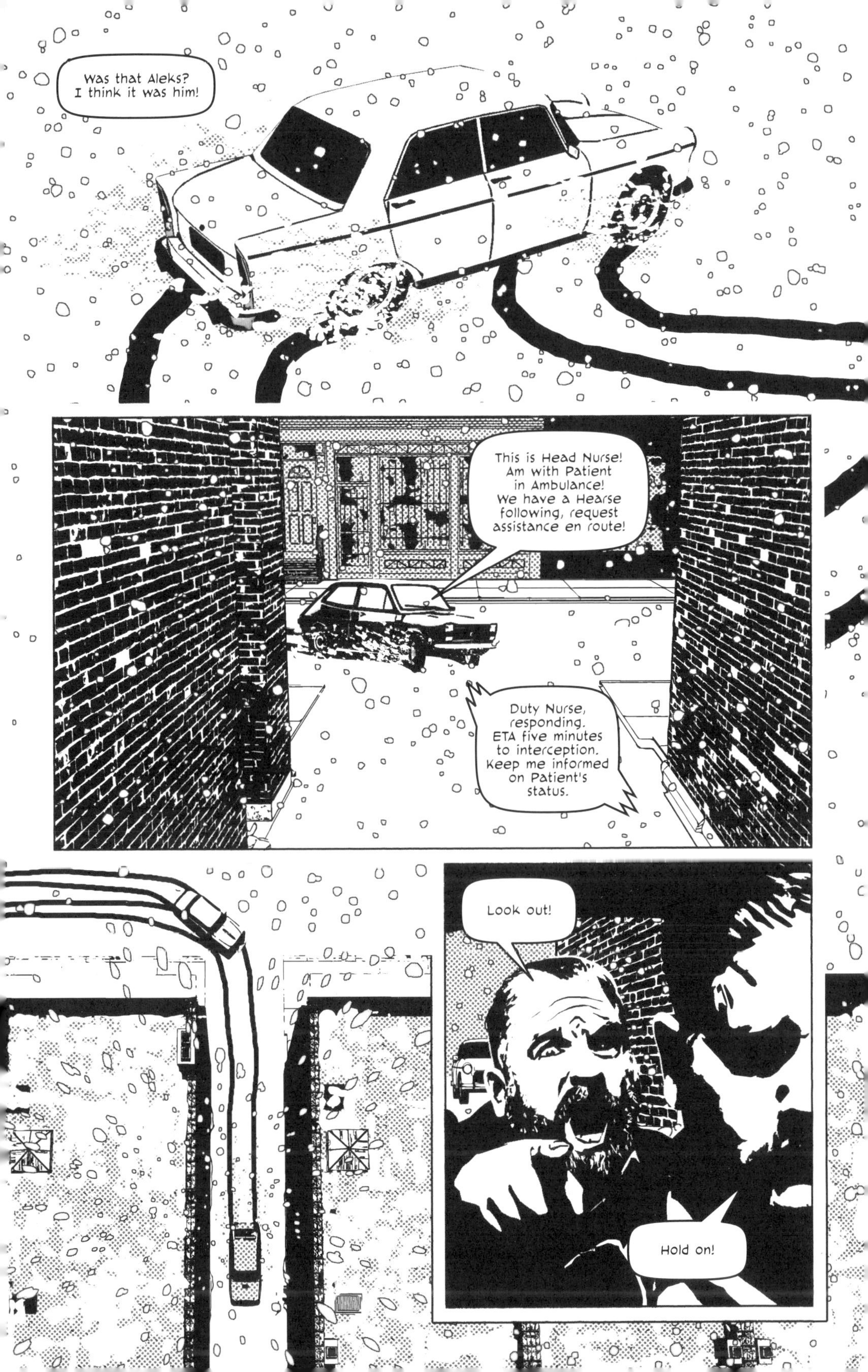
Was that Aleks? I think it was him!
This is Head Nurse! Am with Patient in Ambulance! We have a Hearse following, request assistance en route!
Duty Nurse, responding. ETA five minutes to interception. Keep me informed on Patient's status.
Look out!
Hold on!

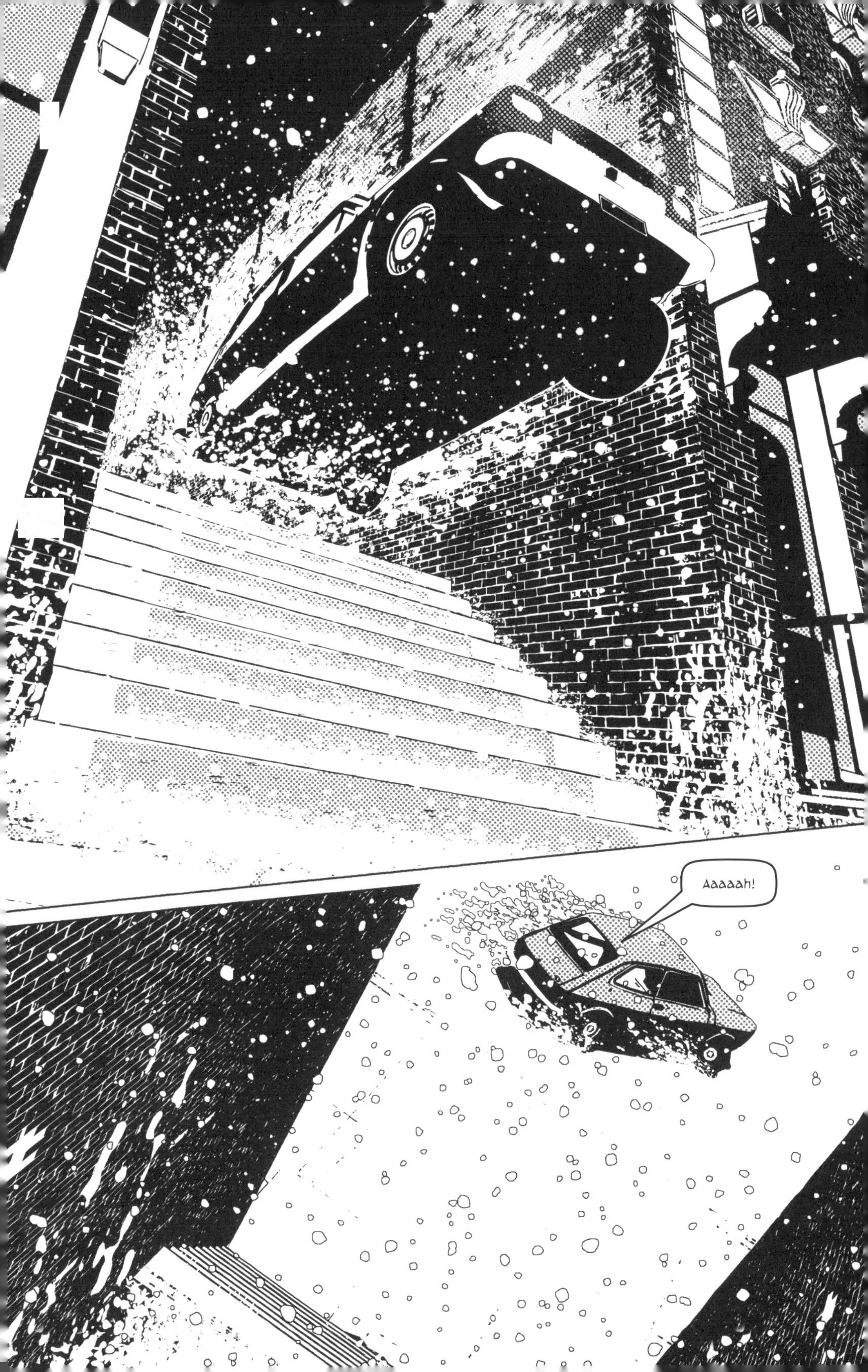
Aaaaah!

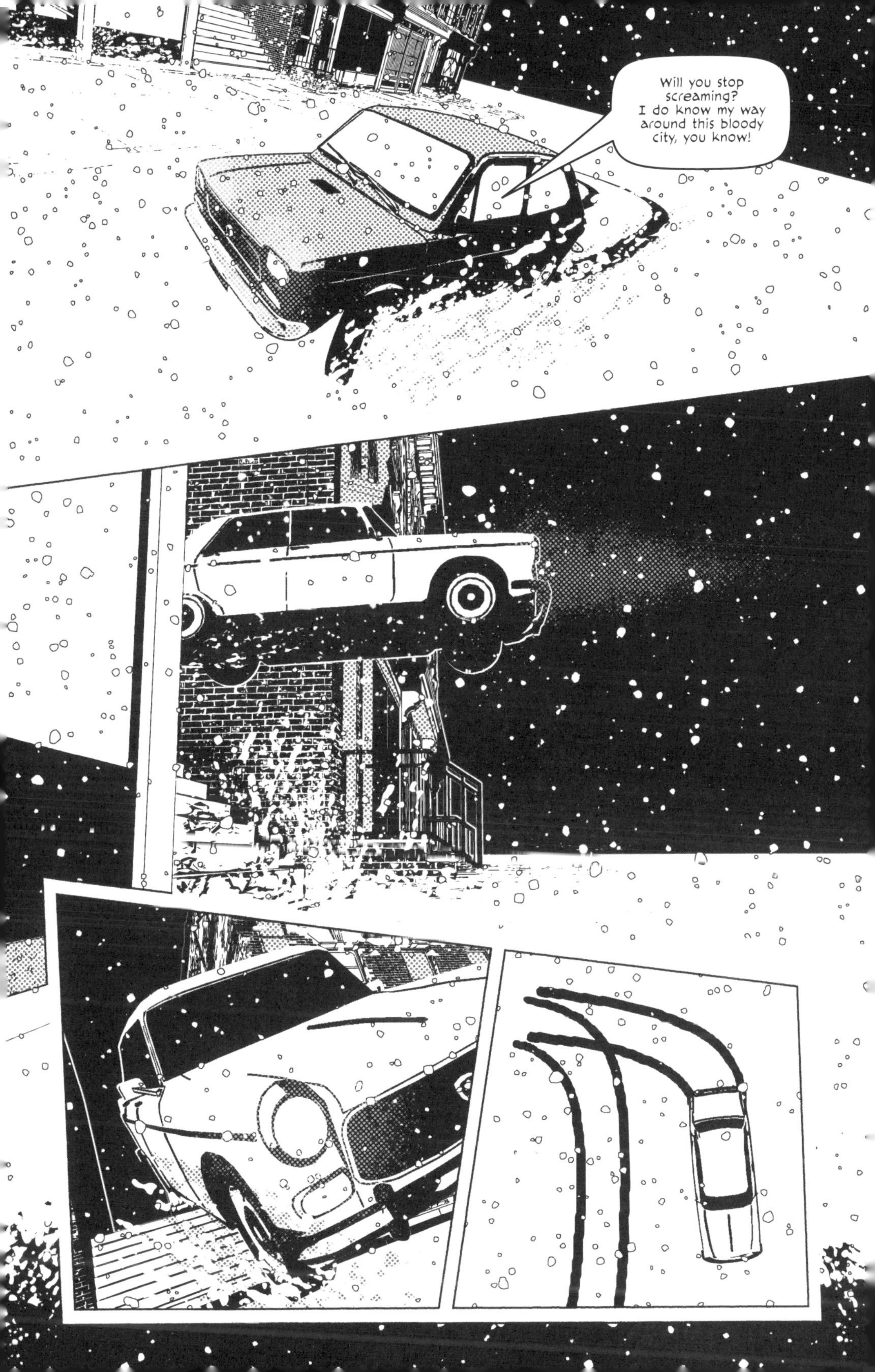
Will you stop screaming? I do know my way around this bloody city, you know!

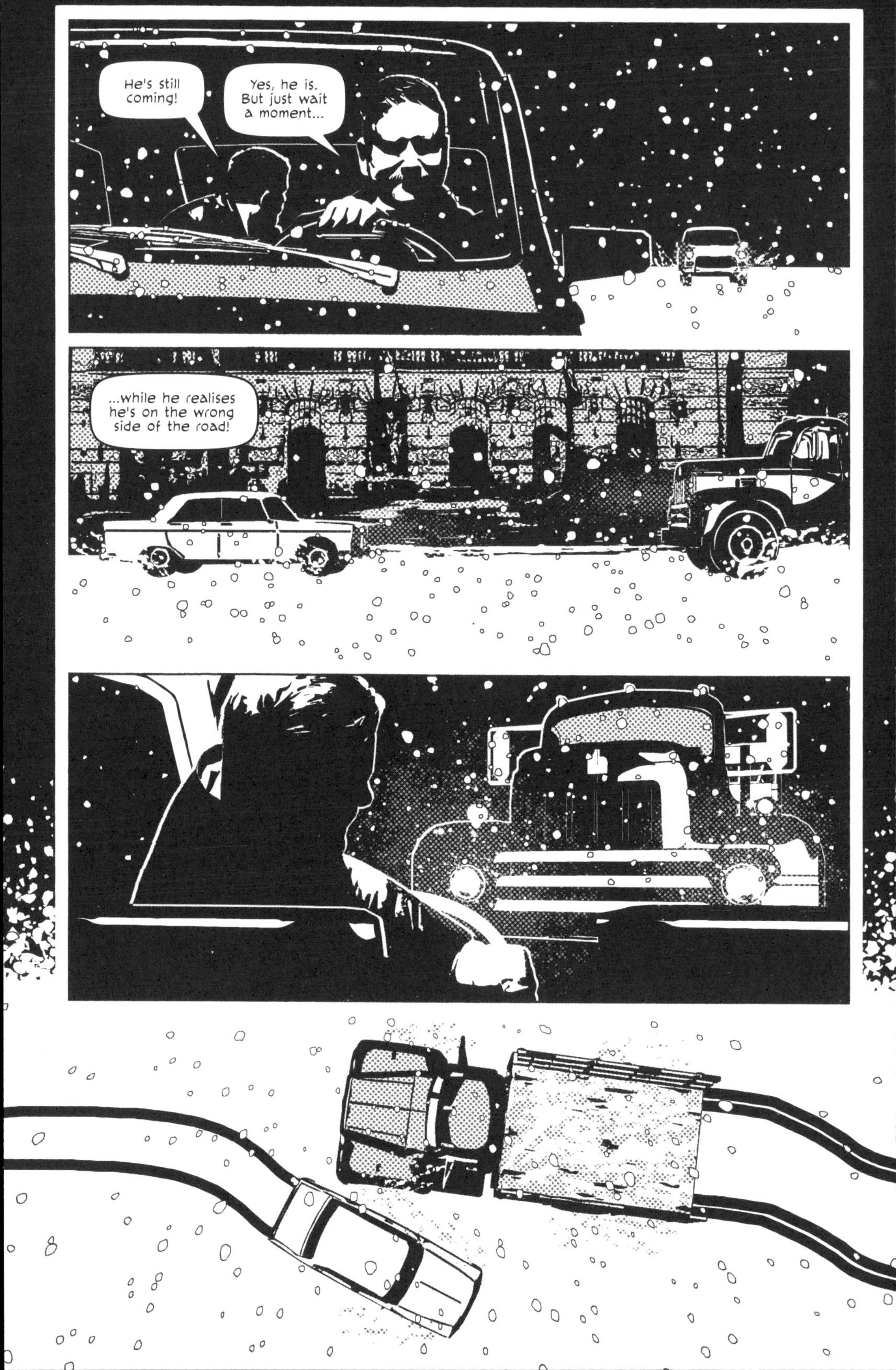
He's still coming!
Yes, he is. But just wait a moment...
...while he realises he's on the wrong side of the road!

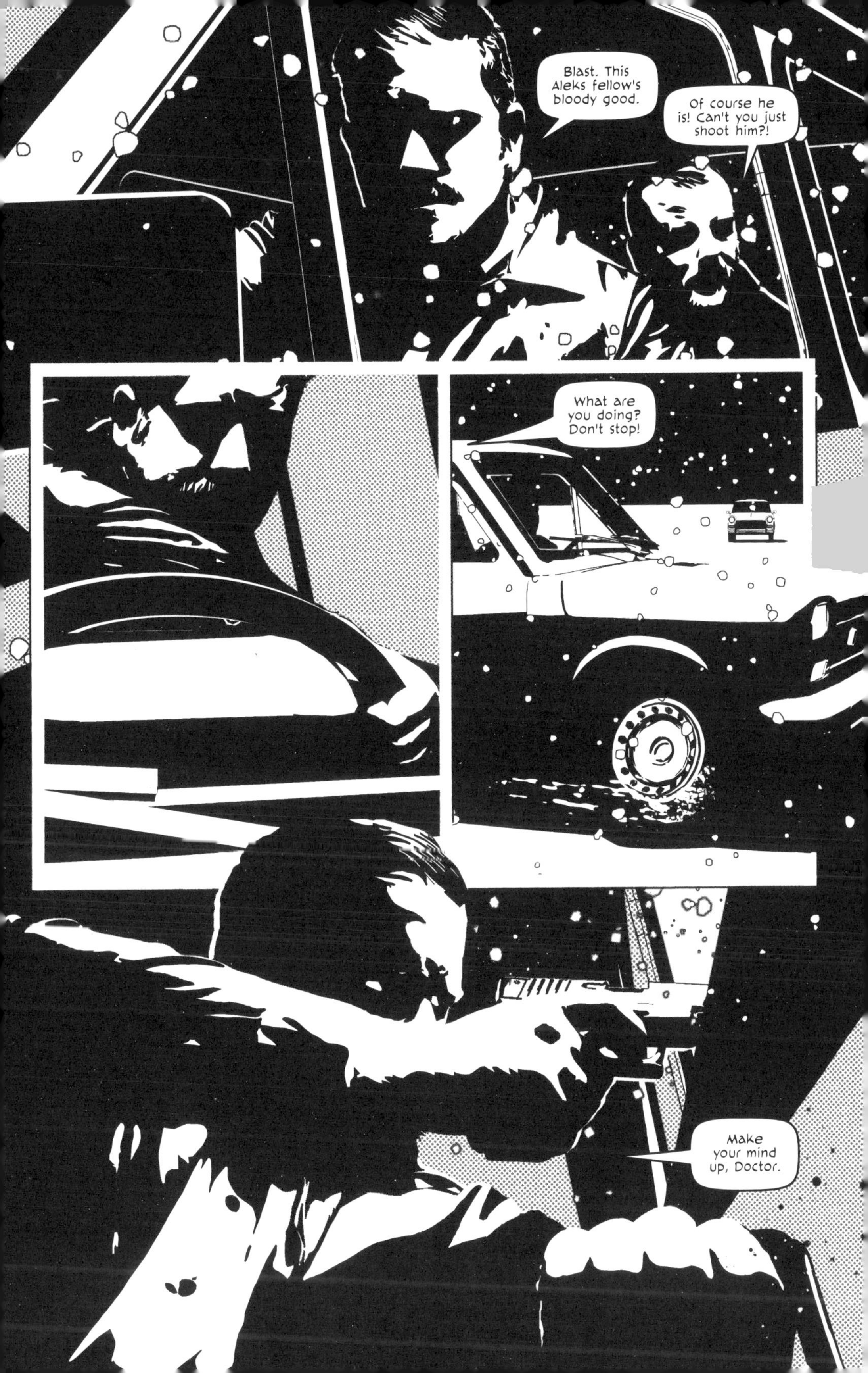
Blast. This Aleks fellow's bloody good.
Of course he is! Can't you just shoot him?!
What are you doing? Don't stop!
Make your mind up, Doctor.

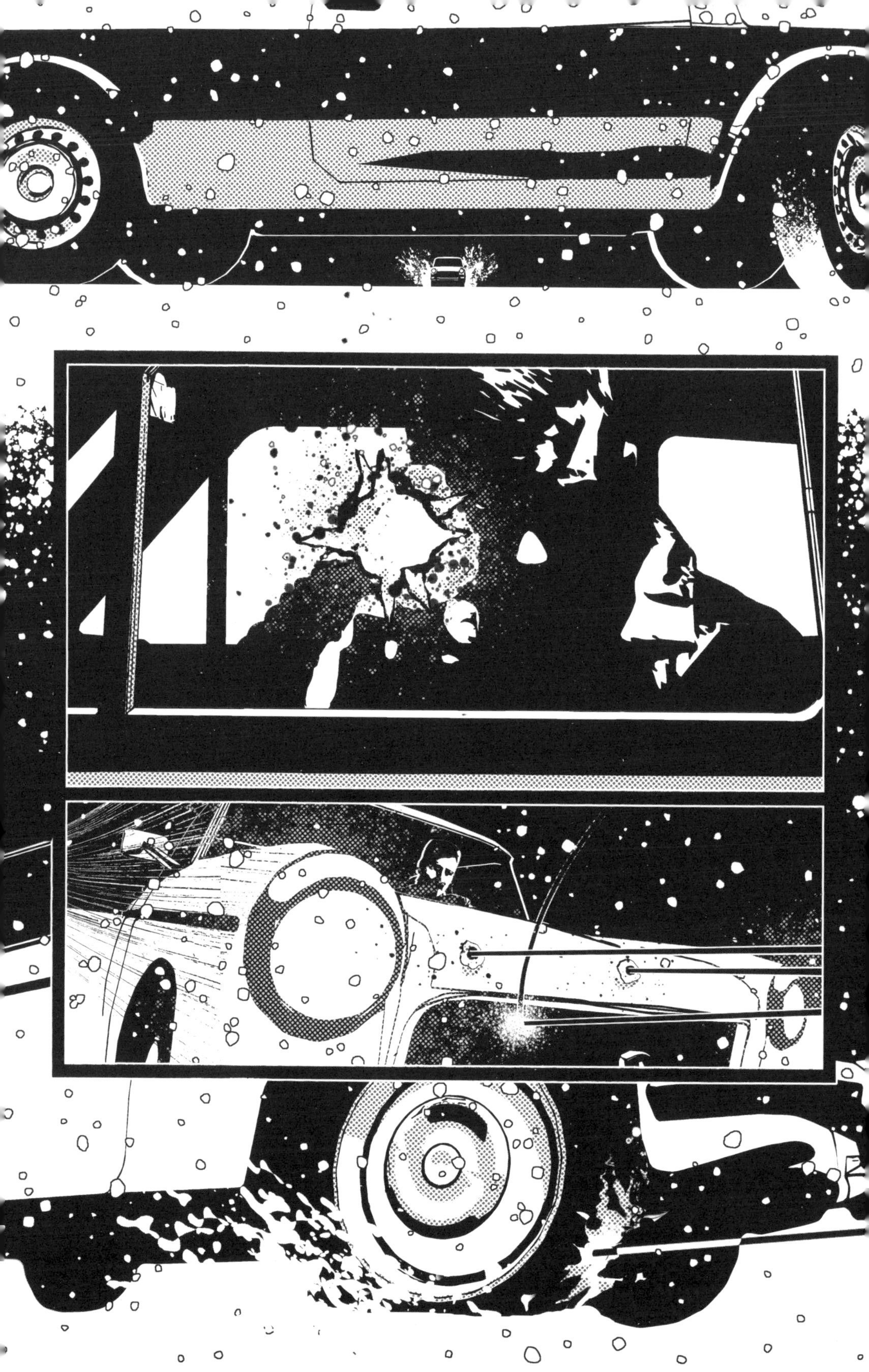

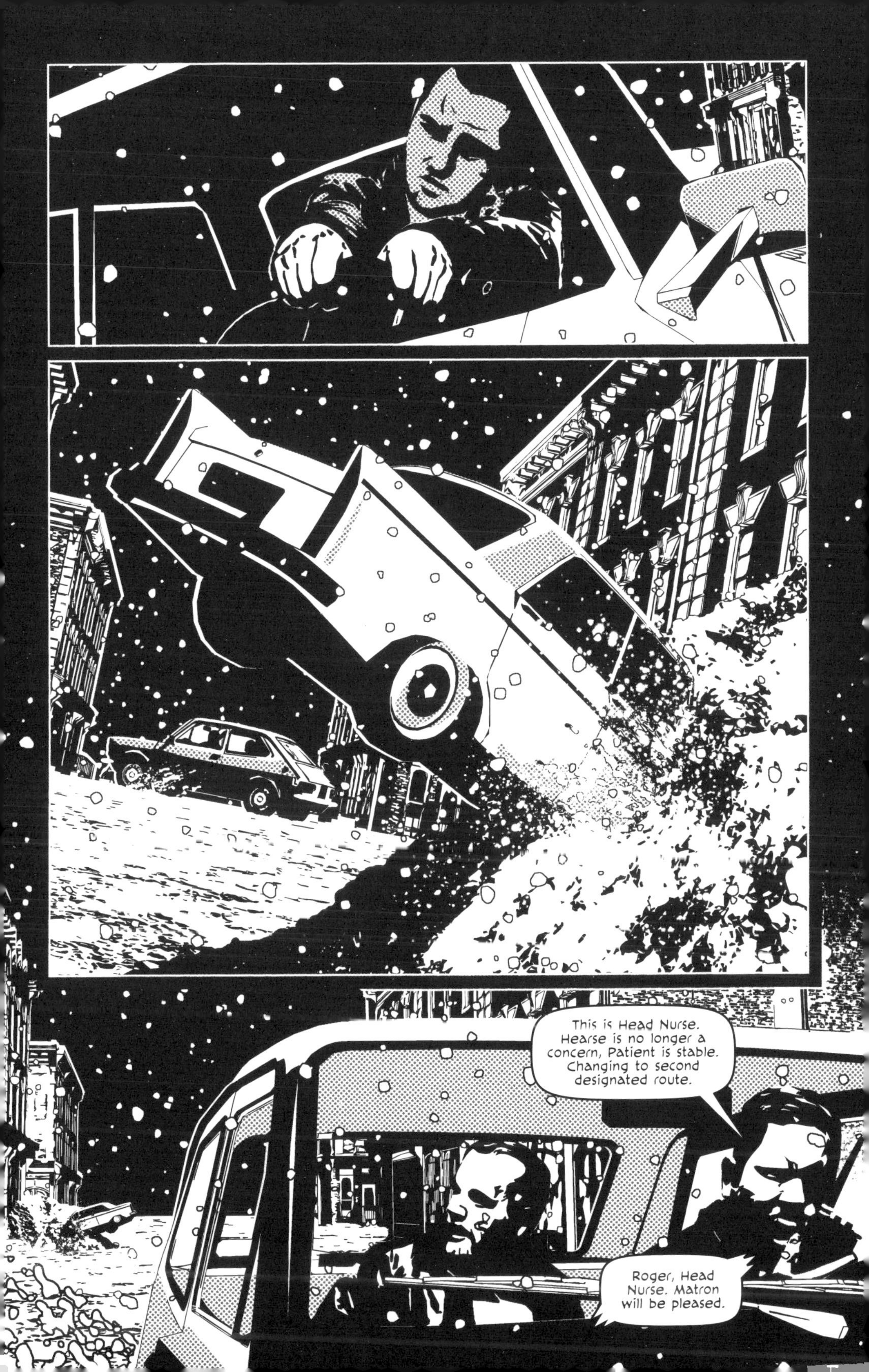
This is Head Nurse. Hearse is no longer a concern, Patient is stable. Changing to second designated route.
Roger, Head Nurse. Matron will be pleased.

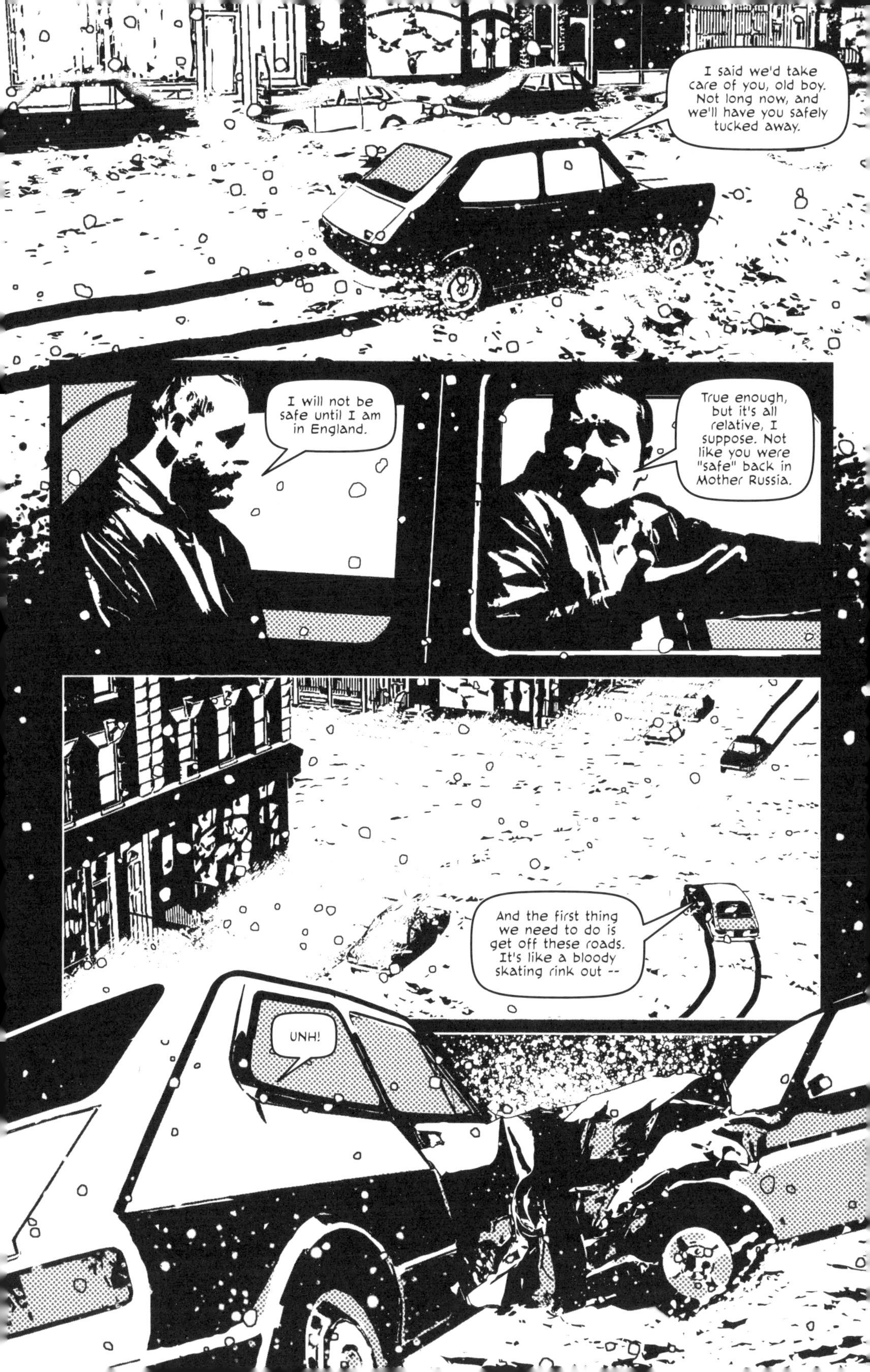
I said we'd take care of you, old boy. Not long now, and we'll have you safely tucked away.
I will not be safe until I am in England.
True enough, but it's all relative, I suppose. Not like you were "safe" back in Mother Russia.
And the first thing we need to do is get off these roads. It's like a bloody skating rink out --
UNH!

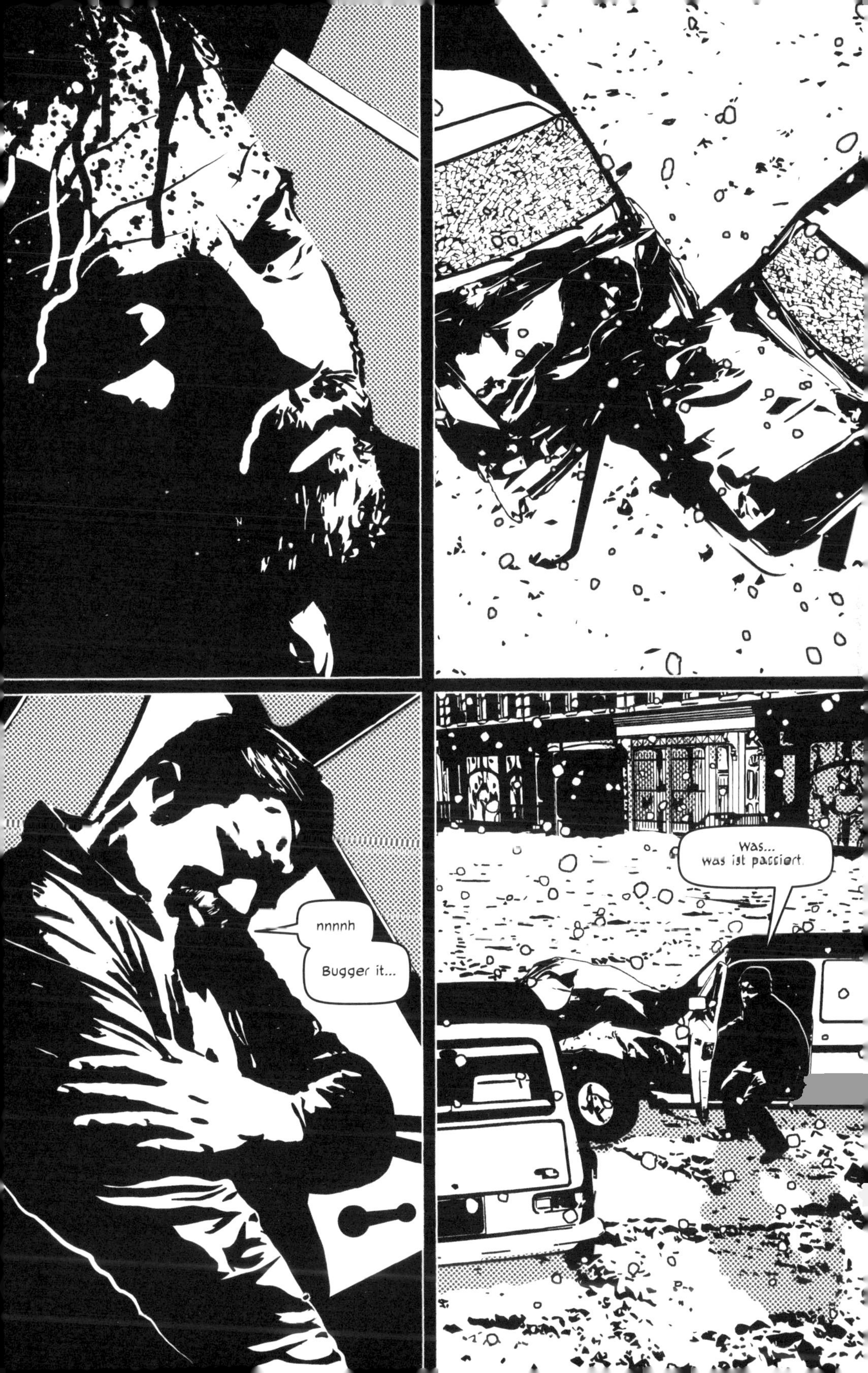
nnnnh
Bugger it...
Was...
was ist passiert.

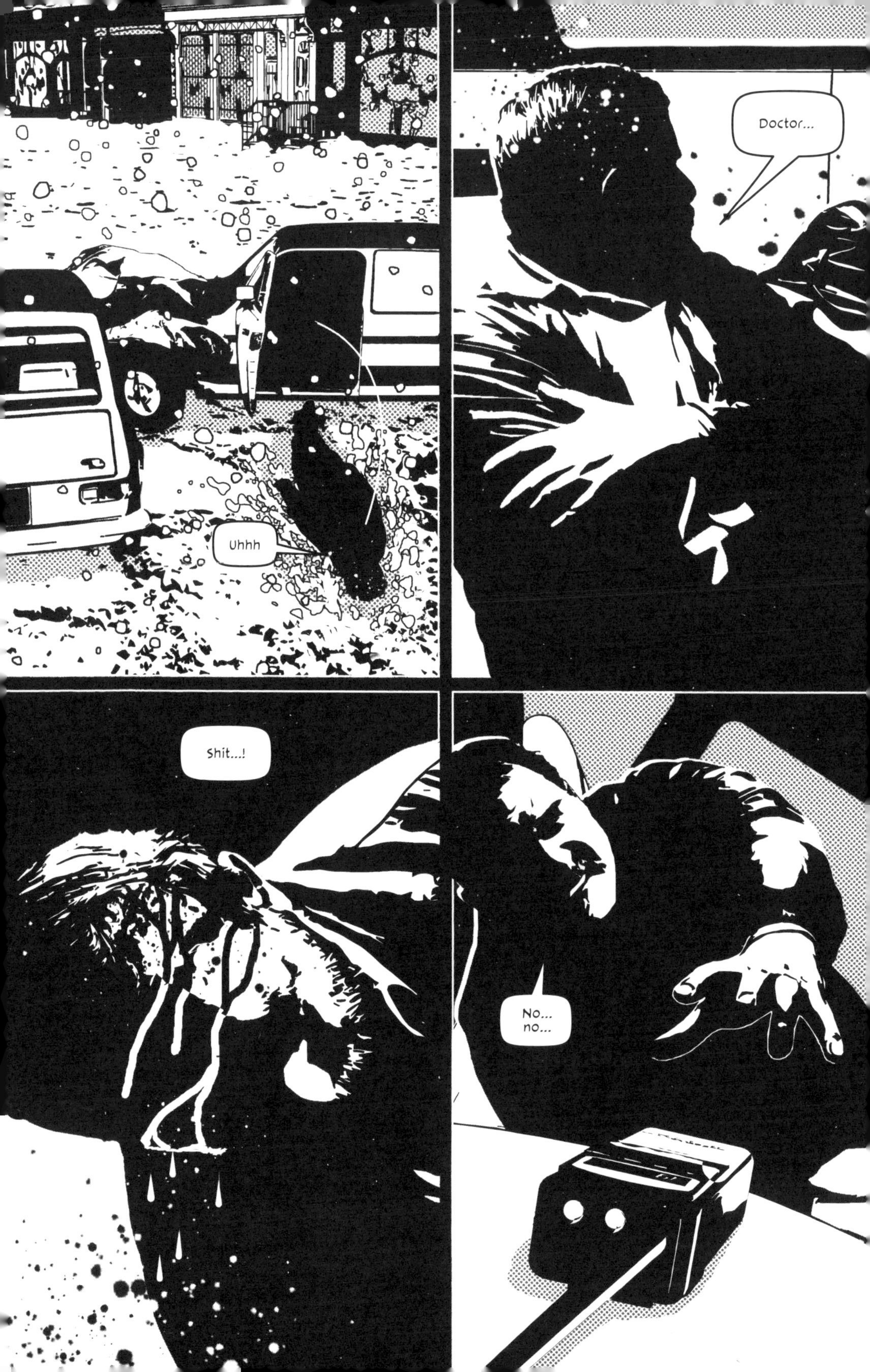
Uhhh
Doctor...
Shit...!
No...
no...

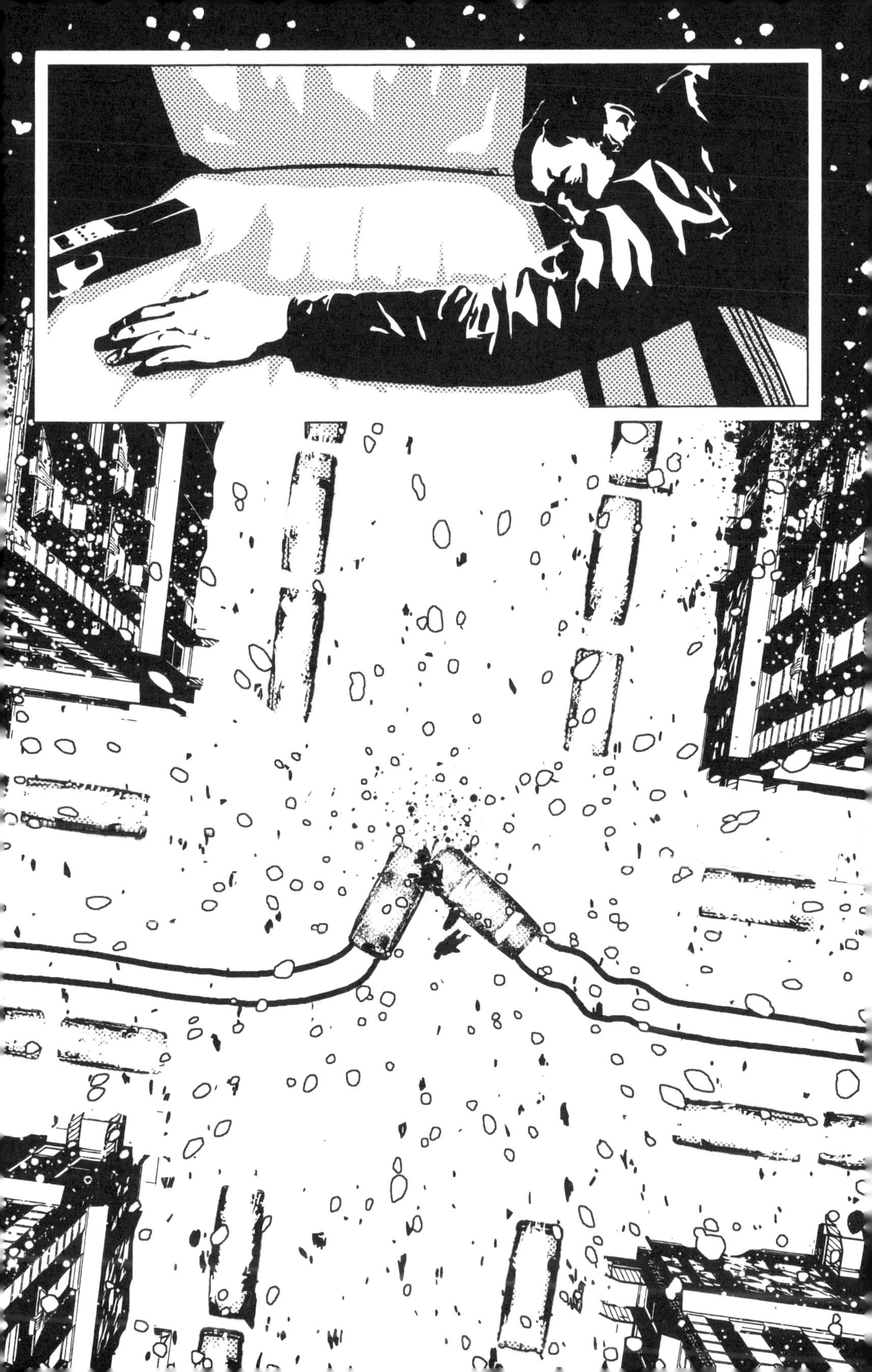

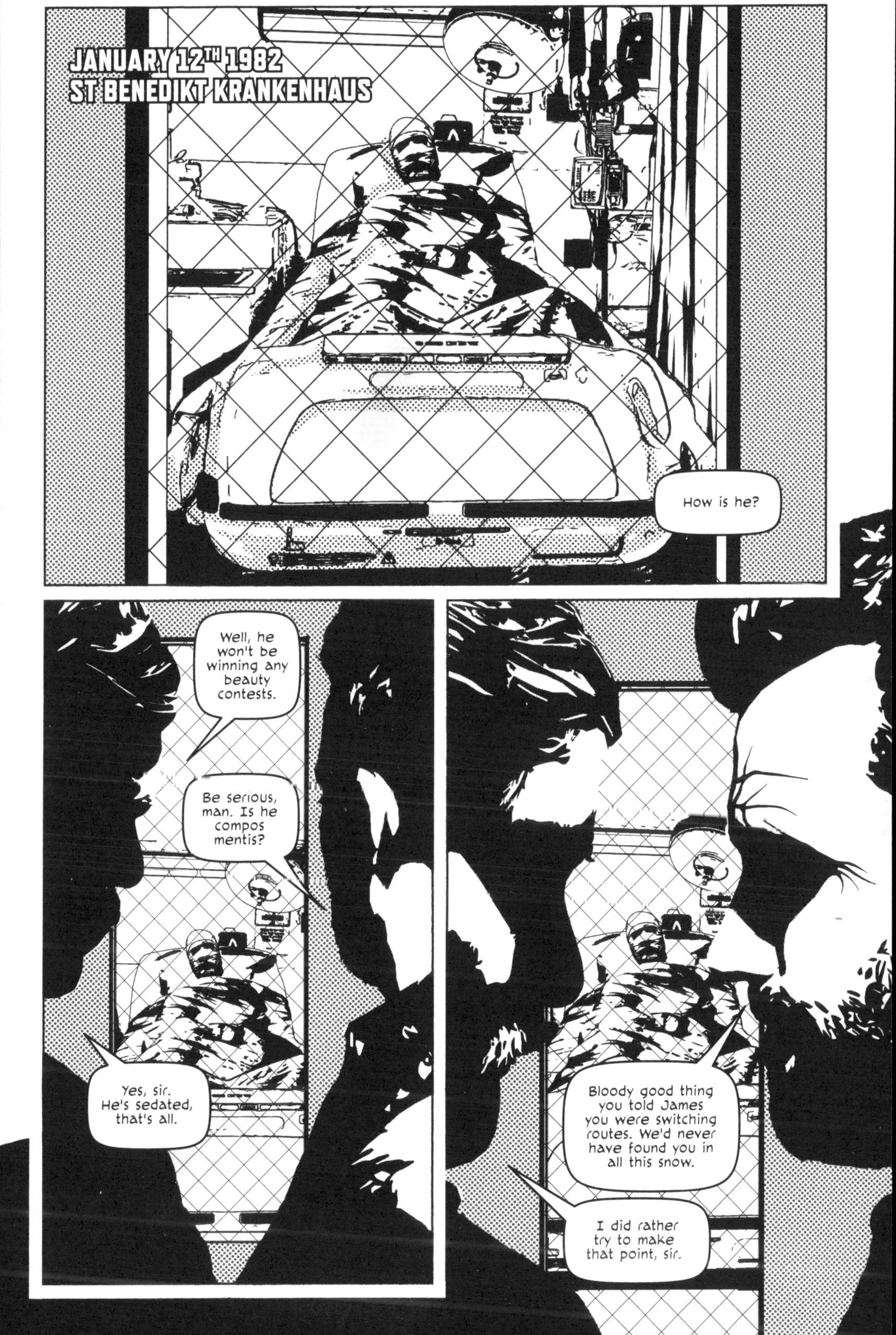
JANUARY 12TH 1982
ST BENEDIKT KRANKENHAUS
How is he?
Well, he won't be winning any beauty contests.
Be serious, man. Is he compos mentis?
Yes, sir. He's sedated, that's all.
Bloody good thing you told James you were switching routes. We'd never have found you in all this snow.
I did rather try to make that point, sir.

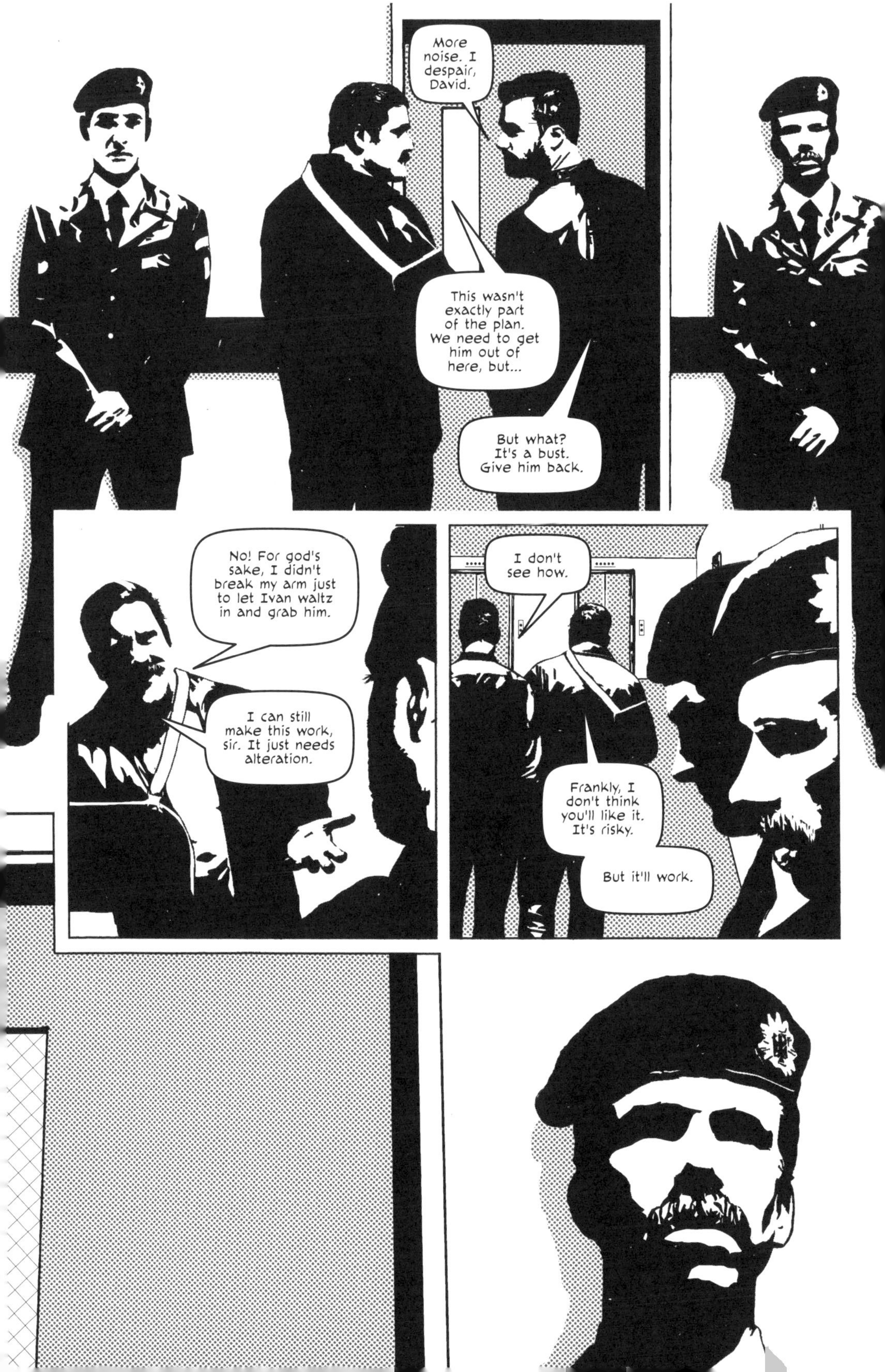
More noise. I despair, David.
This wasn't exactly part of the plan. We need to get him out of here, but...
But what? It's a bust. Give him back.
No! For god's sake, I didn't break my arm just to let Ivan waltz in and grab him.
I can still make this work, sir. It just needs alteration.
I don't see how.
Frankly, I don't think you'll like it. It's risky.
But it'll work.

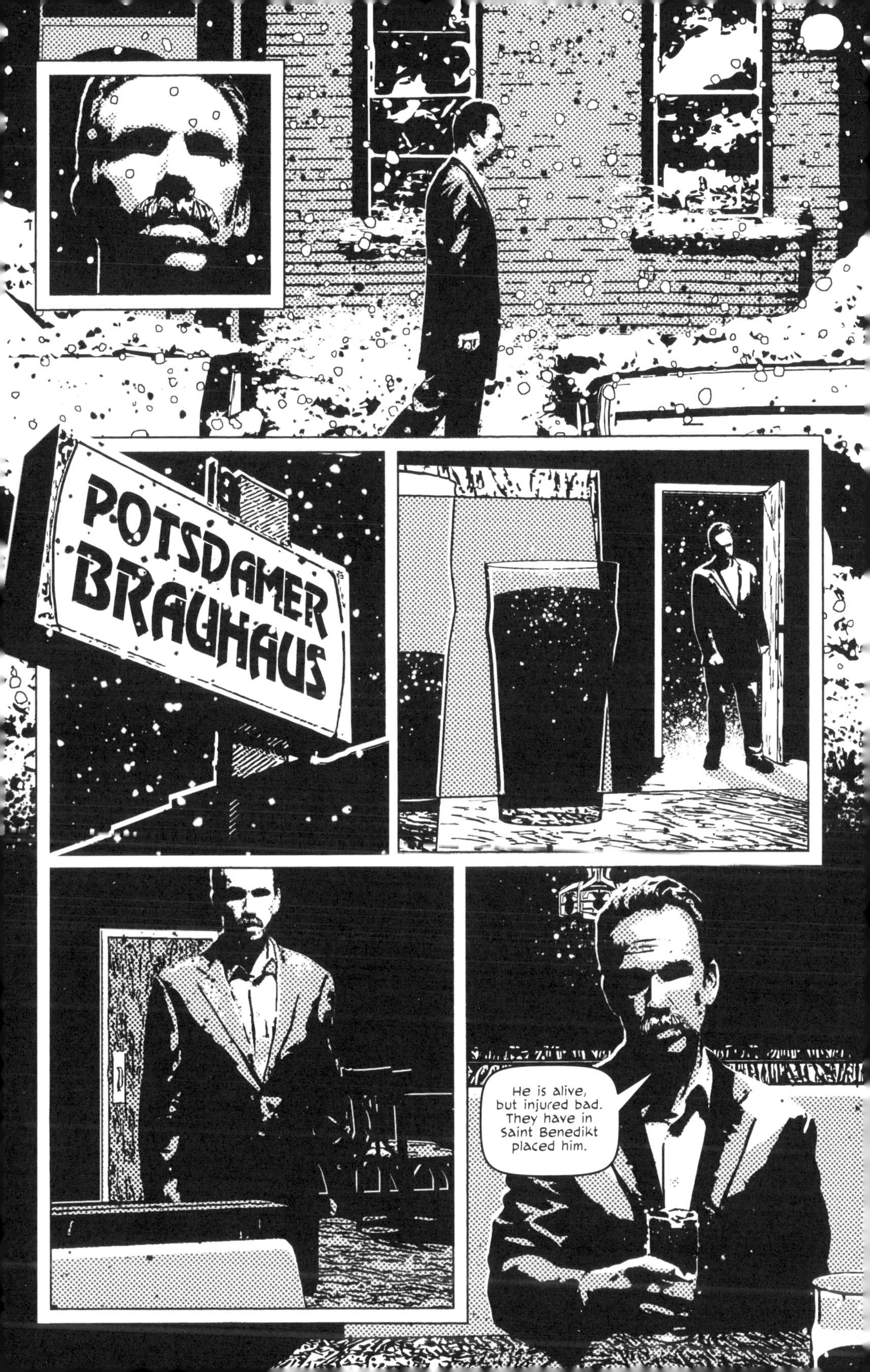
POTSDAMER BRAUHAUS
He is alive, but injured bad. They have in Saint Benedikt placed him.

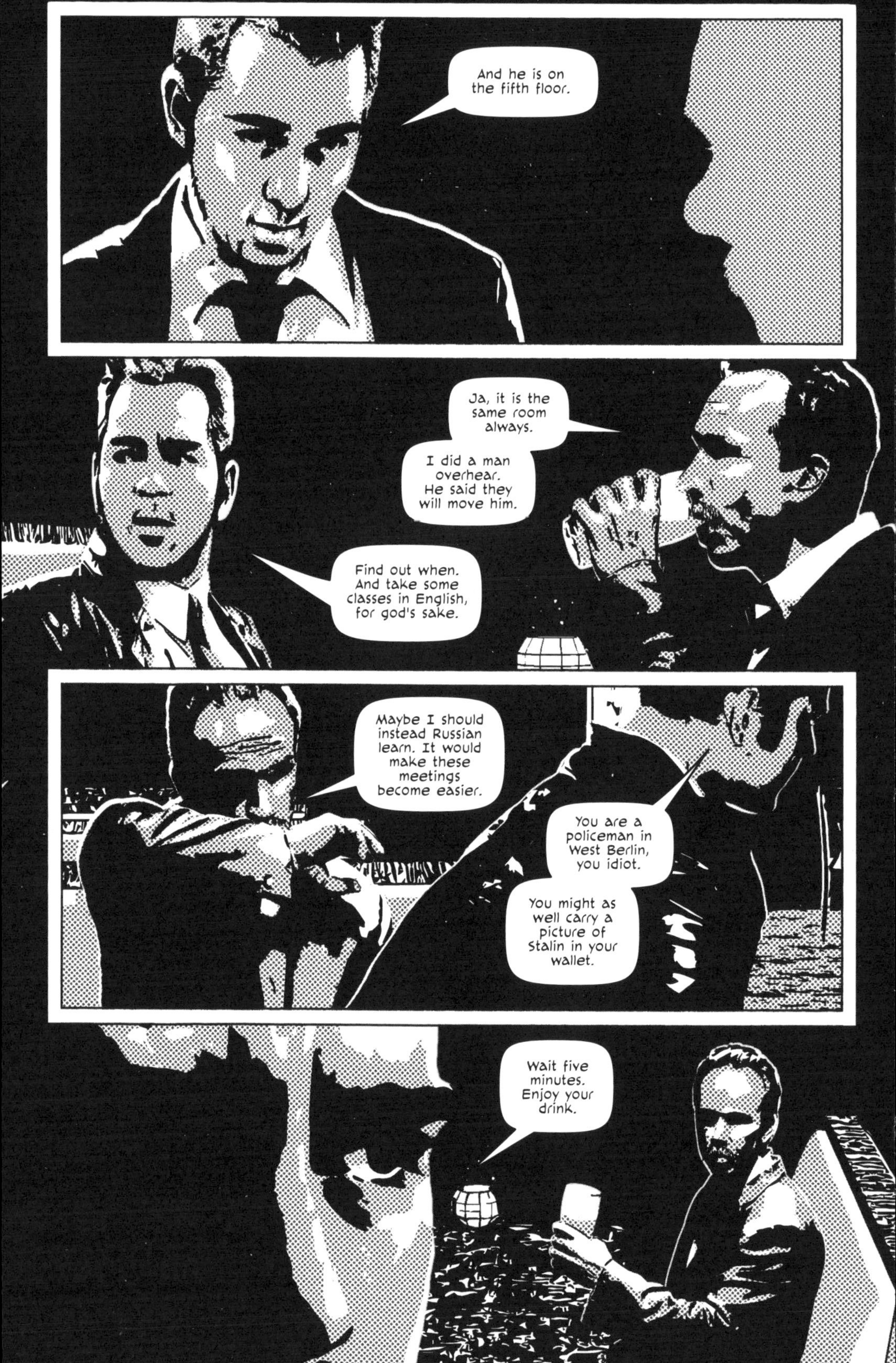
And he is on the fifth floor.
Ja, it is the same room always.
I did a man overhear. He said they will move him.
Find out when. And take some classes in English, for god's sake.
Maybe I should instead Russian learn. It would make these meetings become easier.
You are a policeman in West Berlin, you idiot.
You might as well carry a picture of Stalin in your wallet.
Wait five minutes. Enjoy your drink.

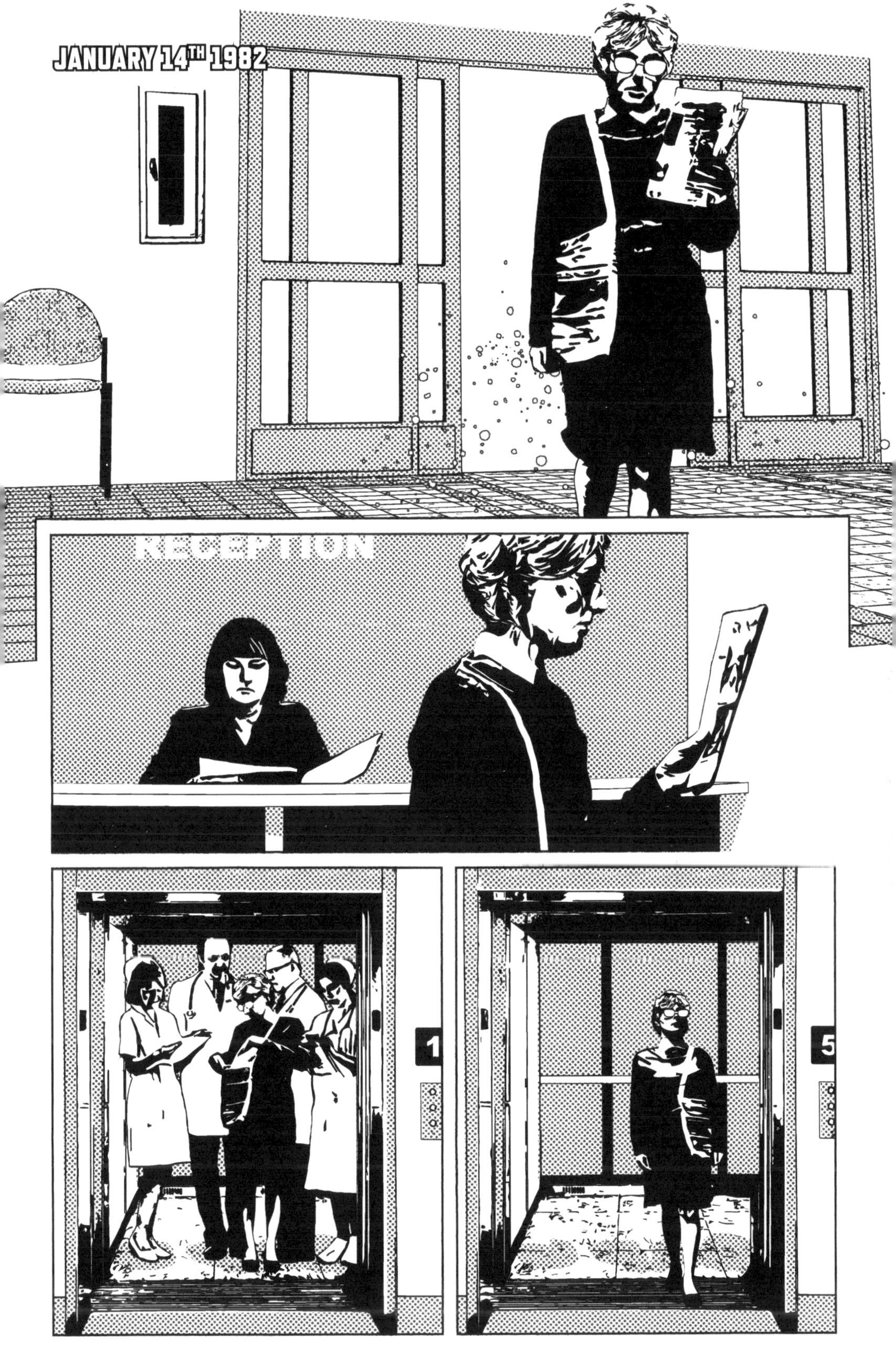
JANUARY 14TH 1982
RECEPTION
1
5

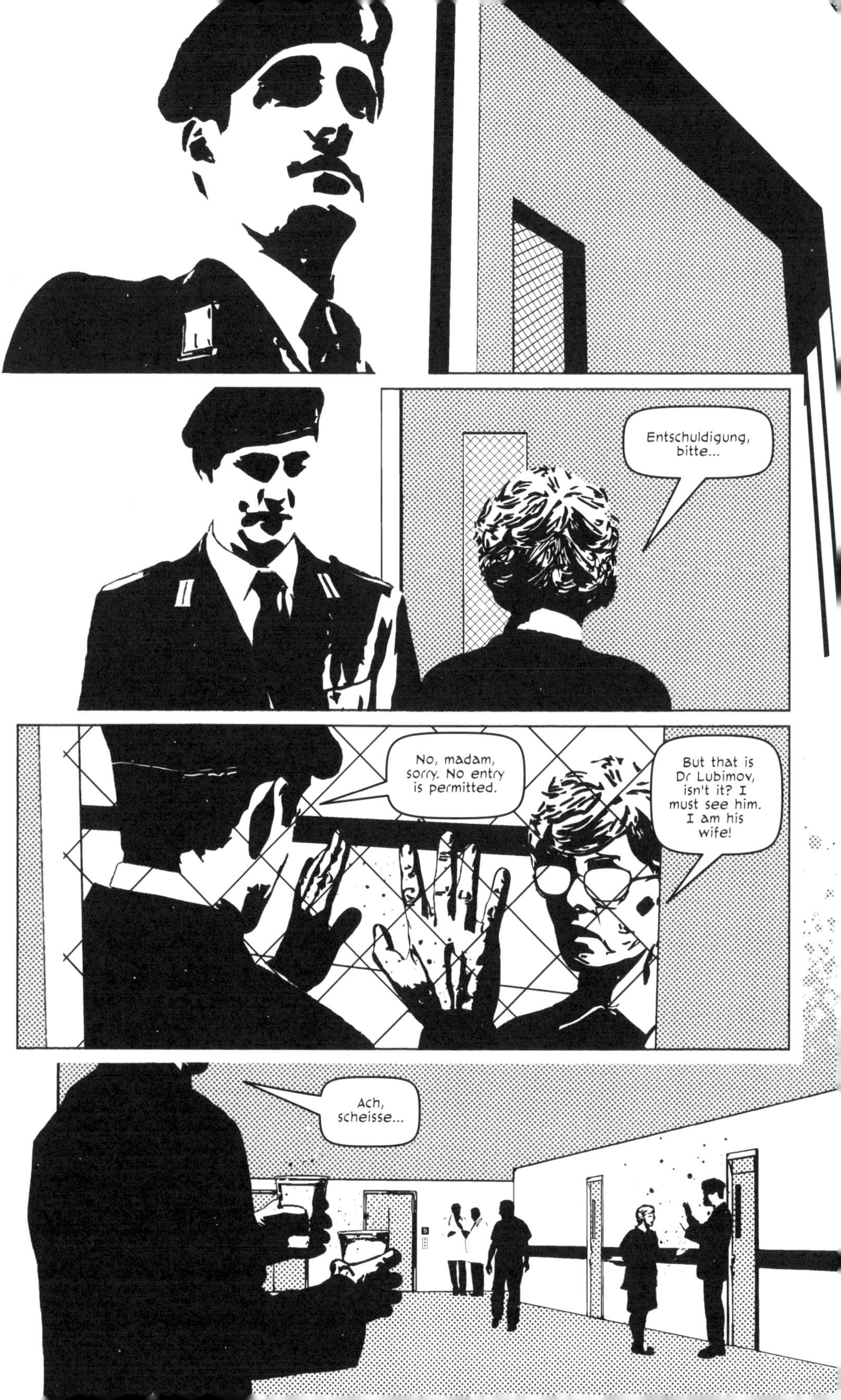
Entschuldigung, bitte...
No, madam, sorry. No entry is permitted.
But that is Dr Lubimov, isn't it? I must see him. I am his wife!
Ach, scheisse...

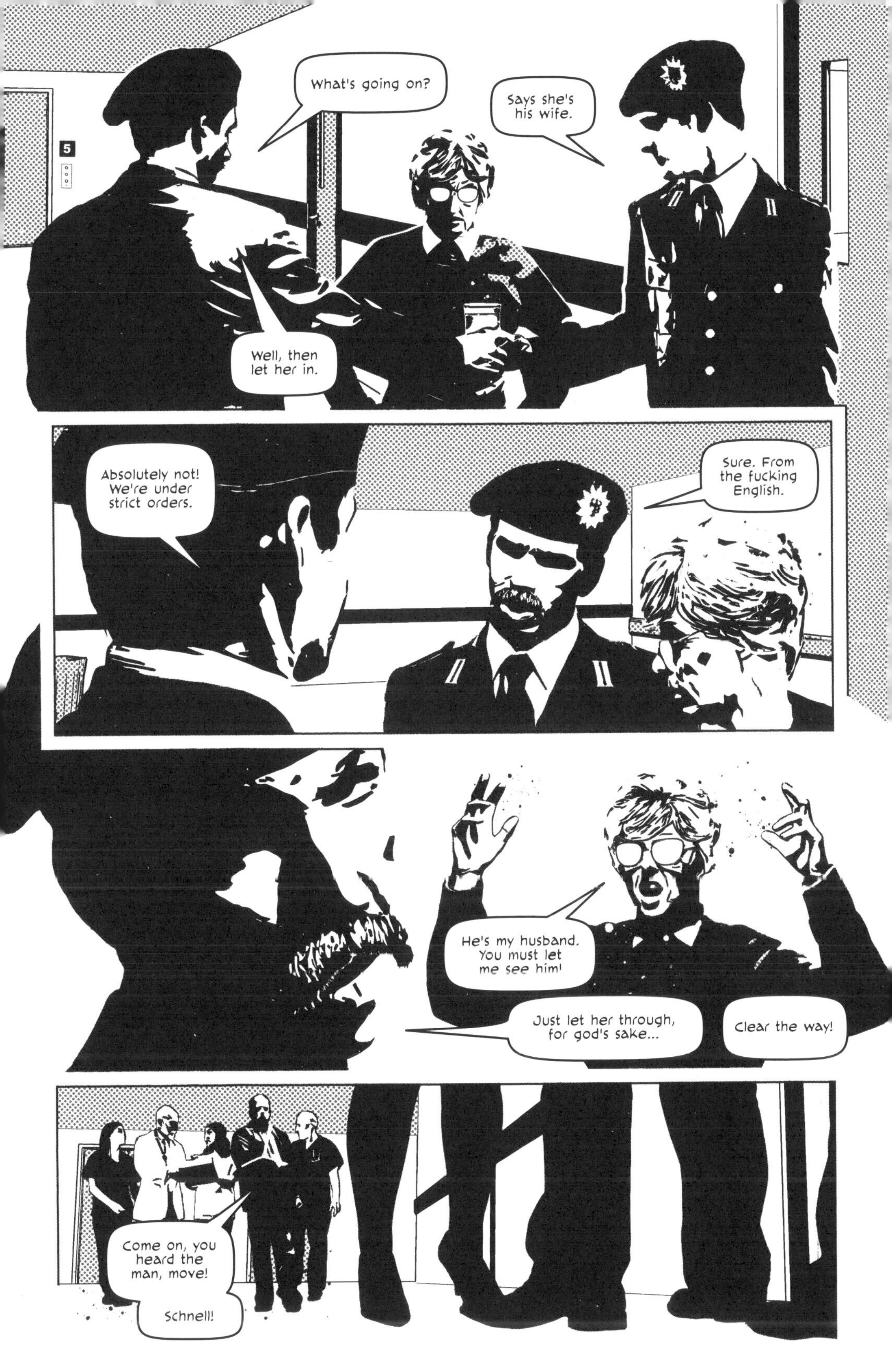
What's going on?
Says she's his wife.
Well, then let her in.
Absolutely not! We're under strict orders.
Sure. From the fucking English.
He's my husband. You must let me see him!
Just let her through, for god's sake...
Clear the way!
Come on, you heard the man, move!
Schnell!

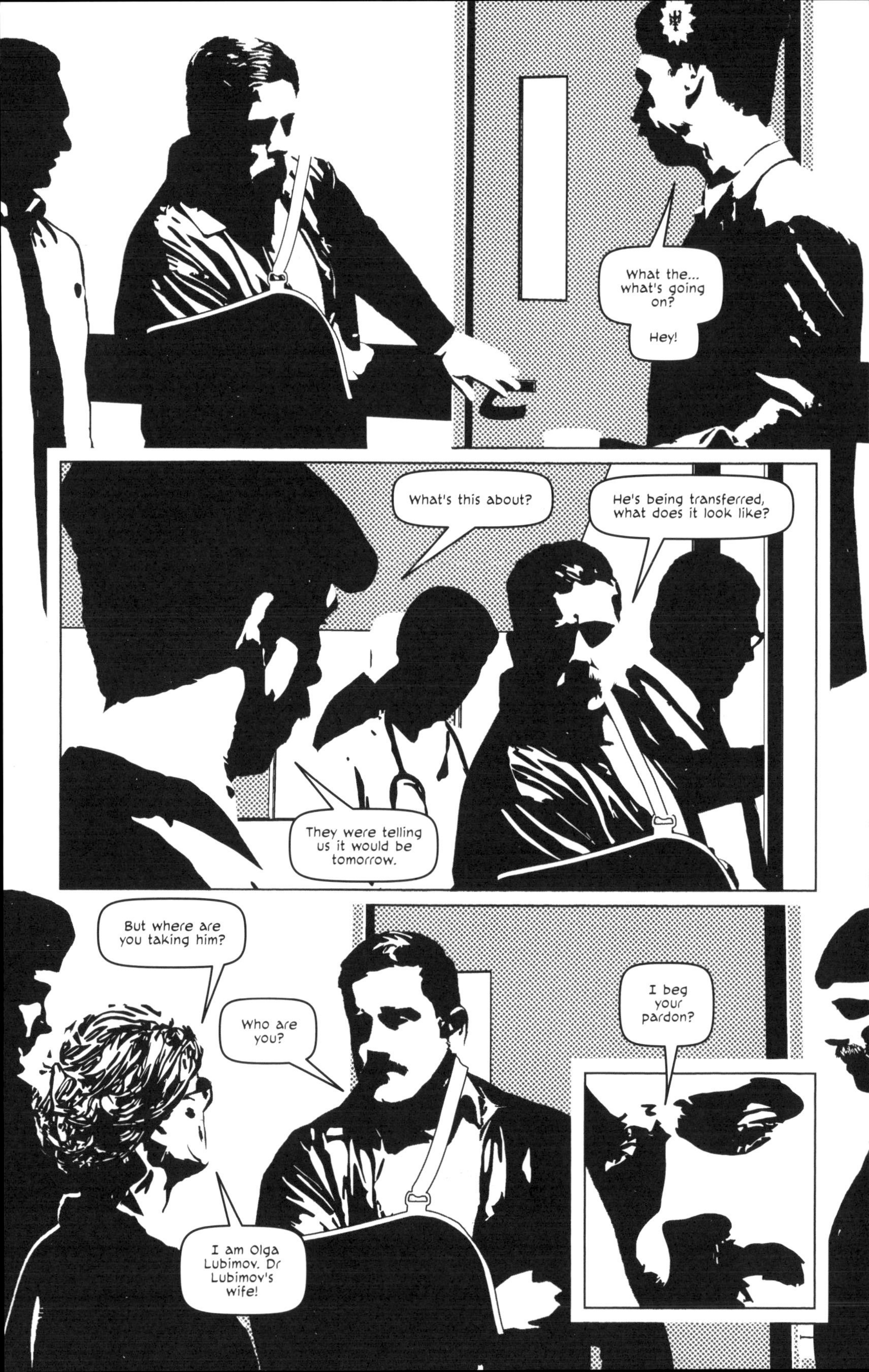
What the... what's going on?
Hey!
What's this about?
He's being transferred, what does it look like?
They were telling us it would be tomorrow.
But where are you taking him?
Who are you?
I am Olga Lubimov. Dr Lubimov's wife!
I beg your pardon?

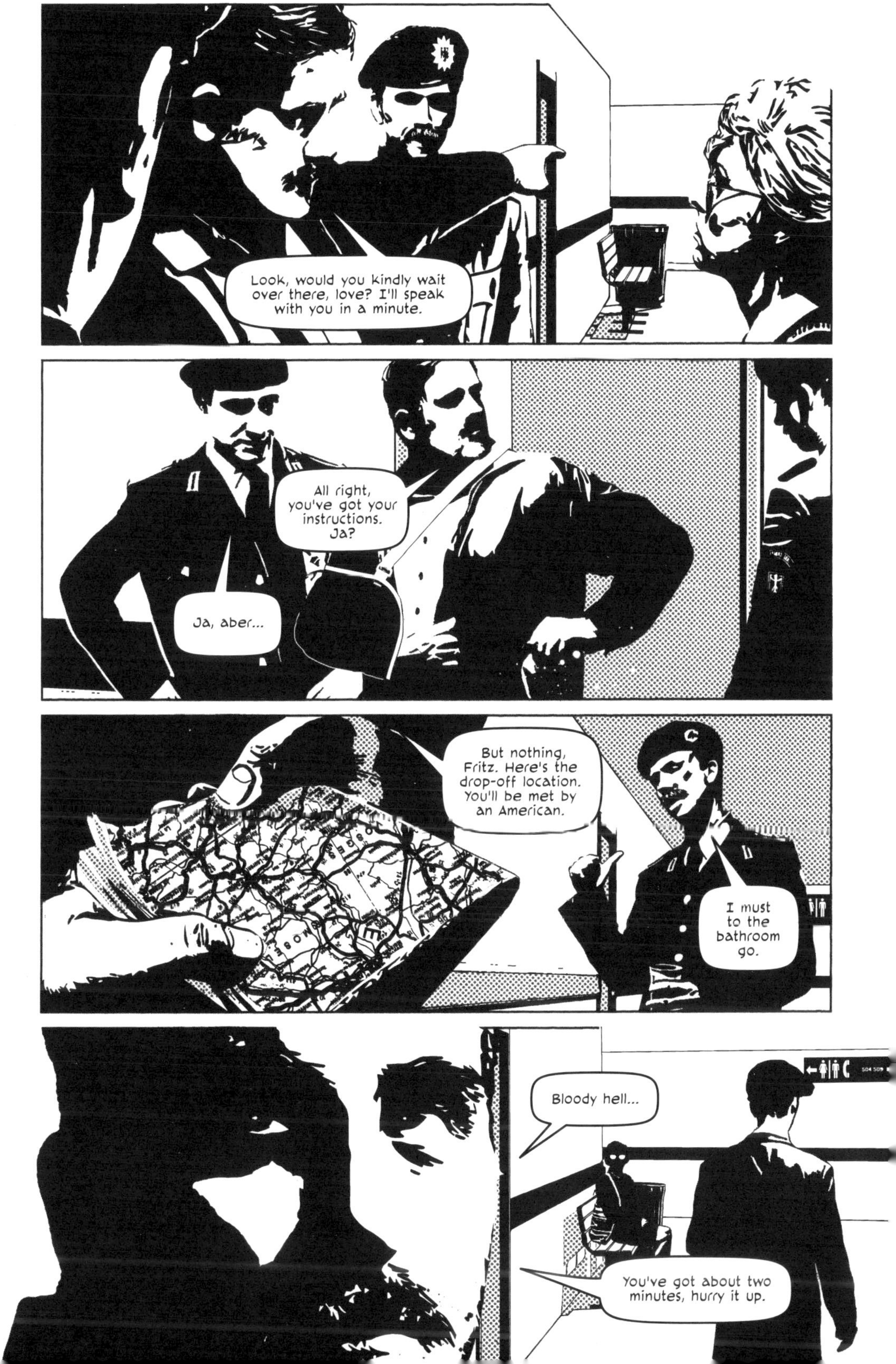
Look, would you kindly wait over there, love? I'll speak with you in a minute.
All right, you've got your instructions. Ja?
Ja, aber...
But nothing, Fritz. Here's the drop-off location. You'll be met by an American.
I must to the bathroom go.
Bloody hell...
You've got about two minutes, hurry it up.

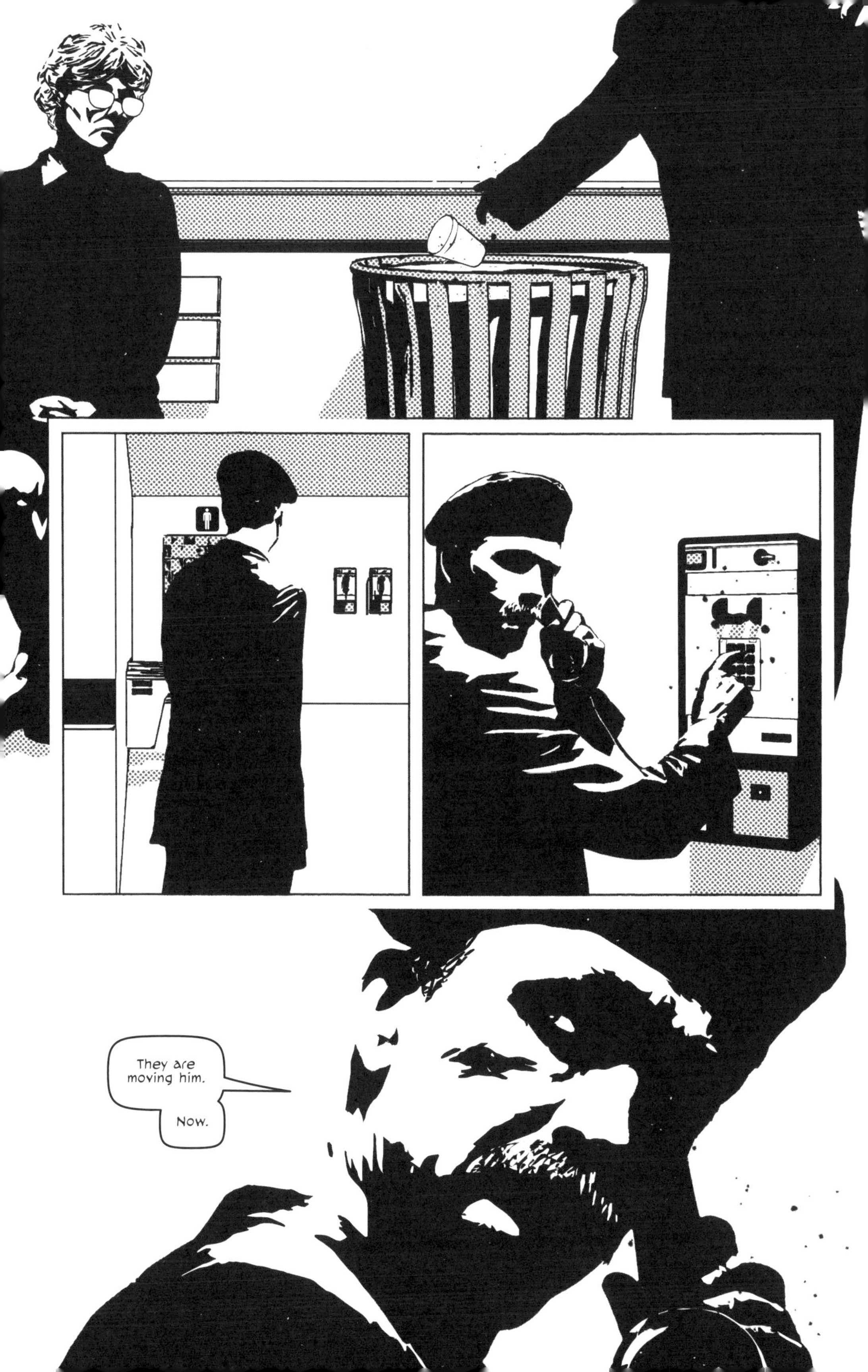
They are moving him.
Now.

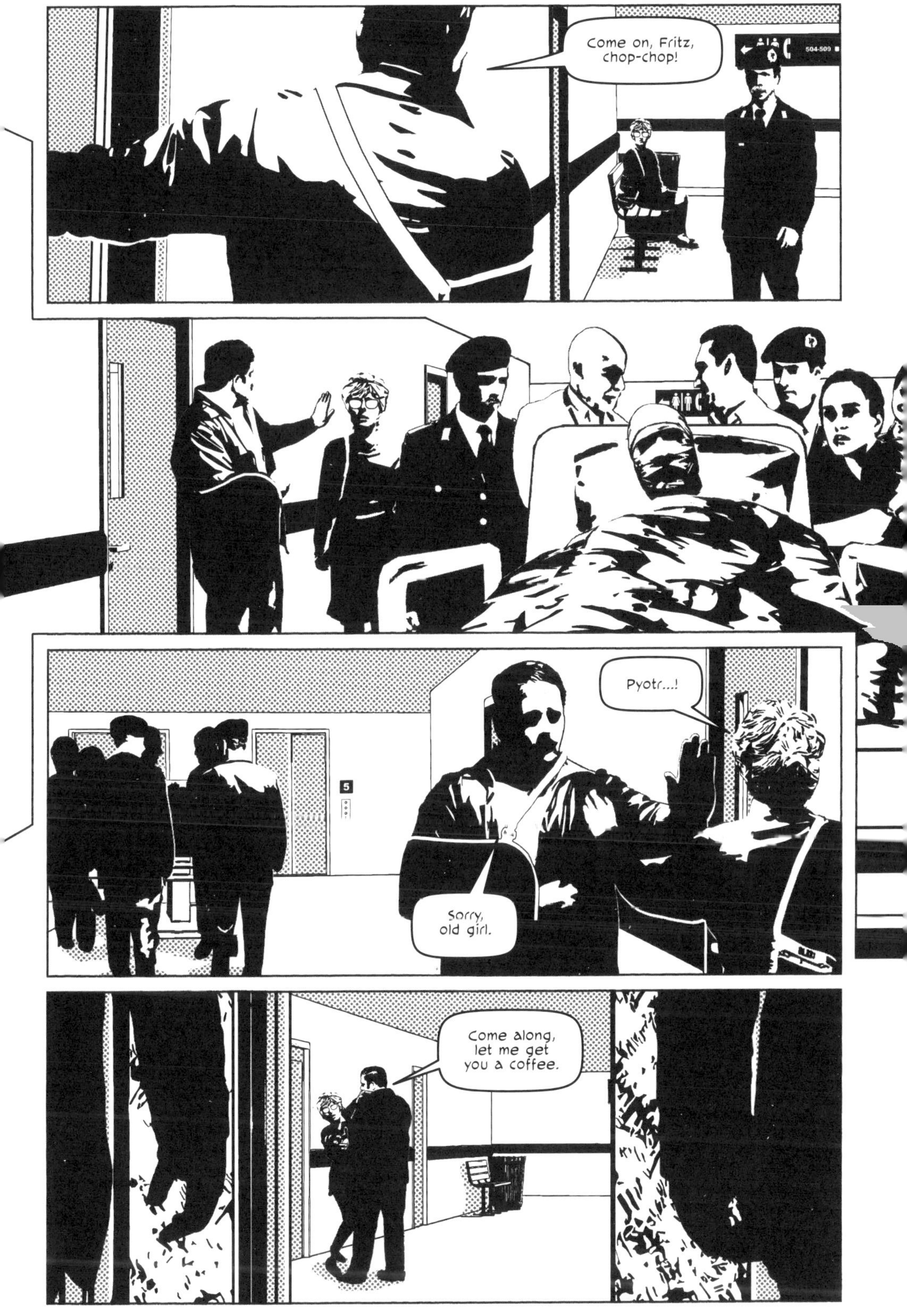
Come on, Fritz, chop-chop!
Pyotr...!
Sorry, old girl.
Come along, let me get you a coffee.

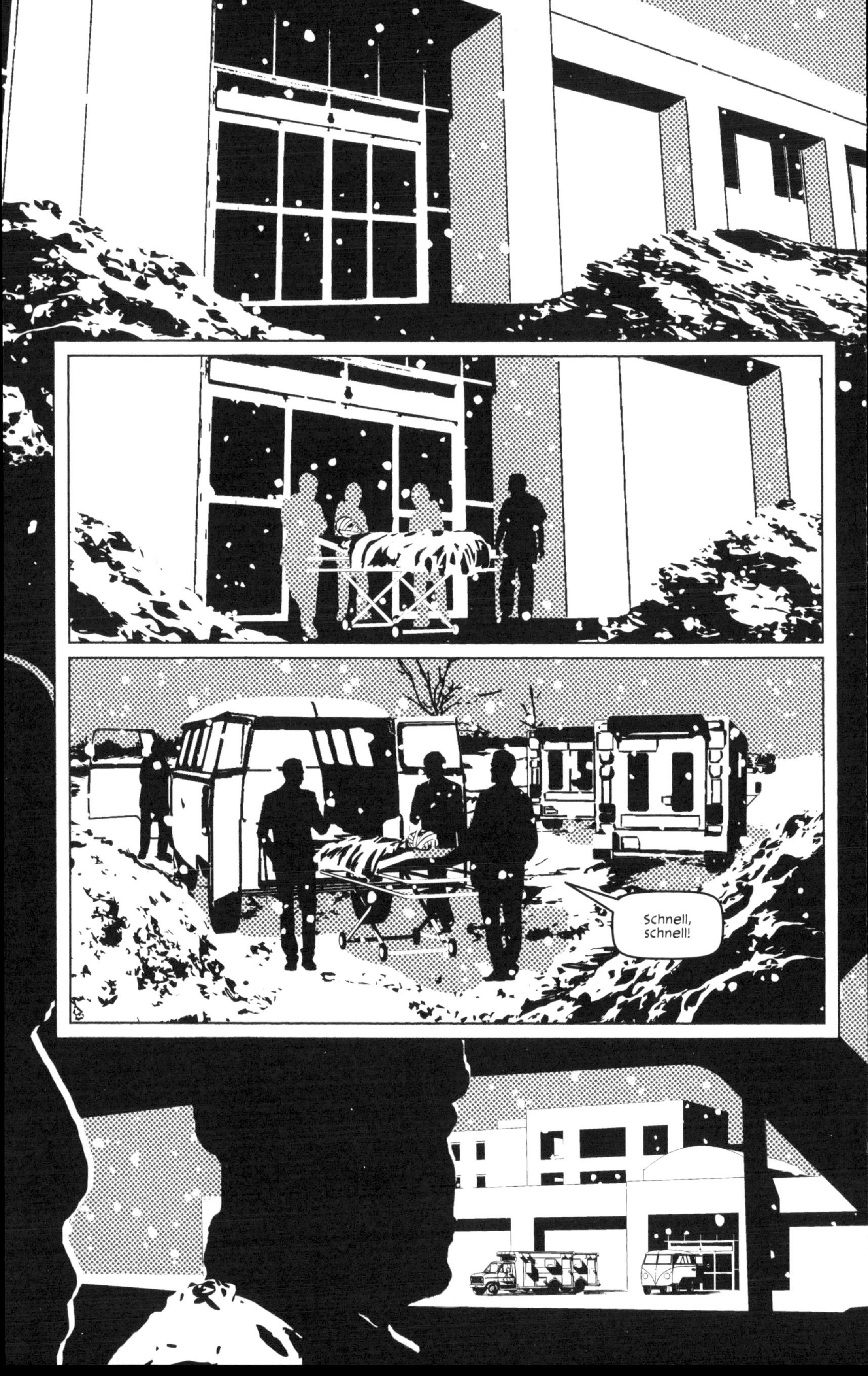
Schnell, schnell!

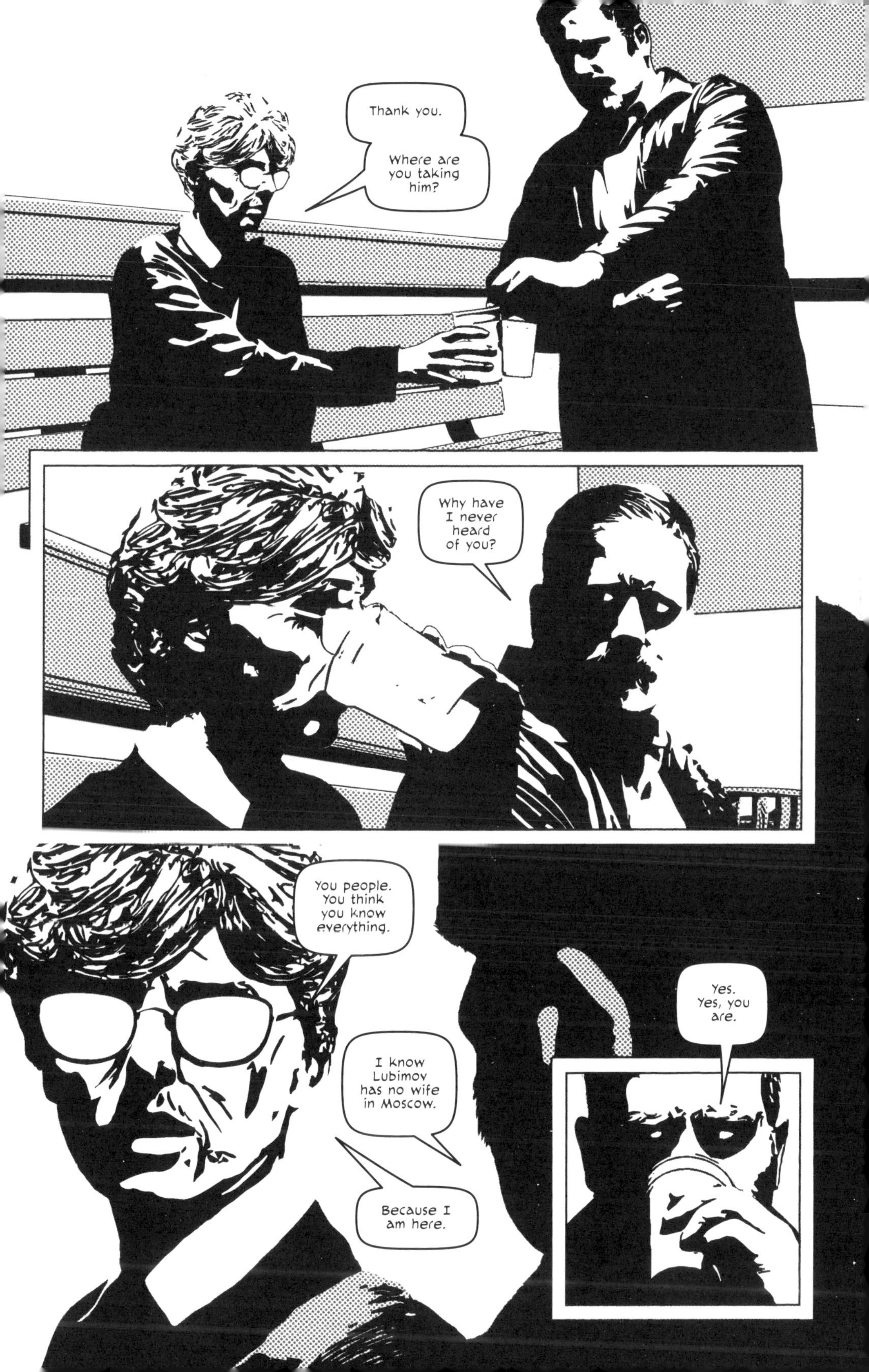
Thank you.
Where are you taking him?
Why have I never heard of you?
You people. You think you know everything.
I know Lubimov has no wife in Moscow.
Because I am here.
Yes. Yes, you are.

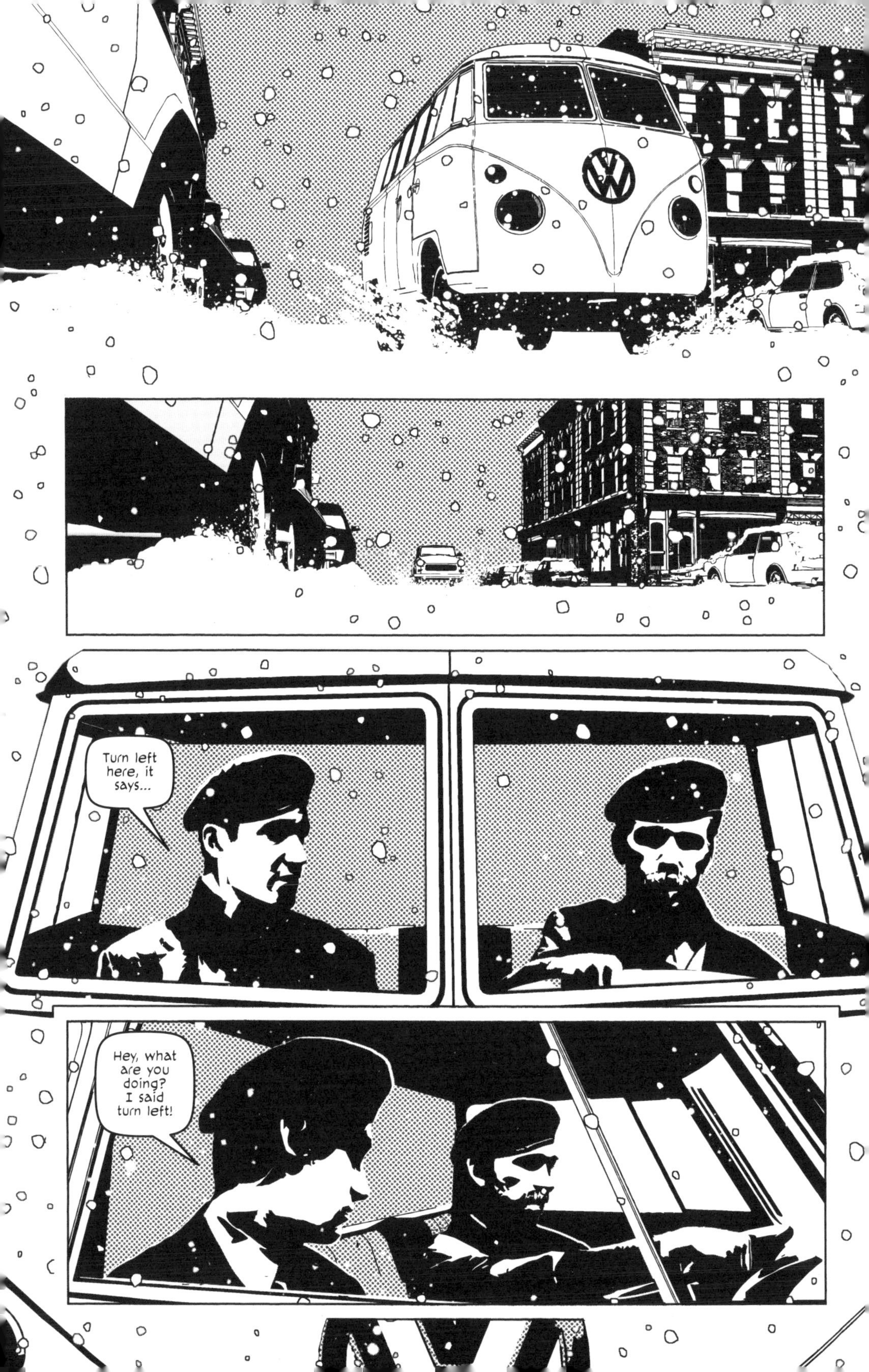
Turn left here, it says...
Hey, what are you doing? I said turn left!

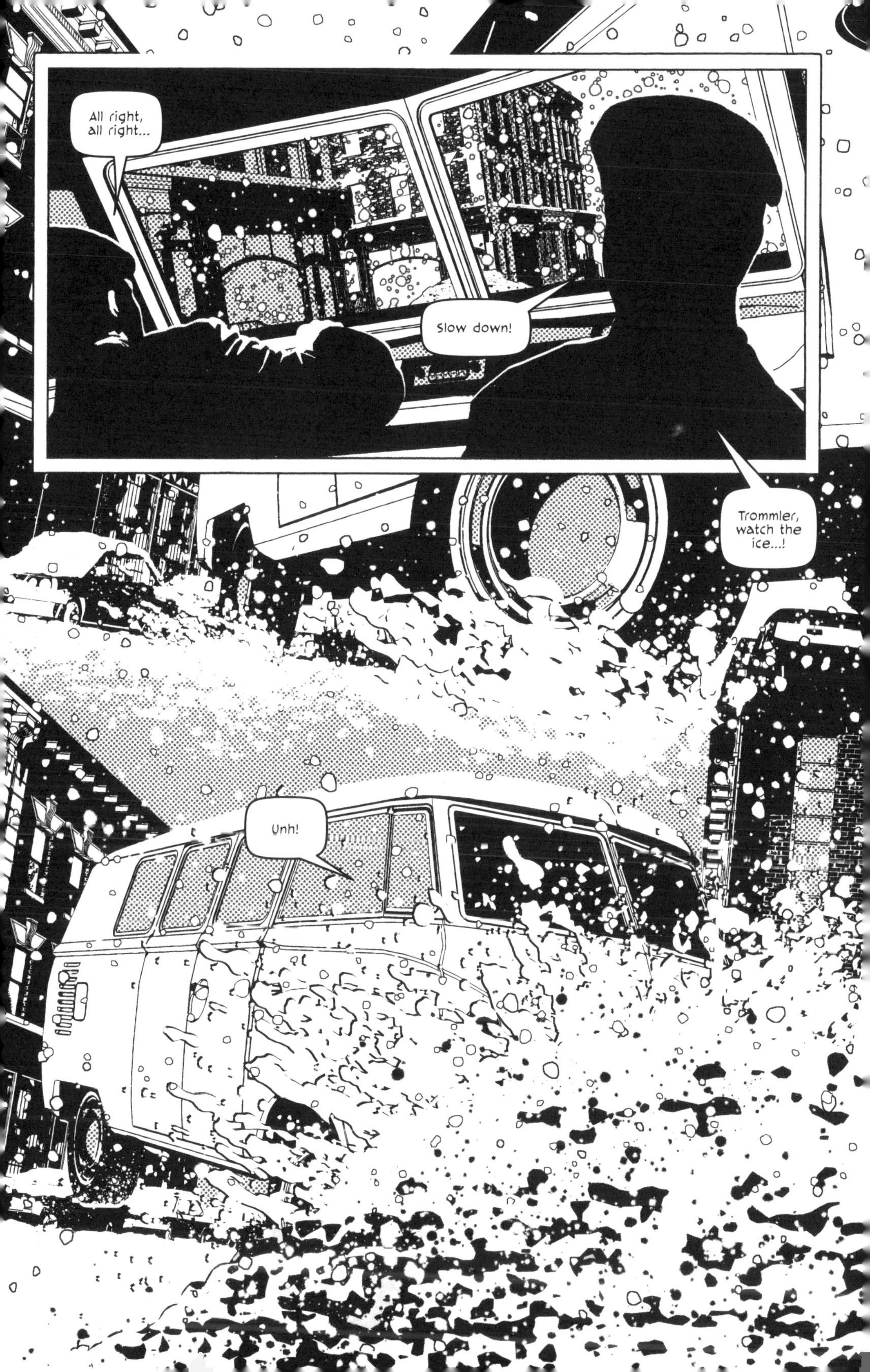
All right, all right...
Slow down!
Trommler, watch the ice...!
Unh!

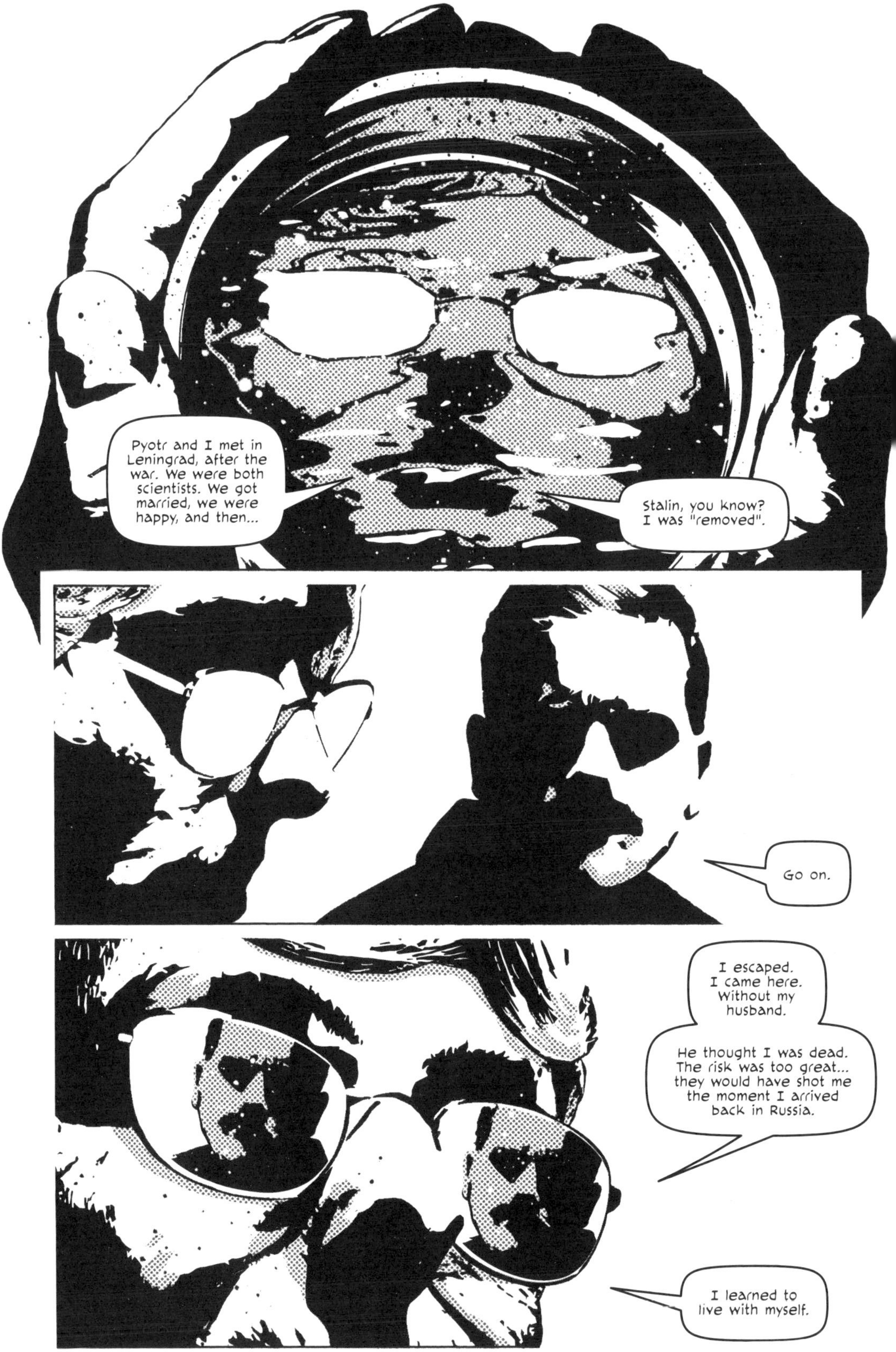
Pyotr and I met in Leningrad, after the war. We were both scientists. We got married, we were happy, and then...
Stalin, you know? I was "removed".
Go on.
I escaped. I came here. Without my husband.
He thought I was dead. The risk was too great... they would have shot me the moment I arrived back in Russia.
I learned to live with myself.

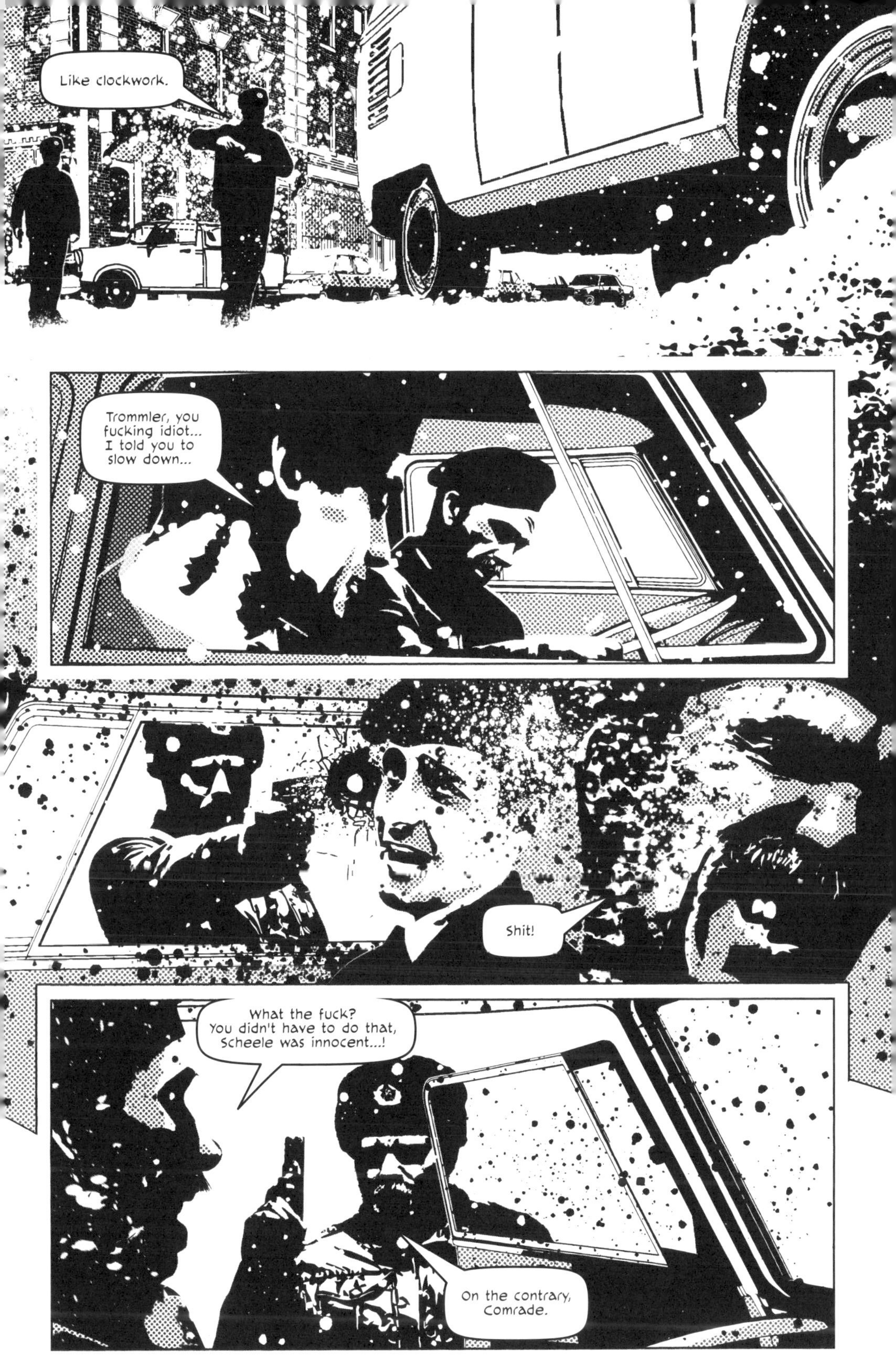
Like clockwork.
Trommler, you fucking idiot... I told you to slow down...
Shit!
What the fuck? You didn't have to do that, Scheele was innocent...!
On the contrary, Comrade.

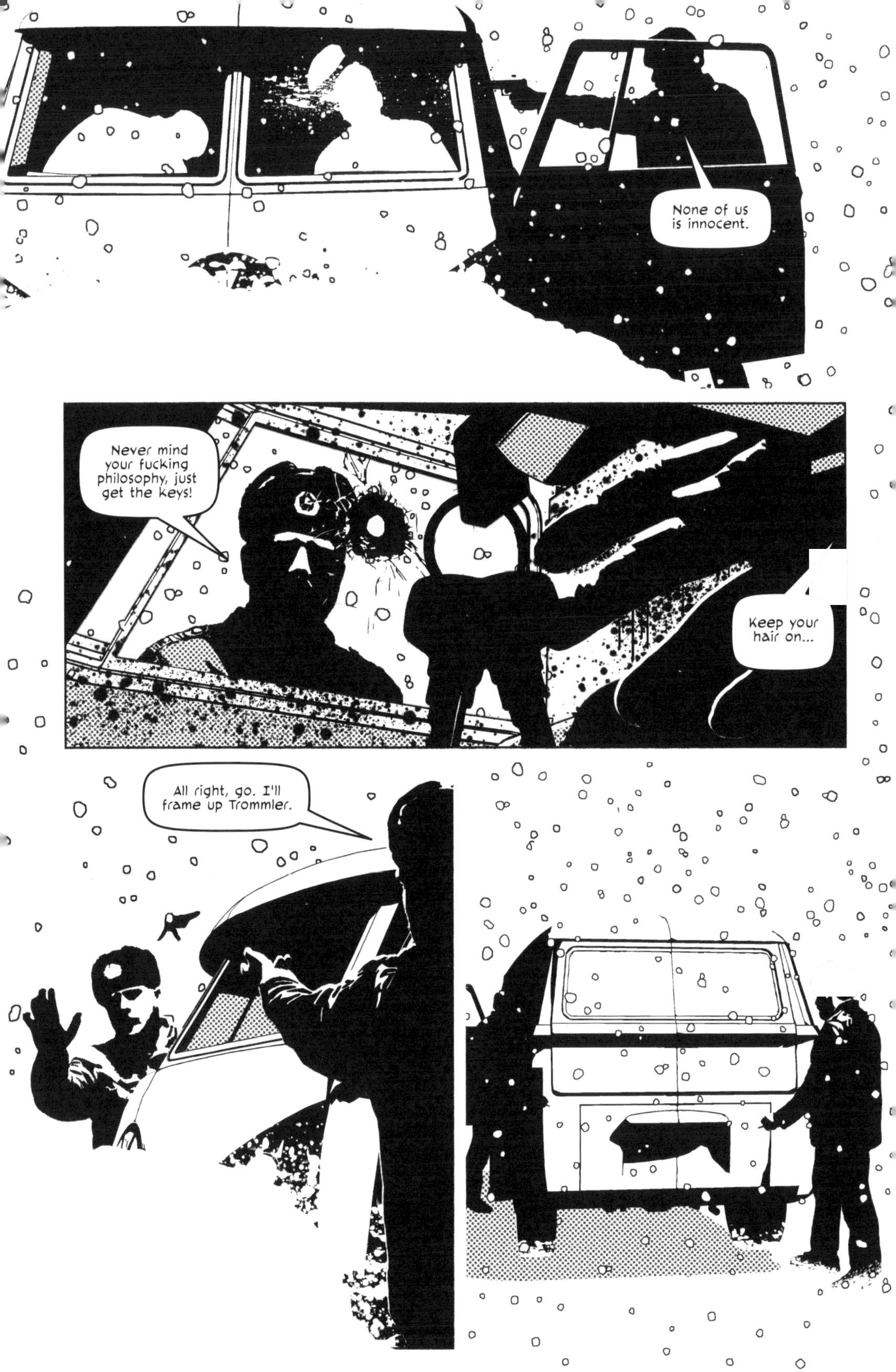
None of us is innocent.
Never mind your fucking philosophy, just get the keys!
Keep your hair on...
All right, go. I'll frame up Trommler.

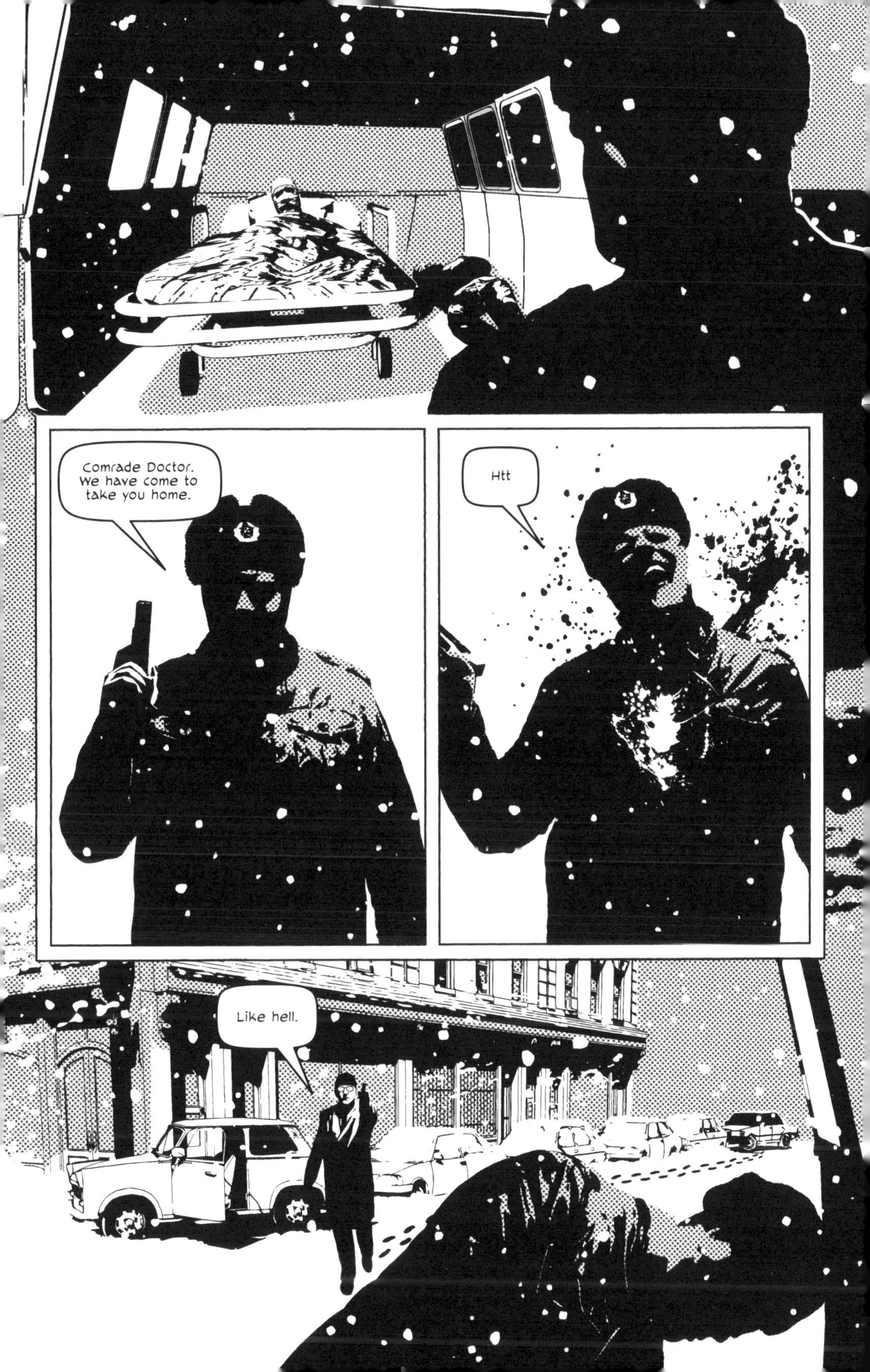
Comrade Doctor. We have come to take you home.
Htt
Like hell.

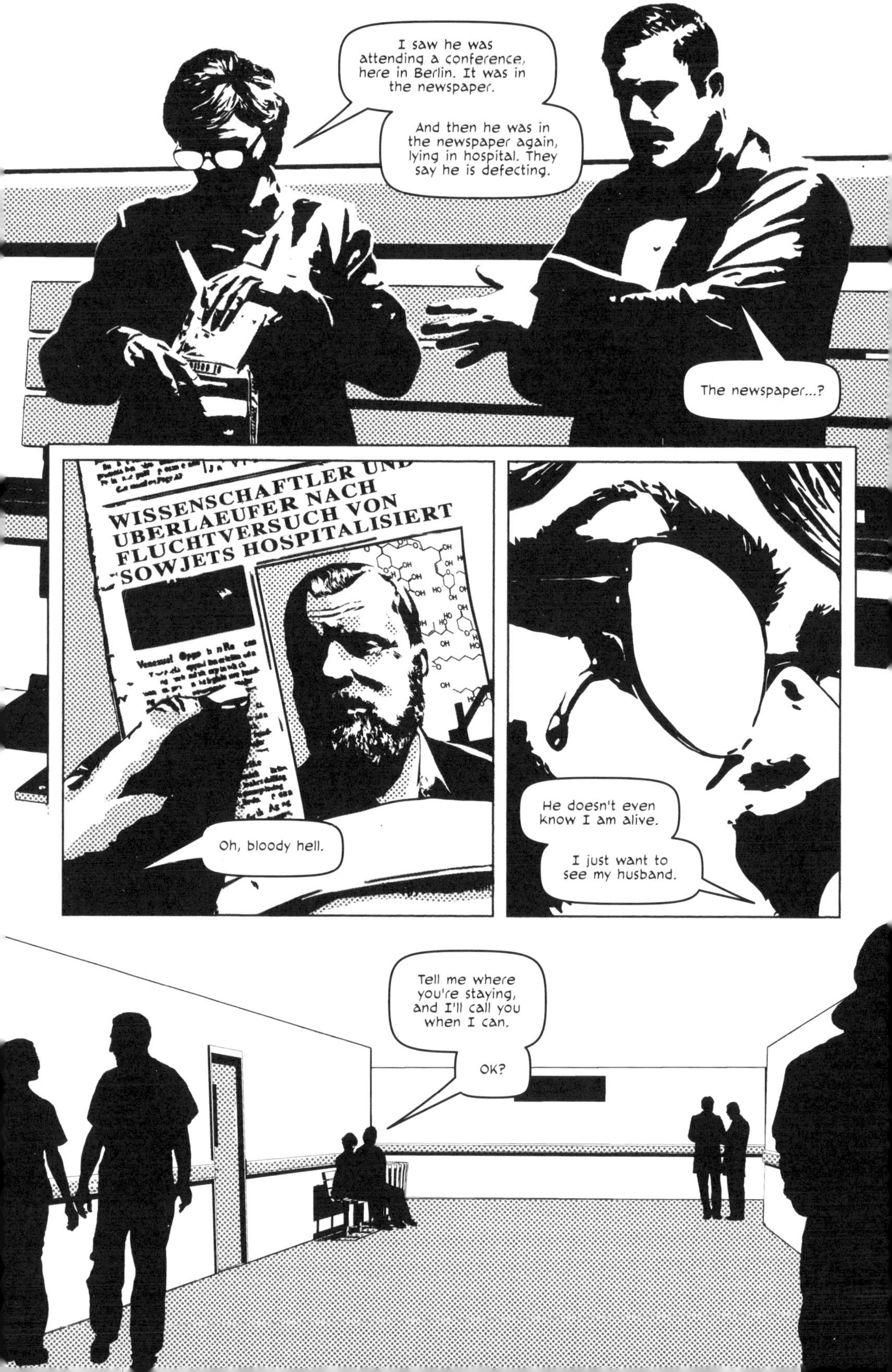

I saw he was attending a conference, here in Berlin. It was in the newspaper.
And then he was in the newspaper again, lying in hospital. They say he is defecting.
The newspaper...?
WISSENSCHAFTLER
UBERLAEUFER NACH
FLUCHTVERSUCH VON
SOWJETS HOSPITALISIERT
Oh, bloody hell.
He doesn't even know I am alive.
I just want to see my husband.
Tell me where you're staying, and I'll call you when I can.
OK?

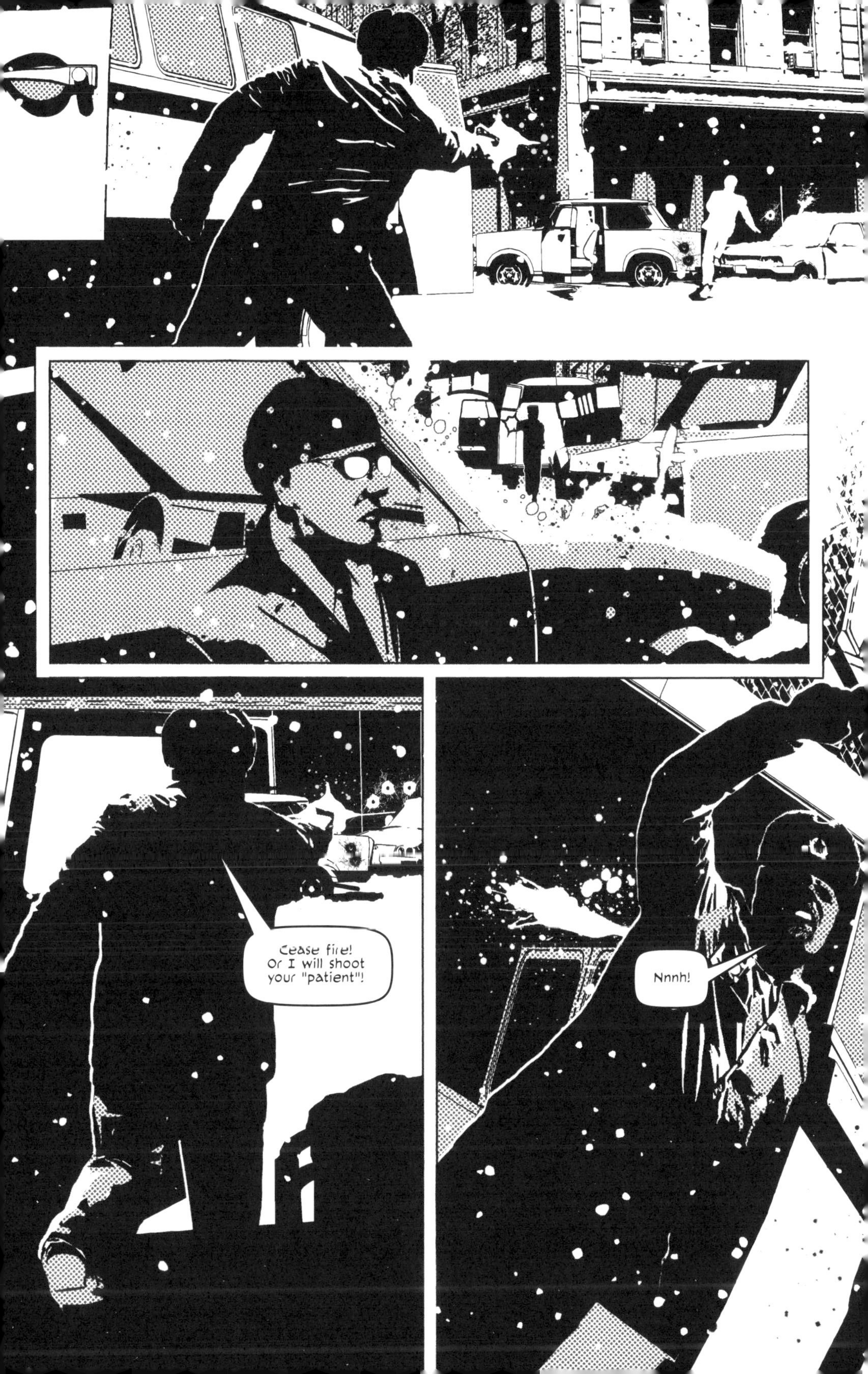
Cease fire! Or I will shoot your "patient"!
Nnnh!

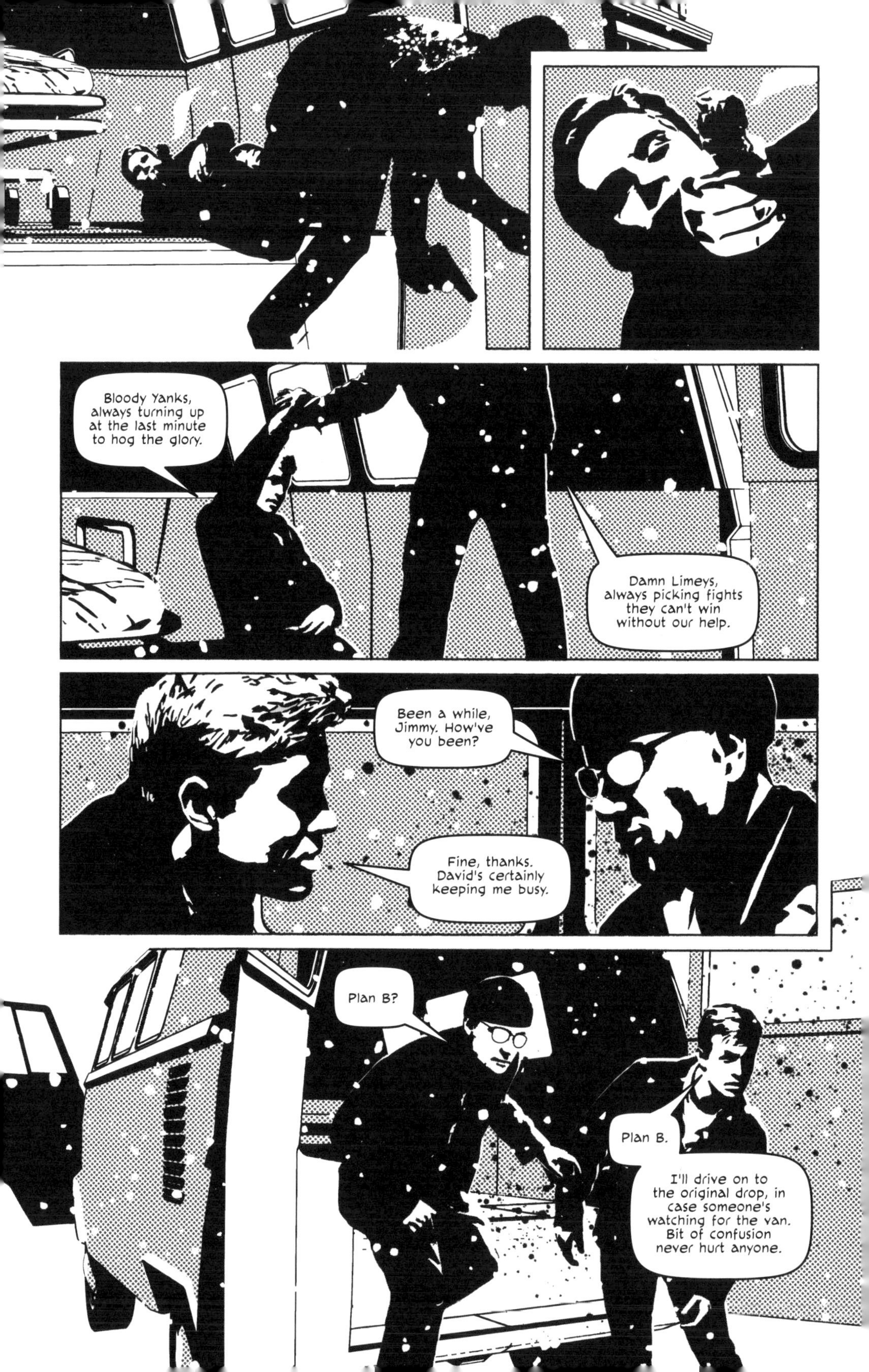
Bloody Yanks, always turning up at the last minute to hog the glory.
Damn Limeys, always picking fights they can't win without our help.
Been a while, Jimmy. How've you been?
Fine, thanks. David's certainly keeping me busy.
Plan B?
Plan B.
I'll drive on to the original drop, in case someone's watching for the van. Bit of confusion never hurt anyone.

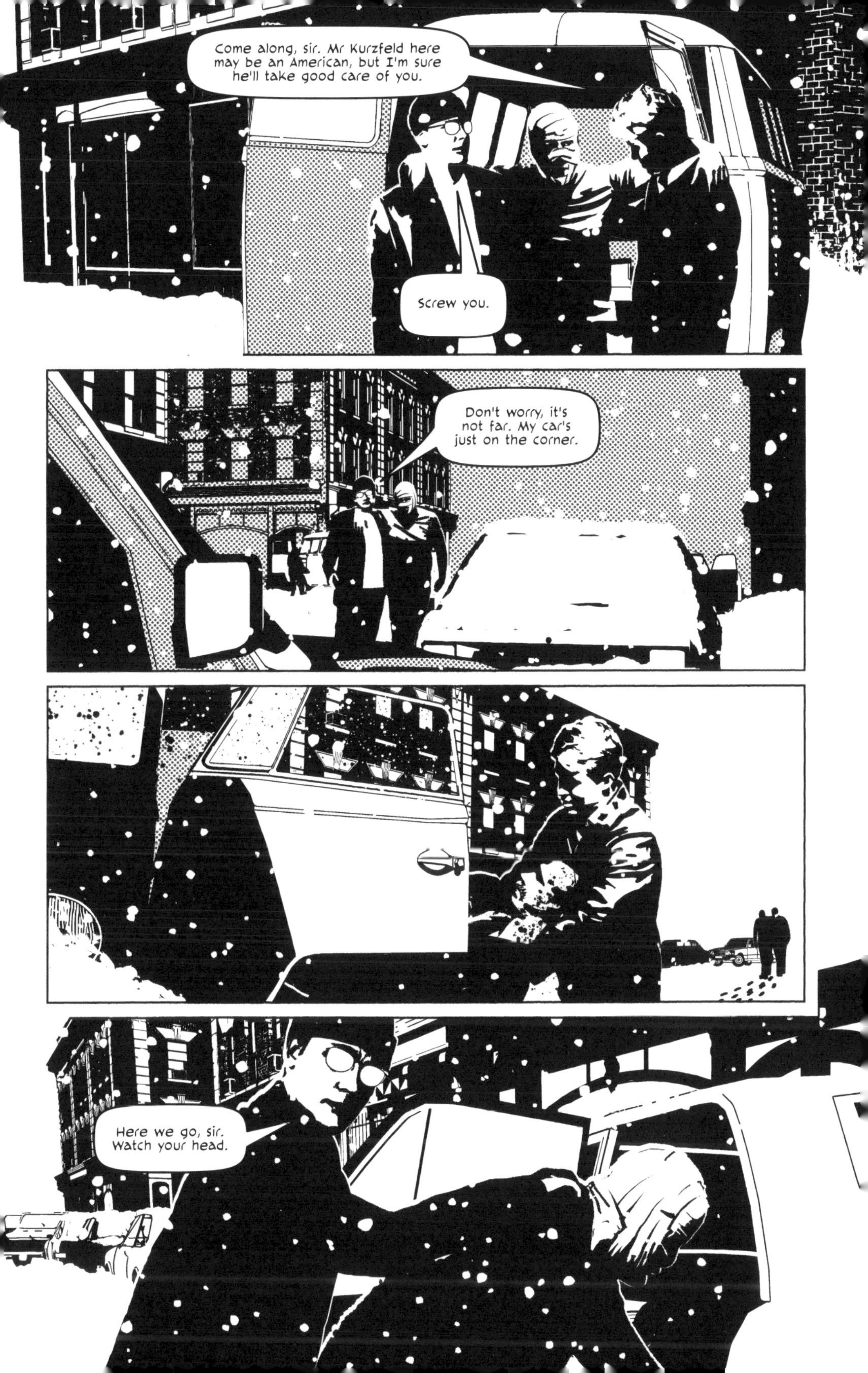
Come along, sir. Mr Kurzfeld here may be an American, but I'm sure he'll take good care of you.
Screw you.
Don't worry, it's not far. My car's just on the corner.
Here we go, sir. Watch your head.

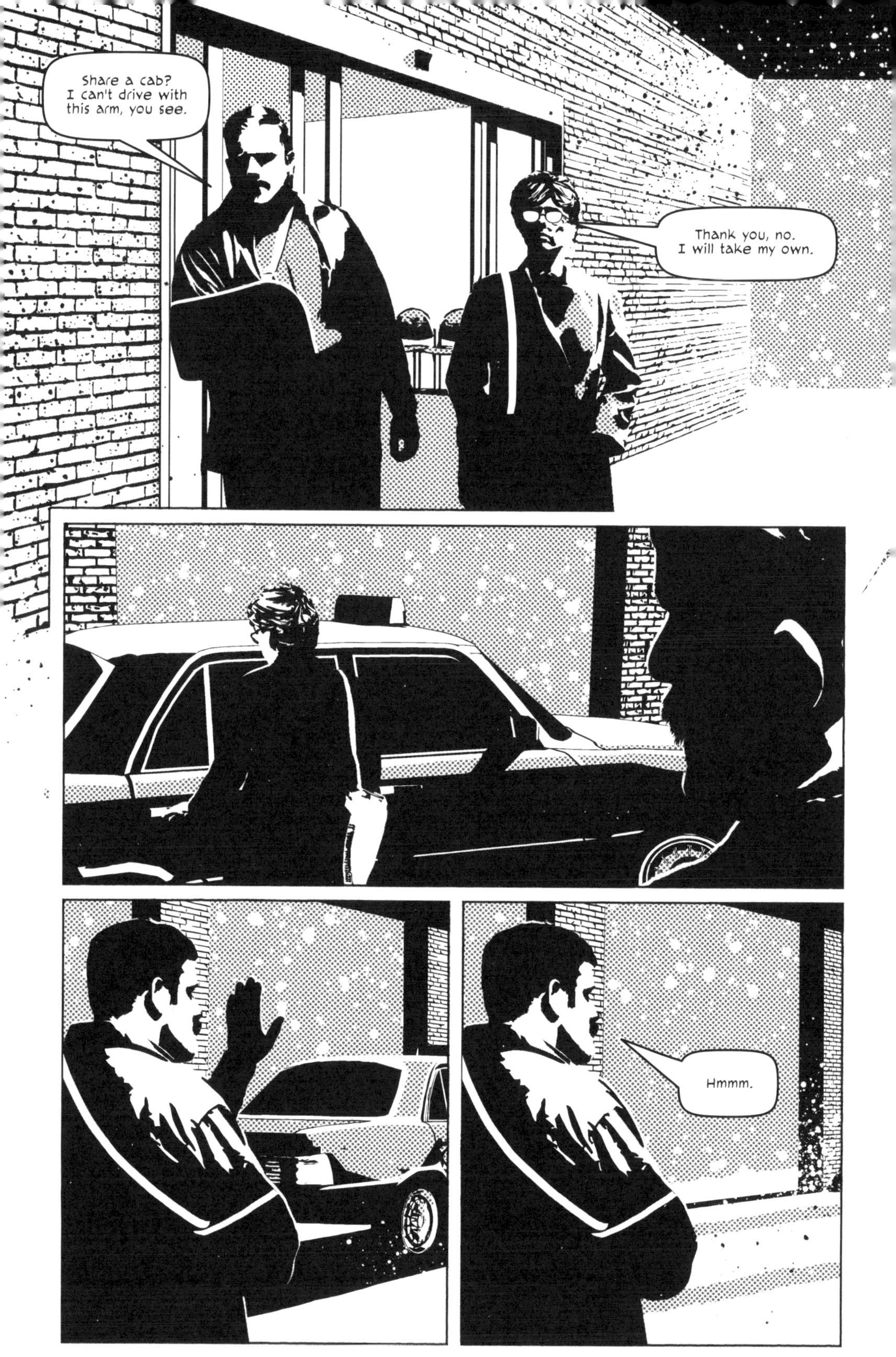
Share a cab? I can't drive with this arm, you see.
Thank you, no. I will take my own.
Hmmm.

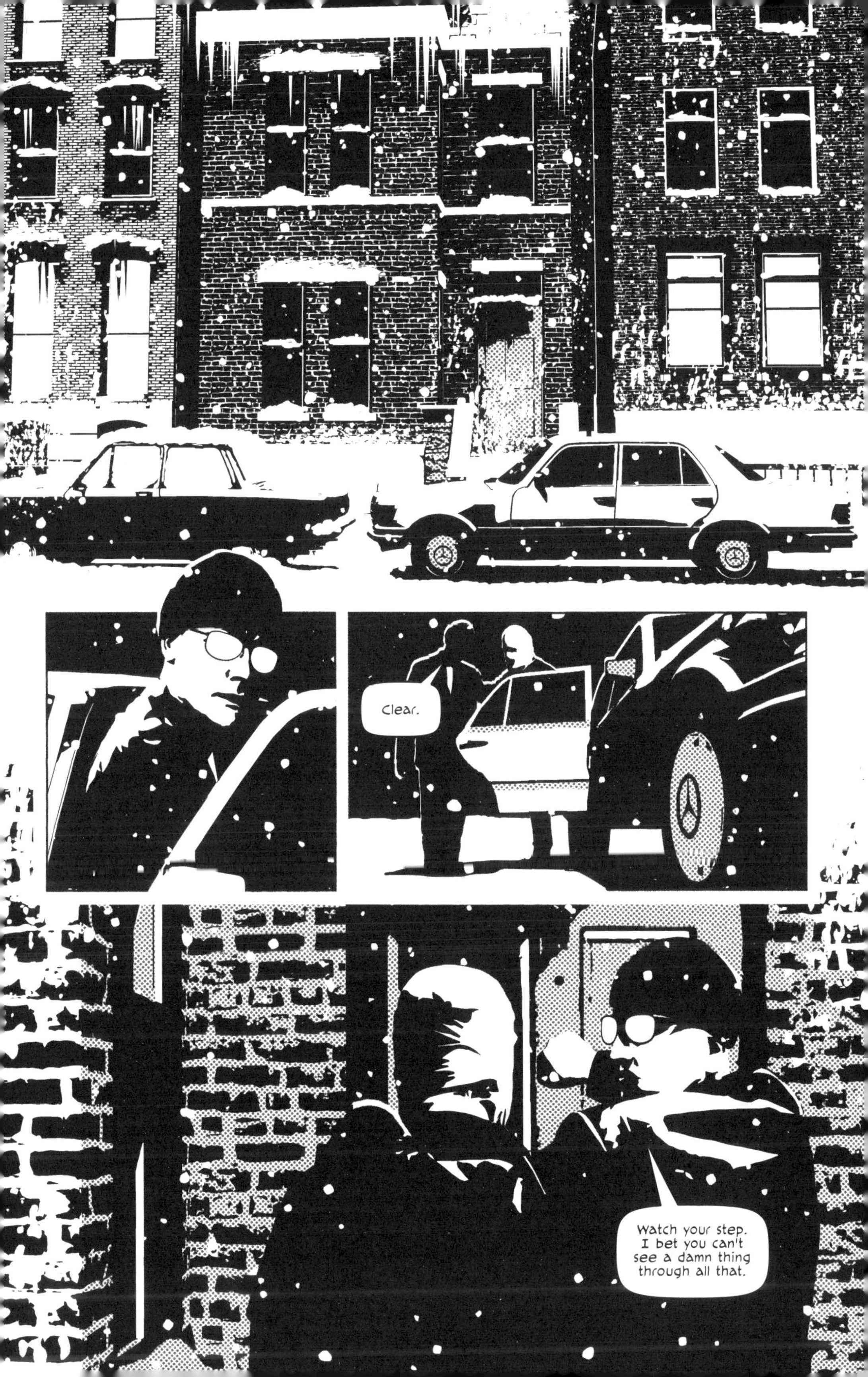

Clear.
Watch your step. I bet you can't see a damn thing through all that.

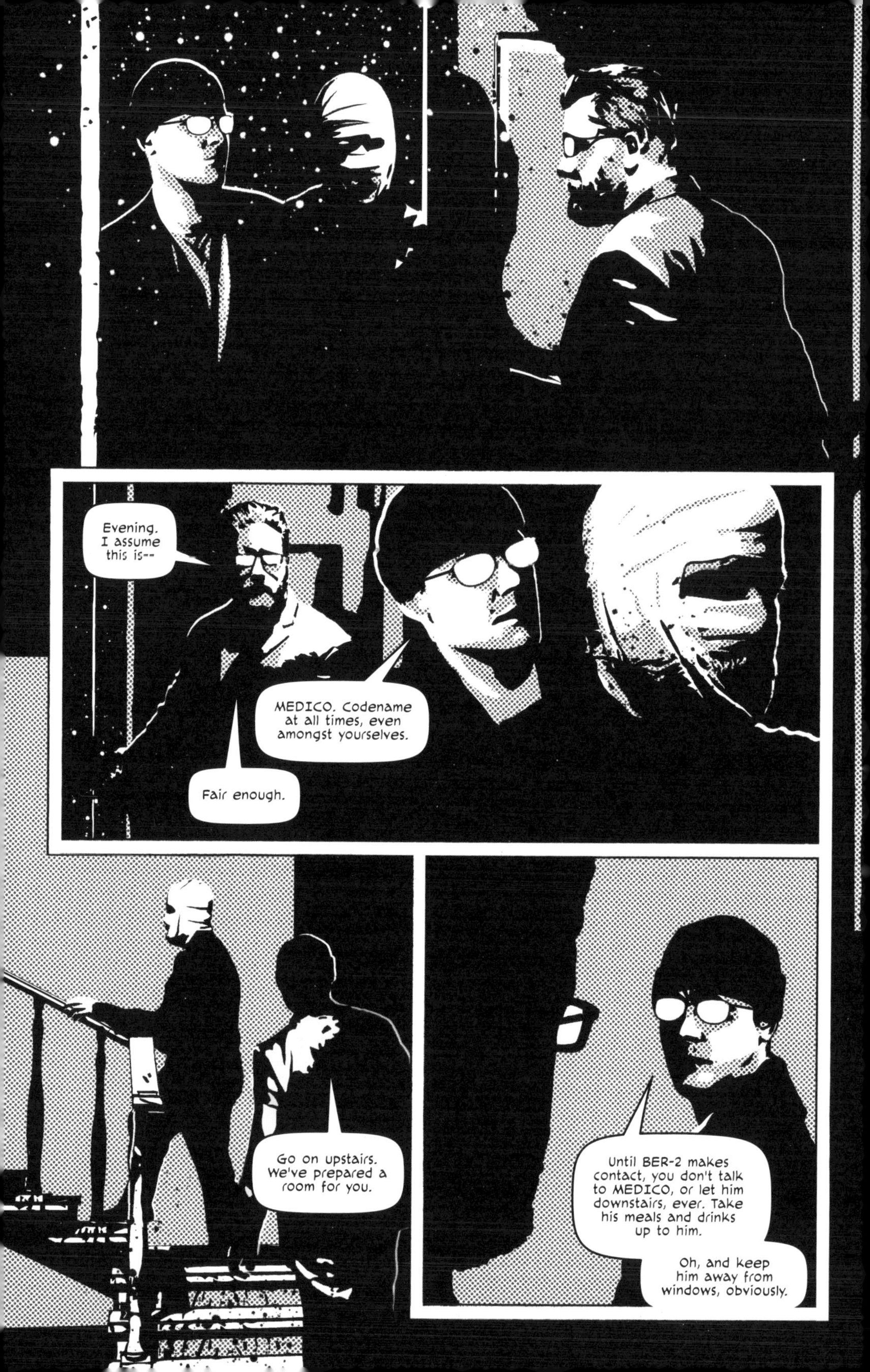

Evening. I assume this is--
MEDICO. Codename at all times, even amongst yourselves.
Fair enough.
Go on upstairs. We've prepared a room for you.
Until BER-2 makes contact, you don't talk to MEDICO, or let him downstairs, ever. Take his meals and drinks up to him.
Oh, and keep him away from windows, obviously.

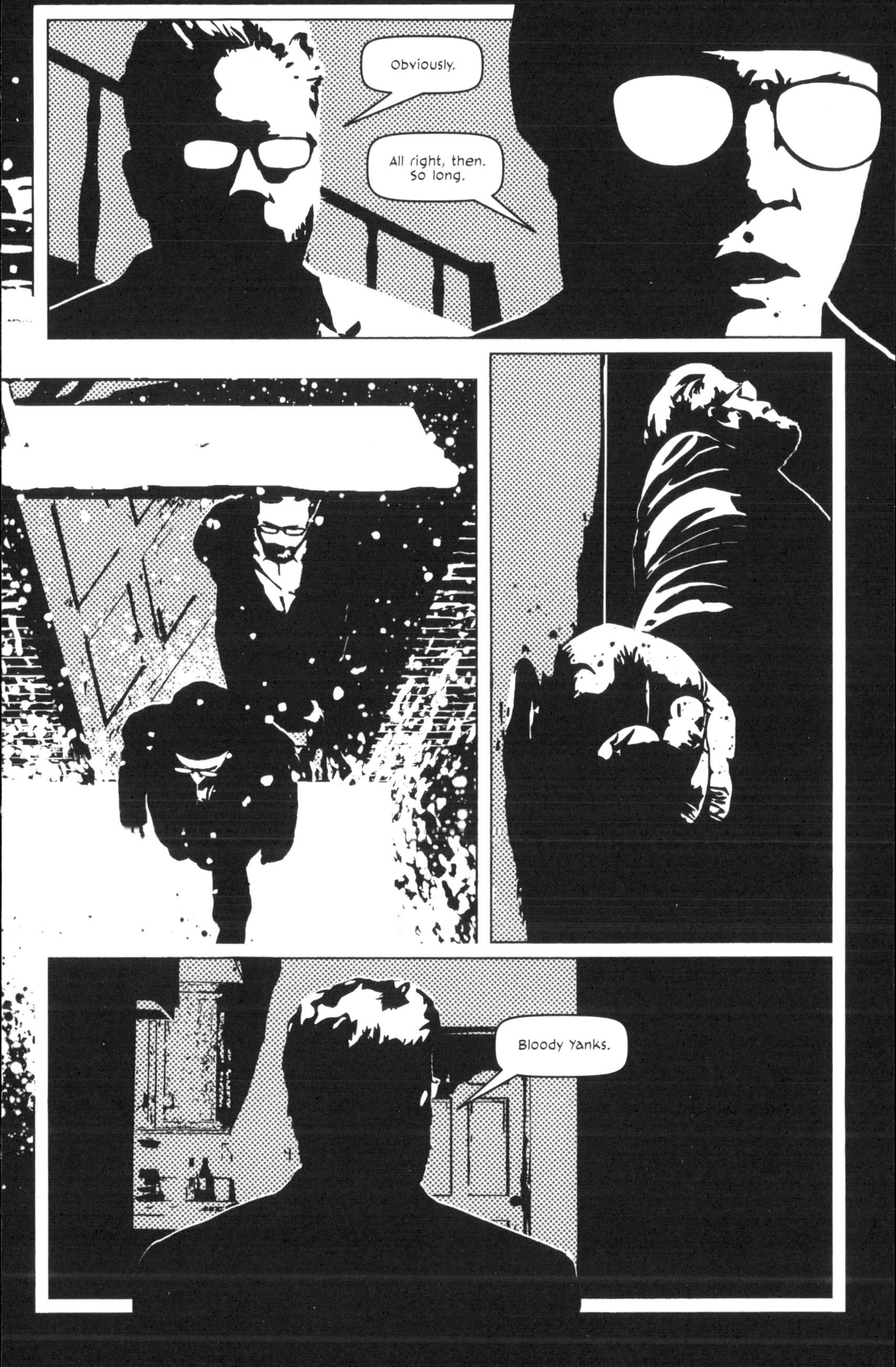
Obviously.
All right, then. So long.
Bloody Yanks.

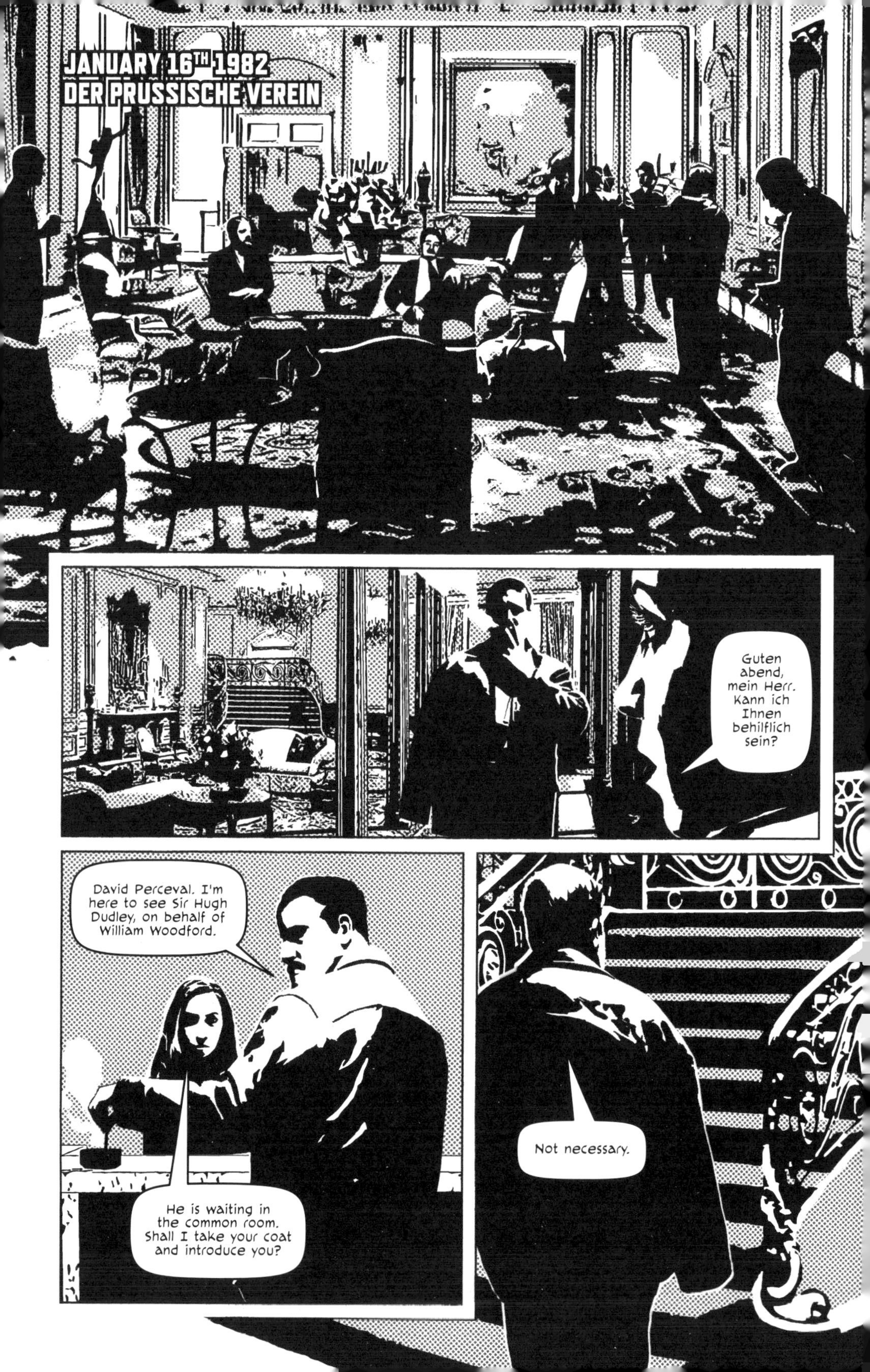
JANUARY 16TH 1982
DER PRUSSISCHE VEREIN
Guten abend, mein Herr. Kann ich Ihnen behilflich sein?
David Perceval. I'm here to see Sir Hugh Dudley, on behalf of William Woodford.
He is waiting in the common room. Shall I take your coat and introduce you?
Not necessary.

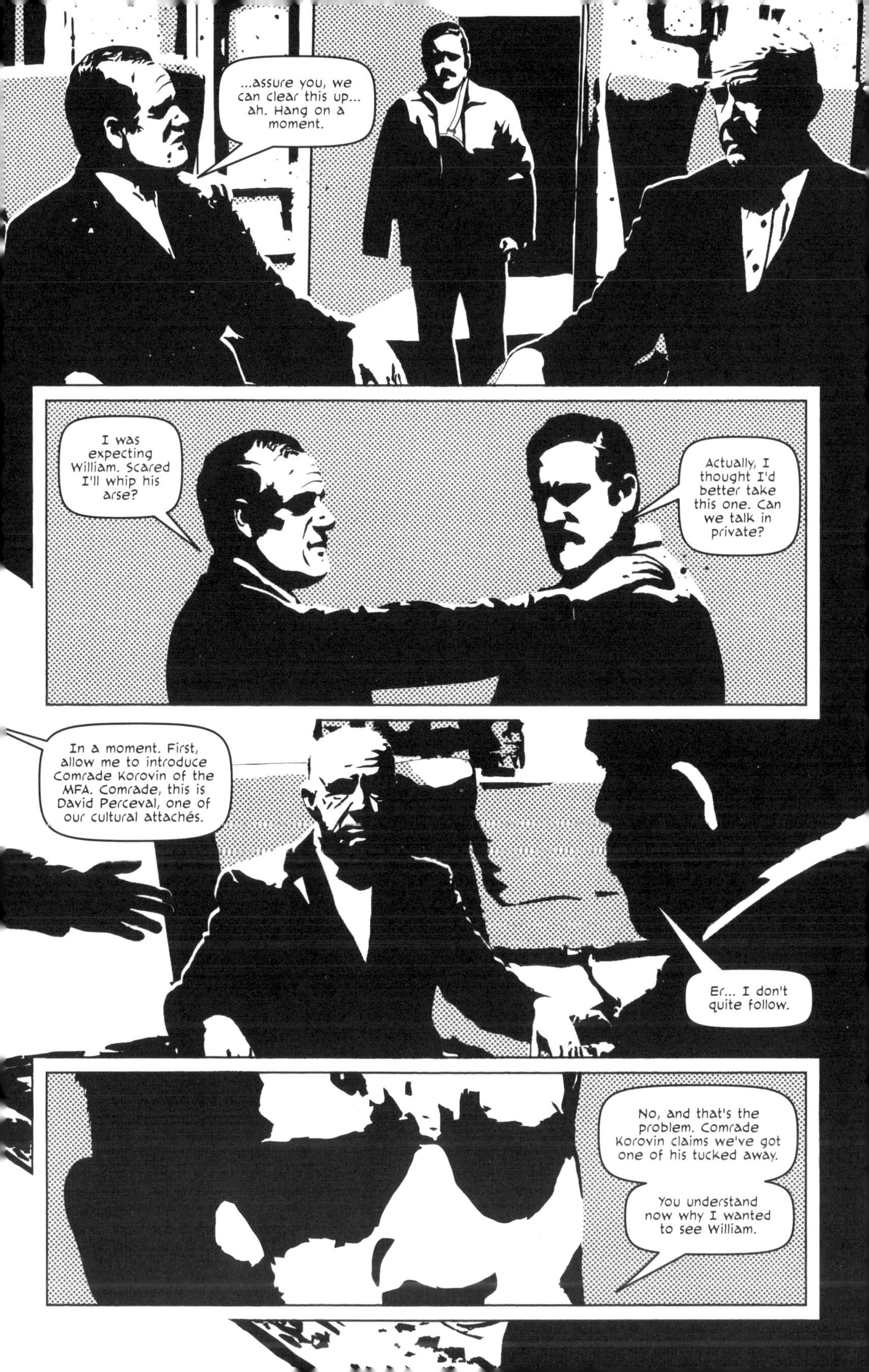
...assure you, we can clear this up... ah. Hang on a moment.
I was expecting William. Scared I'll whip his arse?
Actually, I thought I'd better take this one. Can we talk in private?
In a moment. First, allow me to introduce Comrade Korovin of the MFA. Comrade, this is David Perceval, one of our cultural attachés.
Er... I don't quite follow.
No, and that's the problem. Comrade Korovin claims we've got one of his tucked away.
You understand now why I wanted to see William.

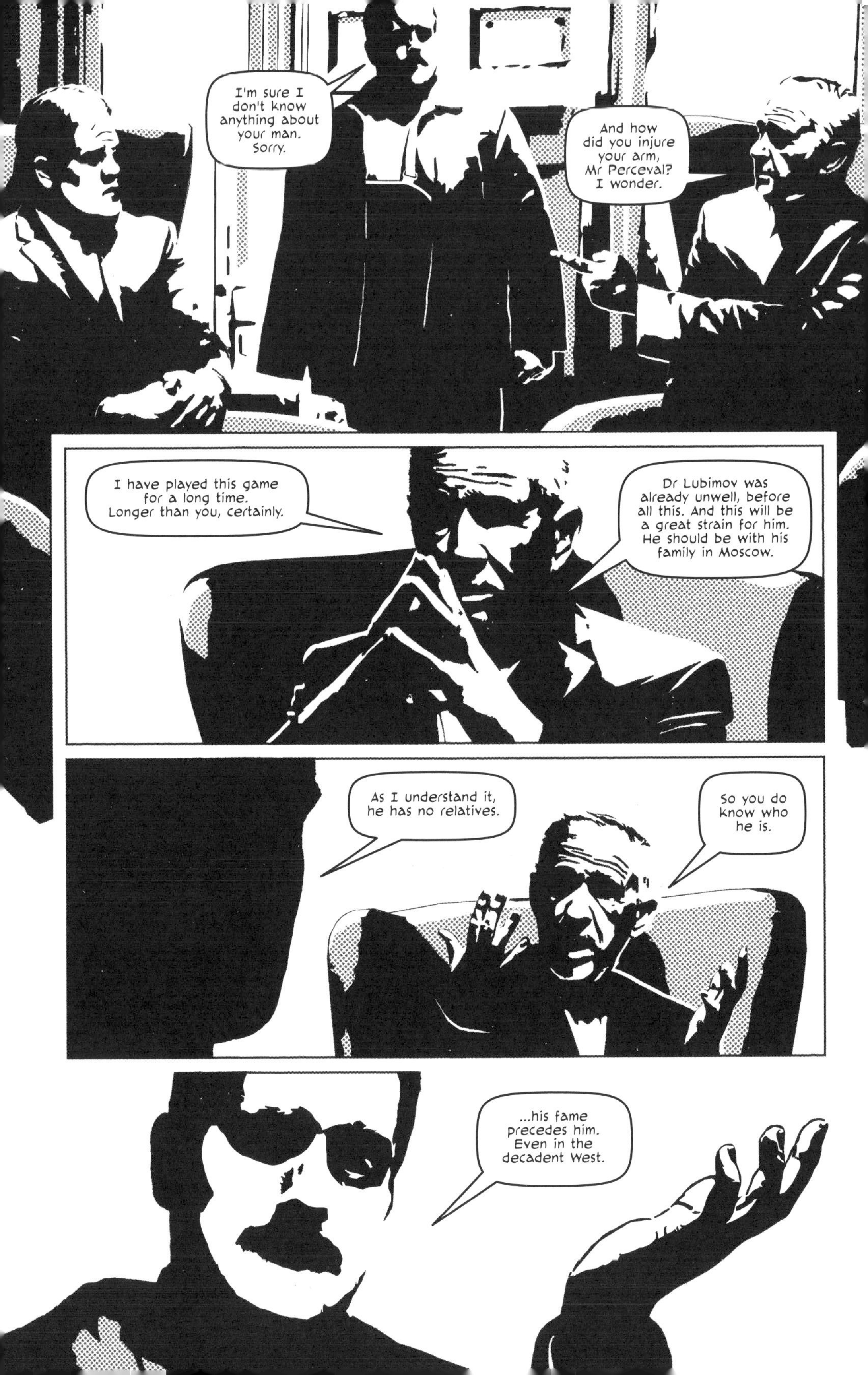
I'm sure I don't know anything about your man. Sorry.
And how did you injure your arm, Mr Perceval? I wonder.
I have played this game for a long time. Longer than you, certainly.
Dr Lubimov was already unwell, before all this. And this will be a great strain for him. He should be with his family in Moscow.
As I understand it, he has no relatives.
So you do know who he is.
...his fame precedes him. Even in the decadent West.

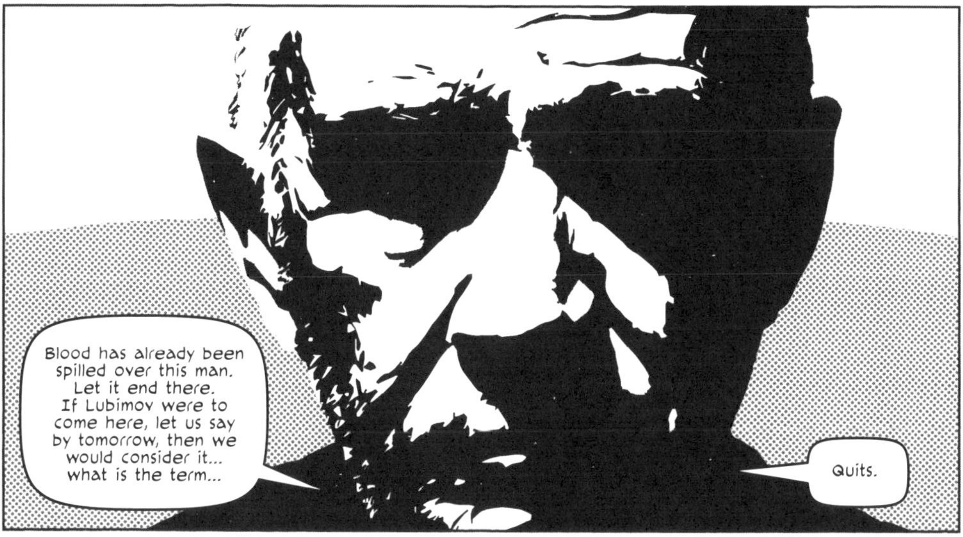
Blood has already been spilled over this man. Let it end there. If Lubimov were to come here, let us say by tomorrow, then we would consider it... what is the term...
Quits.

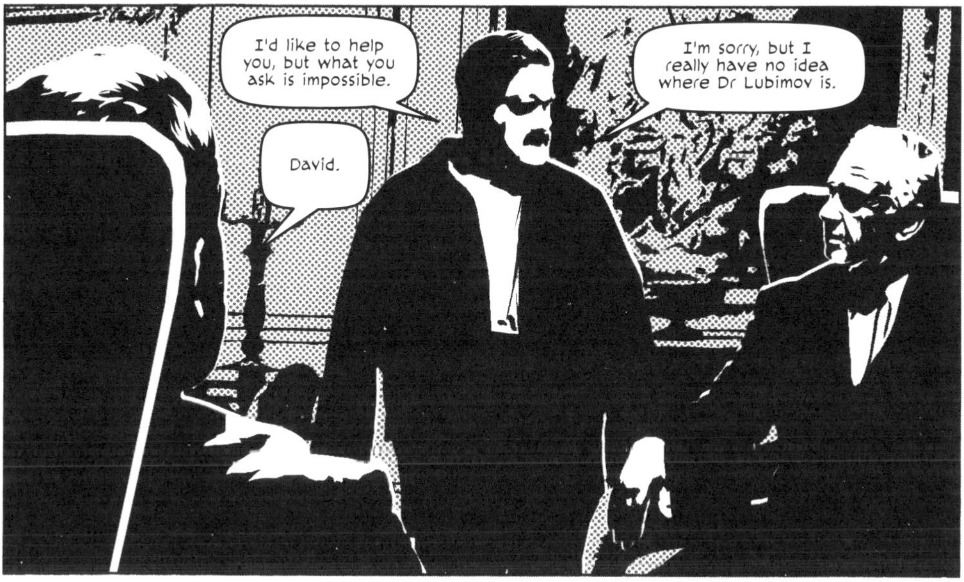
I'd like to help you, but what you ask is impossible.
I'm sorry, but I really have no idea where Dr Lubimov is.
David.

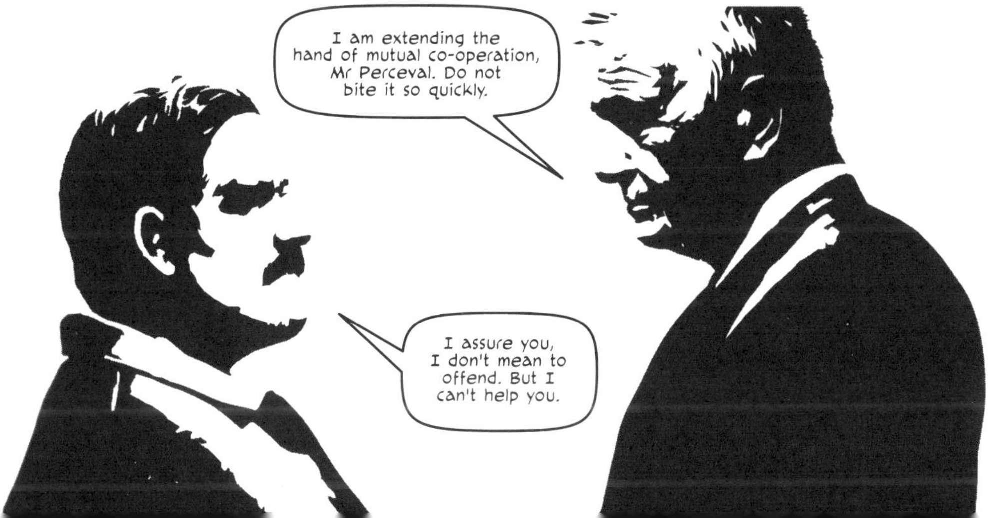
I am extending the hand of mutual co-operation, Mr Perceval. Do not bite it so quickly.
I assure you, I don't mean to offend. But I can't help you.

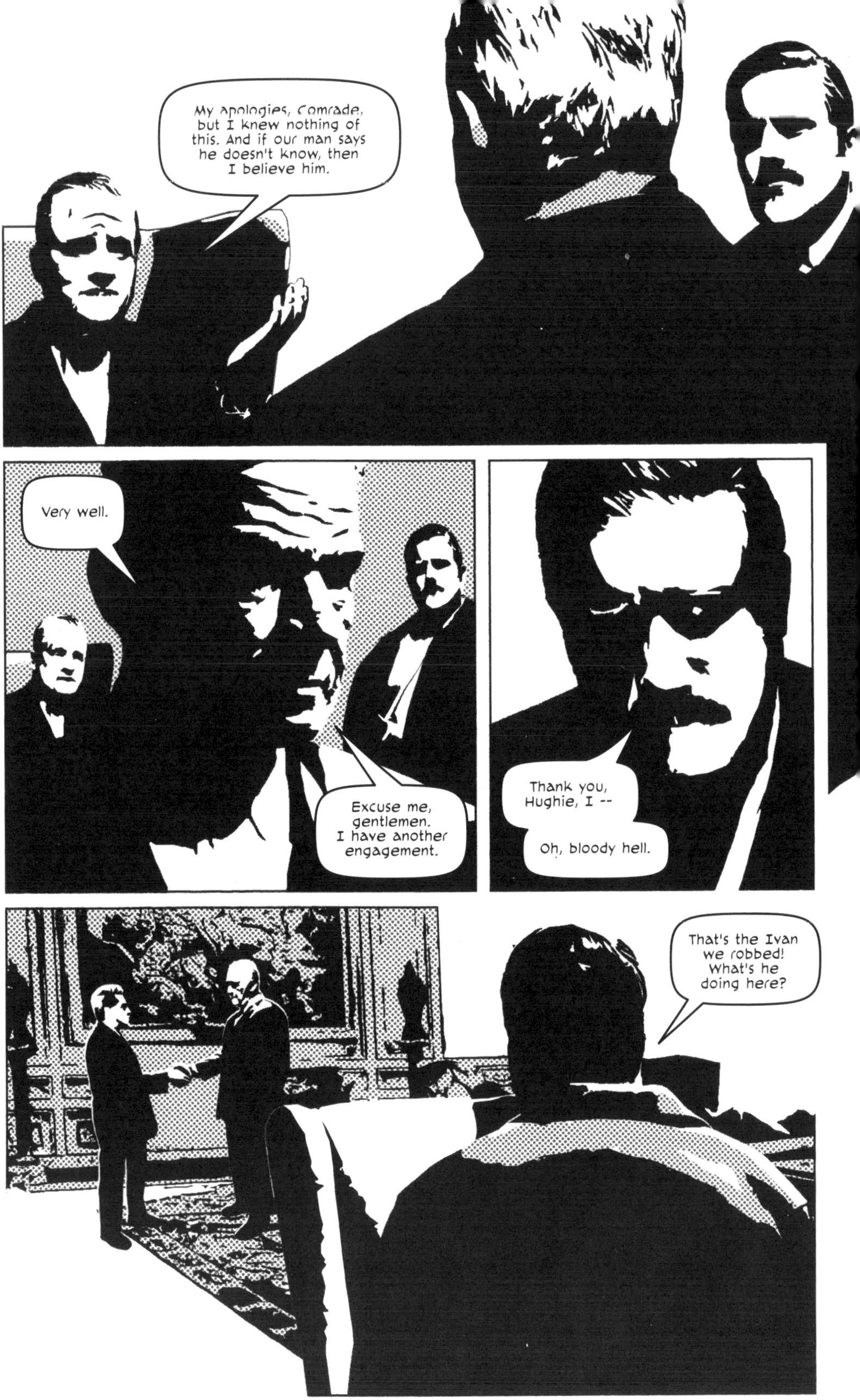
My apologies, Comrade, but I knew nothing of this. And if our man says he doesn't know, then I believe him.
Very well.
Excuse me, gentlemen. I have another engagement.
Thank you, Hughie, I --
Oh, bloody hell.
That's the Ivan we robbed! What's he doing here?

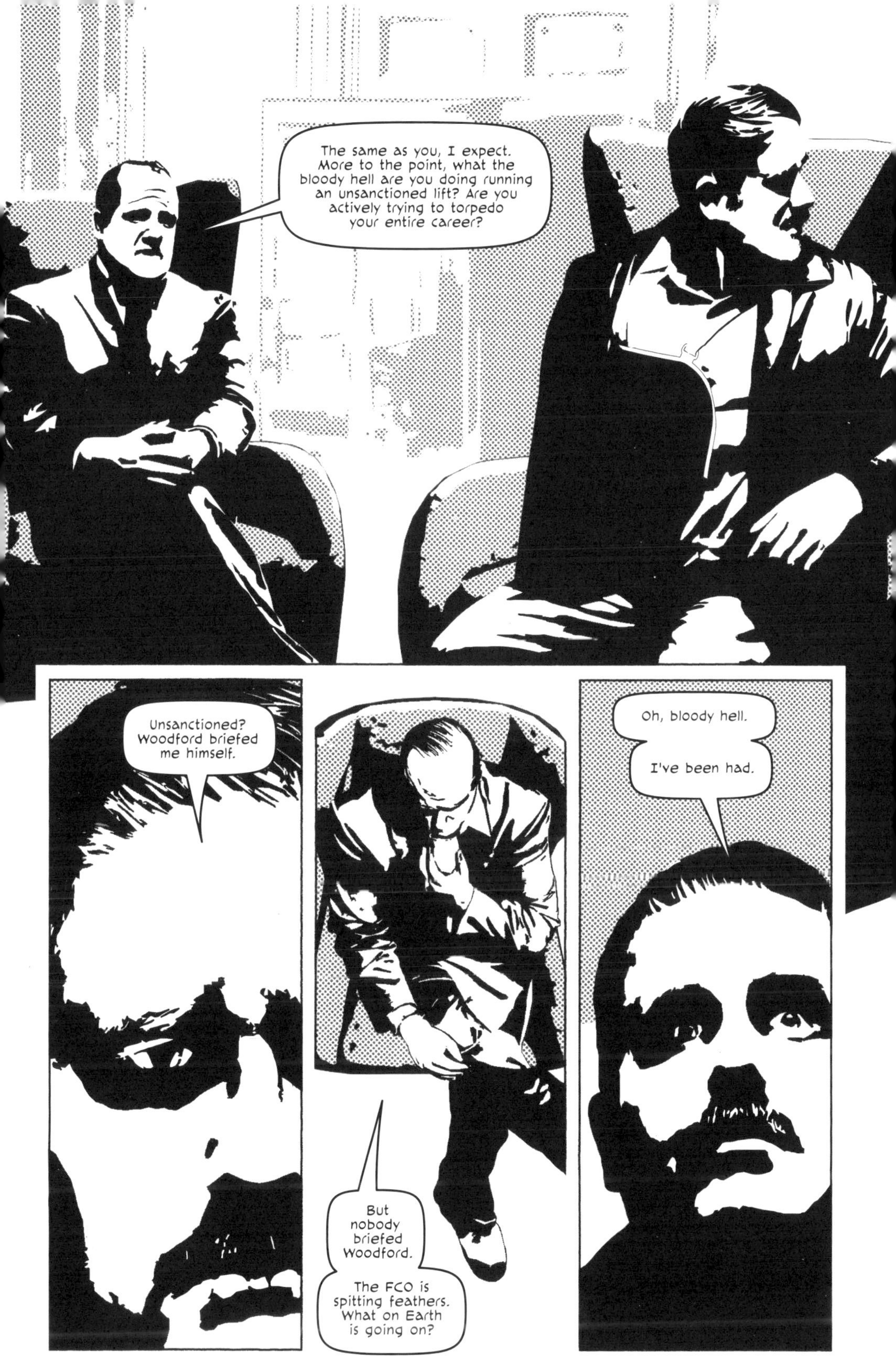
The same as you, I expect. More to the point, what the bloody hell are you doing running an unsanctioned lift? Are you actively trying to torpedo your entire career?
Unsanctioned? Woodford briefed me himself.
But nobody briefed Woodford.
The FCO is spitting feathers. What on Earth is going on?
Oh, bloody hell.
I've been had.

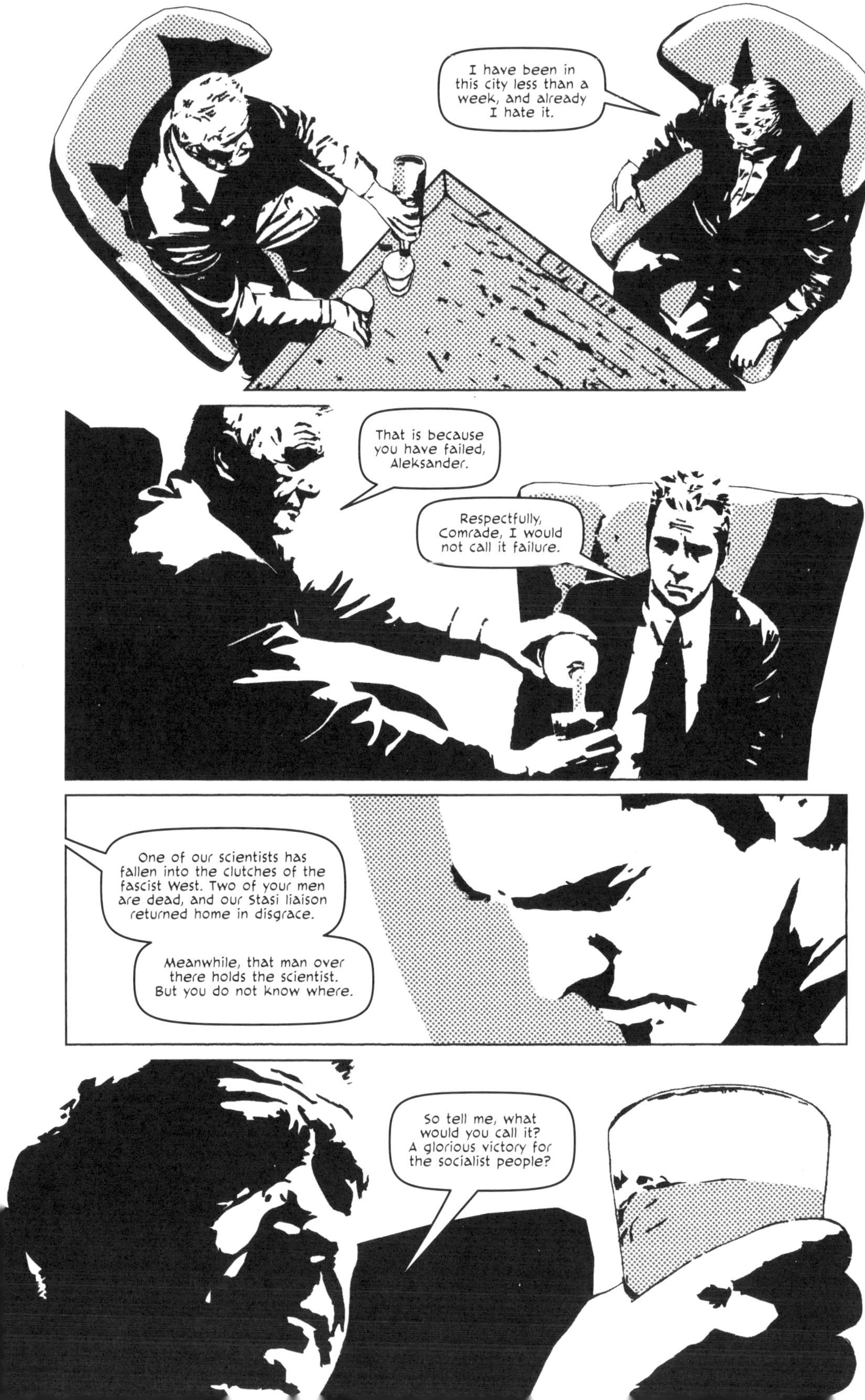
I have been in this city less than a week, and already I hate it.
That is because you have failed, Aleksander.
Respectfully, Comrade, I would not call it failure.
One of our scientists has fallen into the clutches of the fascist West. Two of your men are dead, and our Stasi liaison returned home in disgrace.
Meanwhile, that man over there holds the scientist. But you do not know where.
So tell me, what would you call it? A glorious victory for the socialist people?

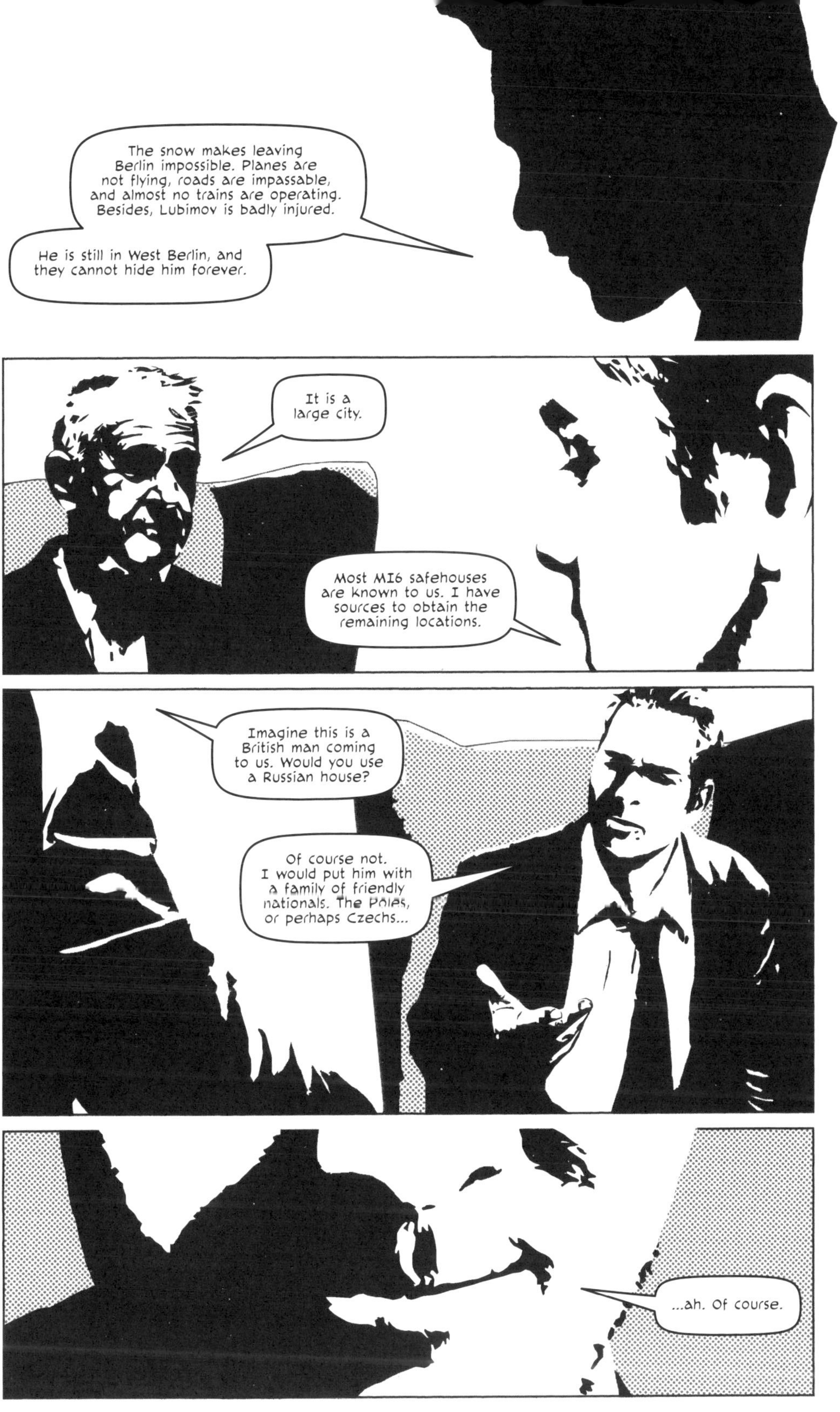

The snow makes leaving Berlin impossible. Planes are not flying, roads are impassable, and almost no trains are operating. Besides, Lubimov is badly injured.
He is still in West Berlin, and they cannot hide him forever.
It is a large city.
Most MI6 safehouses are known to us. I have sources to obtain the remaining locations.
Imagine this is a British man coming to us. Would you use a Russian house?
Of course not. I would put him with a family of friendly nationals. The Poles, or perhaps Czechs...
...ah. Of course.

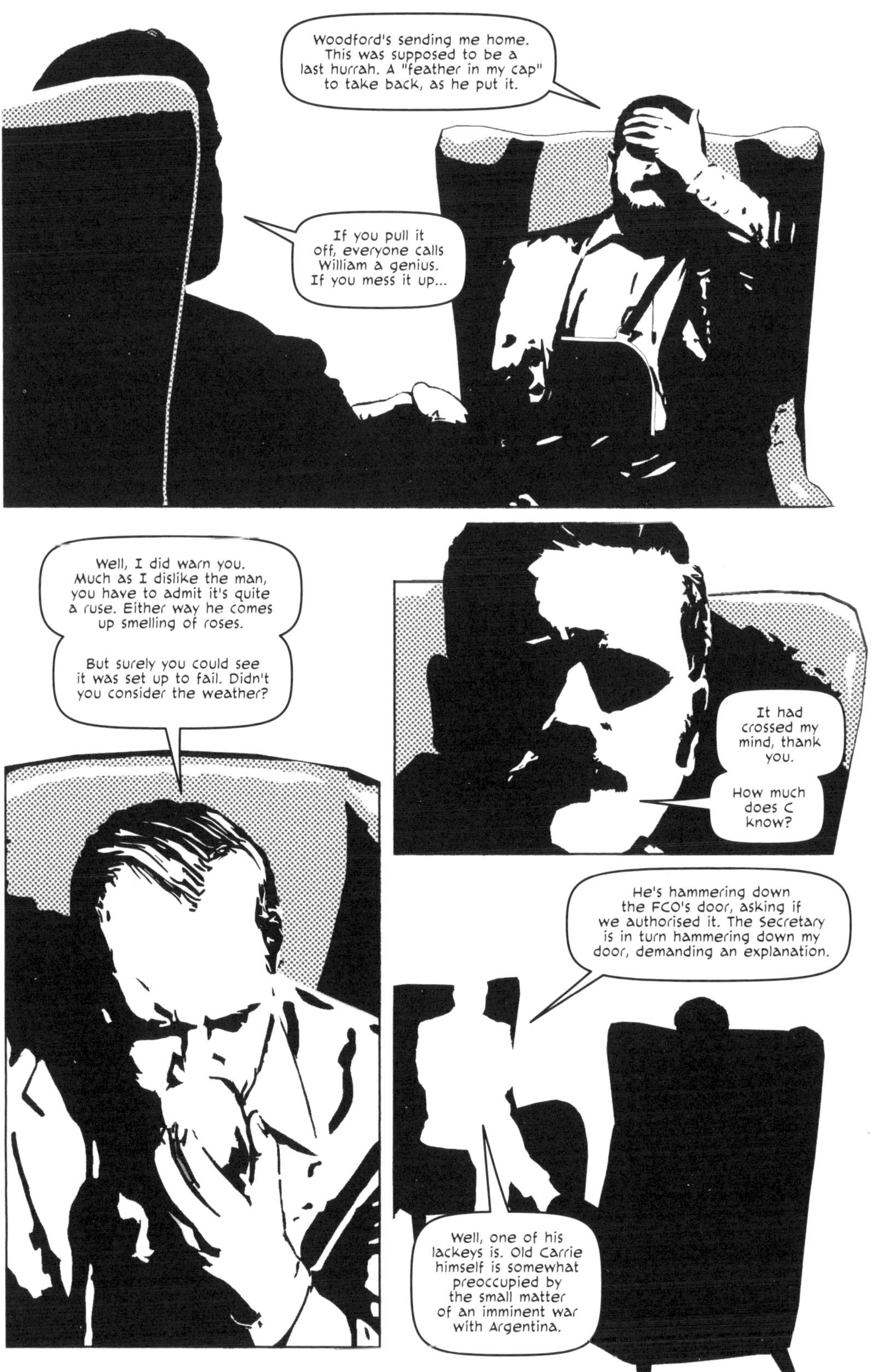
Woodford's sending me home. This was supposed to be a last hurrah. A "feather in my cap" to take back, as he put it.
If you pull it off, everyone calls William a genius. If you mess it up...
Well, I did warn you. Much as I dislike the man, you have to admit it's quite a ruse. Either way he comes up smelling of roses.
But surely you could see it was set up to fail. Didn't you consider the weather?
It had crossed my mind, thank you.
How much does C know?
He's hammering down the FCO's door, asking if we authorised it. The Secretary is in turn hammering down my door, demanding an explanation.
Well, one of his lackeys is. Old Carrie himself is somewhat preoccupied by the small matter of an imminent war with Argentina.

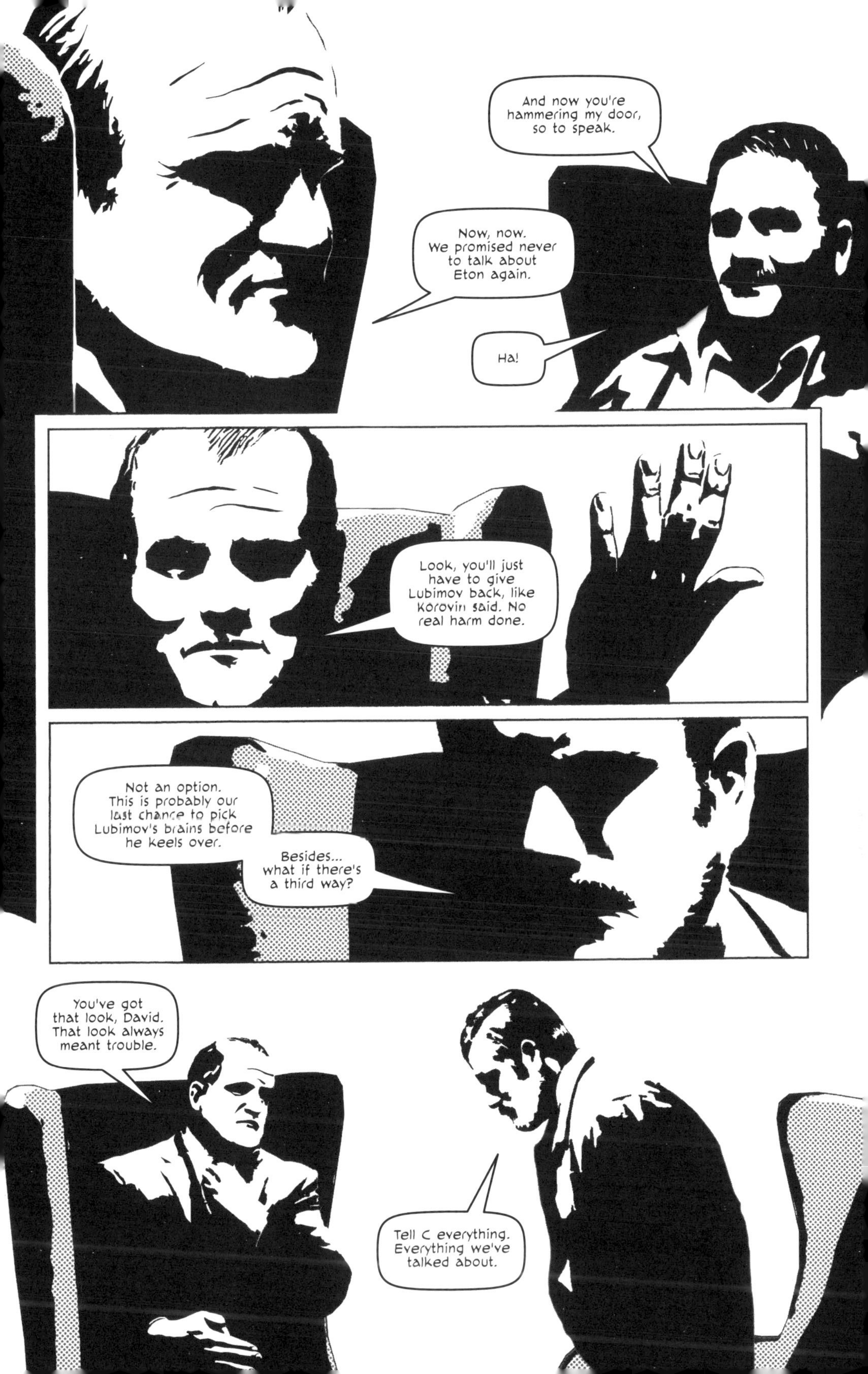
And now you're hammering my door, so to speak.
Now, now. We promised never to talk about Eton again.
Ha!
Look, you'll just have to give Lubimov back, like Korovin said. No real harm done.
Not an option. This is probably our last chance to pick Lubimov's brains before he keels over.
Besides... what if there's a third way?
You've got that look, David. That look always meant trouble.
Tell C everything. Everything we've talked about.

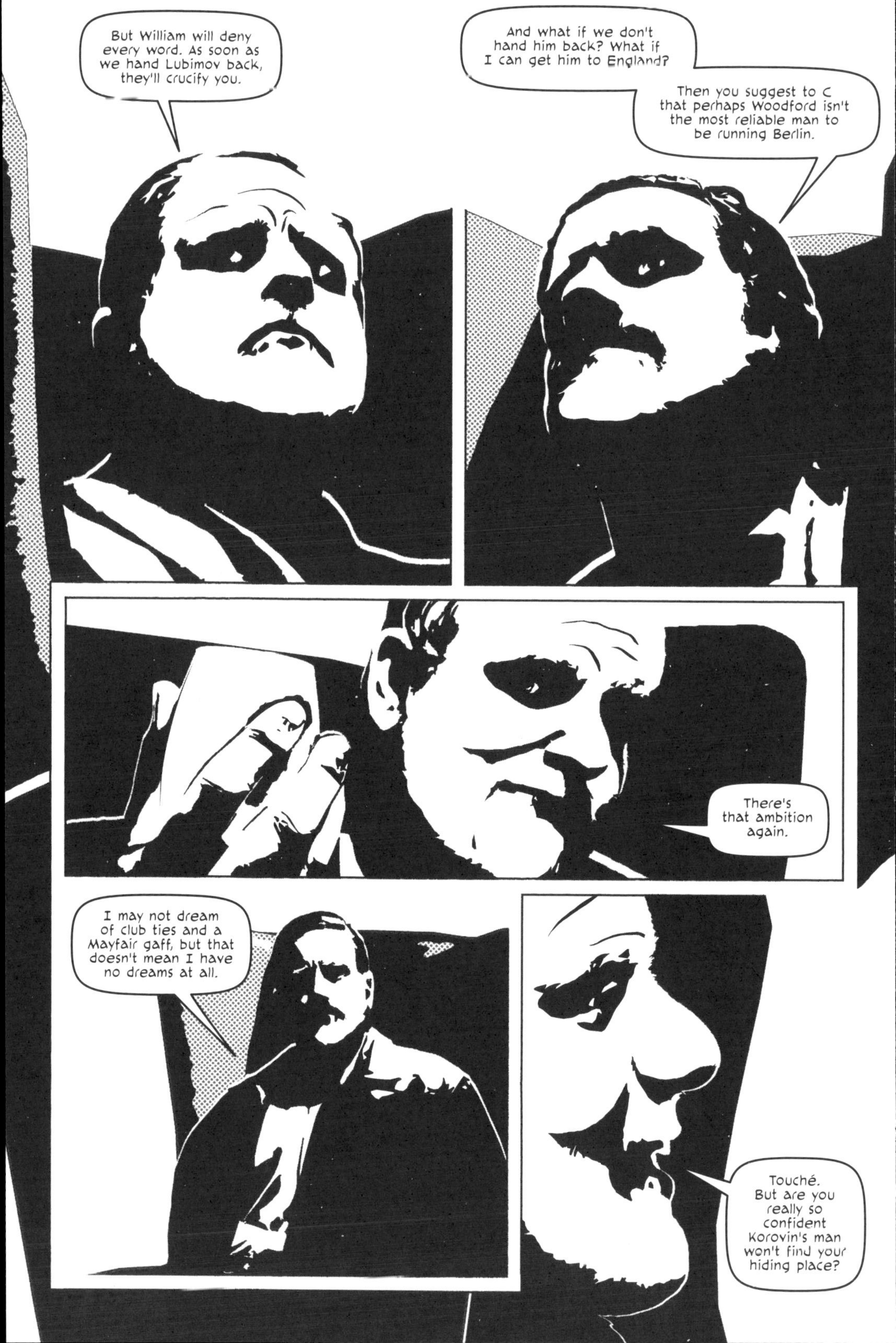

But William will deny every word. As soon as we hand Lubimov back, they'll crucify you.
And what if we don't hand him back? What if I can get him to England?
Then you suggest to C that perhaps Woodford isn't the most reliable man to be running Berlin.
There's that ambition again.
I may not dream of club ties and a Mayfair gaff, but that doesn't mean I have no dreams at all.
Touché. But are you really so confident Korovin's man won't find your hiding place?

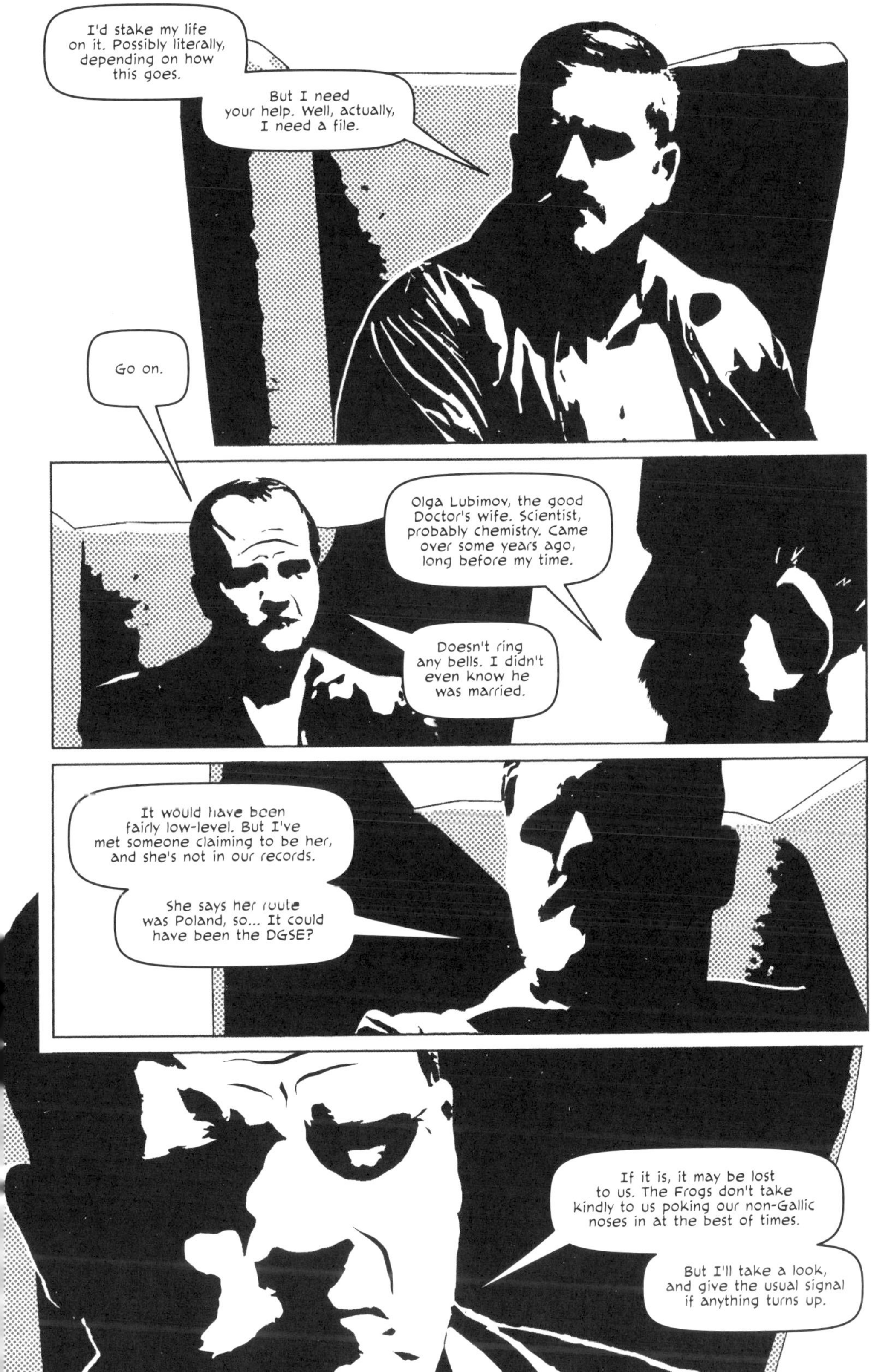

I'd stake my life on it. Possibly literally, depending on how this goes.
But I need your help. Well, actually, I need a file.
Go on.
Olga Lubimov, the good Doctor's wife. Scientist, probably chemistry. Came over some years ago, long before my time.
Doesn't ring any bells. I didn't even know he was married.
It would have been fairly low-level. But I've met someone claiming to be her, and she's not in our records.
She says her route was Poland, so... It could have been the DGSE?
If it is, it may be lost to us. The Frogs don't take kindly to us poking our non-Gallic noses in at the best of times.
But I'll take a look, and give the usual signal if anything turns up.

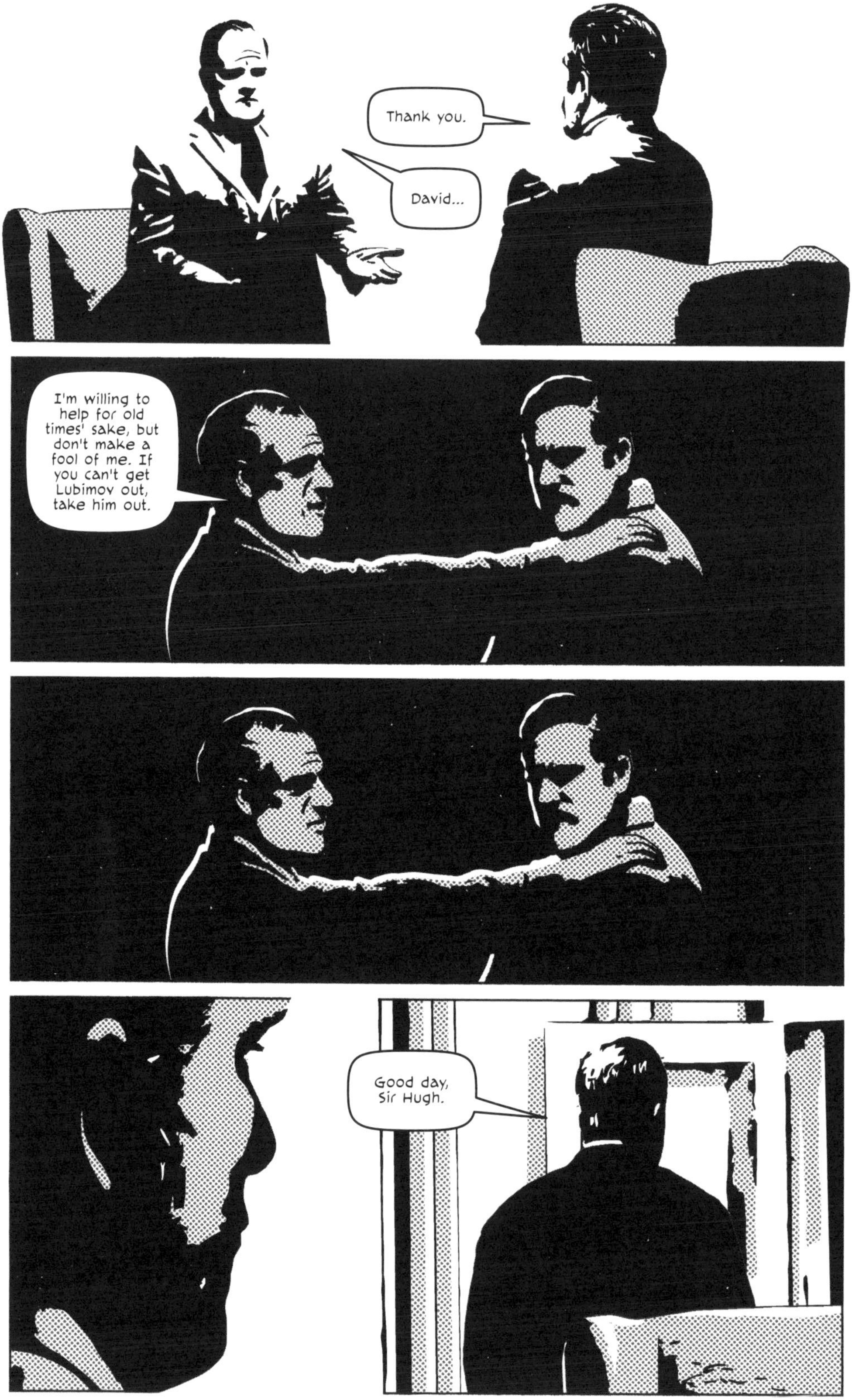
Thank you.
David...
I'm willing to help for old times' sake, but don't make a fool of me. If you can't get Lubimov out, take him out.
Good day, Sir Hugh.

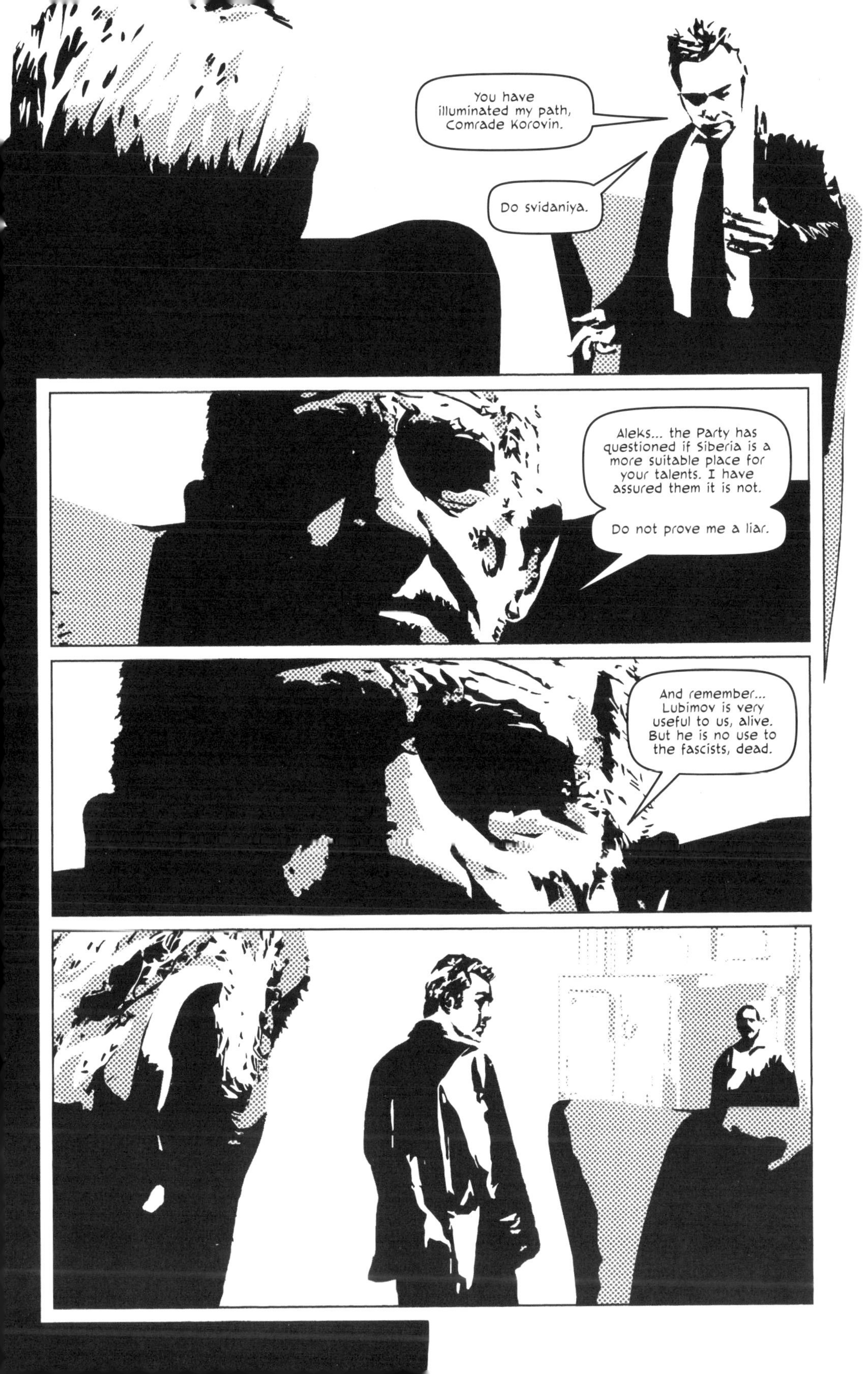
You have illuminated my path, Comrade Korovin.
Do svidaniya.
Aleks... the Party has questioned if Siberia is a more suitable place for your talents. I have assured them it is not.
Do not prove me a liar.
And remember... Lubimov is very useful to us, alive. But he is no use to the fascists, dead.

Posli vas, tovarishch.

Your German accent was better.

So was my driving.

Hmph.

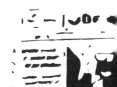

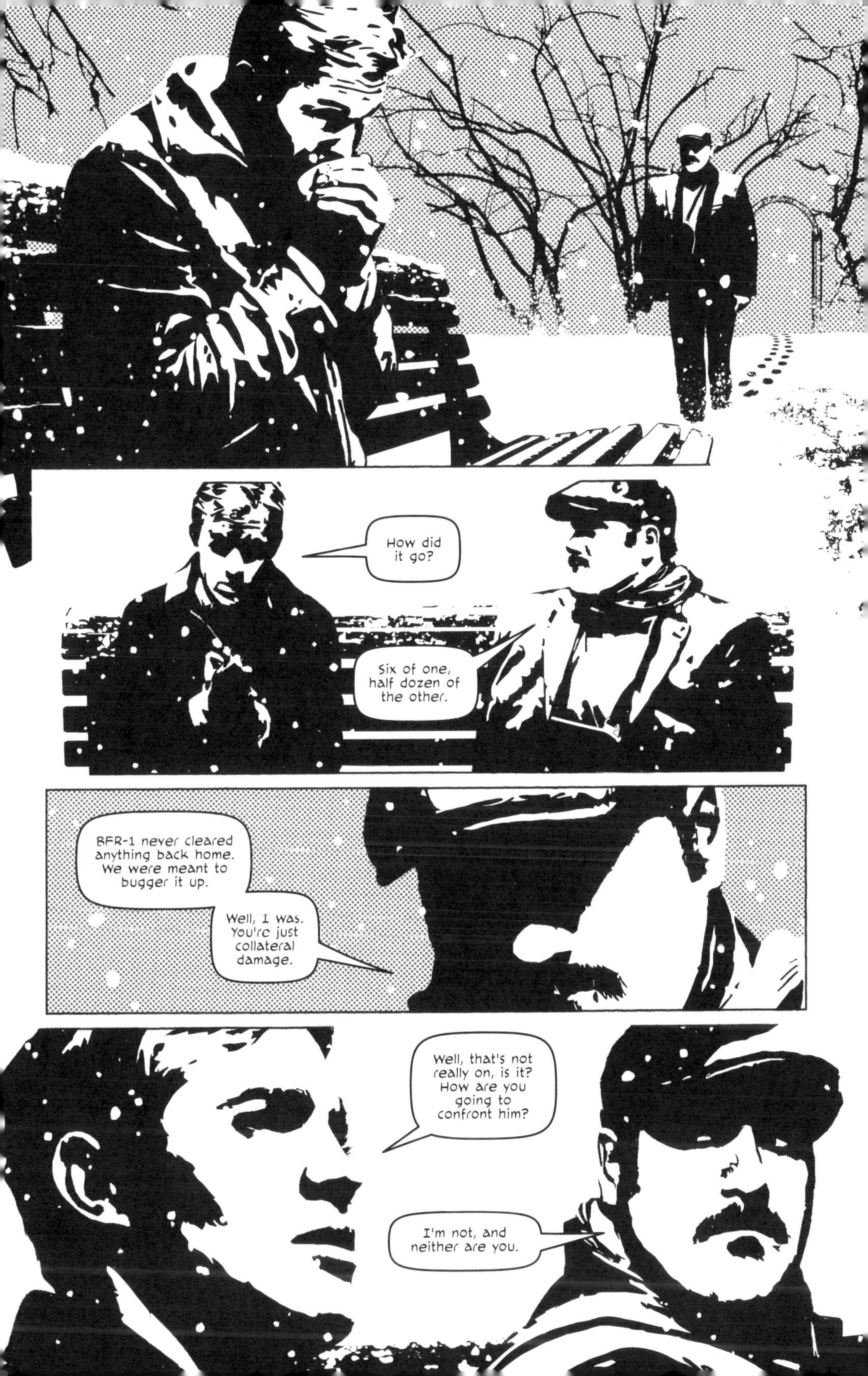

How did it go?
Six of one, half dozen of the other.
BFR-1 never cleared anything back home. We were meant to bugger it up.
Well, I was. You're just collateral damage.
Well, that's not really on, is it? How are you going to confront him?
I'm not, and neither are you.

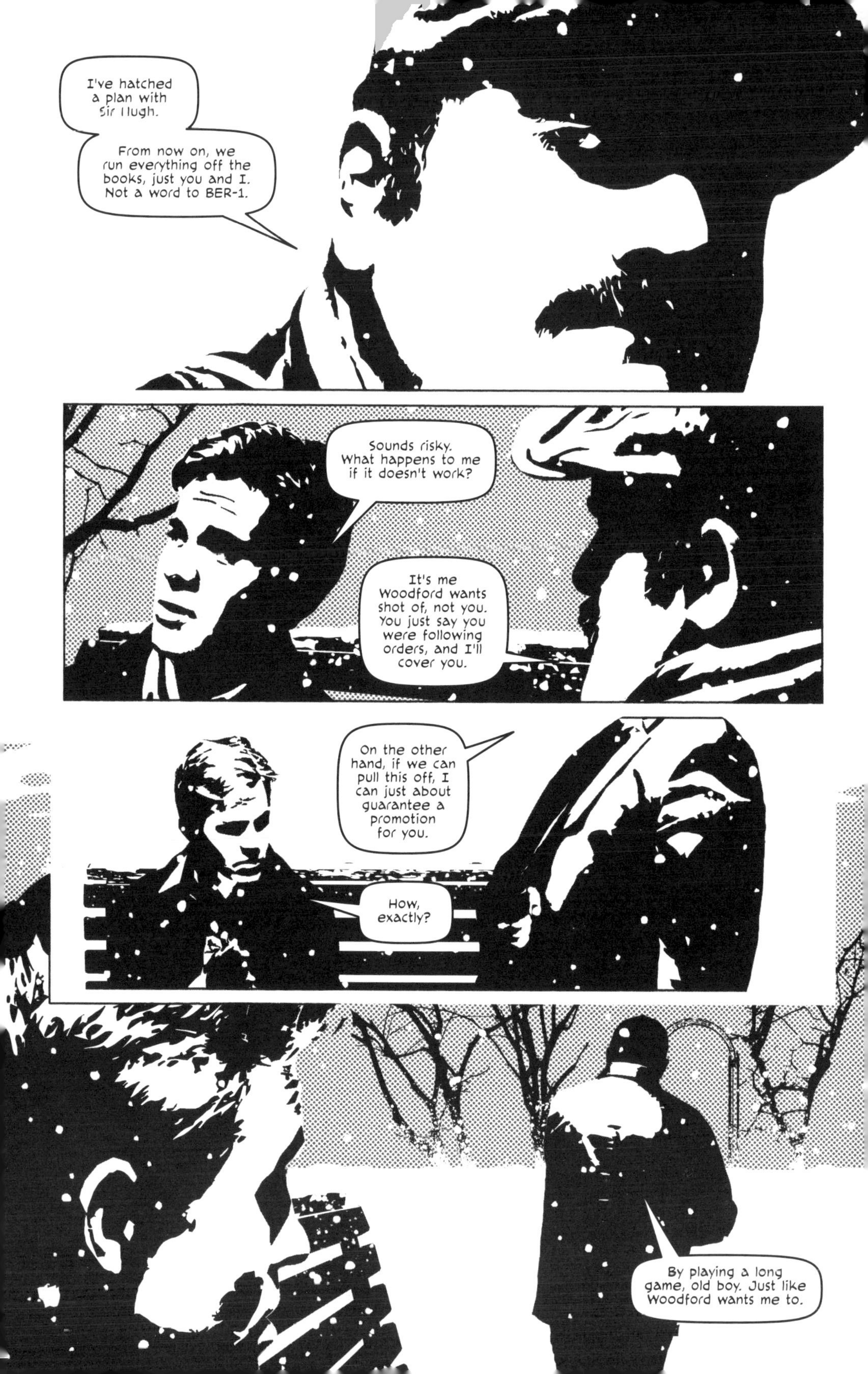
I've hatched a plan with Sir Hugh.
From now on, we run everything off the books, just you and I. Not a word to BER-1.
Sounds risky. What happens to me if it doesn't work?
It's me Woodford wants shot of, not you. You just say you were following orders, and I'll cover you.
On the other hand, if we can pull this off, I can just about guarantee a promotion for you.
How, exactly?
By playing a long game, old boy. Just like Woodford wants me to.

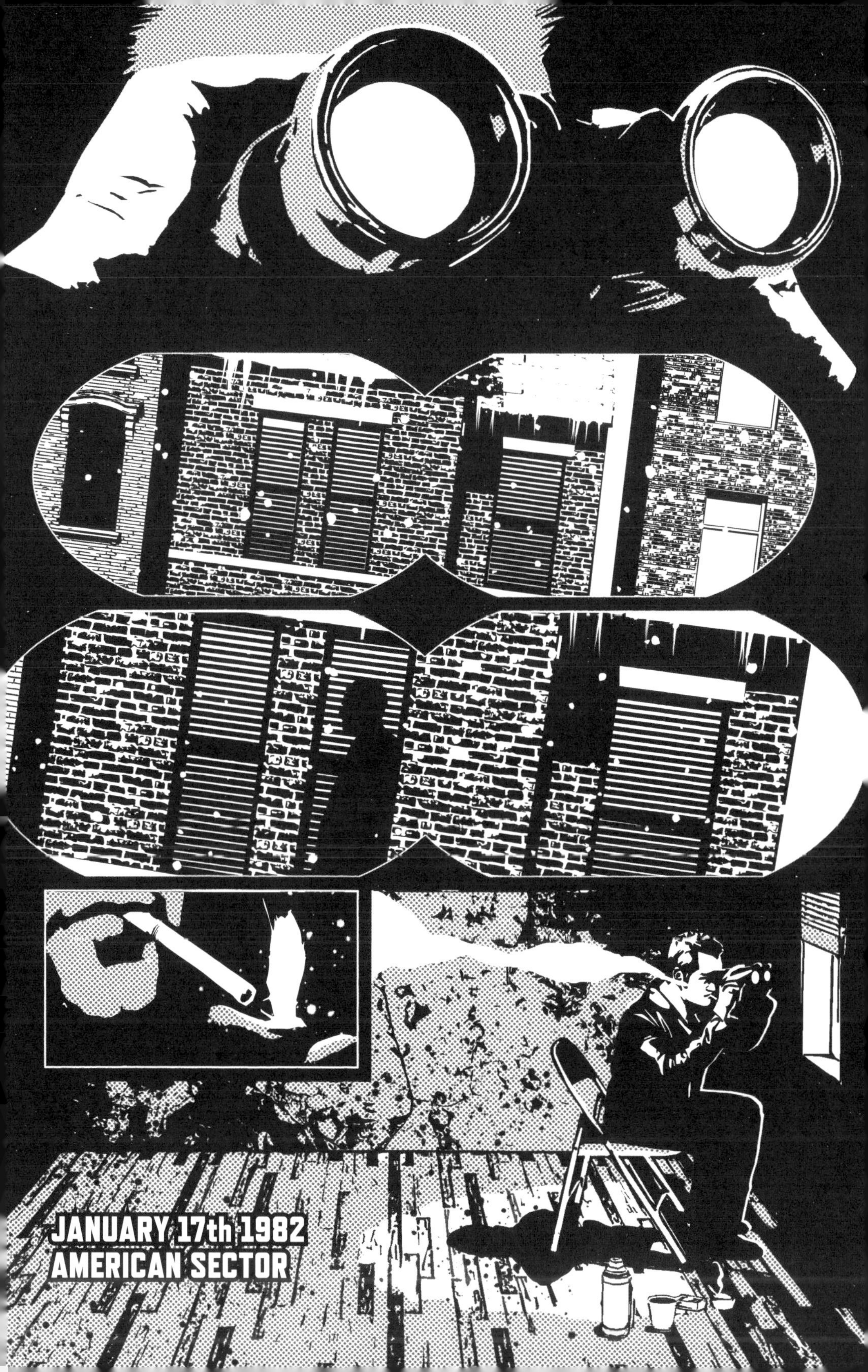
JANUARY 17th 1982
AMERICAN SECTOR

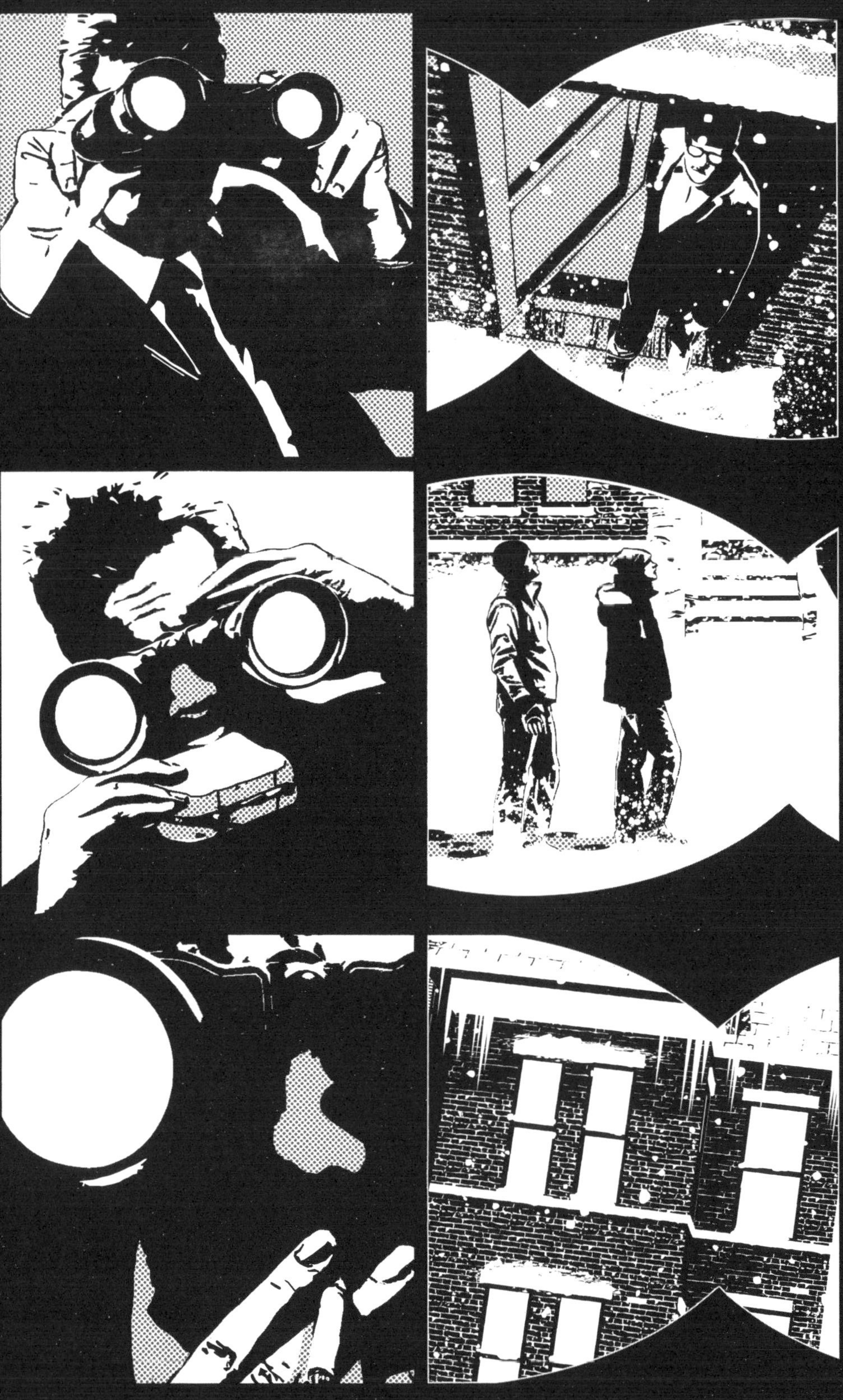

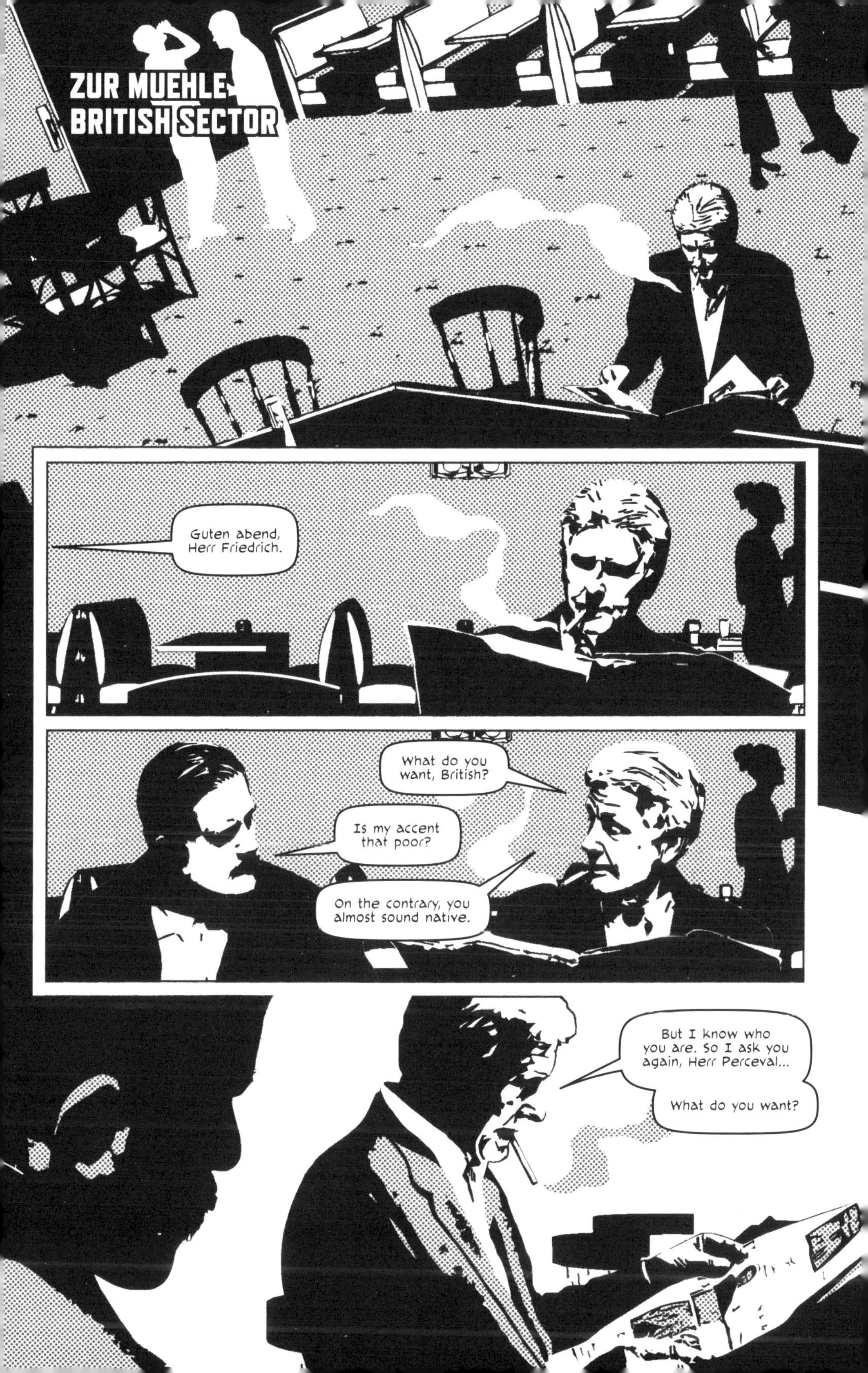
ZUR MUEHLE BRITISH SECTOR
Guten abend, Herr Friedrich.
What do you want, British?
Is my accent that poor?
On the contrary, you almost sound native.
But I know who you are. So I ask you again, Herr Perceval...
What do you want?

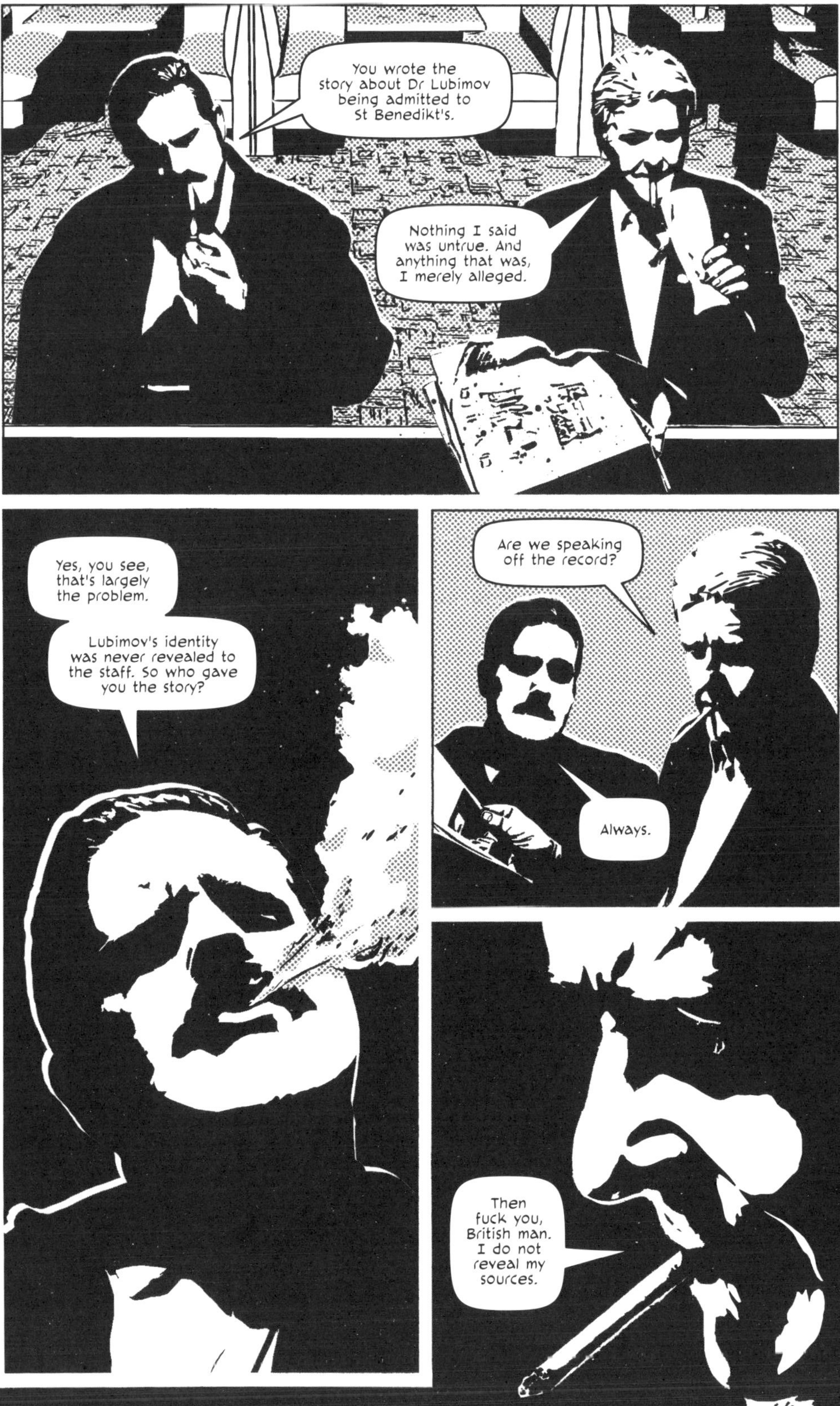
You wrote the story about Dr Lubimov being admitted to St Benedikt's.
Nothing I said was untrue. And anything that was, I merely alleged.
Yes, you see, that's largely the problem.
Lubimov's identity was never revealed to the staff. So who gave you the story?
Are we speaking off the record?
Always.
Then fuck you, British man. I do not reveal my sources.

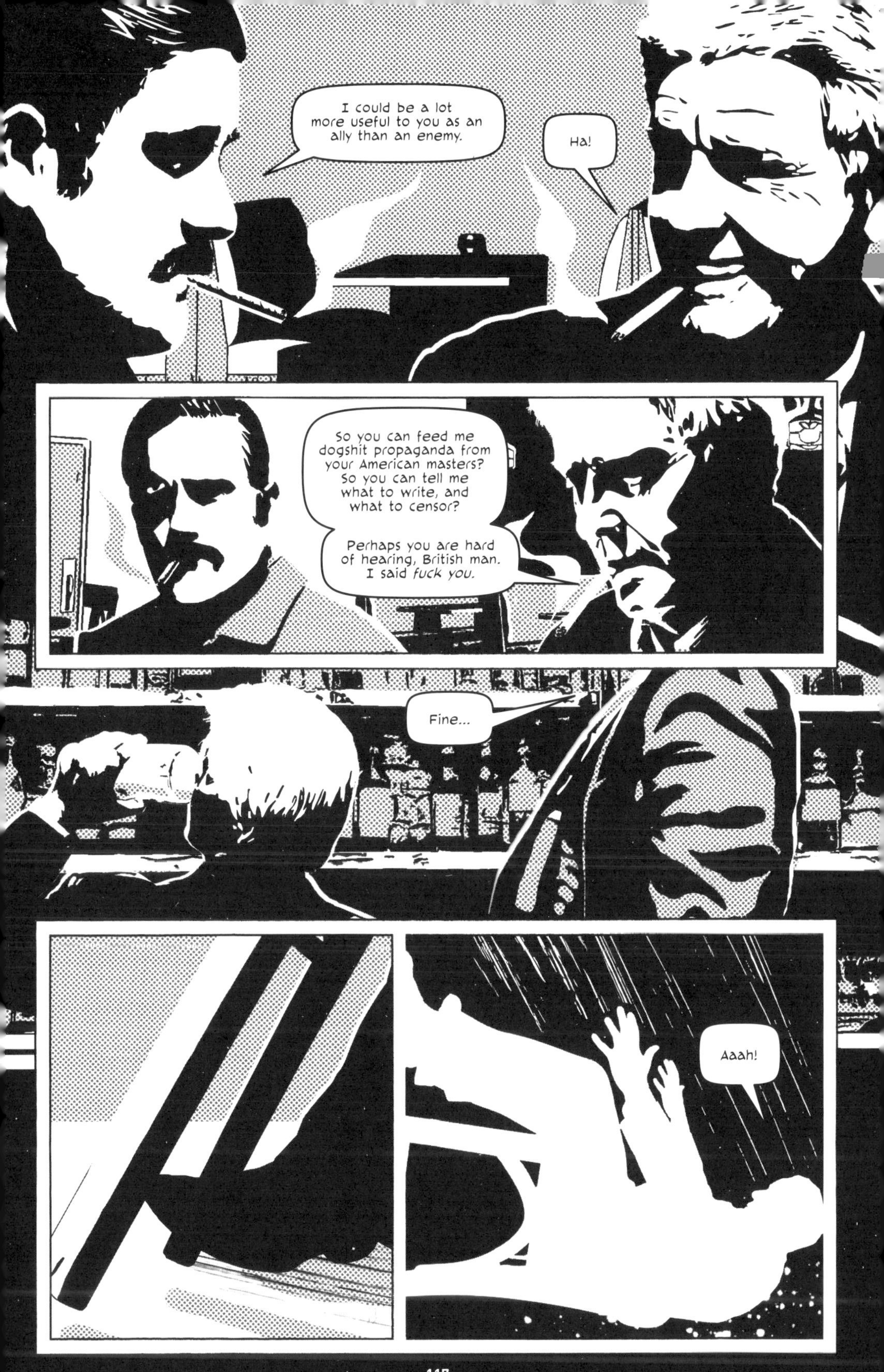
I could be a lot more useful to you as an ally than an enemy.
Ha!
So you can feed me dogshit propaganda from your American masters? So you can tell me what to write, and what to censor?
Perhaps you are hard of hearing, British man. I said *fuck you.*
Fine...
Aaah!

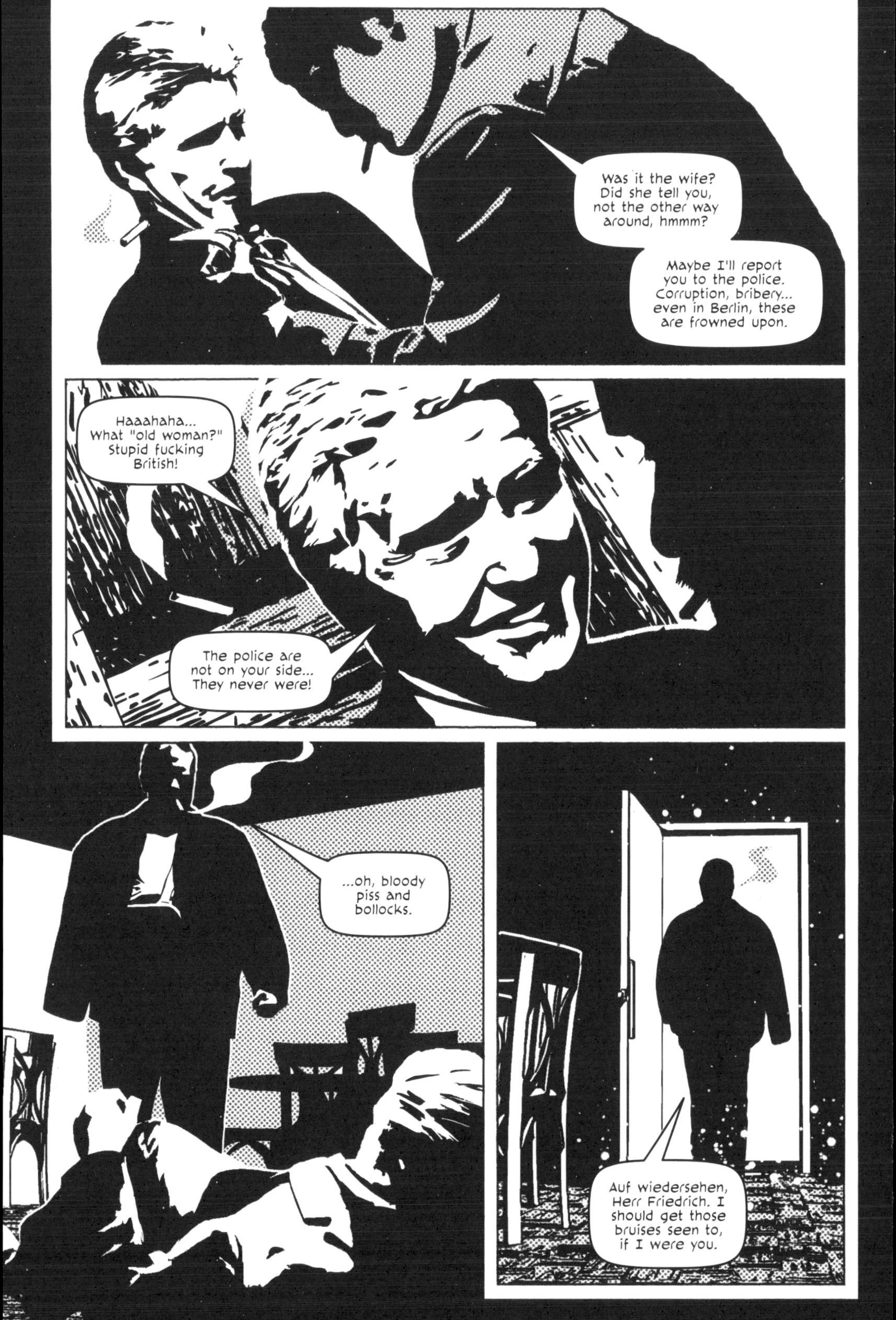
Was it the wife? Did she tell you, not the other way around, hmmm?
Maybe I'll report you to the police. Corruption, bribery... even in Berlin, these are frowned upon.
Haaahaha... What "old woman?" Stupid fucking British!
The police are not on your side... They never were!
...oh, bloody piss and bollocks.
Auf wiedersehen, Herr Friedrich. I should get those bruises seen to, if I were you.

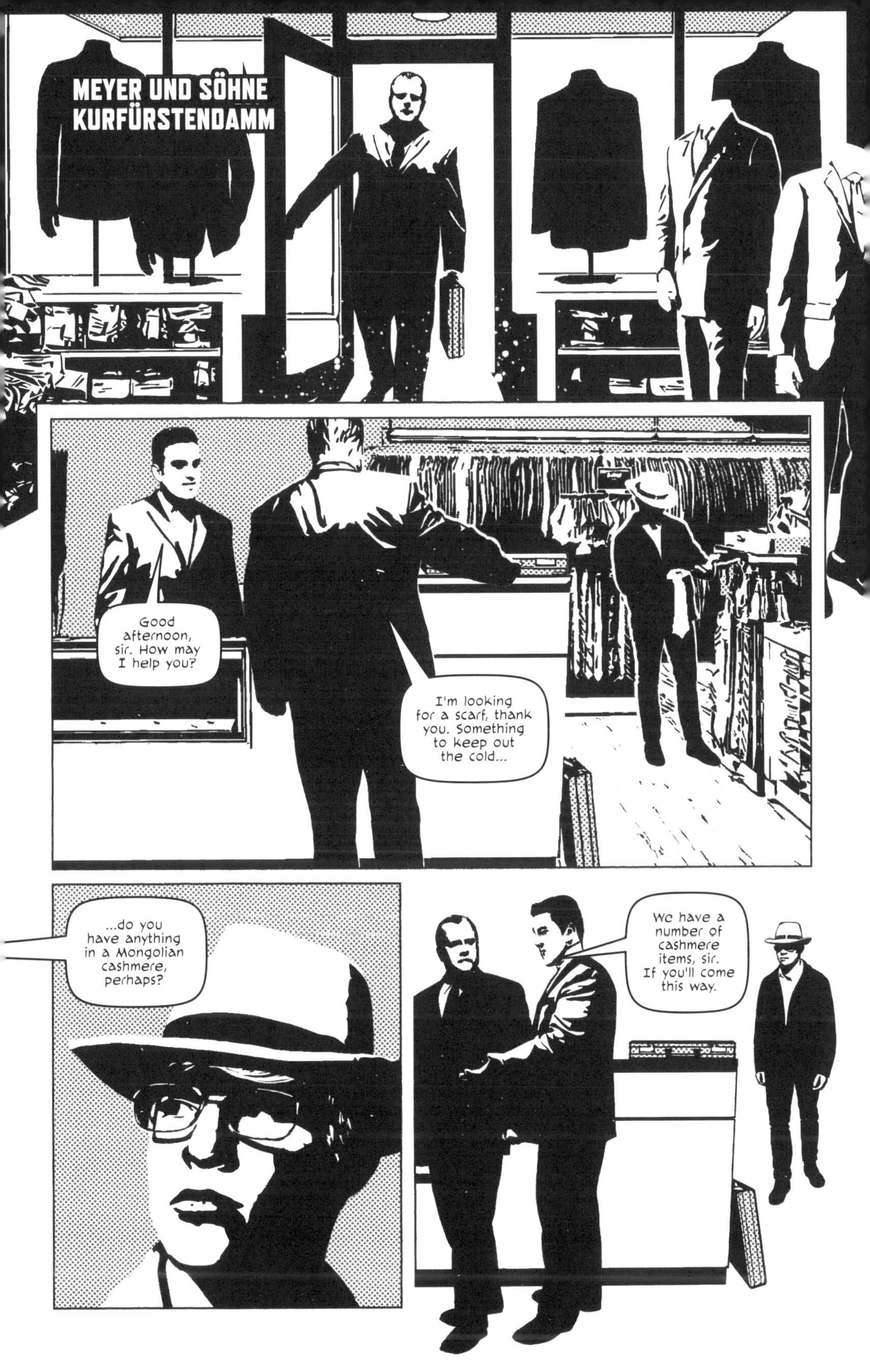
MEYER UND SÖHNE
KURFÜRSTENDAMM
Good afternoon, sir. How may I help you?
I'm looking for a scarf, thank you. Something to keep out the cold...
...do you have anything in a Mongolian cashmere, perhaps?
We have a number of cashmere items, sir. If you'll come this way.

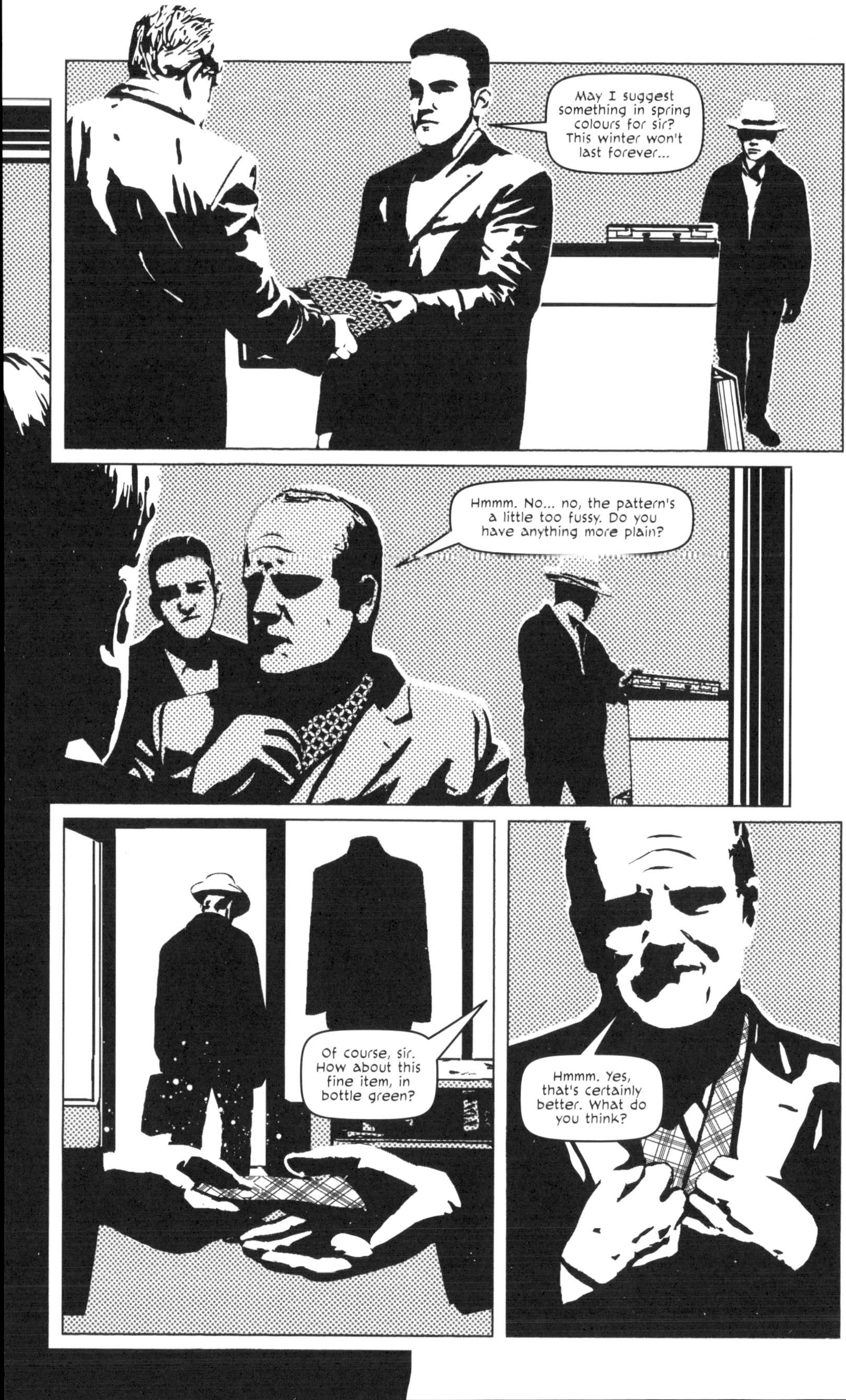
May I suggest something in spring colours for sir? This winter won't last forever...
Hmmm. No... no, the pattern's a little too fussy. Do you have anything more plain?
Of course, sir. How about this fine item, in bottle green?
Hmmm. Yes, that's certainly better. What do you think?

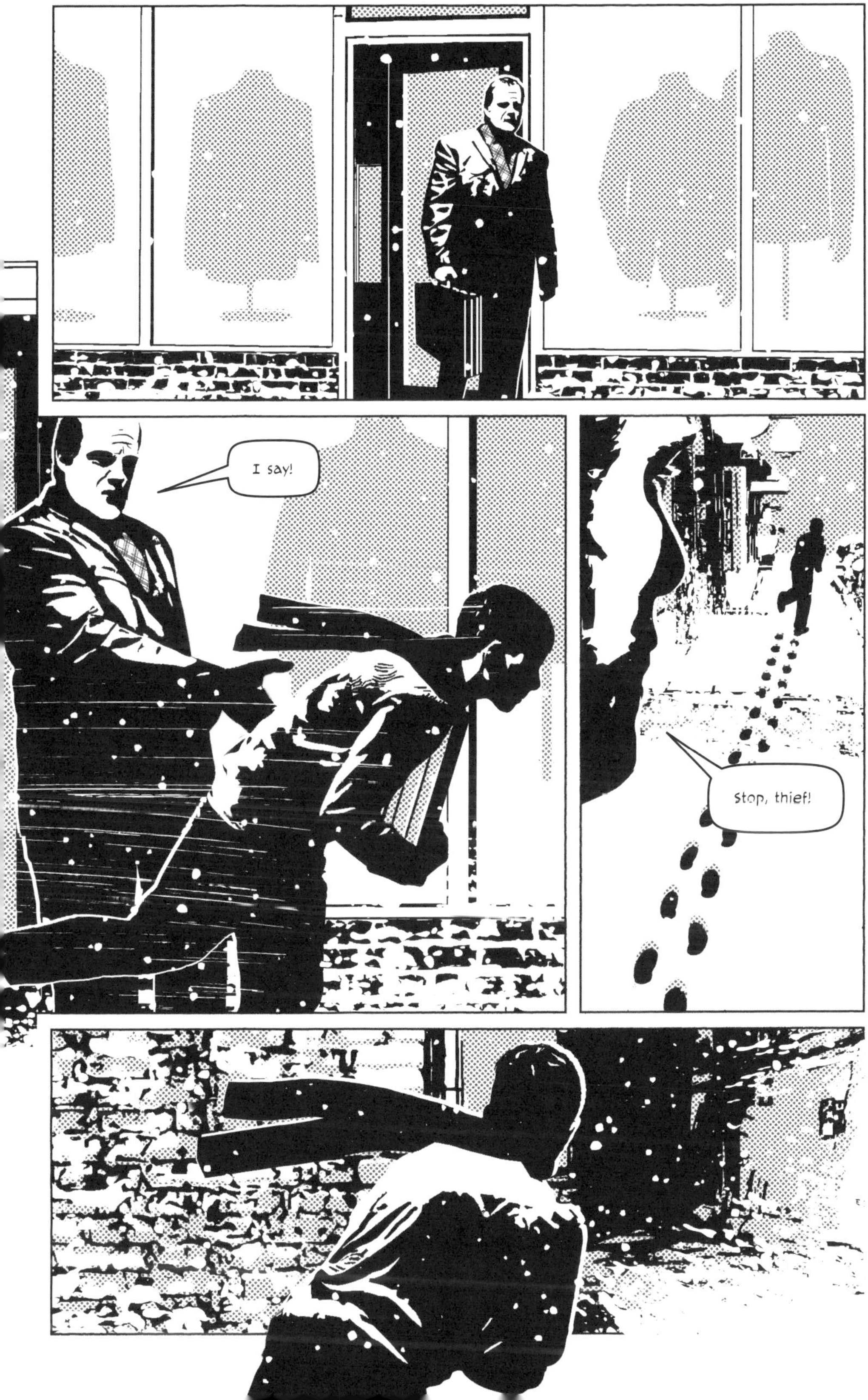

I say!
Stop, thief!

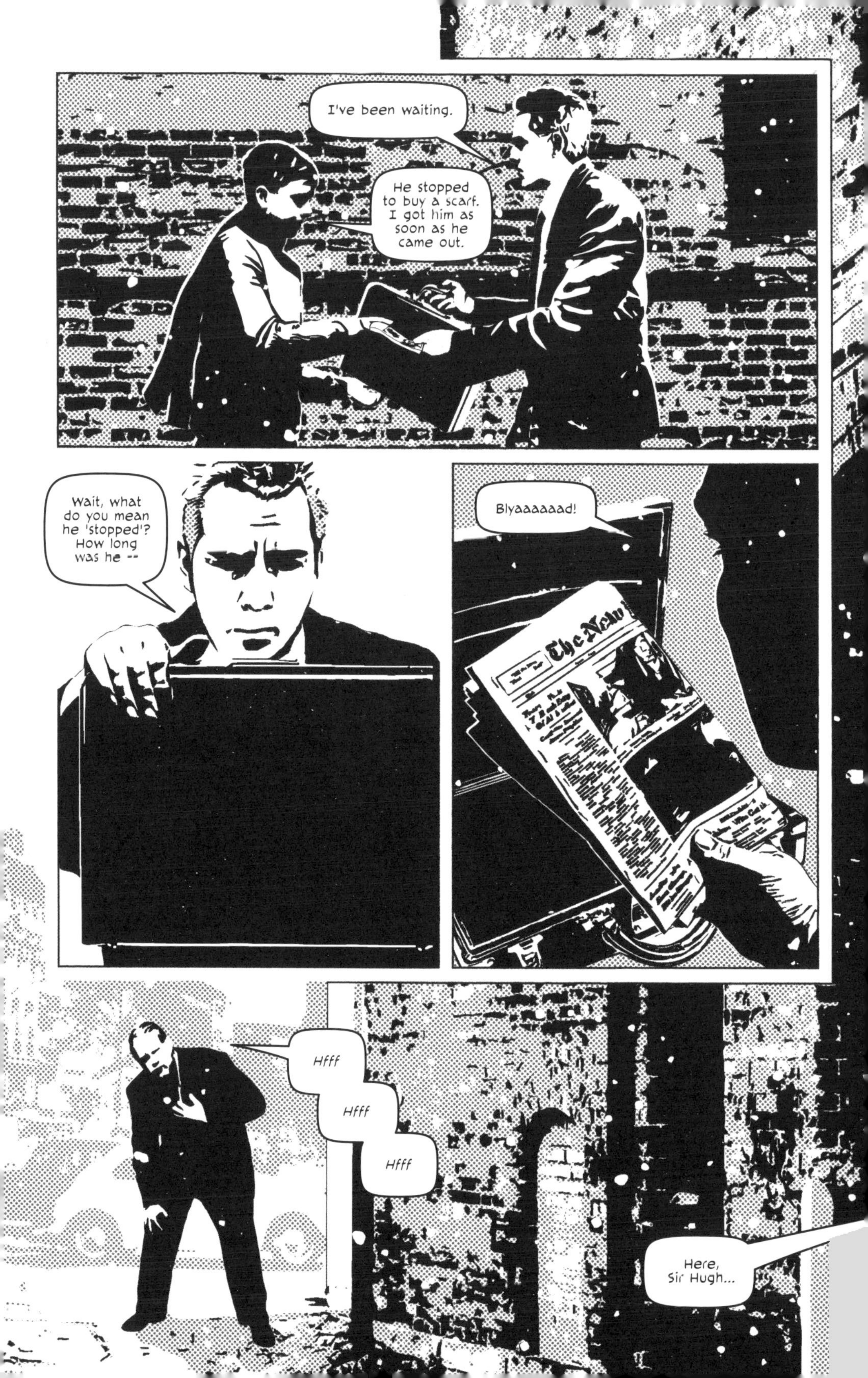
I've been waiting.
He stopped to buy a scarf. I got him as soon as he came out.
Wait, what do you mean he 'stopped'? How long was he --
Blyaaaaaad!
Hfff
Hfff
Hfff
Here, Sir Hugh...

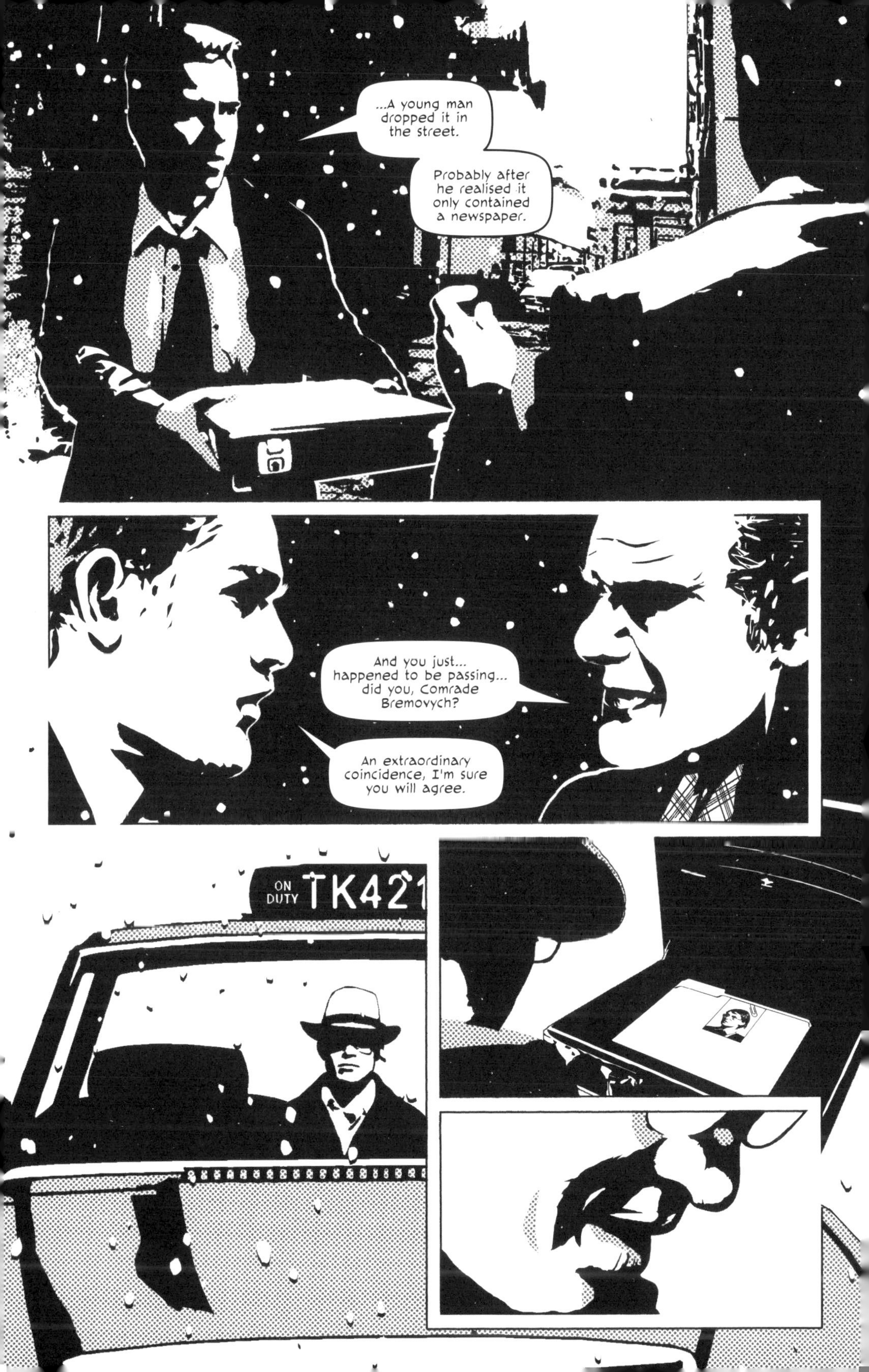
...A young man dropped it in the street.
Probably after he realised it only contained a newspaper.
And you just... happened to be passing... did you, Comrade Bremovych?
An extraordinary coincidence, I'm sure you will agree.
ON DUTY TK421

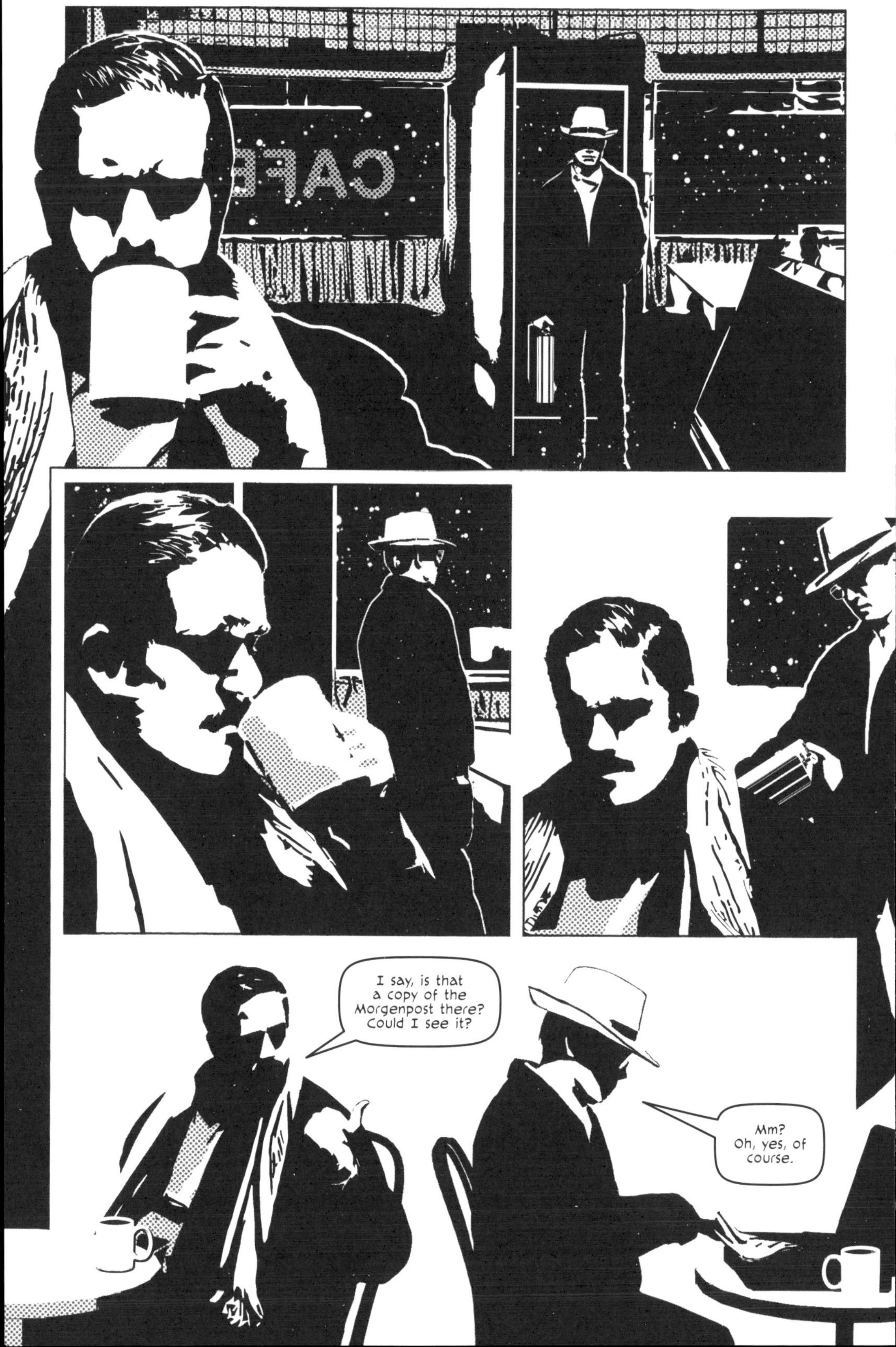
CAFE
I say, is that a copy of the Morgenpost there? Could I see it?
Mm? Oh, yes, of course.

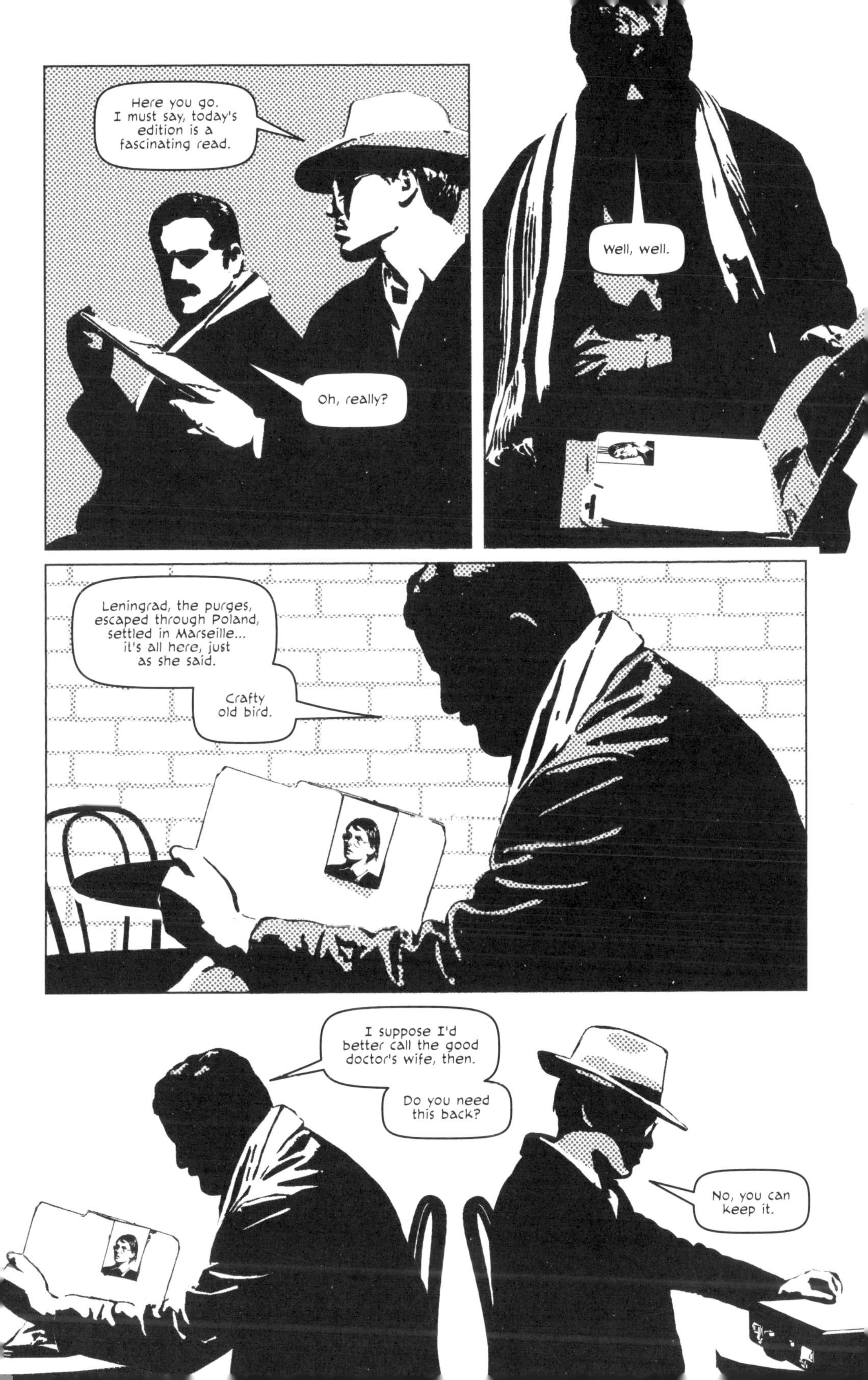

Here you go. I must say, today's edition is a fascinating read.
Oh, really?
Well, well.
Leningrad, the purges, escaped through Poland, settled in Marseille... it's all here, just as she said.
Crafty old bird.
I suppose I'd better call the good doctor's wife, then.
Do you need this back?
No, you can keep it.

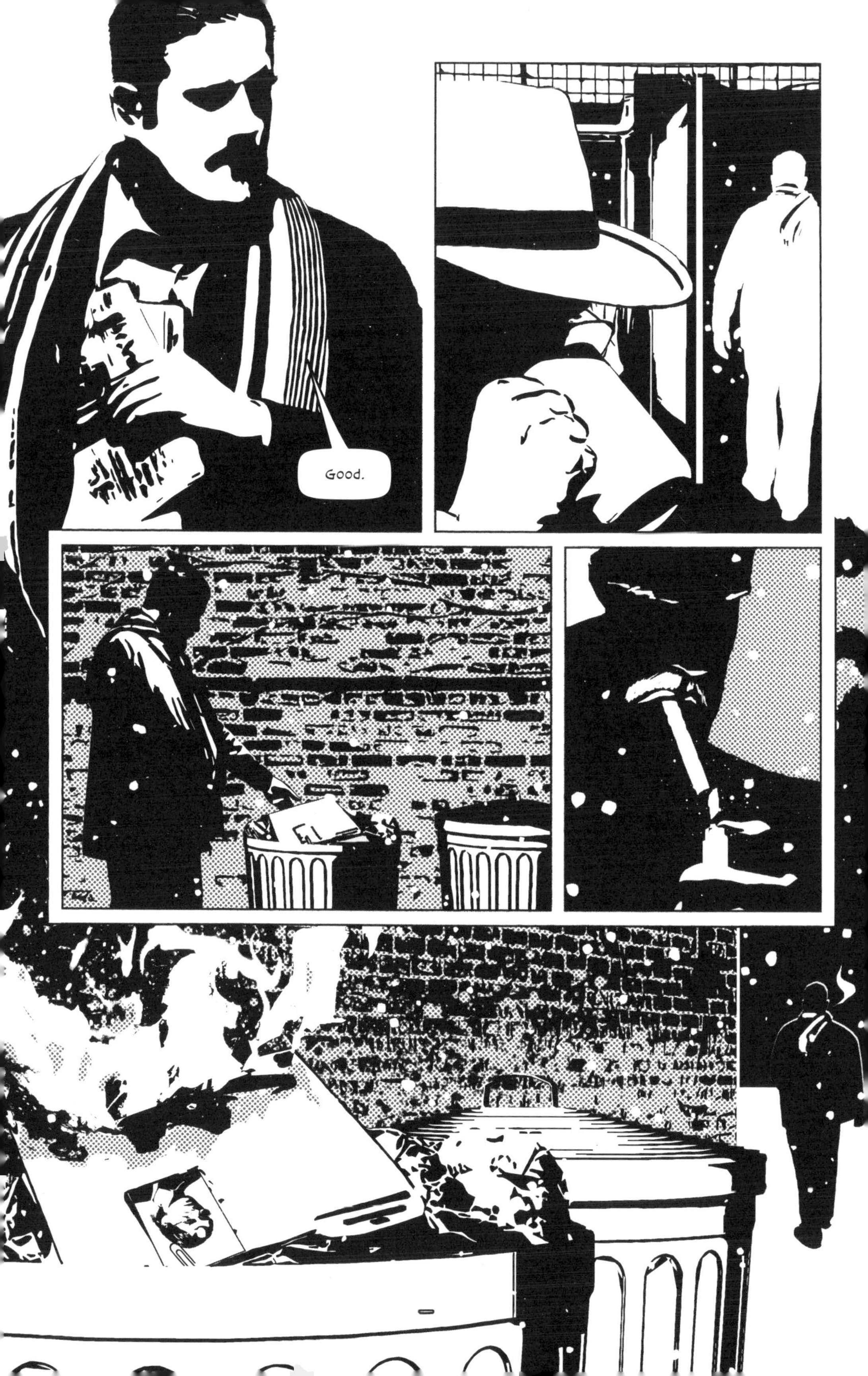
Good.

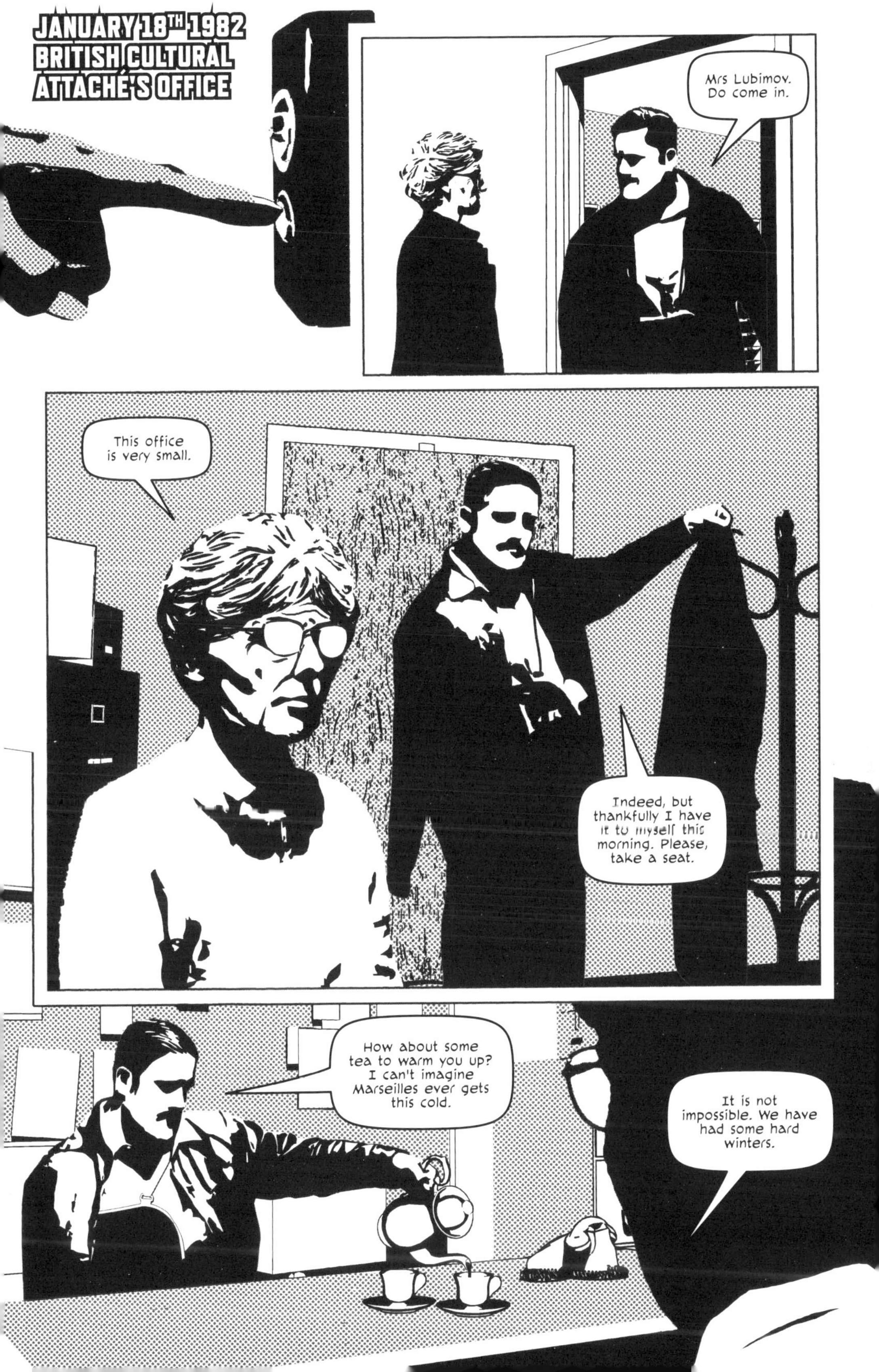
JANUARY 18TH 1982 BRITISH CULTURAL ATTACHÉ'S OFFICE
Mrs Lubimov. Do come in.
This office is very small.
Indeed, but thankfully I have it to myself this morning. Please, take a seat.
How about some tea to warm you up? I can't imagine Marseilles ever gets this cold.
It is not impossible. We have had some hard winters.

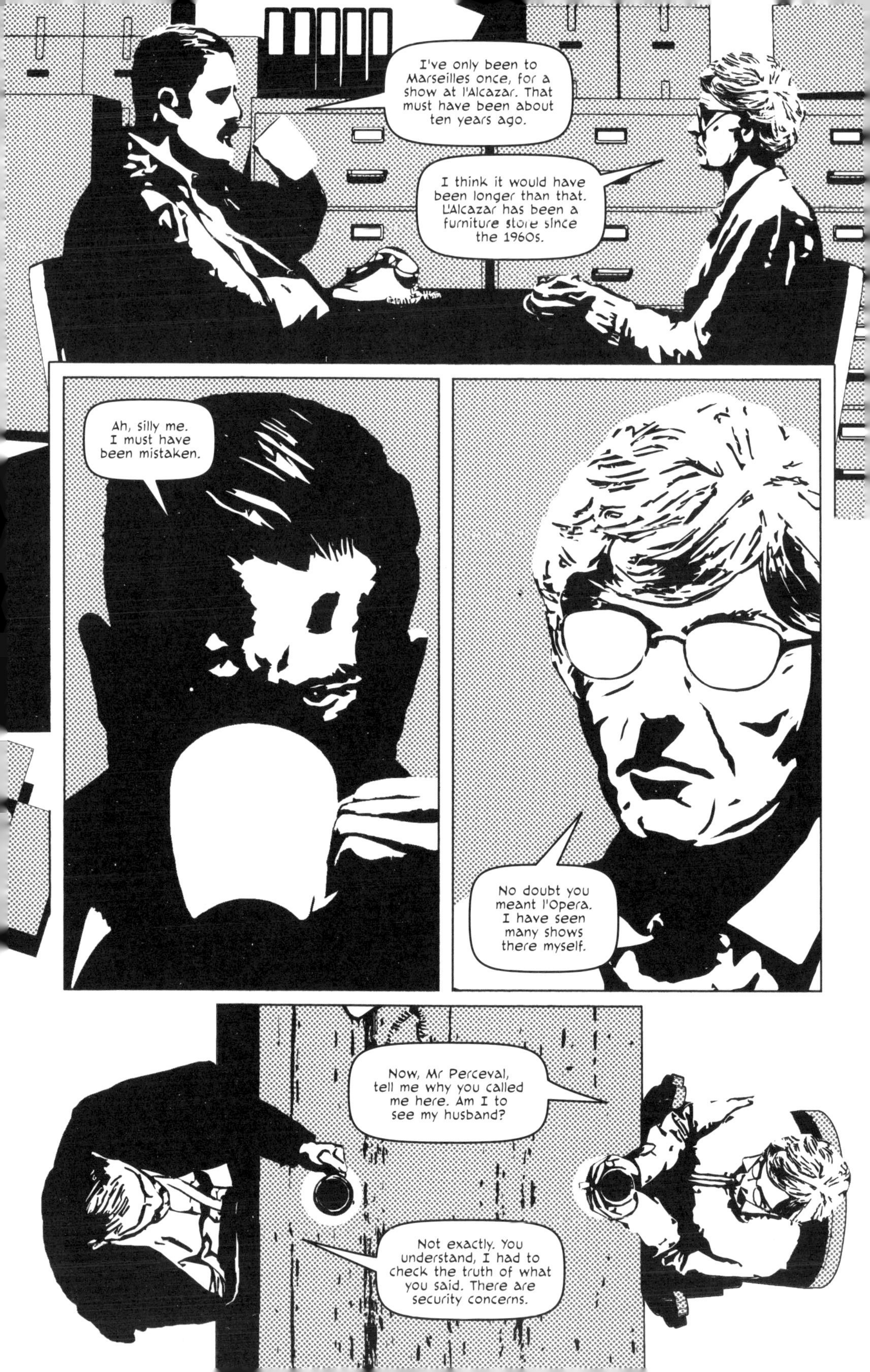
I've only been to Marseilles once, for a show at l'Alcazar. That must have been about ten years ago.
I think it would have been longer than that. L'Alcazar has been a furniture store since the 1960s.
Ah, silly me. I must have been mistaken.
No doubt you meant l'Opera. I have seen many shows there myself.
Now, Mr Perceval, tell me why you called me here. Am I to see my husband?
Not exactly. You understand, I had to check the truth of what you said. There are security concerns.

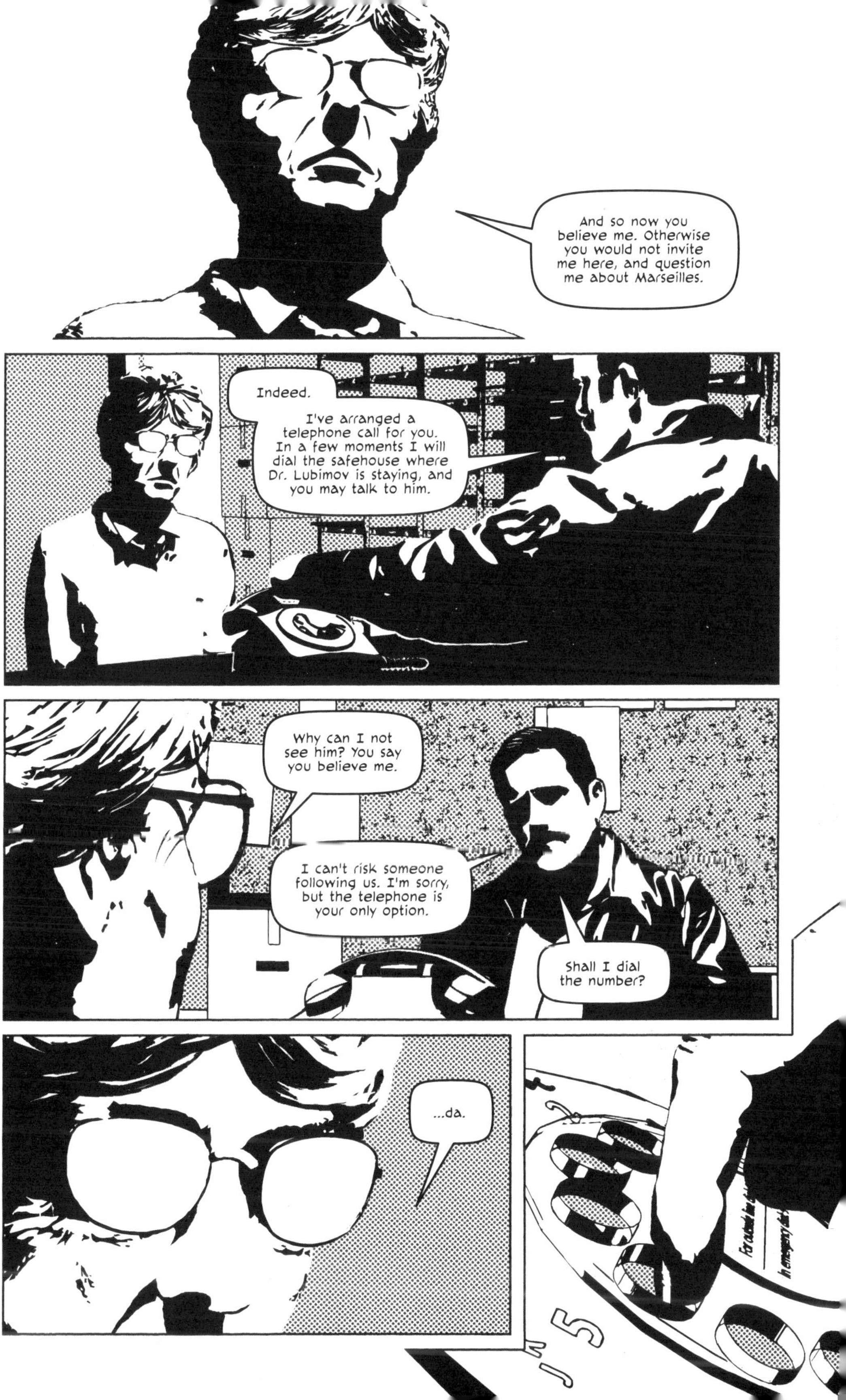
And so now you believe me. Otherwise you would not invite me here, and question me about Marseilles.
Indeed.
I've arranged a telephone call for you. In a few moments I will dial the safehouse where Dr. Lubimov is staying, and you may talk to him.
Why can I not see him? You say you believe me.
I can't risk someone following us. I'm sorry, but the telephone is your only option.
Shall I dial the number?
...da.

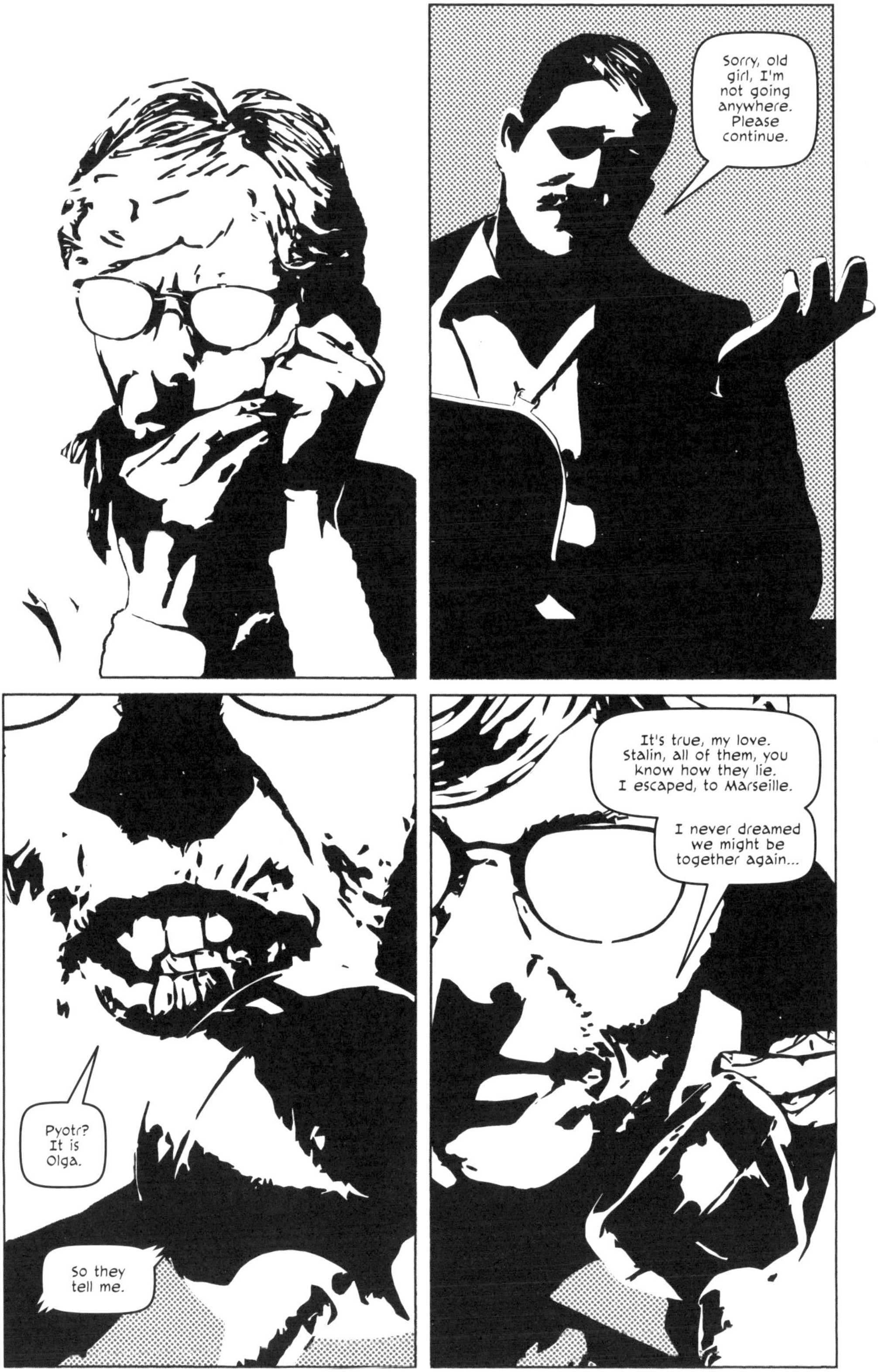
Sorry, old girl, I'm not going anywhere. Please continue.
Pyotr? It is Olga.
So they tell me.
It's true, my love. Stalin, all of them, you know how they lie. I escaped, to Marseille.
I never dreamed we might be together again...

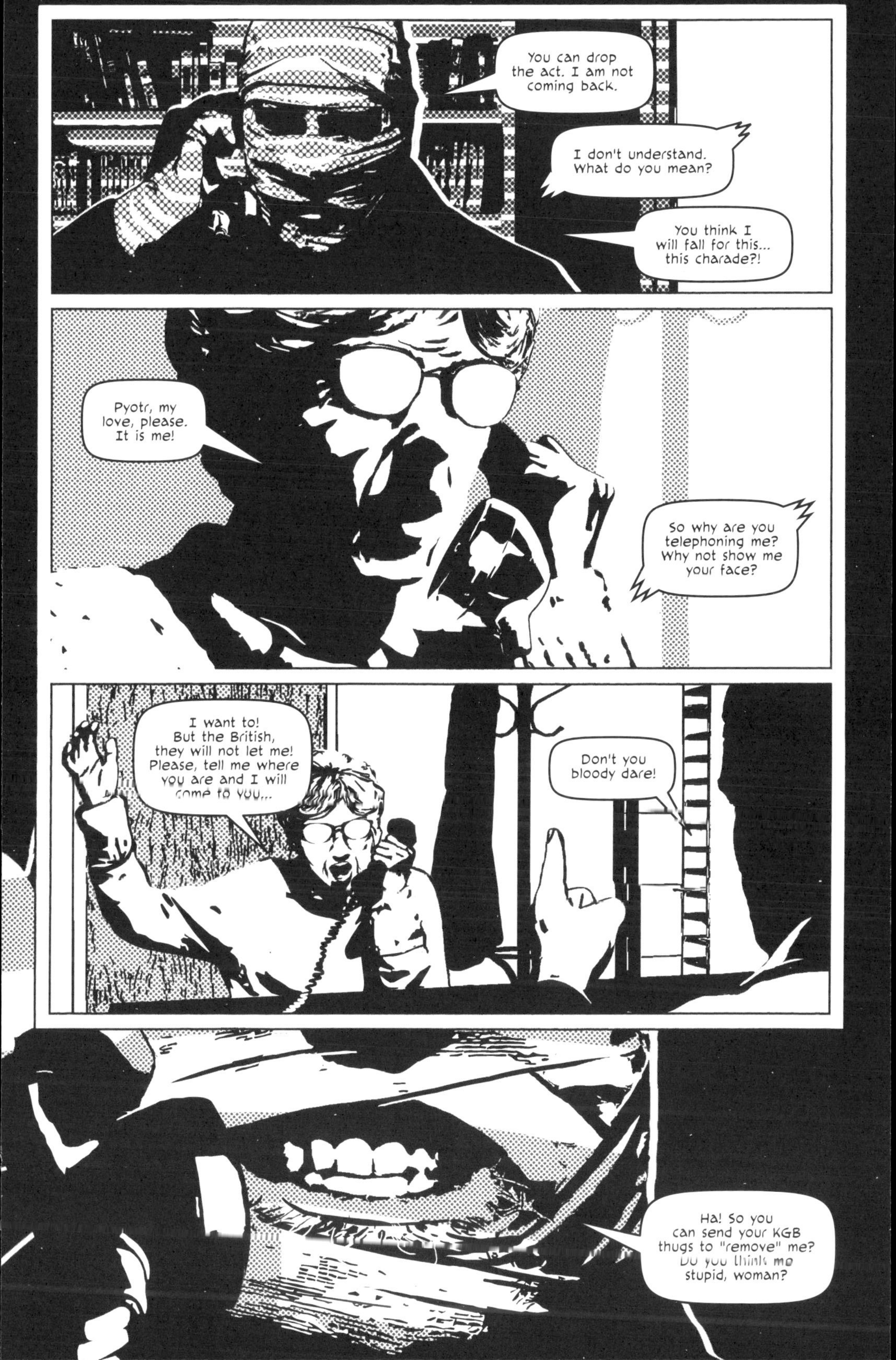
You can drop the act. I am not coming back.
I don't understand. What do you mean?
You think I will fall for this... this charade?!
Pyotr, my love, please. It is me!
So why are you telephoning me? Why not show me your face?
I want to! But the British, they will not let me! Please, tell me where you are and I will come to you...
Don't you bloody dare!
Ha! So you can send your KGB thugs to "remove" me? Do you think me stupid, woman?

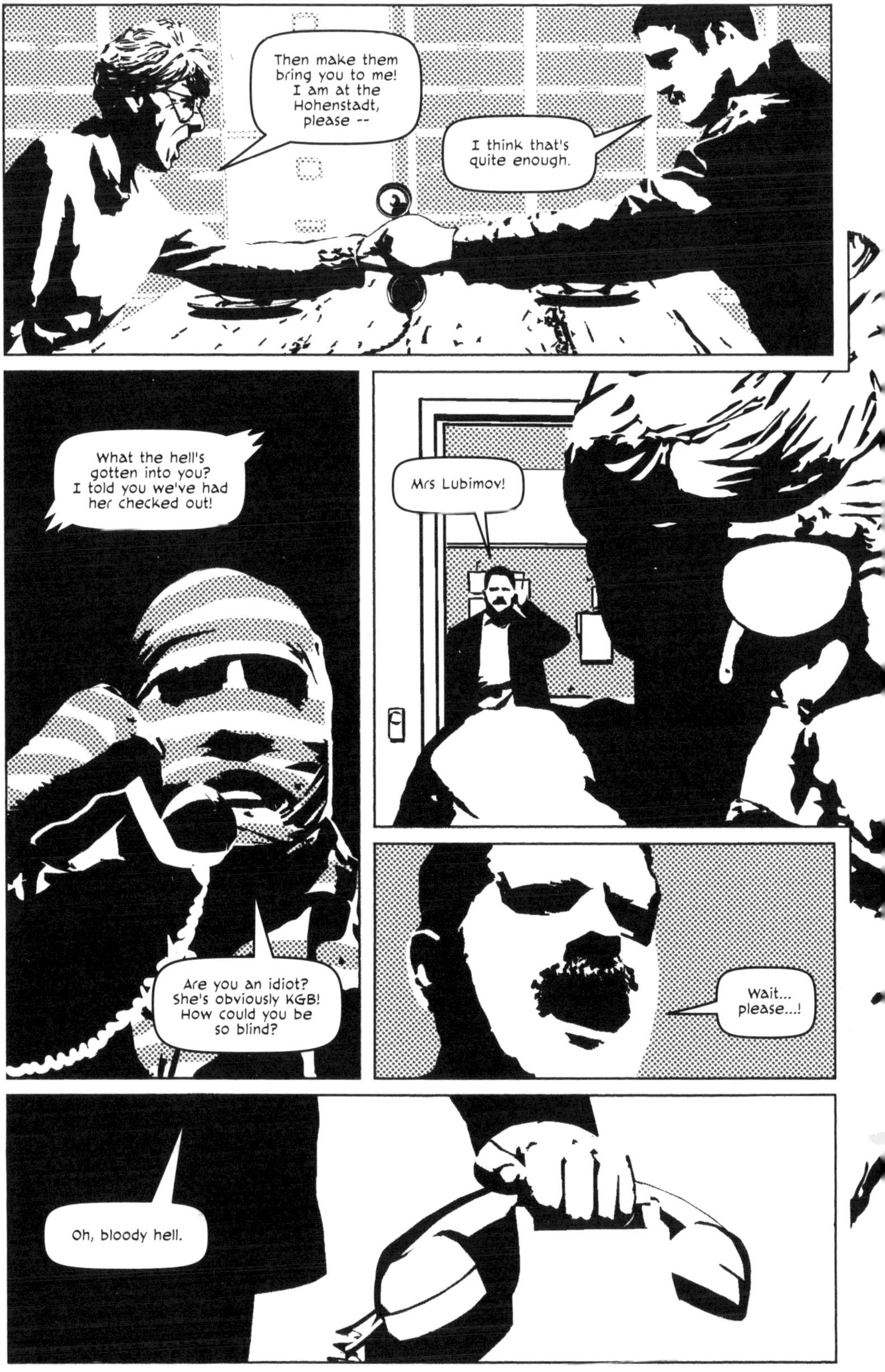

Then make them bring you to me! I am at the Hohenstadt, please --
I think that's quite enough.
What the hell's gotten into you? I told you we've had her checked out!
Are you an idiot? She's obviously KGB! How could you be so blind?
Mrs Lubimov!
Wait... please...!
Oh, bloody hell.

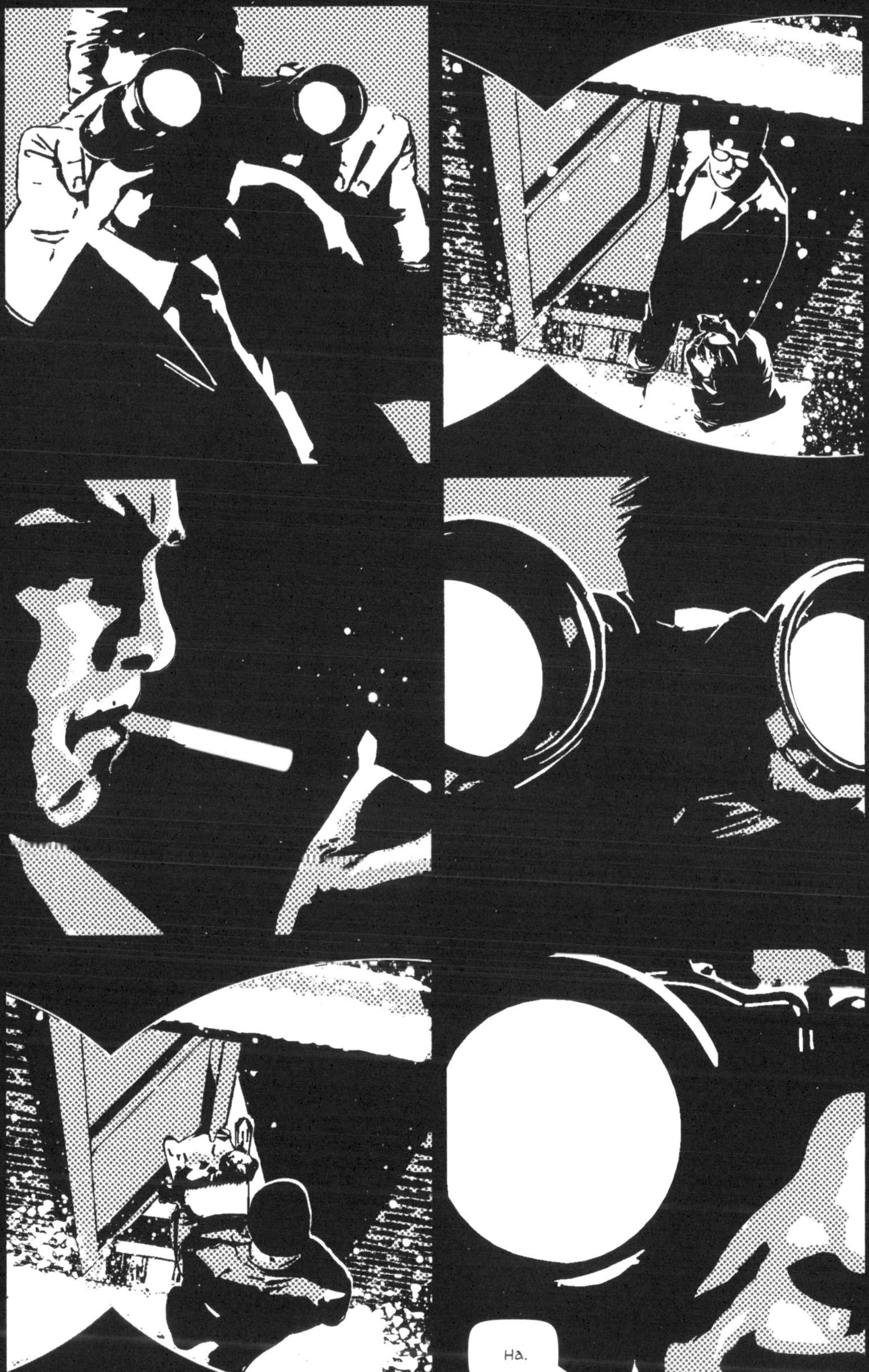
Ha.

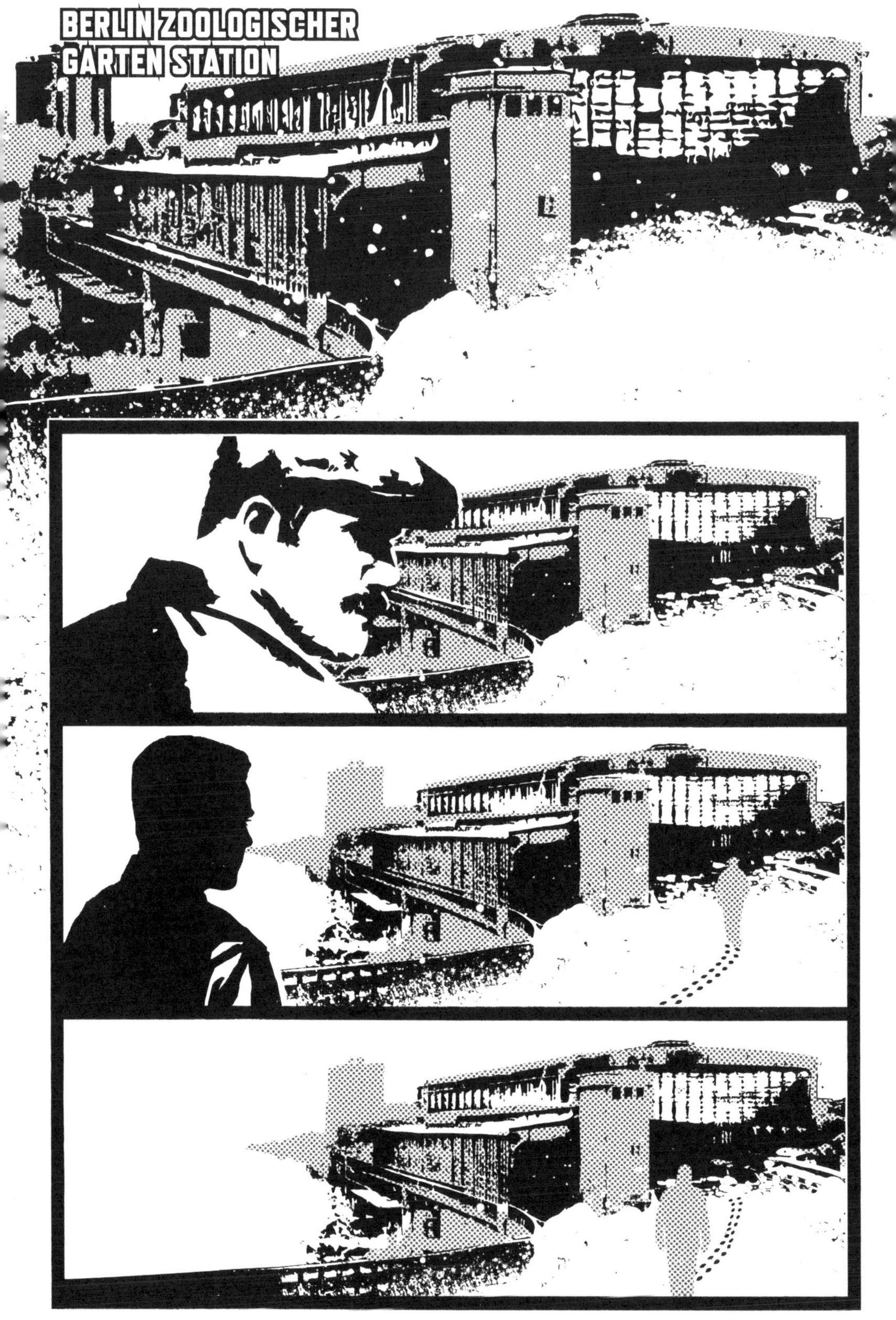
BERLIN ZOOLOGISCHER GARTEN STATION

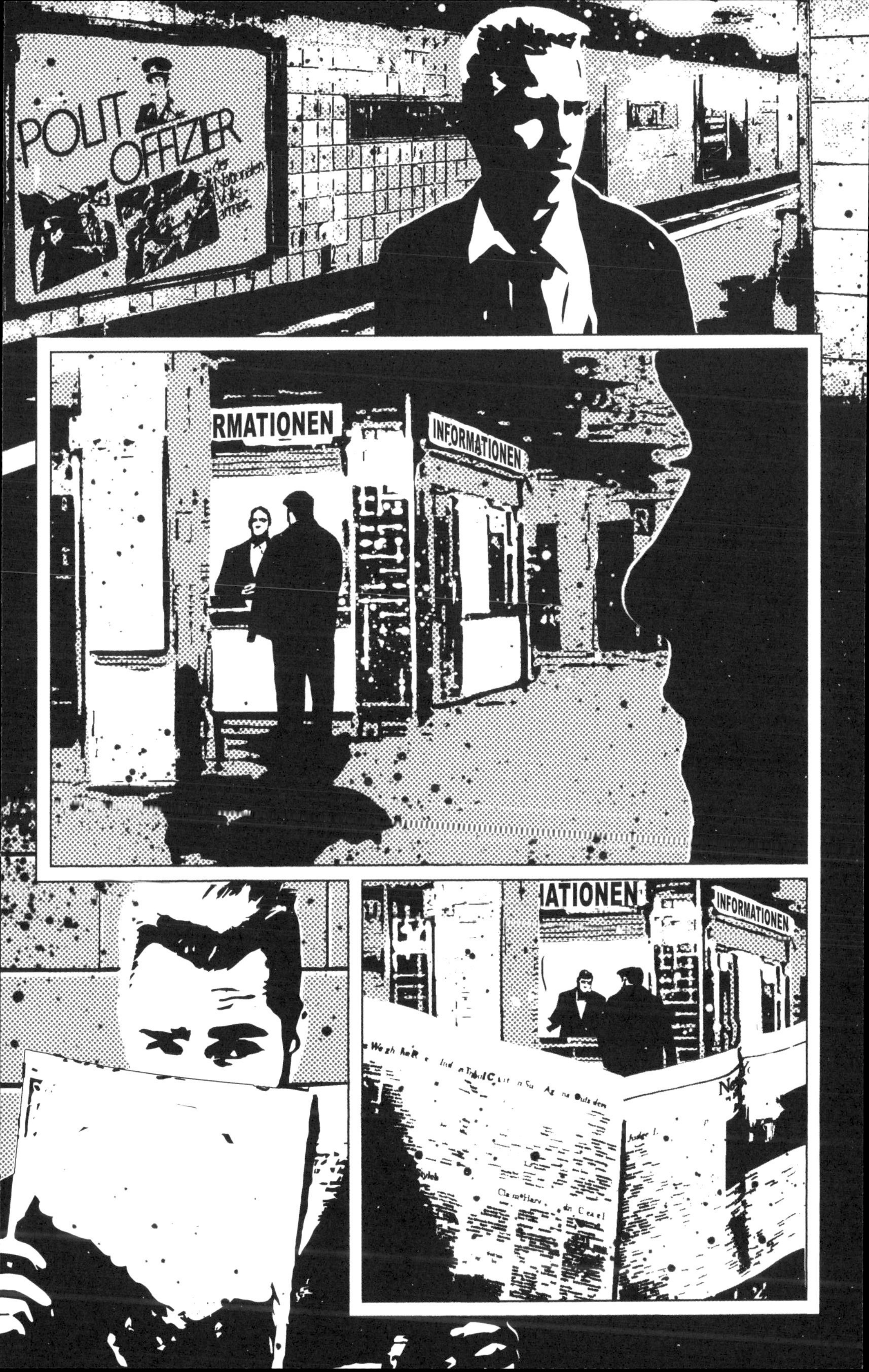
POLIT OFFIZIER
RMATIONEN
INFORMATIONEN
ATIONEN
INFORMATIONEN

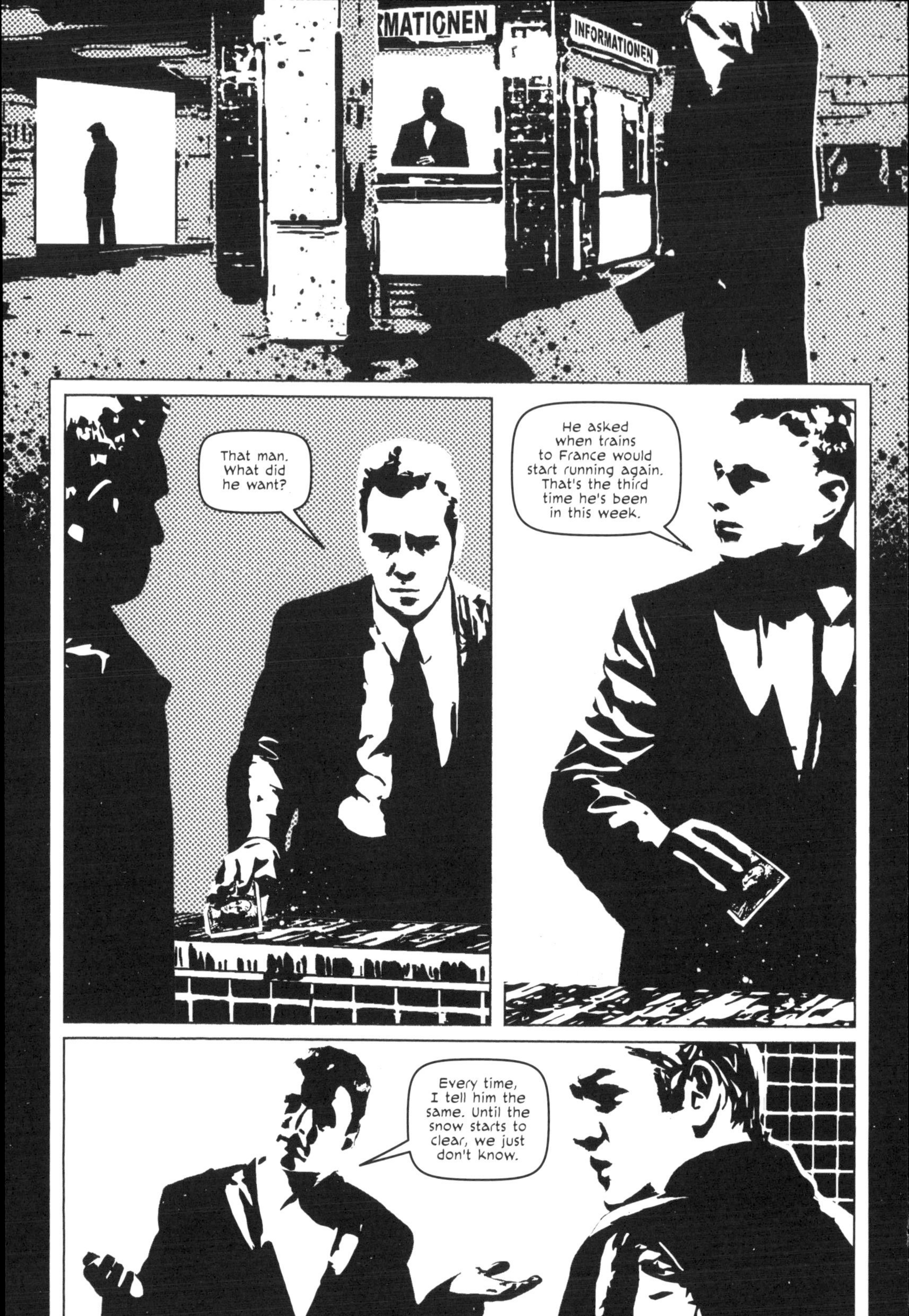
RMATIONEN
INFORMATIONEN
That man. What did he want?
He asked when trains to France would start running again. That's the third time he's been in this week.
Every time, I tell him the same. Until the snow starts to clear, we just don't know.

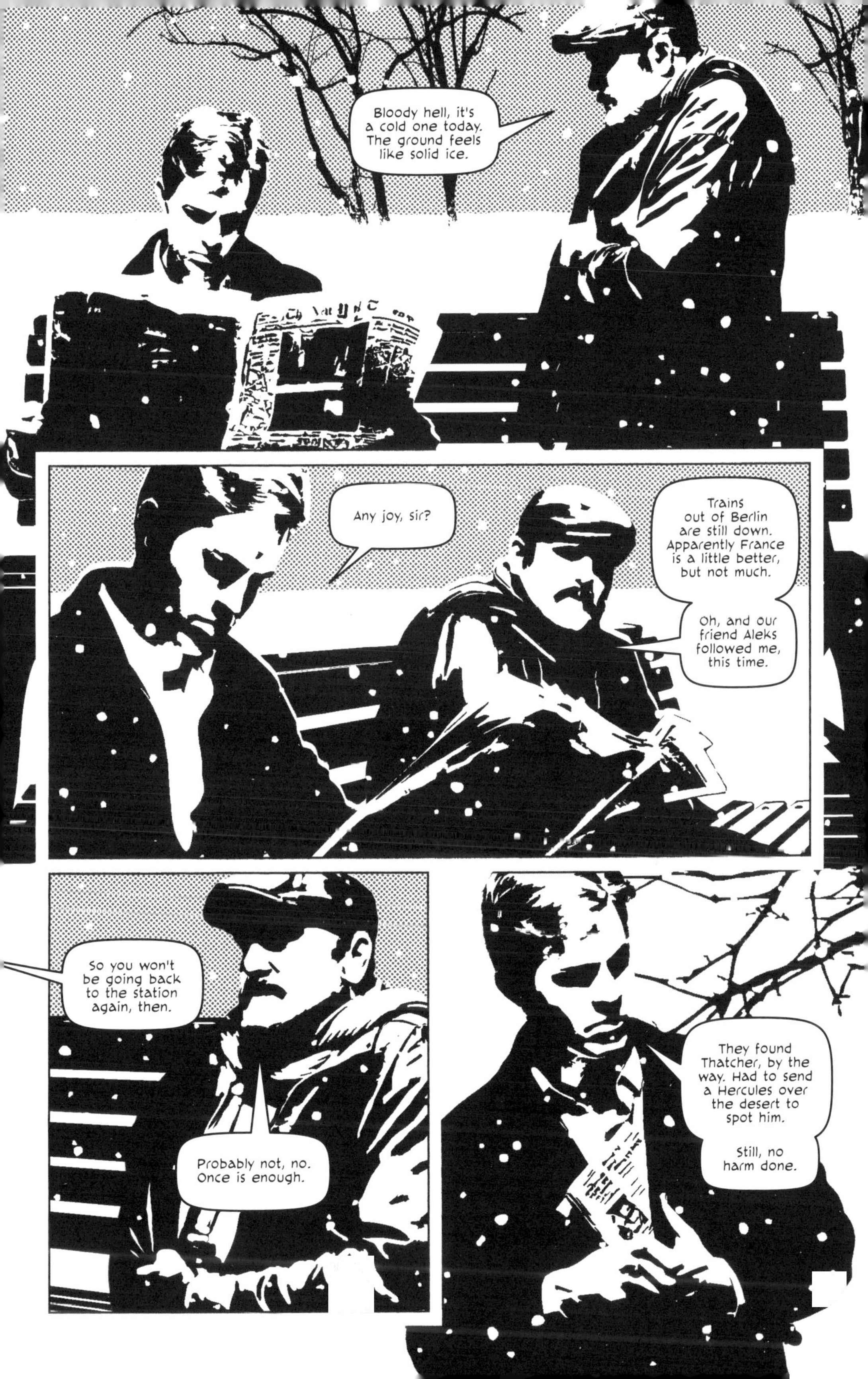
Bloody hell, it's a cold one today. The ground feels like solid ice.
Any joy, sir?
Trains out of Berlin are still down. Apparently France is a little better, but not much.
Oh, and our friend Aleks followed me, this time.
So you won't be going back to the station again, then.
Probably not, no. Once is enough.
They found Thatcher, by the way. Had to send a Hercules over the desert to spot him.
Still, no harm done.

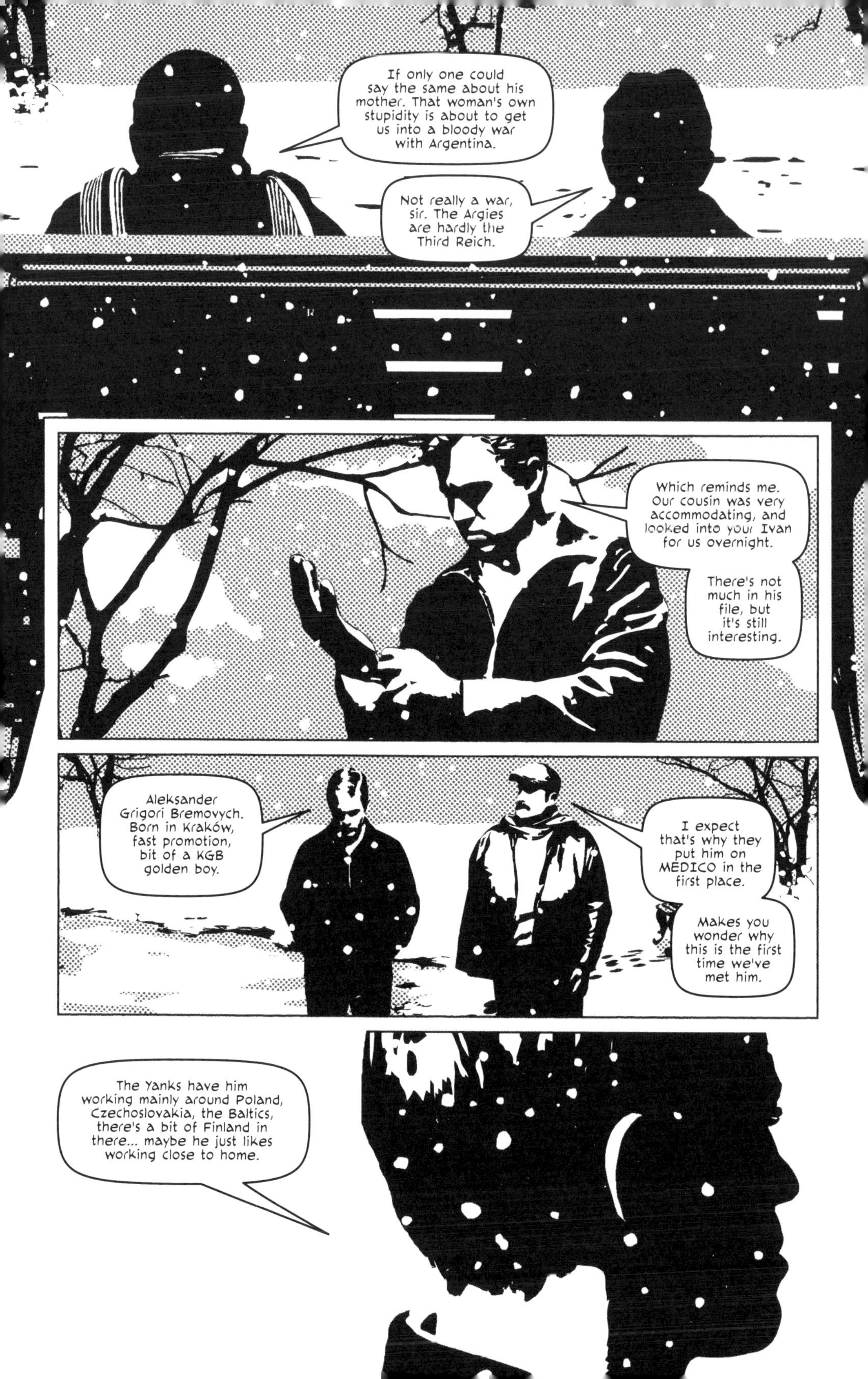
If only one could say the same about his mother. That woman's own stupidity is about to get us into a bloody war with Argentina.
Not really a war, sir. The Argies are hardly the Third Reich.
Which reminds me. Our cousin was very accommodating, and looked into your Ivan for us overnight.
There's not much in his file, but it's still interesting.
Aleksander Grigori Bremovych. Born in Kraków, fast promotion, bit of a KGB golden boy.
I expect that's why they put him on MEDICO in the first place.
Makes you wonder why this is the first time we've met him.
The Yanks have him working mainly around Poland, Czechoslovakia, the Baltics, there's a bit of Finland in there... maybe he just likes working close to home.

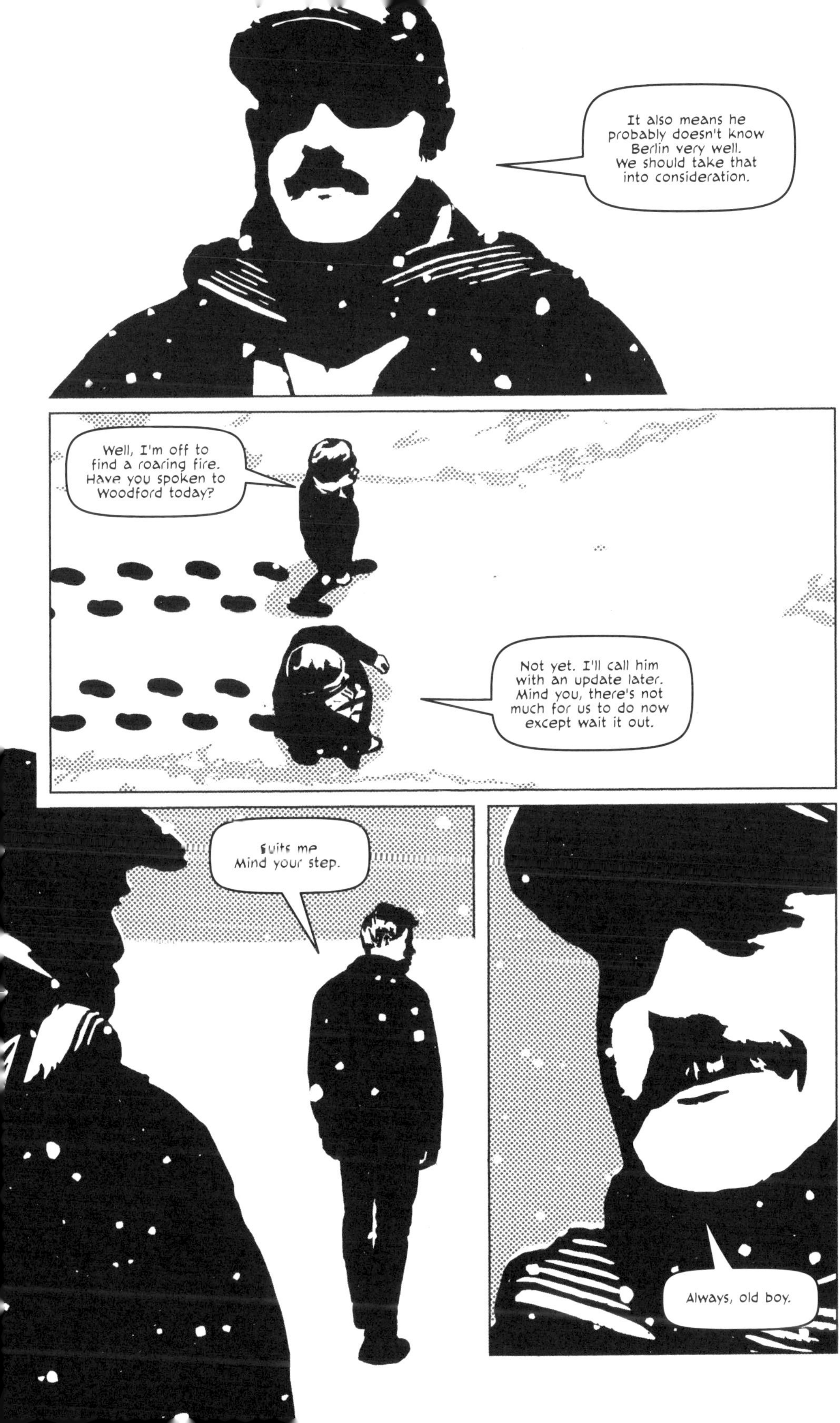

It also means he probably doesn't know Berlin very well. We should take that into consideration.
Well, I'm off to find a roaring fire. Have you spoken to Woodford today?
Not yet. I'll call him with an update later. Mind you, there's not much for us to do now except wait it out.
Suits me. Mind your step.
Always, old boy.

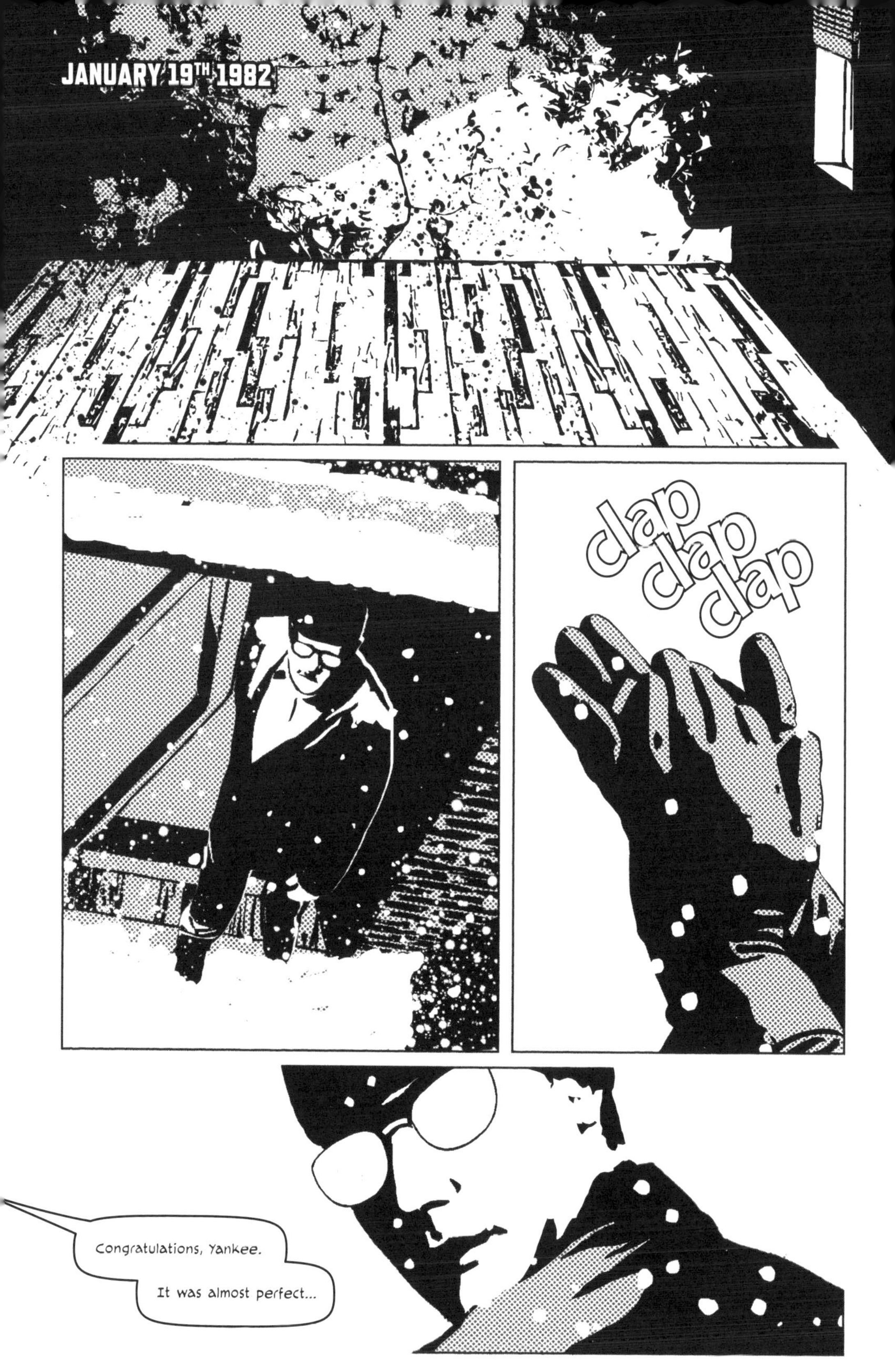
JANUARY 19TH 1982
clap clap clap
Congratulations, Yankee.
It was almost perfect...

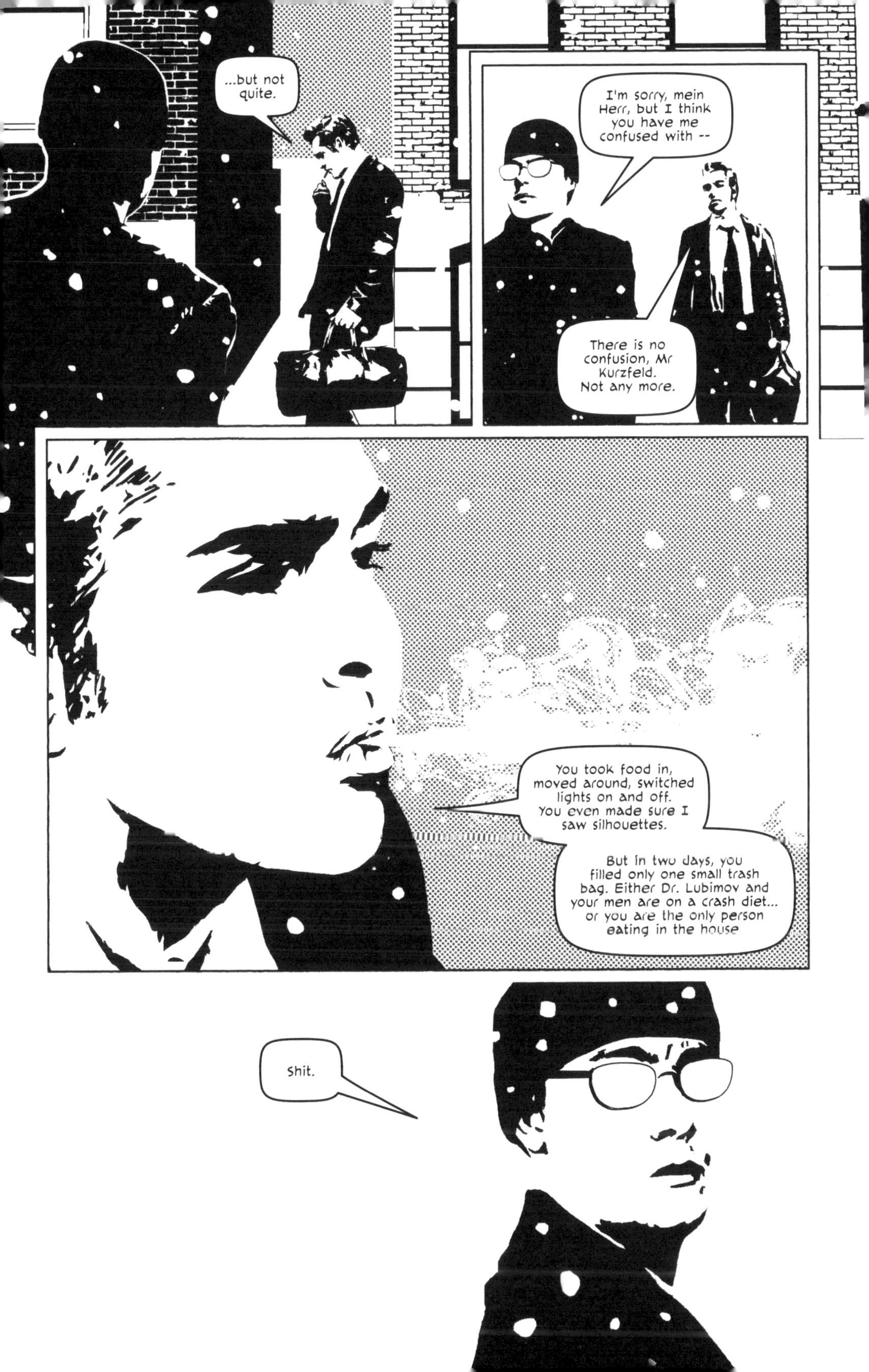
...but not quite.
I'm sorry, mein Herr, but I think you have me confused with --
There is no confusion, Mr Kurzfeld. Not any more.
You took food in, moved around, switched lights on and off. You even made sure I saw silhouettes.
But in two days, you filled only one small trash bag. Either Dr. Lubimov and your men are on a crash diet... or you are the only person eating in the house
Shit.

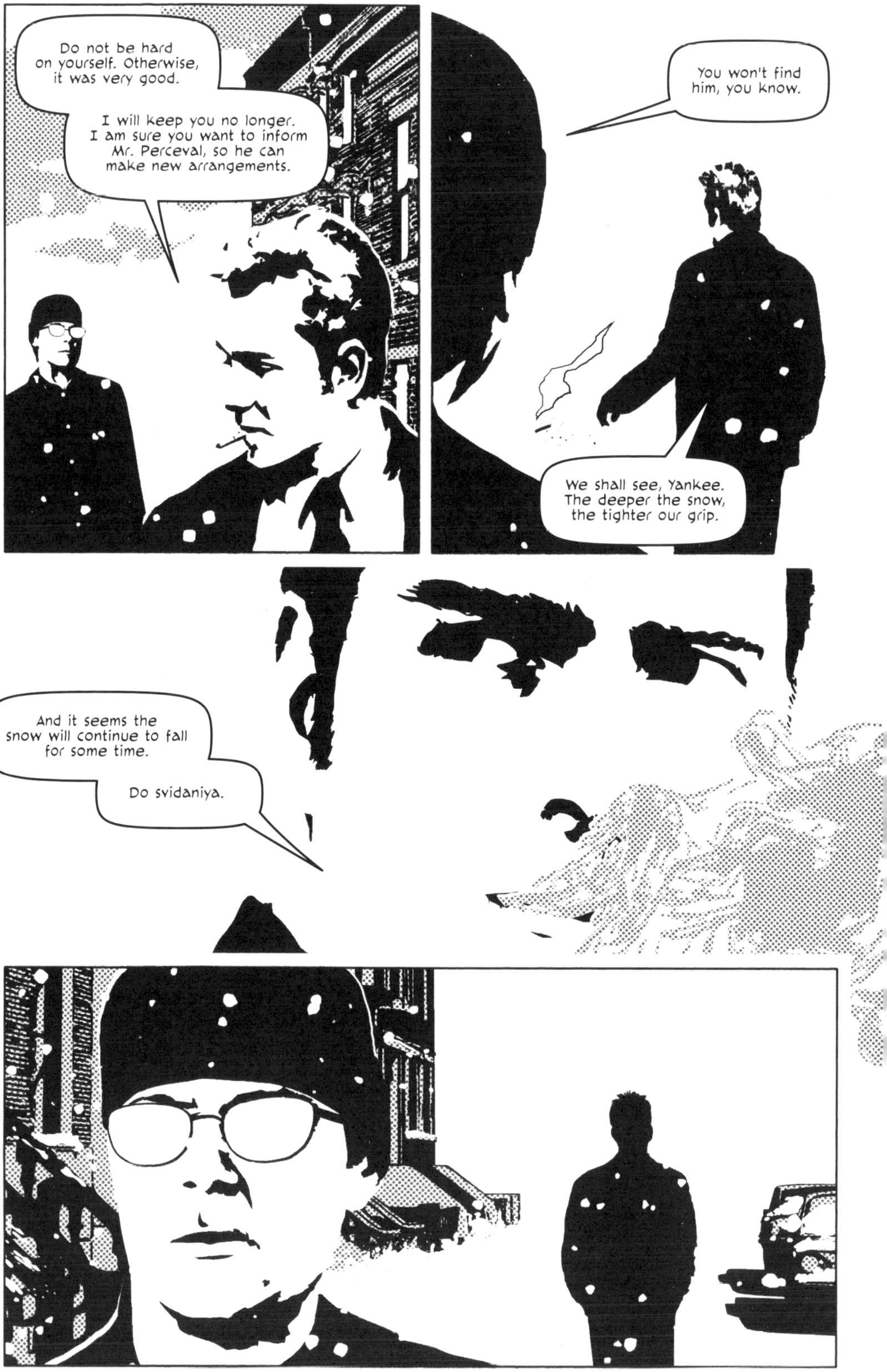
Do not be hard on yourself. Otherwise, it was very good.
I will keep you no longer. I am sure you want to inform Mr. Perceval, so he can make new arrangements.
You won't find him, you know.
We shall see, Yankee. The deeper the snow, the tighter our grip.
And it seems the snow will continue to fall for some time.
Do svidaniya.

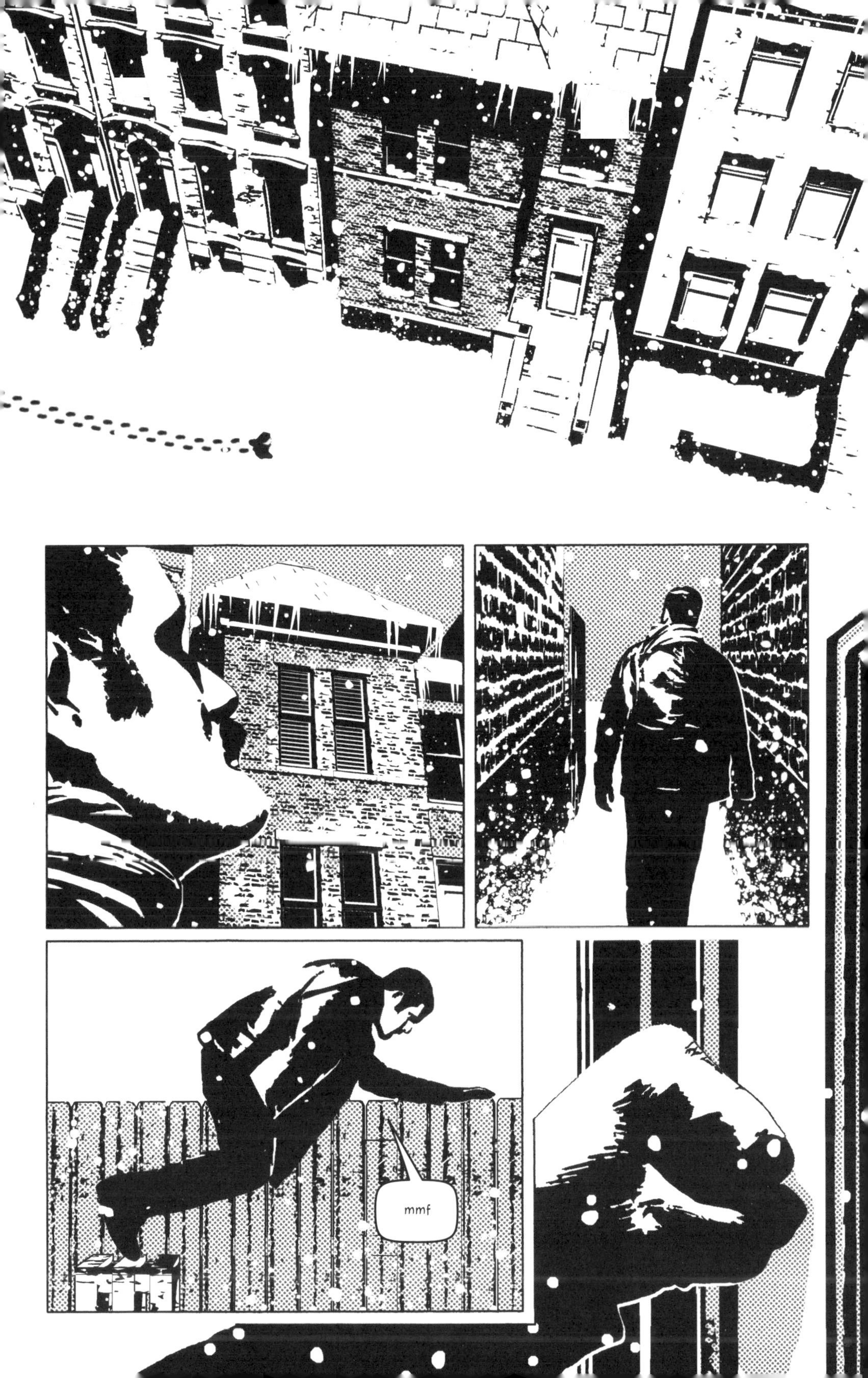
mmf

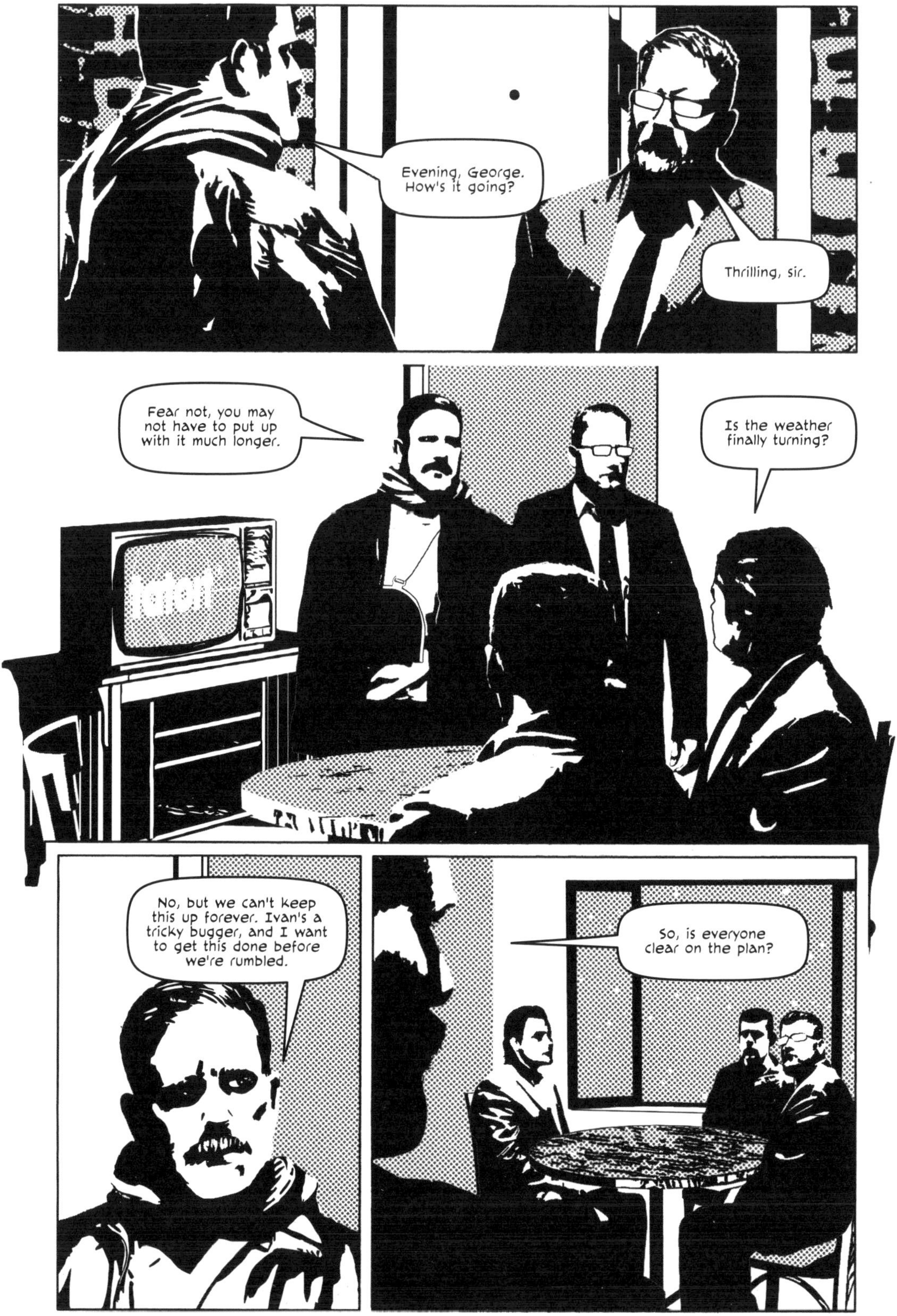
Evening, George. How's it going?
Thrilling, sir.
Fear not, you may not have to put up with it much longer.
Is the weather finally turning?
No, but we can't keep this up forever. Ivan's a tricky bugger, and I want to get this done before we're rumbled.
So, is everyone clear on the plan?

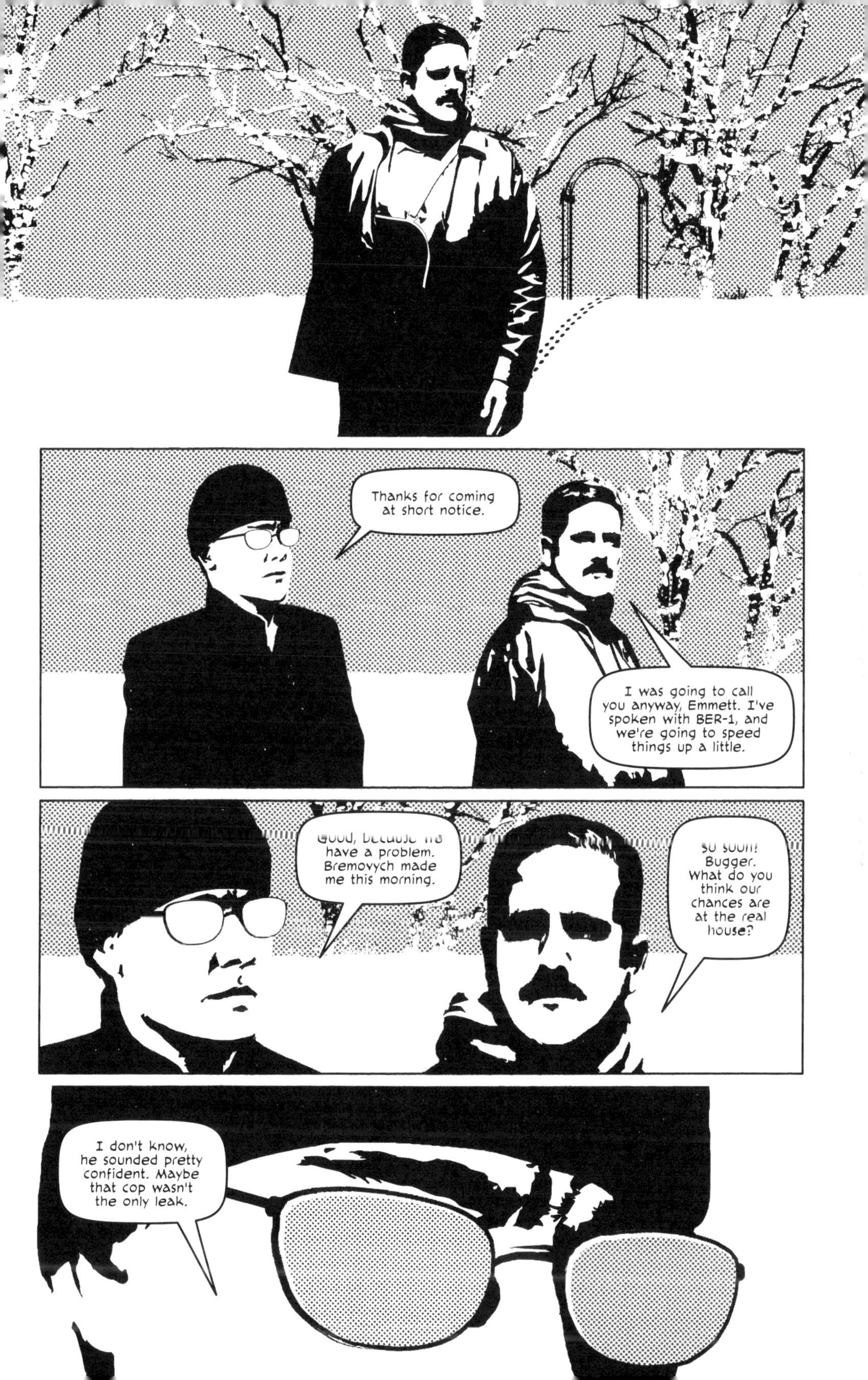
Thanks for coming at short notice.
I was going to call you anyway, Emmett. I've spoken with BER-1, and we're going to speed things up a little.
have a problem. Bremovych made me this morning.
Bugger. What do you think our chances are at the real house?
I don't know, he sounded pretty confident. Maybe that cop wasn't the only leak.

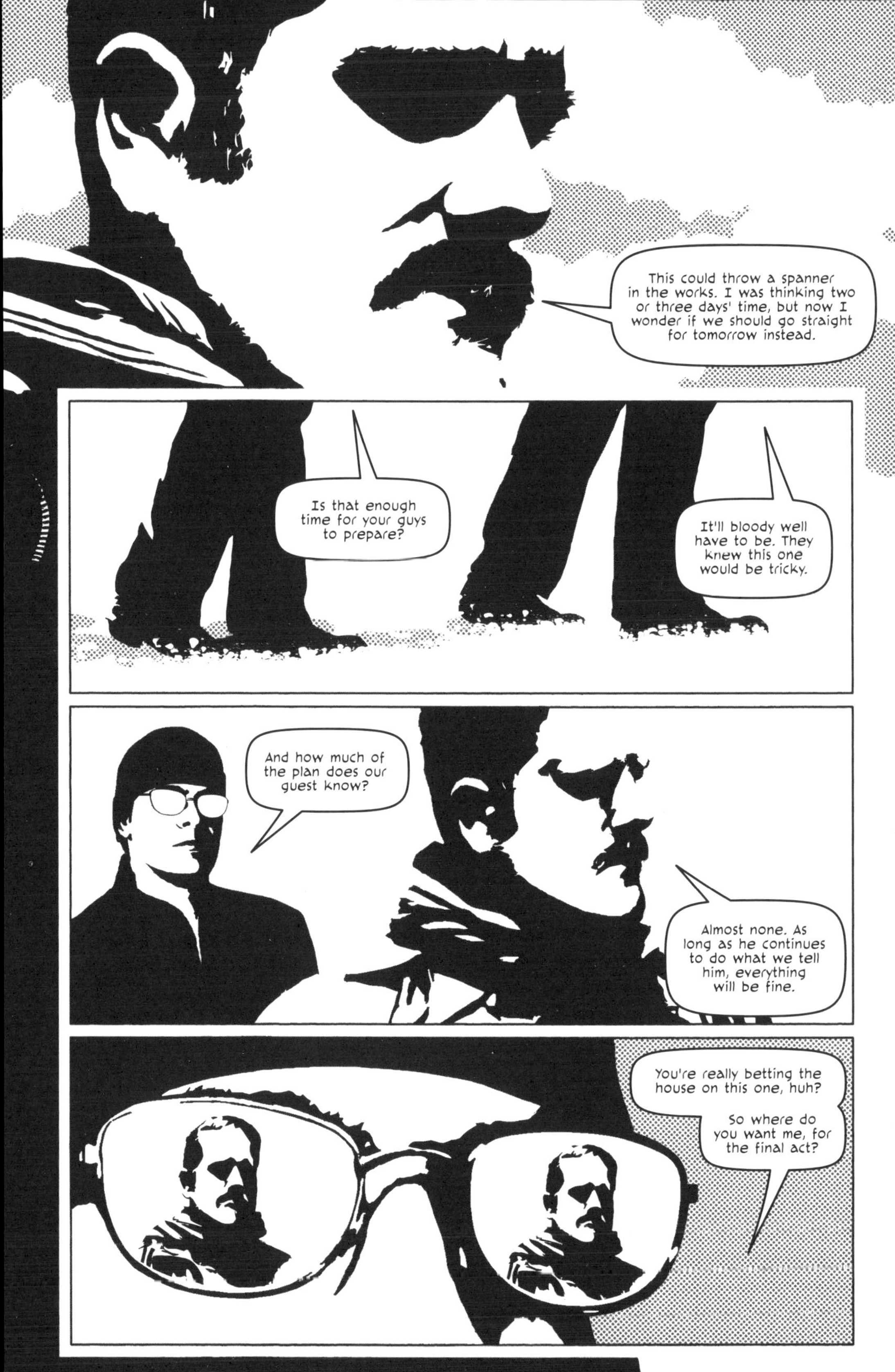
This could throw a spanner in the works. I was thinking two or three days' time, but now I wonder if we should go straight for tomorrow instead.
Is that enough time for your guys to prepare?
It'll bloody well have to be. They knew this one would be tricky.
And how much of the plan does our guest know?
Almost none. As long as he continues to do what we tell him, everything will be fine.
You're really betting the house on this one, huh?
So where do you want me, for the final act?

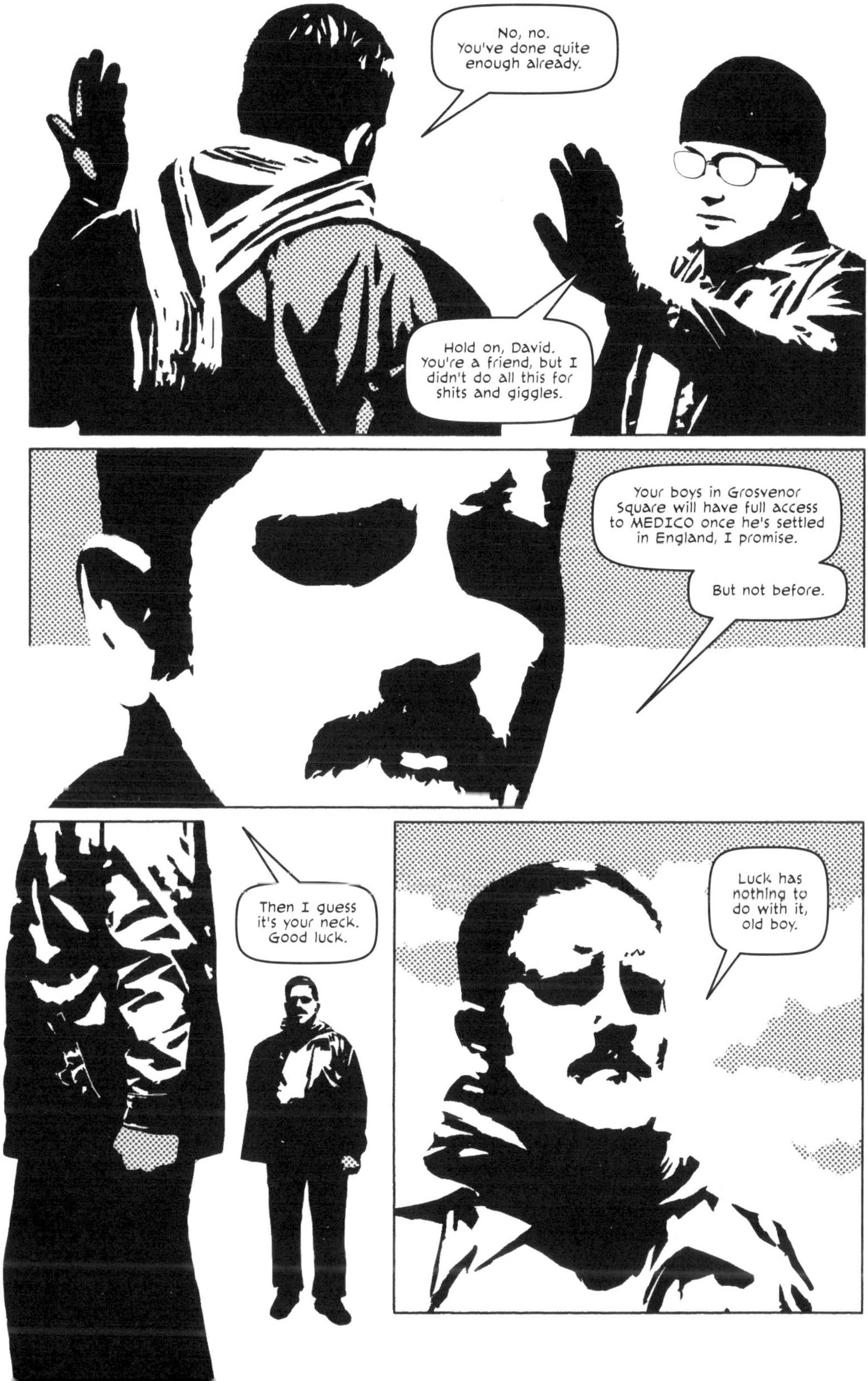
No, no. You've done quite enough already.
Hold on, David. You're a friend, but I didn't do all this for shits and giggles.
Your boys in Grosvenor Square will have full access to MEDICO once he's settled in England, I promise.
But not before.
Then I guess it's your neck. Good luck.
Luck has nothing to do with it, old boy.

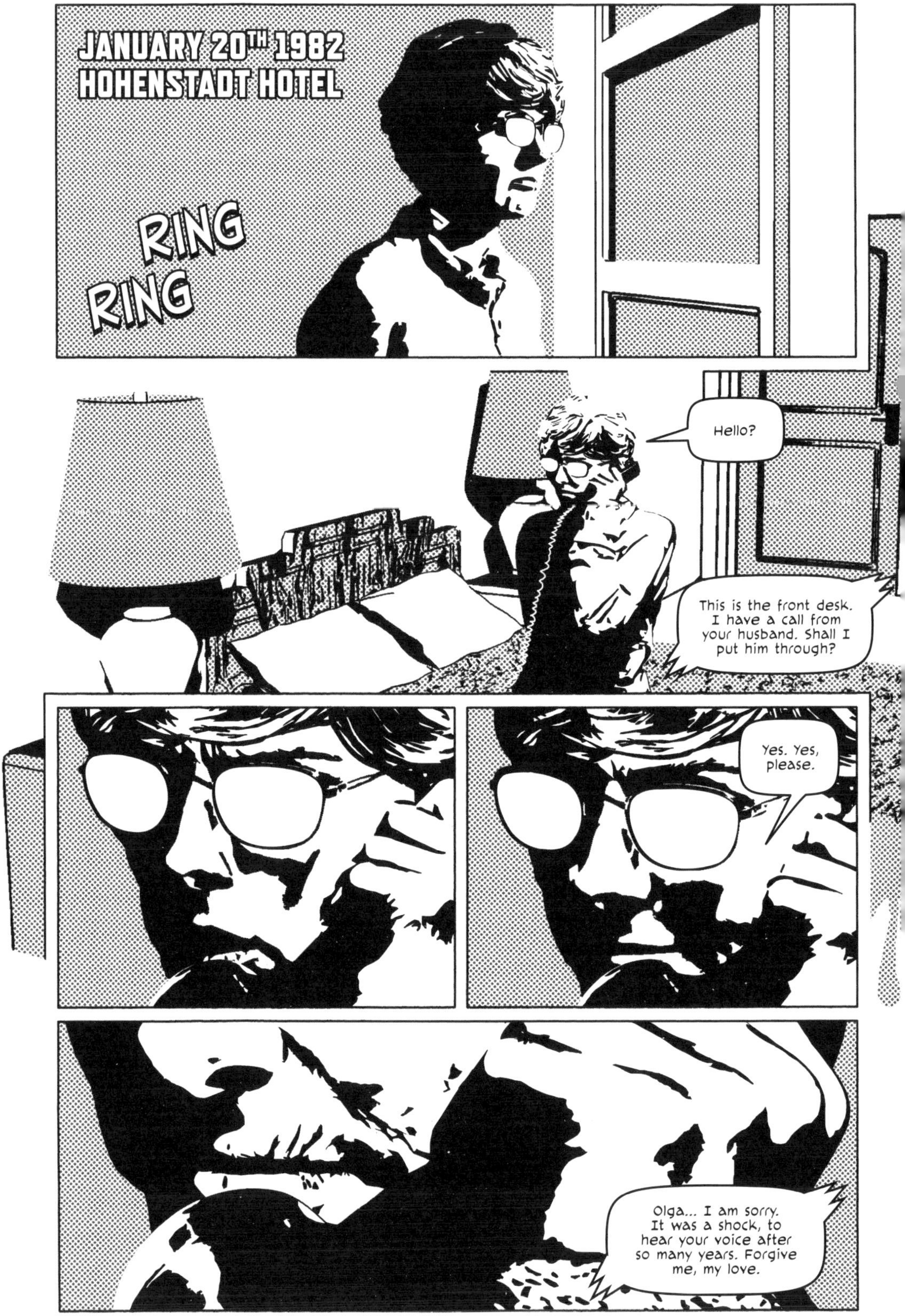
JANUARY 20TH 1982
HOHENSTADT HOTEL
RING
RING
Hello?
This is the front desk. I have a call from your husband. Shall I put him through?
Yes. Yes, please.
Olga... I am sorry. It was a shock, to hear your voice after so many years. Forgive me, my love.

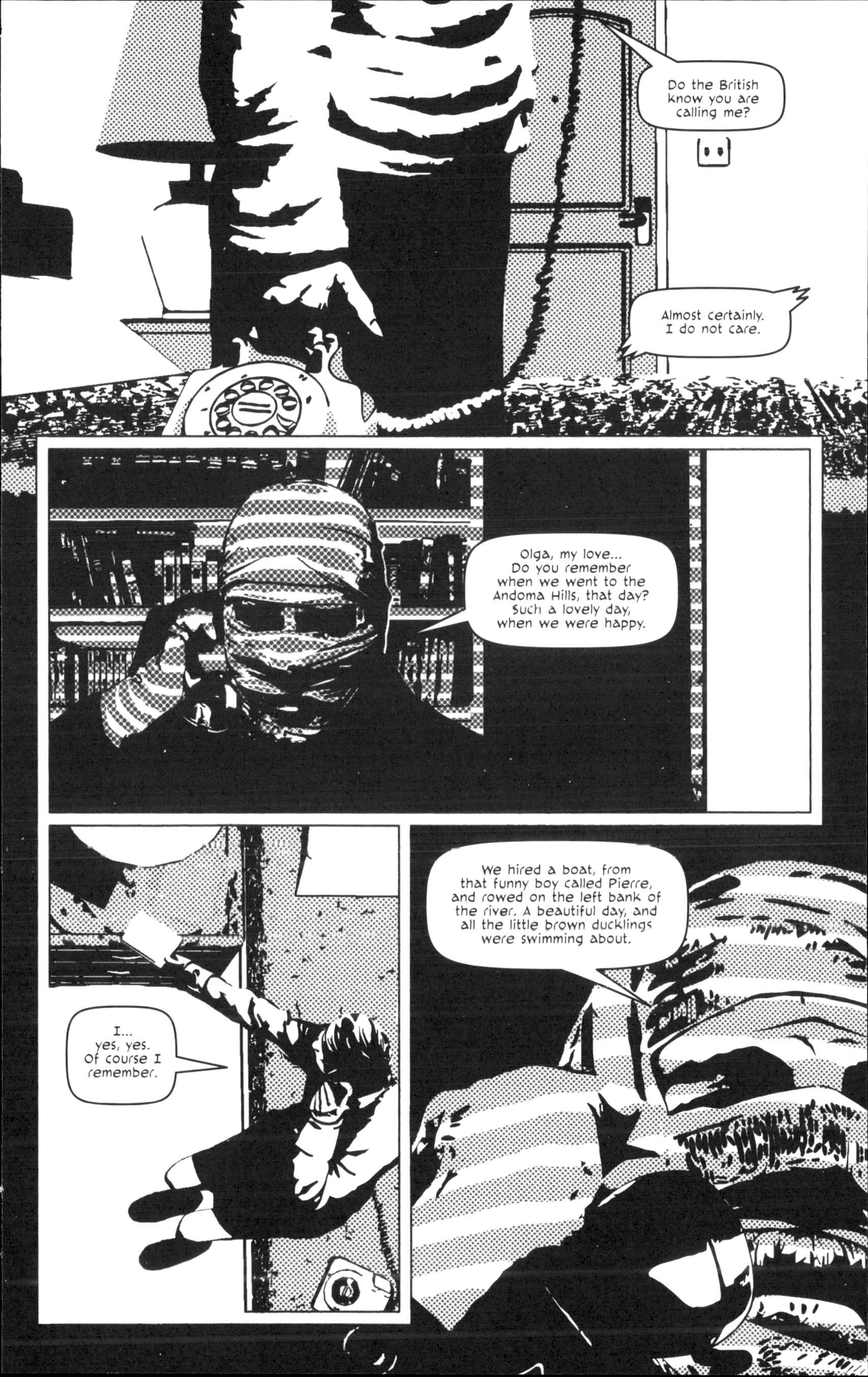
Do the British know you are calling me?
Almost certainly. I do not care.
Olga, my love... Do you remember when we went to the Andoma Hills, that day? Such a lovely day, when we were happy.
I... yes, yes. Of course I remember.
We hired a boat, from that funny boy called Pierre, and rowed on the left bank of the river. A beautiful day, and all the little brown ducklings were swimming about.

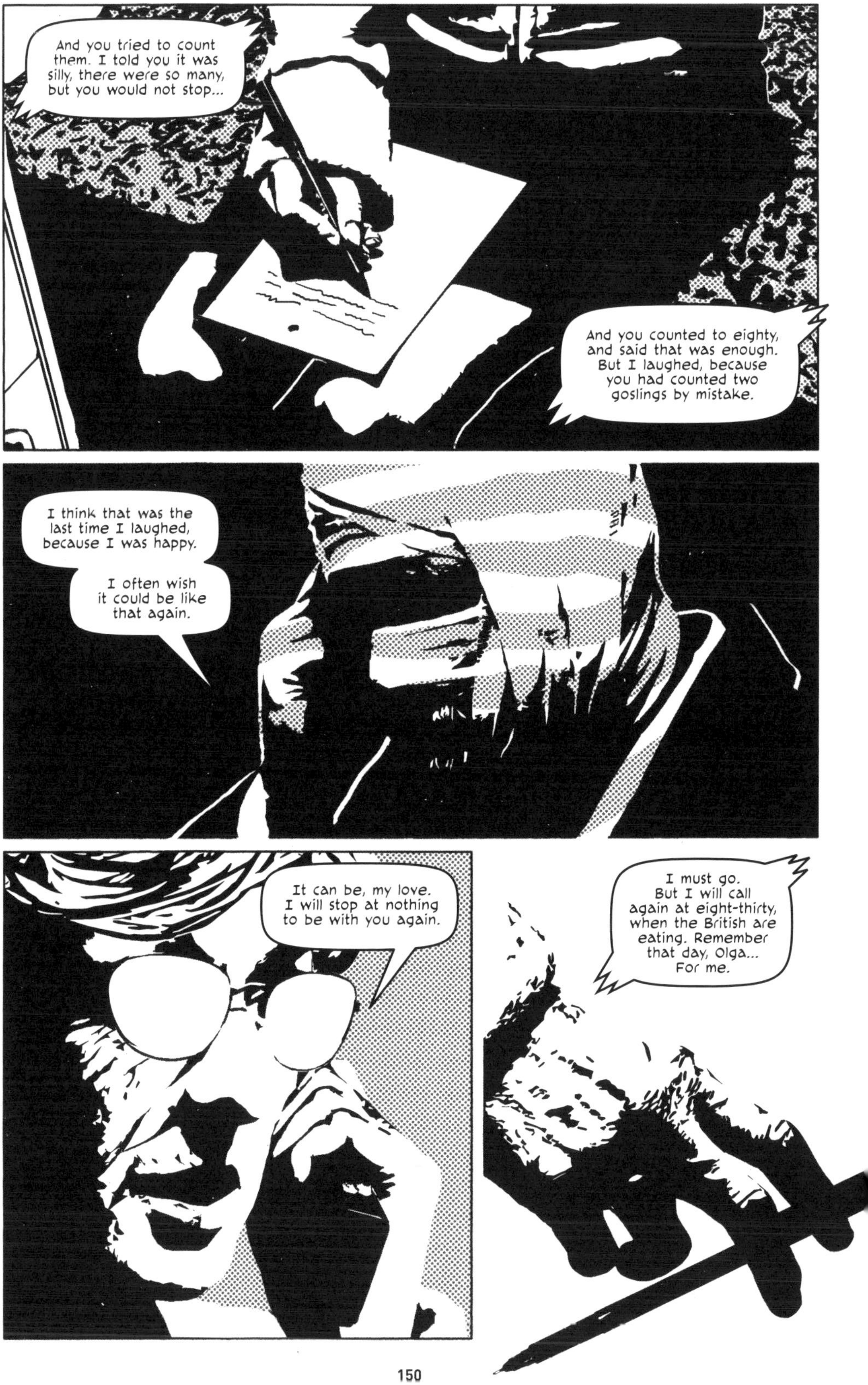
And you tried to count them. I told you it was silly, there were so many, but you would not stop...
And you counted to eighty, and said that was enough. But I laughed, because you had counted two goslings by mistake.
I think that was the last time I laughed, because I was happy.
I often wish it could be like that again.
It can be, my love. I will stop at nothing to be with you again.
I must go. But I will call again at eight-thirty, when the British are eating. Remember that day, Olga... For me.

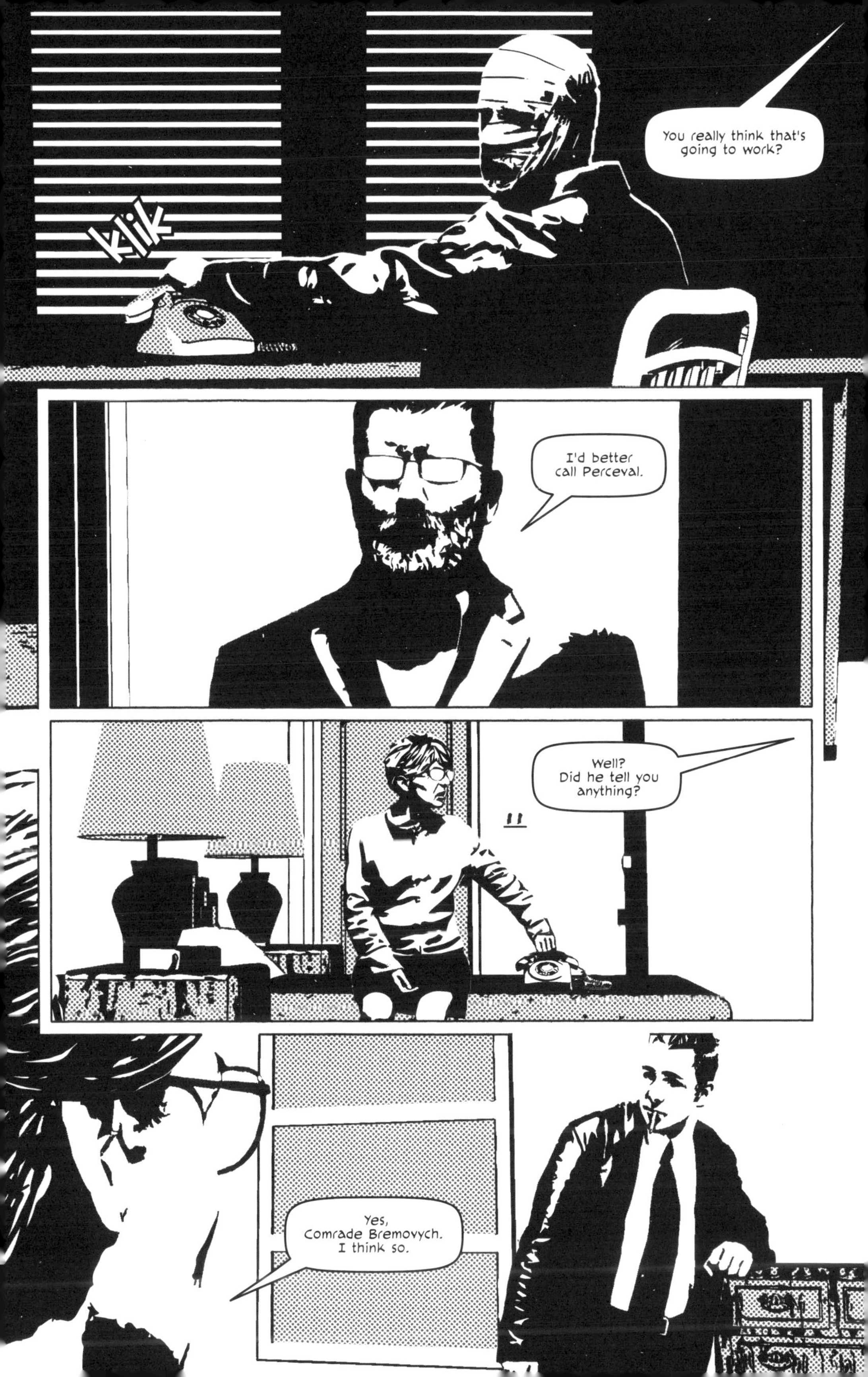
You really think that's going to work?
klik
I'd better call Perceval.
Well? Did he tell you anything?
Yes, Comrade Bremovych. I think so.

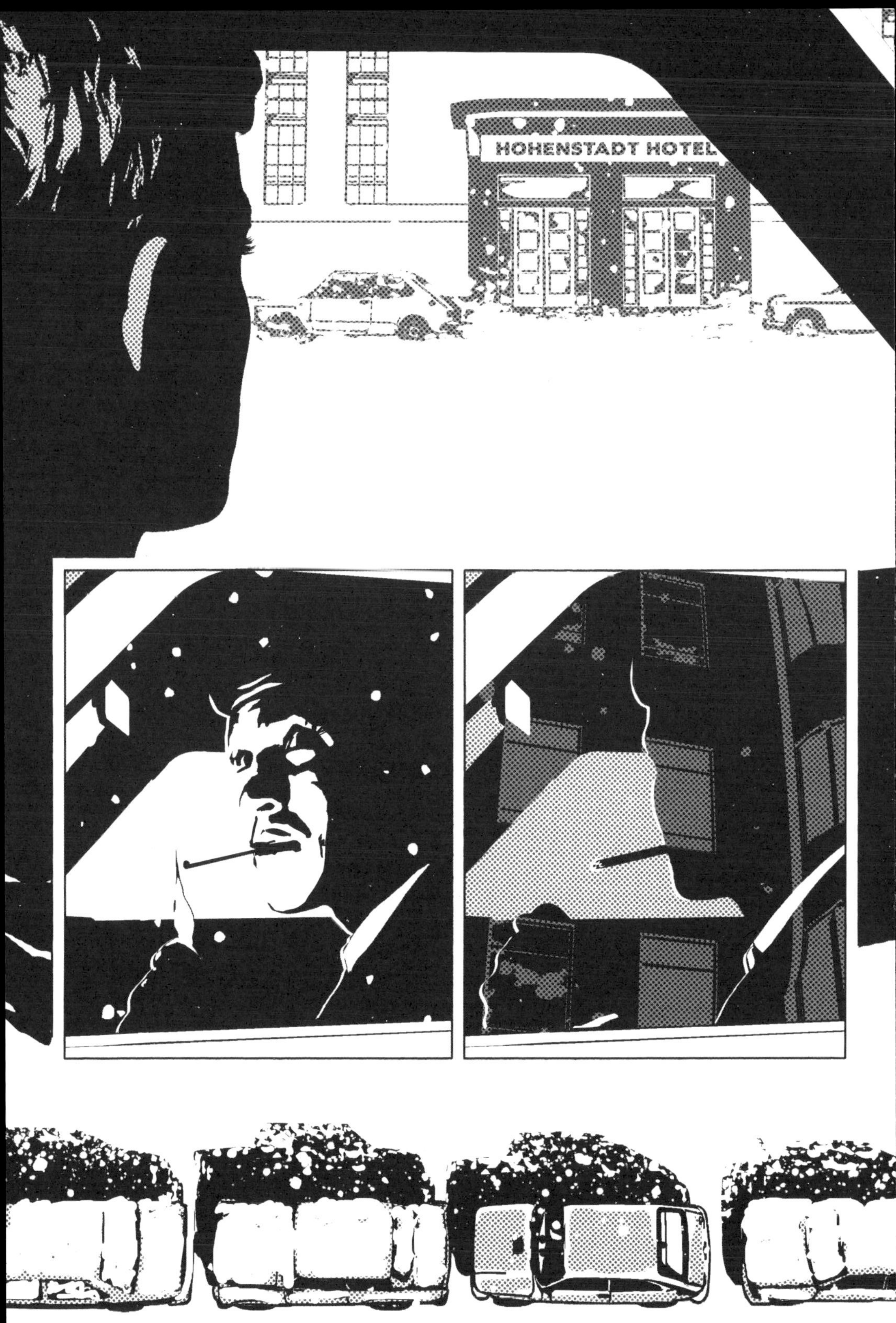
HOHENSTADT HOTEL

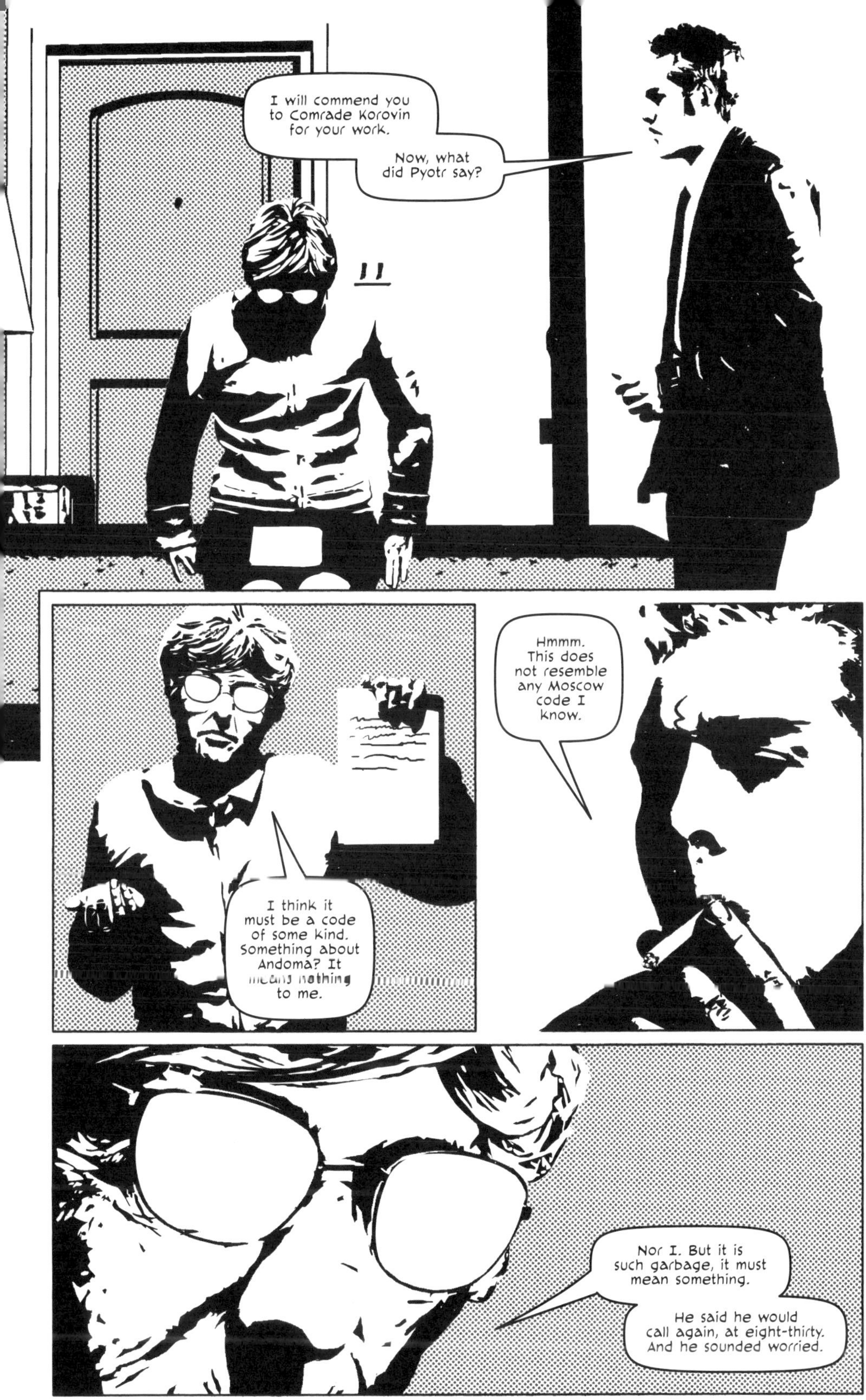
I will commend you to Comrade Korovin for your work.
Now, what did Pyotr say?
I think it must be a code of some kind. Something about Andoma? It means nothing to me.
Hmmm. This does not resemble any Moscow code I know.
Nor I. But it is such garbage, it must mean something.
He said he would call again, at eight-thirty. And he sounded worried.

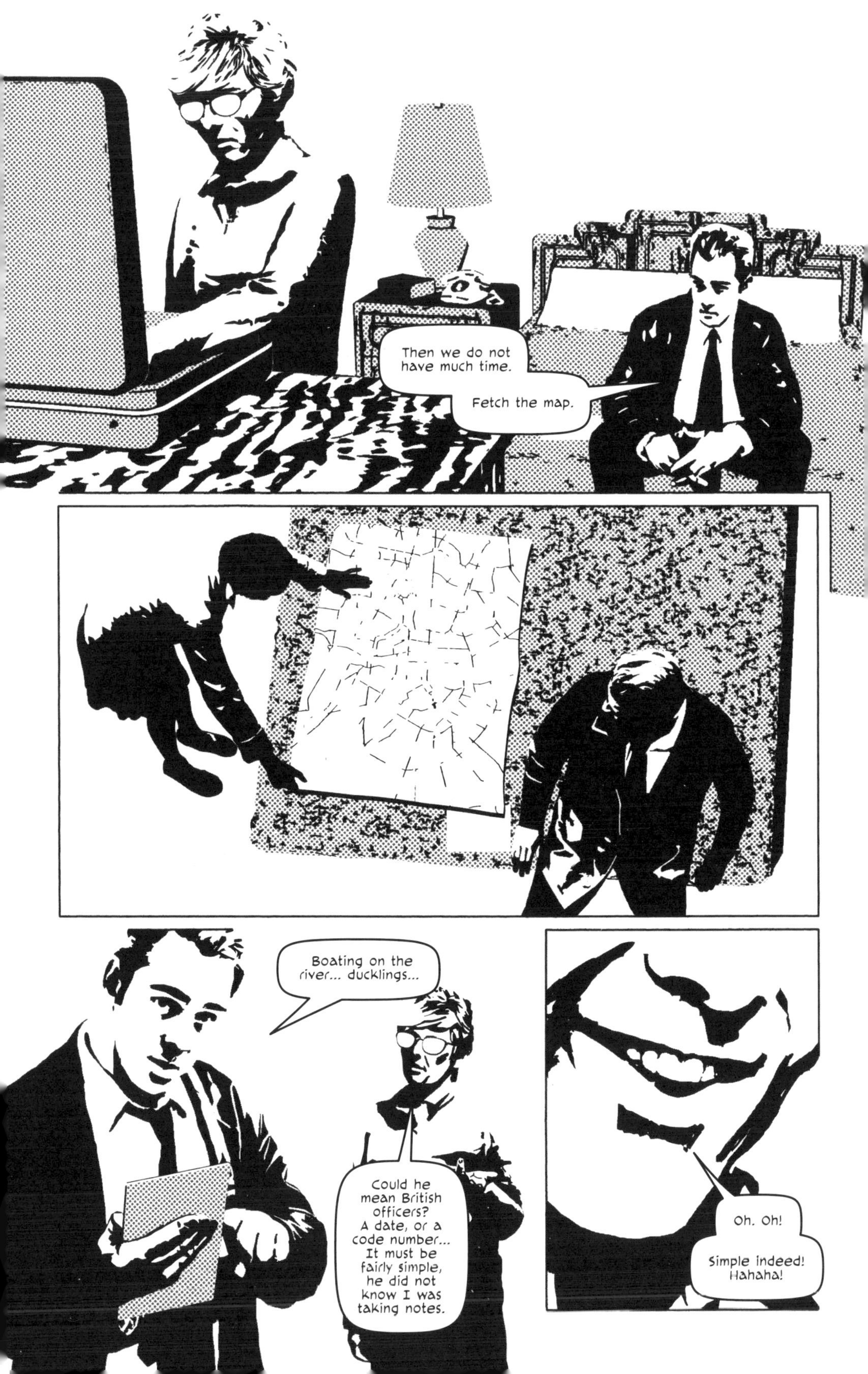
Then we do not have much time.
Fetch the map.
Boating on the river... ducklings...
Could he mean British officers? A date, or a code number... It must be fairly simple, he did not know I was taking notes.
Oh. Oh!
Simple indeed! Hahaha!

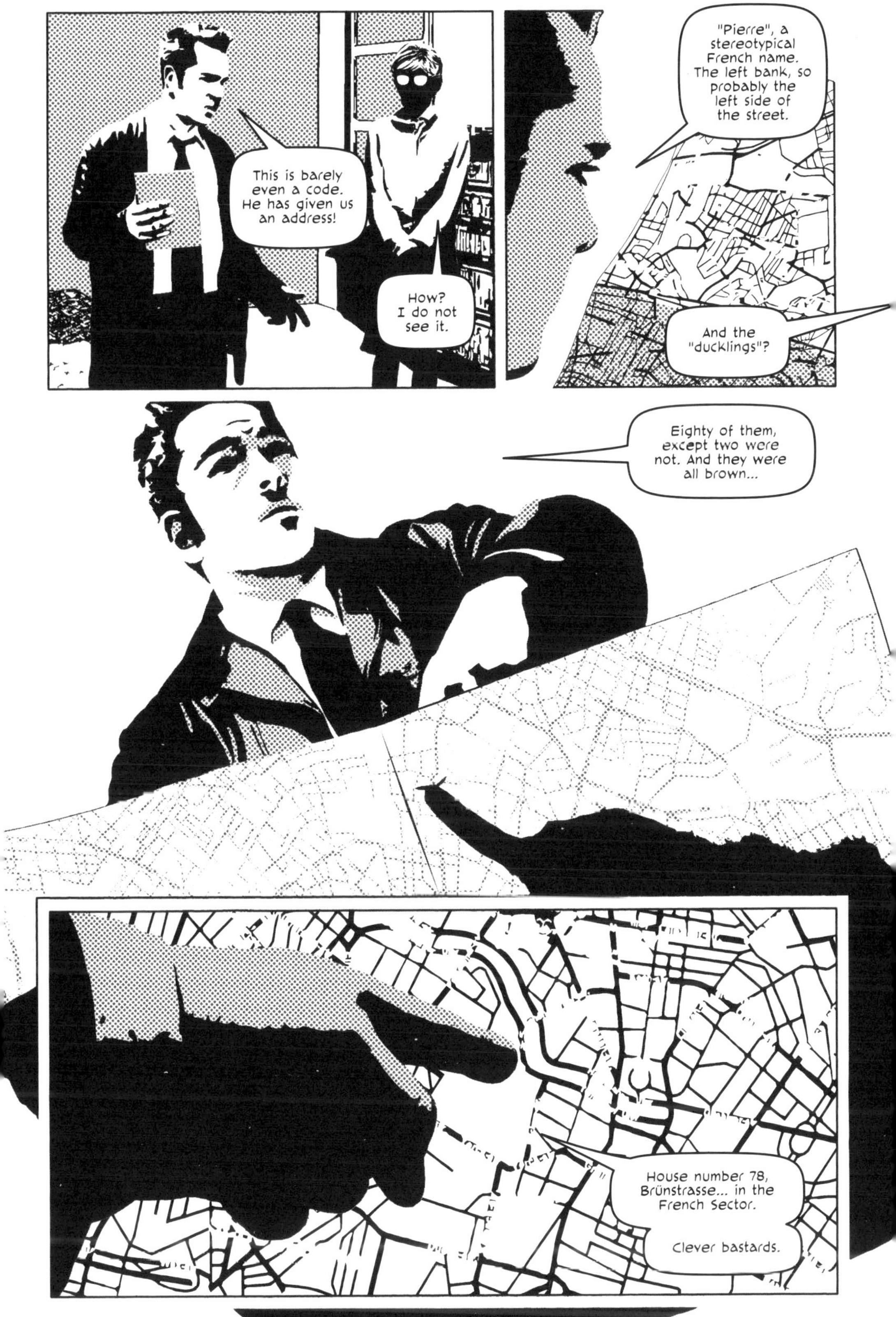
This is barely even a code. He has given us an address!
How? I do not see it.
"Pierre", a stereotypical French name. The left bank, so probably the left side of the street.
And the "ducklings"?
Eighty of them, except two were not. And they were all brown...
House number 78, Brünstrasse... in the French Sector.
Clever bastards.

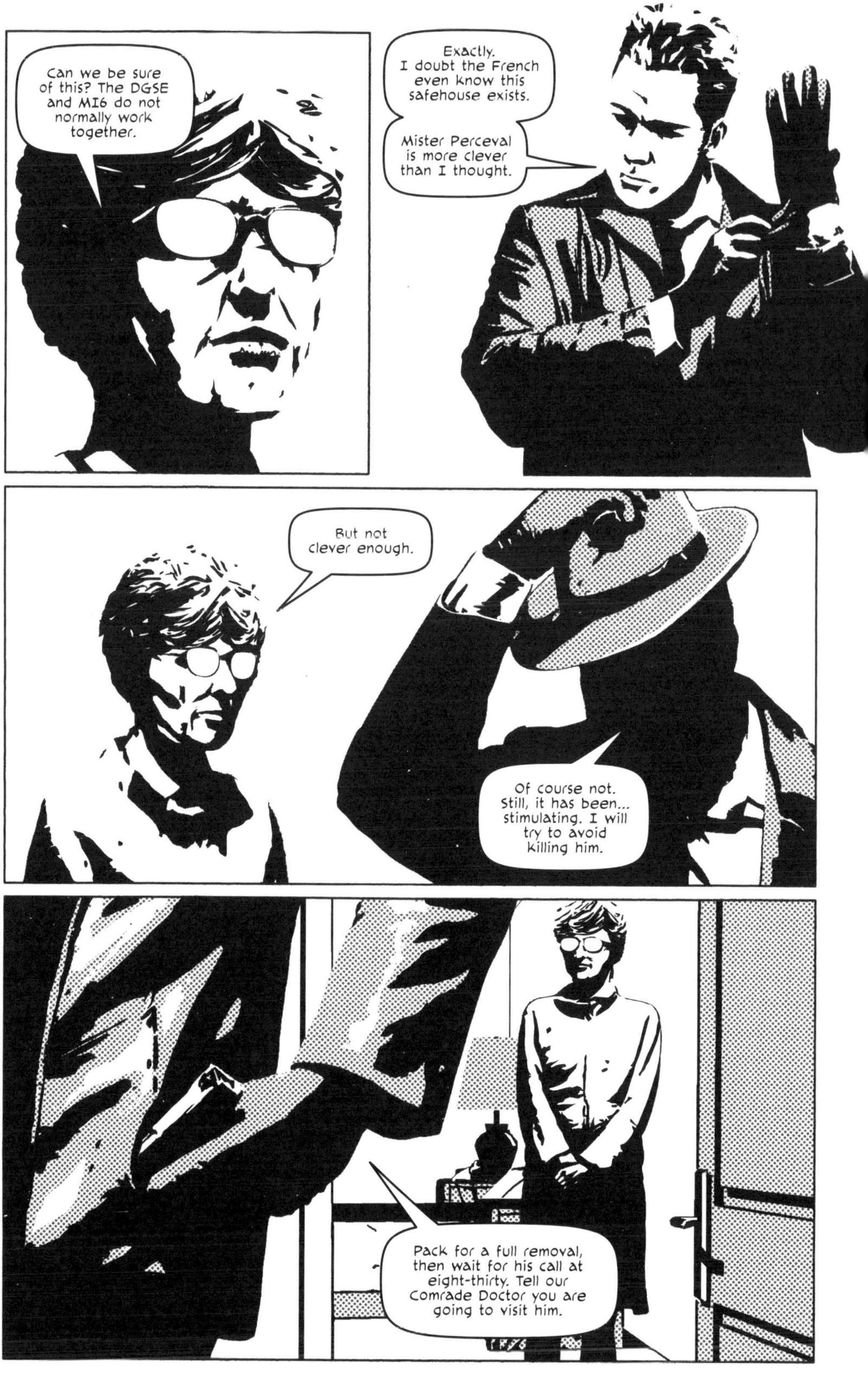
Can we be sure of this? The DGSE and MI6 do not normally work together.
Exactly. I doubt the French even know this safehouse exists.
Mister Perceval is more clever than I thought.
But not clever enough.
Of course not. Still, it has been... stimulating. I will try to avoid killing him.
Pack for a full removal, then wait for his call at eight-thirty. Tell our Comrade Doctor you are going to visit him.

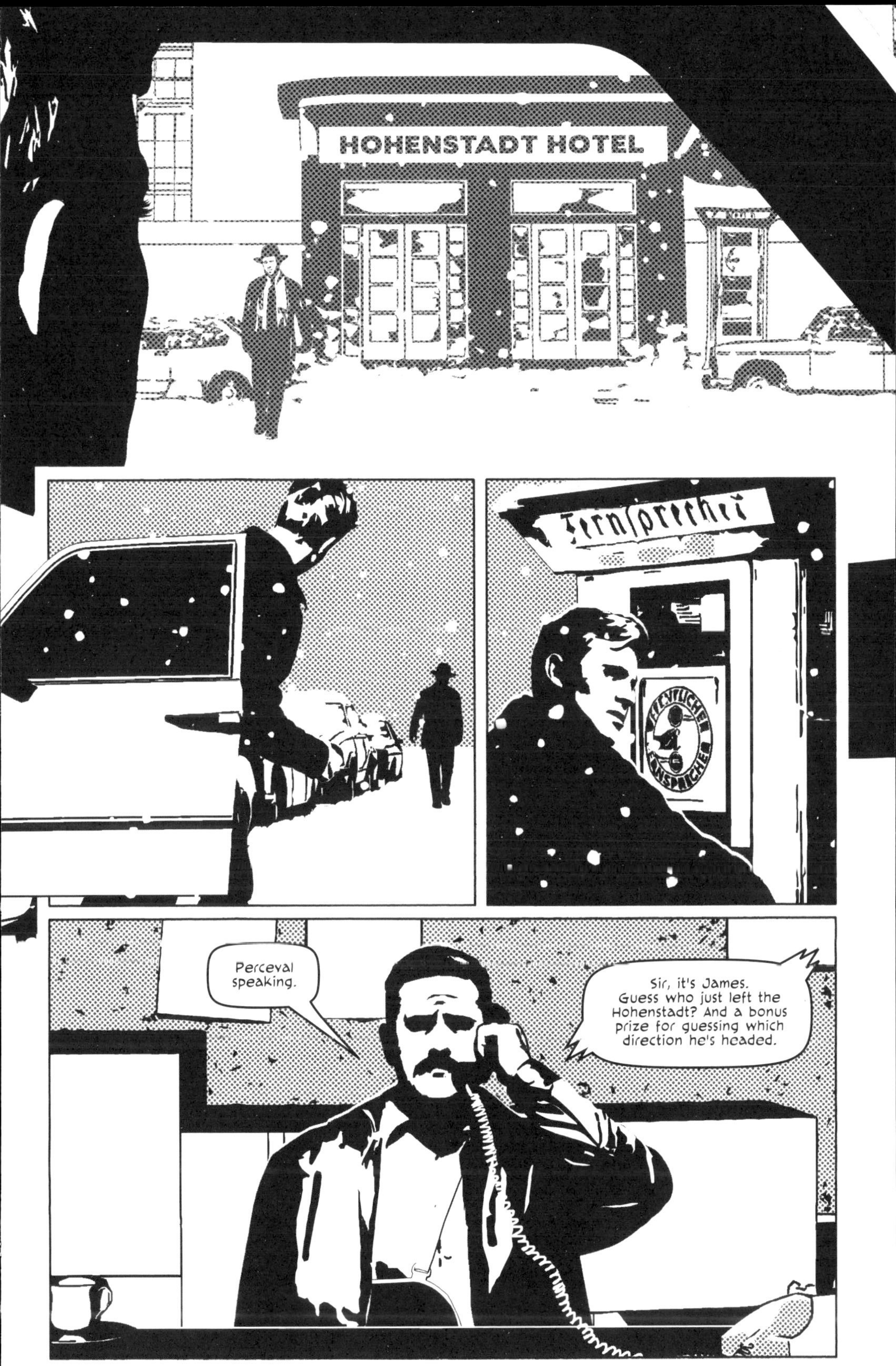
HOHENSTADT HOTEL
Fernsprecher
Perceval speaking.
Sir, it's James. Guess who just left the Hohenstadt? And a bonus prize for guessing which direction he's headed.

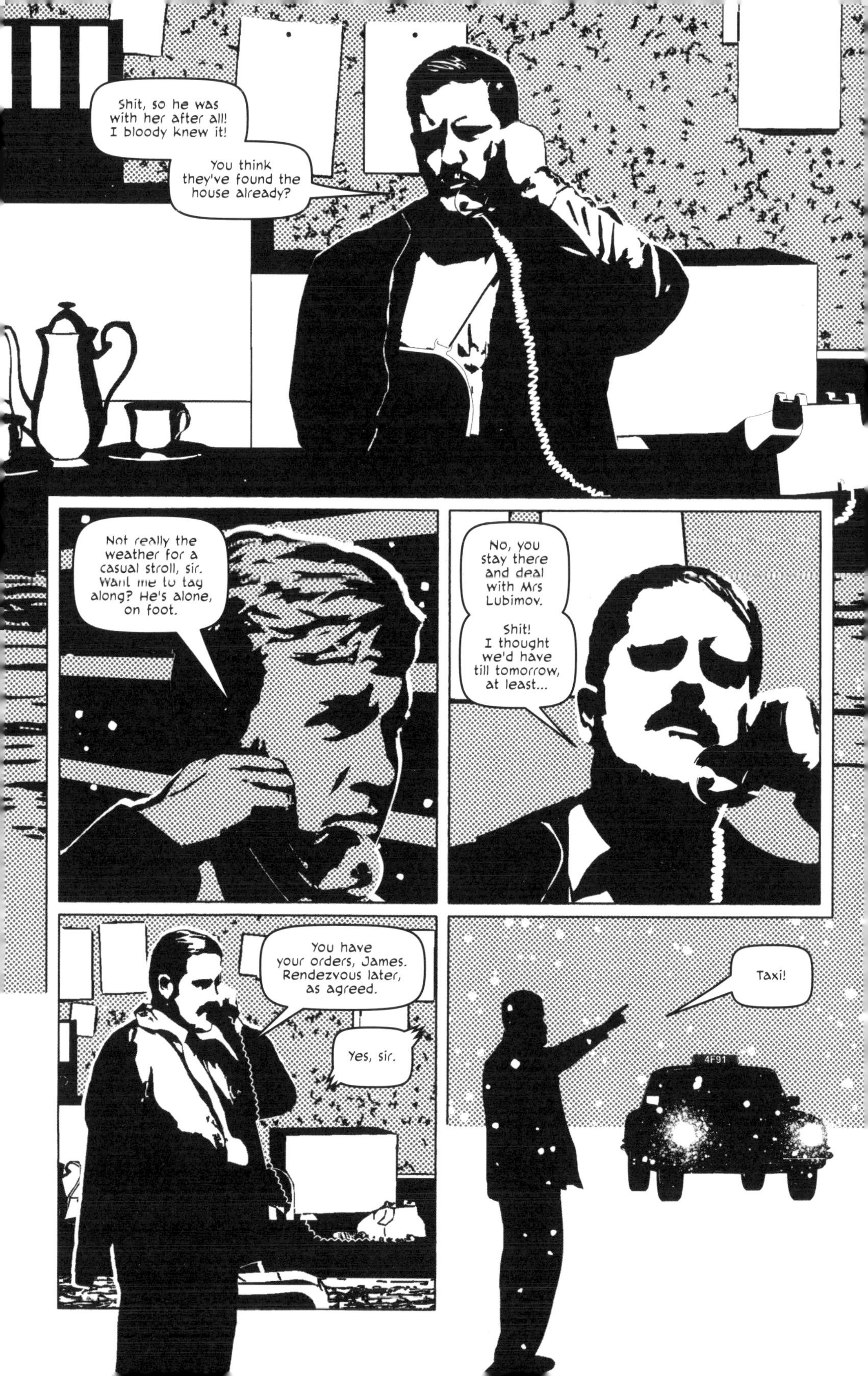
Shit, so he was with her after all! I bloody knew it!
You think they've found the house already?
Not really the weather for a casual stroll, sir. Want me to tag along? He's alone, on foot.
No, you stay there and deal with Mrs Lubimov.
Shit! I thought we'd have till tomorrow, at least...
You have your orders, James. Rendezvous later, as agreed.
Yes, sir.
Taxi!
4F91

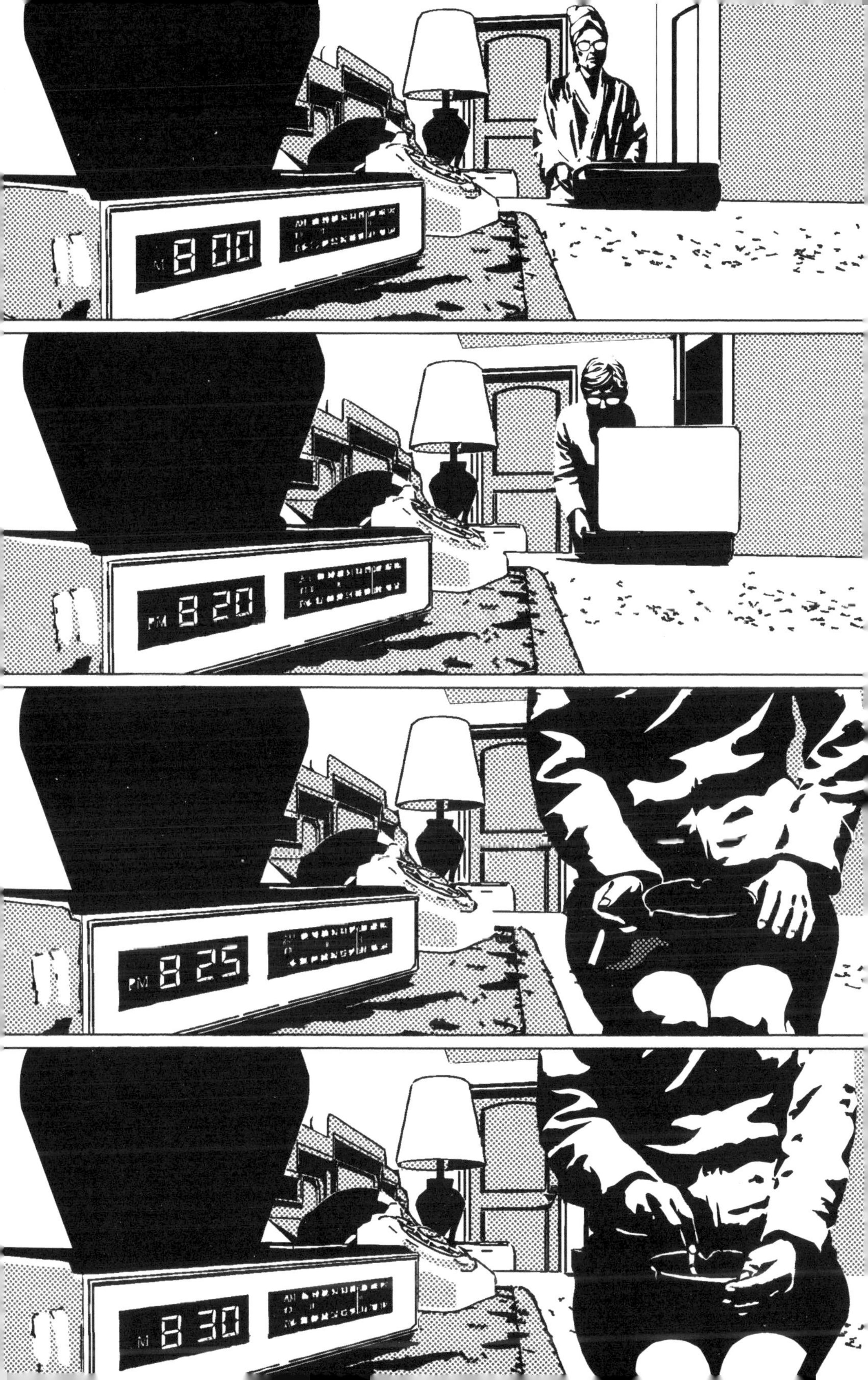
8 00
PM 8 20
PM 8 25
8 30

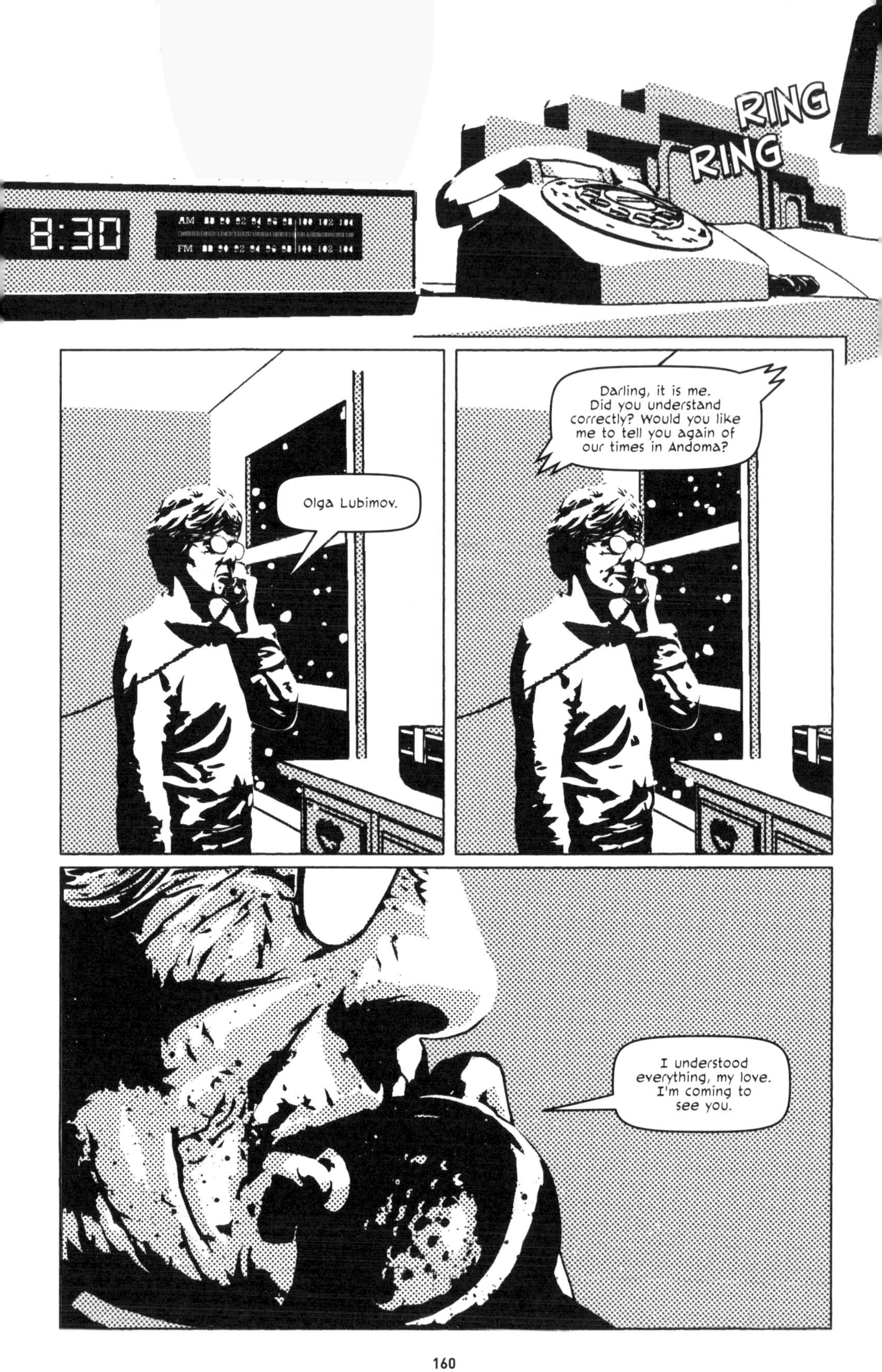
8:30
RING
RING
Olga Lubimov.
Darling, it is me. Did you understand correctly? Would you like me to tell you again of our times in Andoma?
I understood everything, my love. I'm coming to see you.

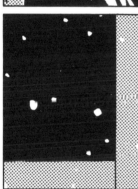

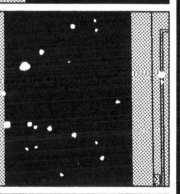

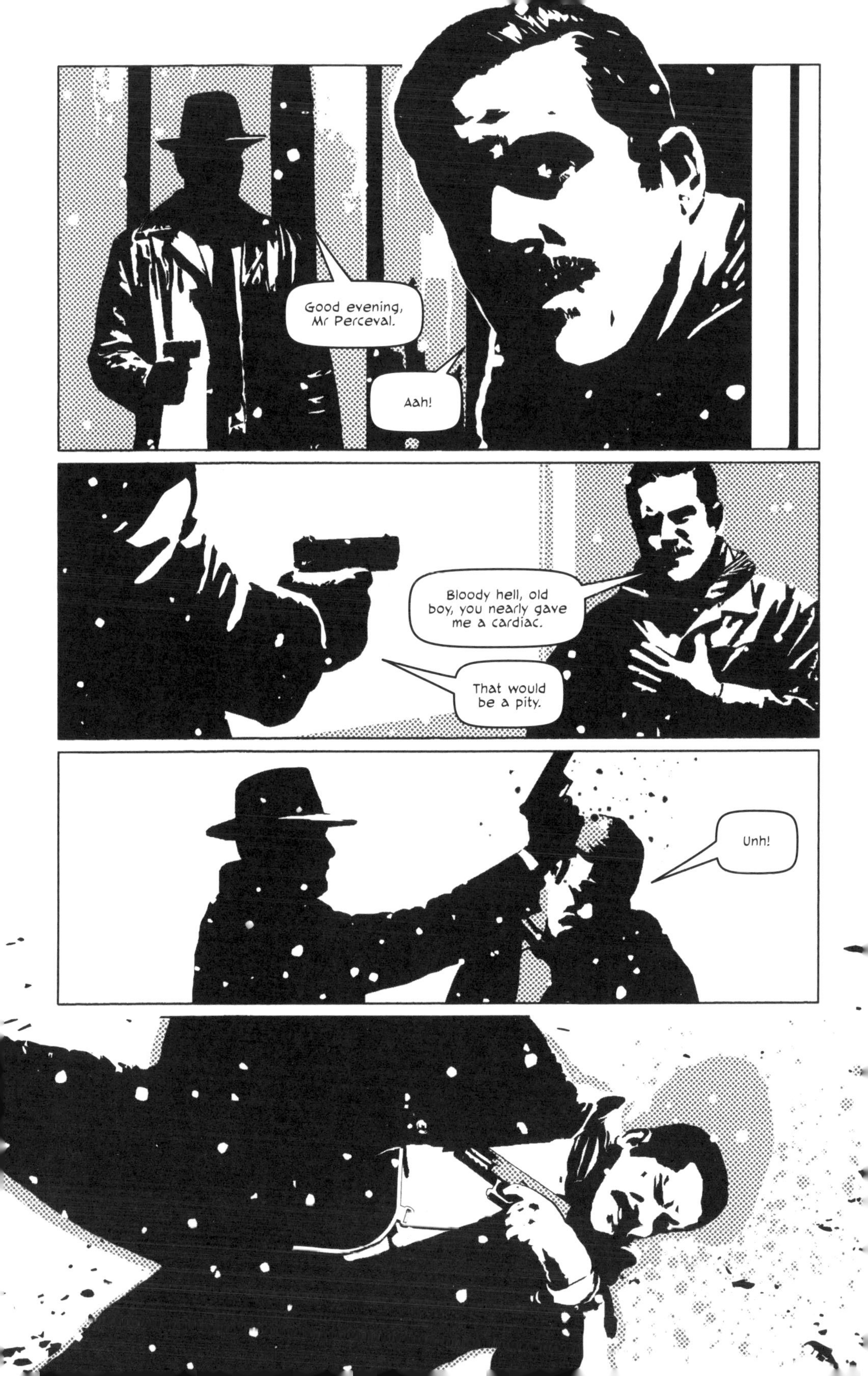
Good evening, Mr Perceval.
Aah!
Bloody hell, old boy, you nearly gave me a cardiac.
That would be a pity.
Unh!

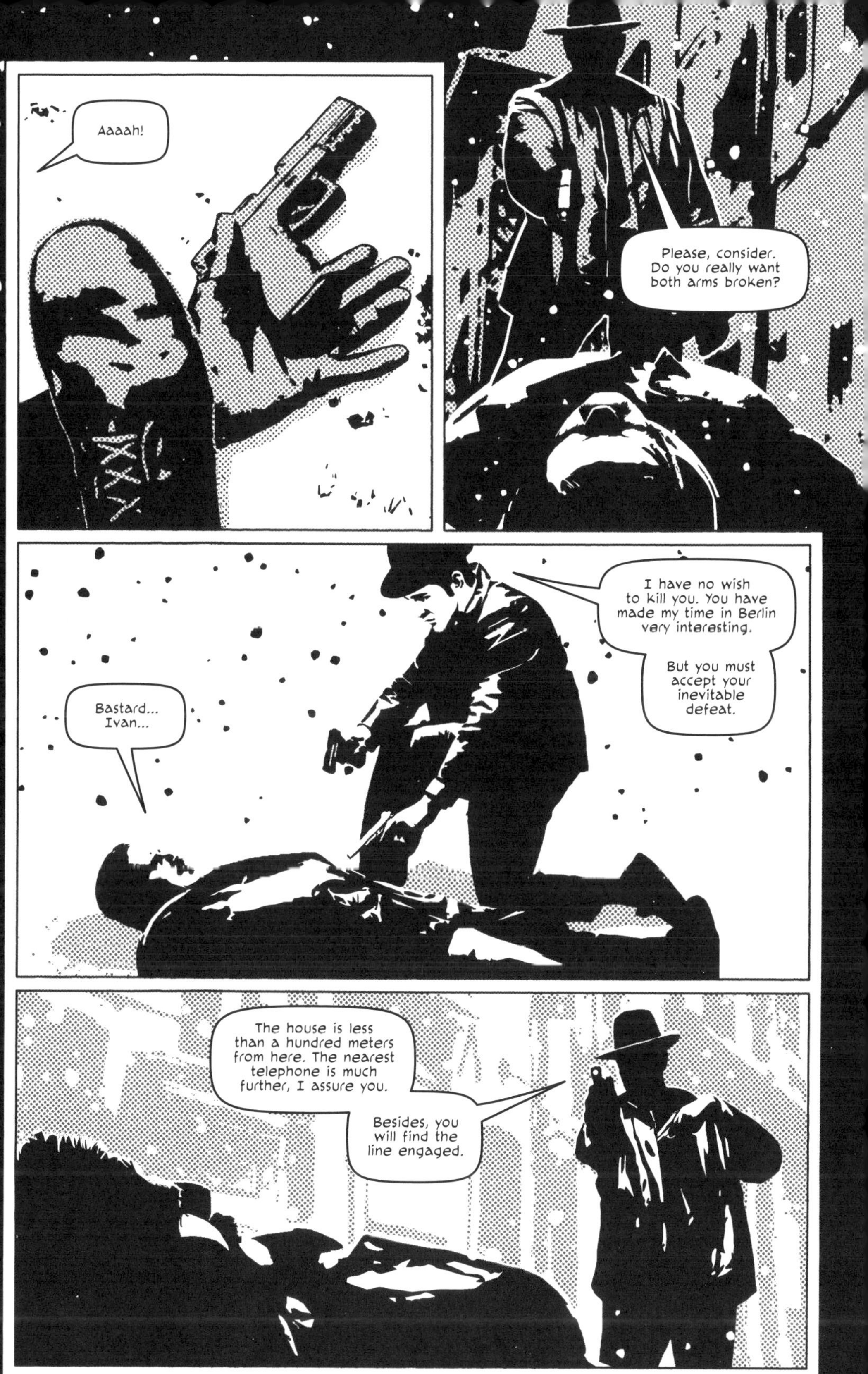
Aaaah!
Please, consider. Do you really want both arms broken?
Bastard... Ivan...
I have no wish to kill you. You have made my time in Berlin very interesting.
But you must accept your inevitable defeat.
The house is less than a hundred meters from here. The nearest telephone is much further, I assure you.
Besides, you will find the line engaged.

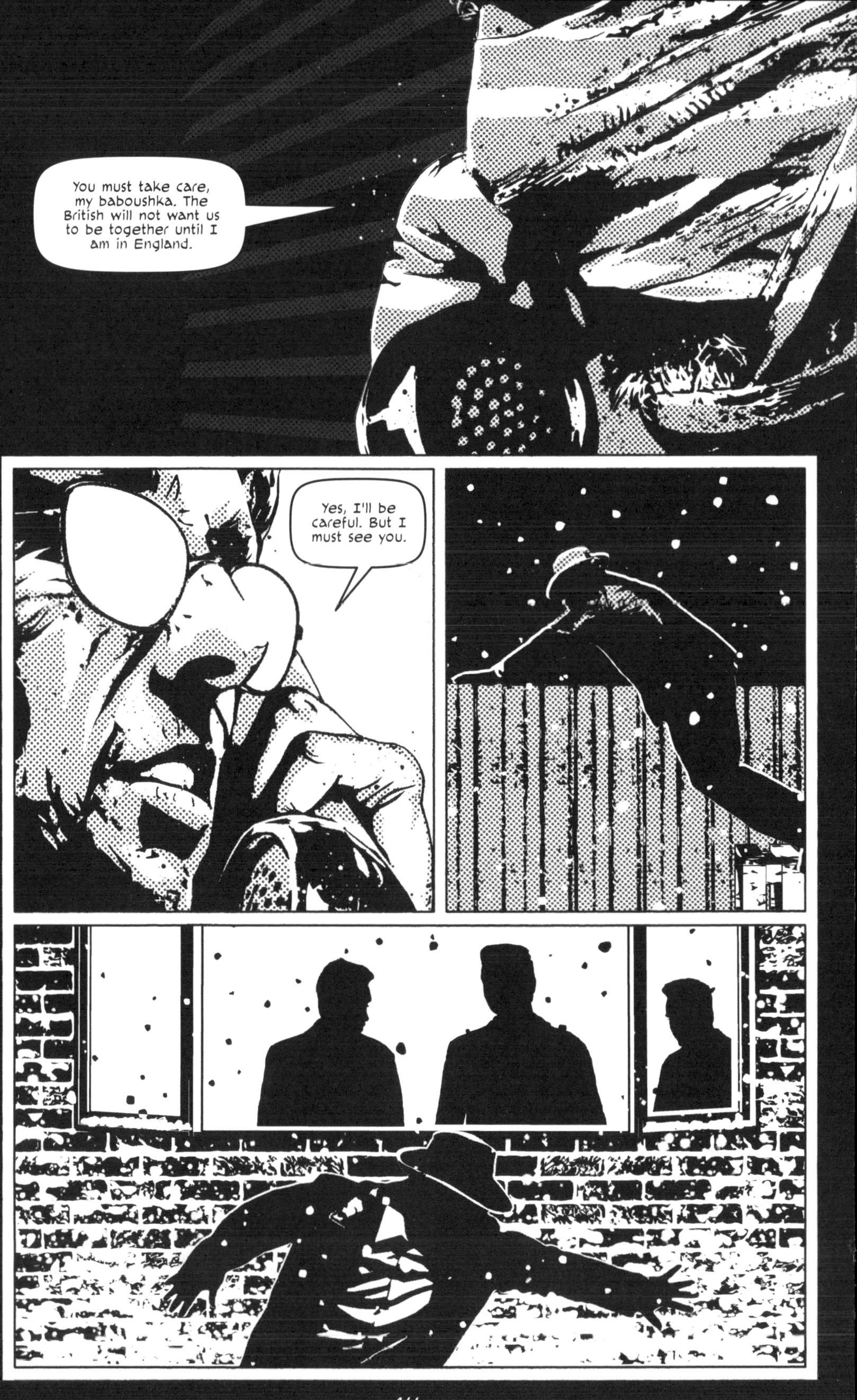
You must take care, my baboushka. The British will not want us to be together until I am in England.
Yes, I'll be careful. But I must see you.

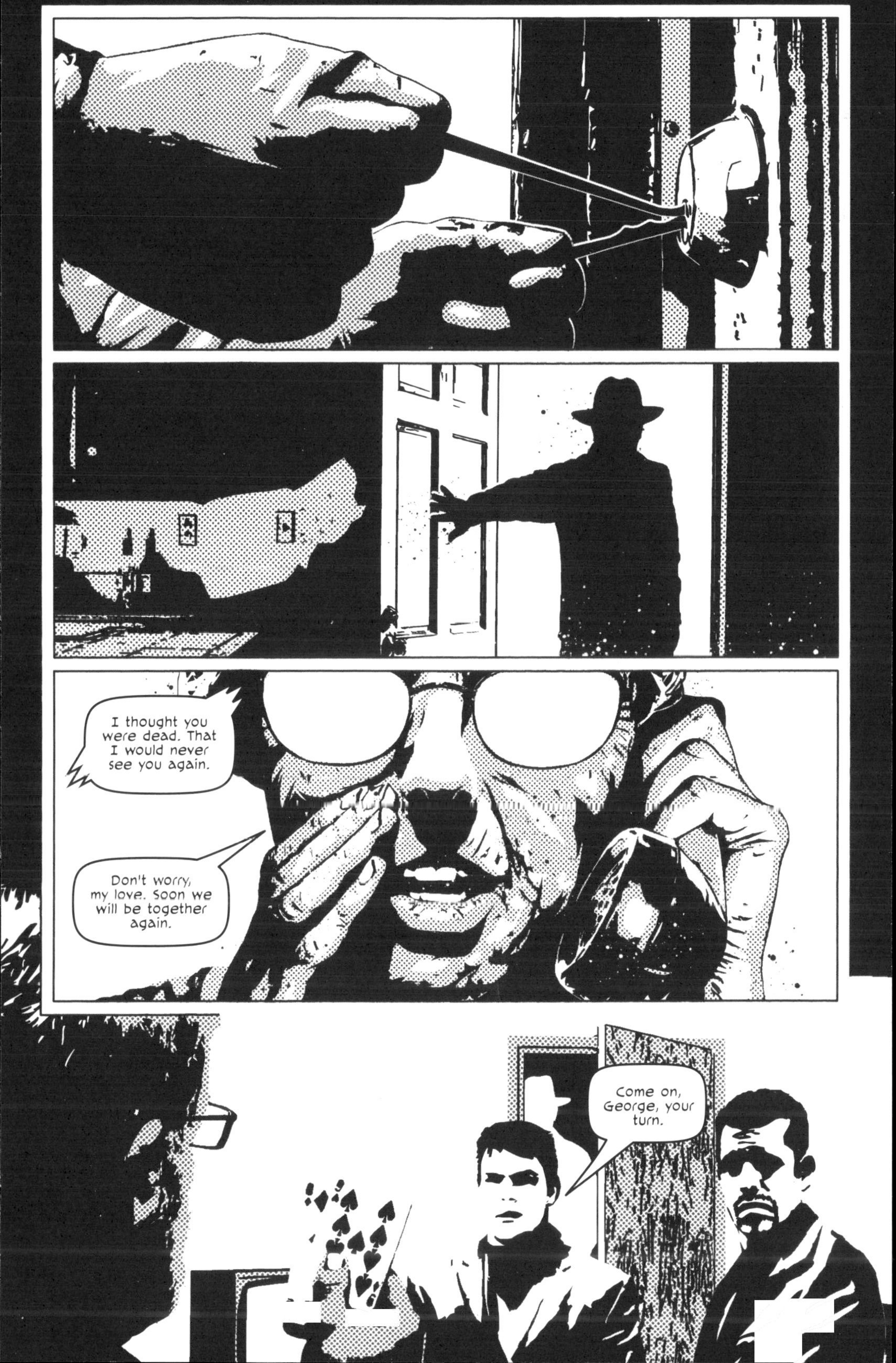
I thought you were dead. That I would never see you again.
Don't worry, my love. Soon we will be together again.
Come on, George, your turn.

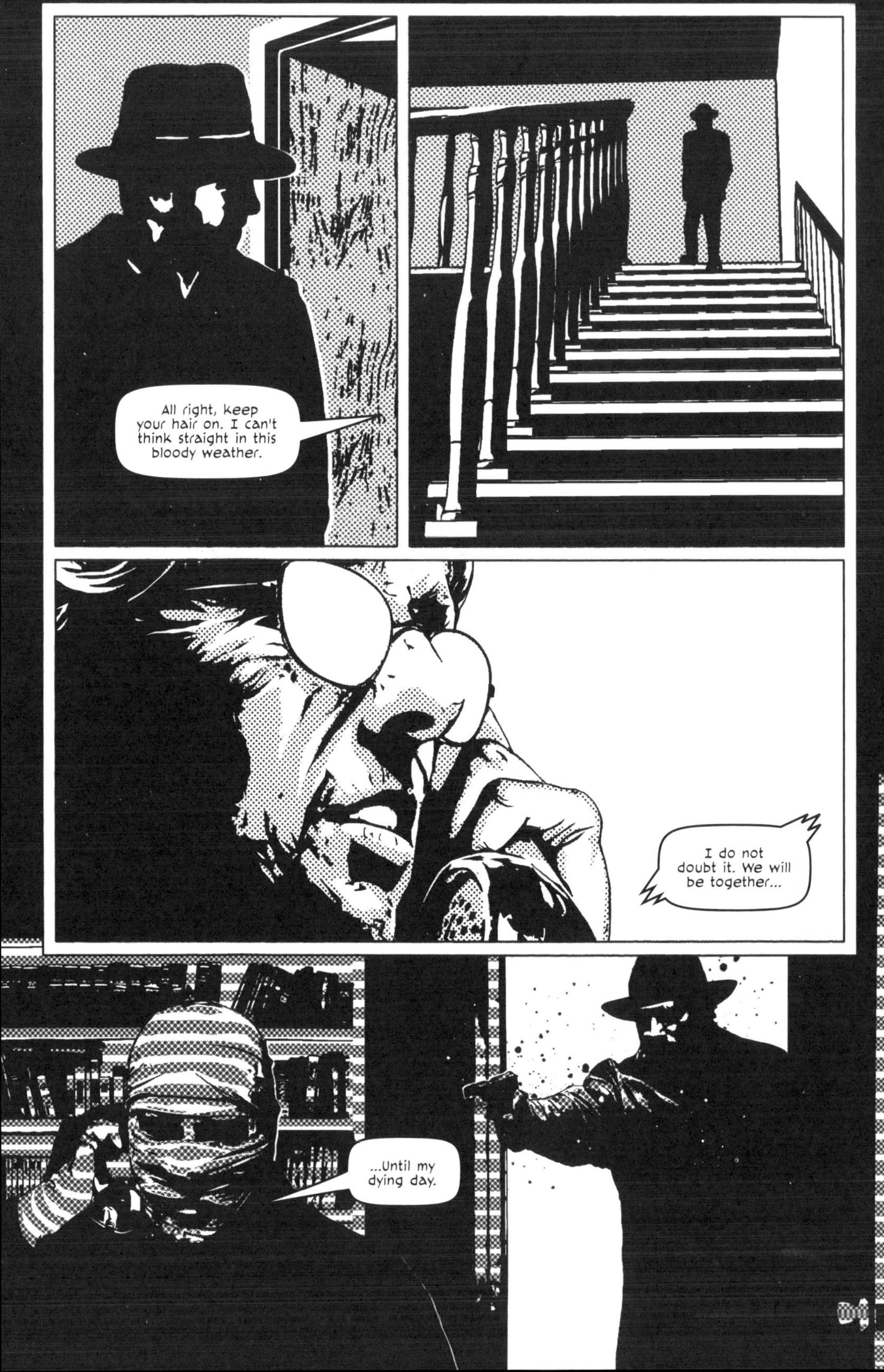
All right, keep your hair on. I can't think straight in this bloody weather.
I do not doubt it. We will be together...
...Until my dying day.

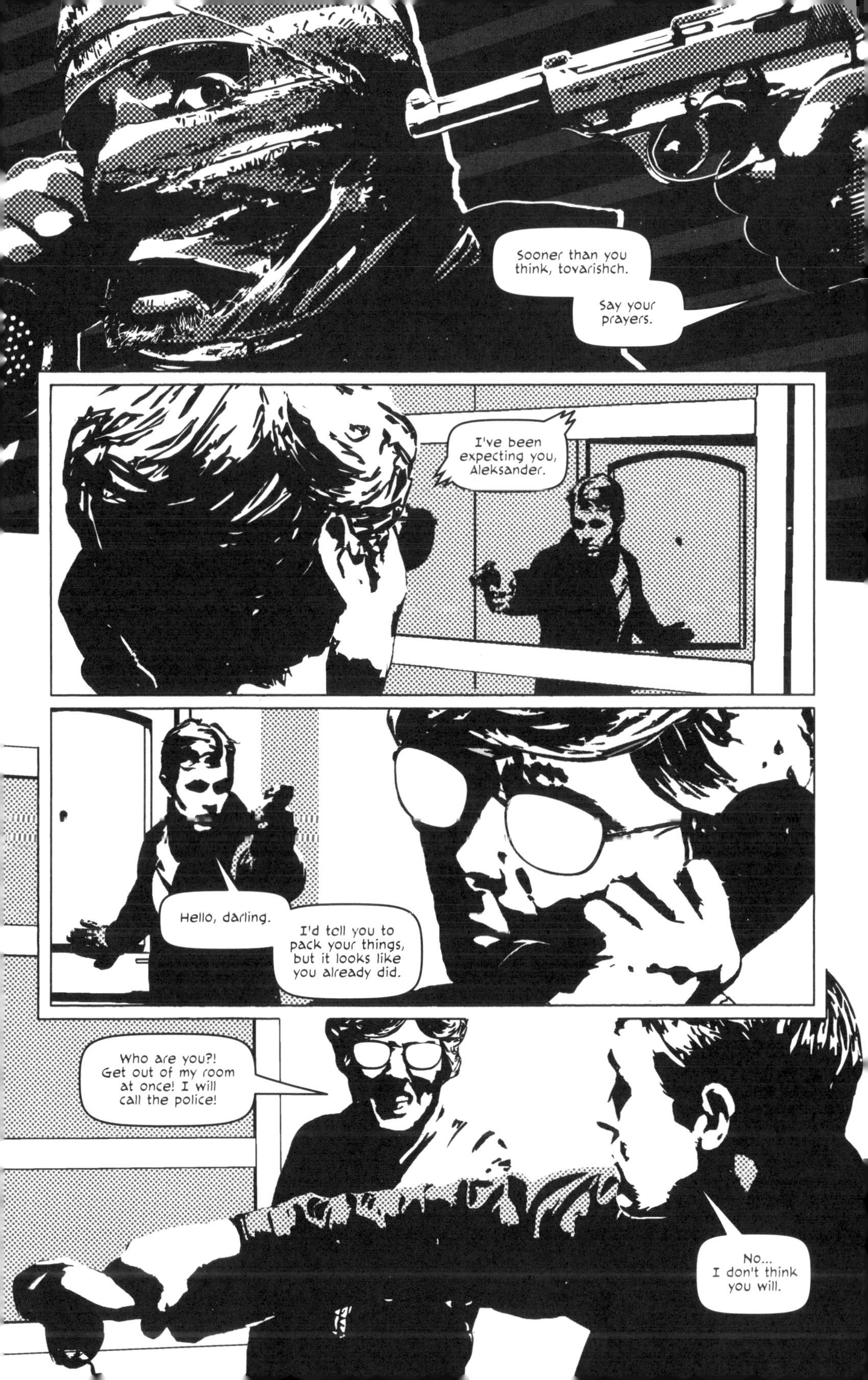
Sooner than you think, tovarishch.
Say your prayers.
I've been expecting you, Aleksander.
Hello, darling.
I'd tell you to pack your things, but it looks like you already did.
Who are you?! Get out of my room at once! I will call the police!
No... I don't think you will.

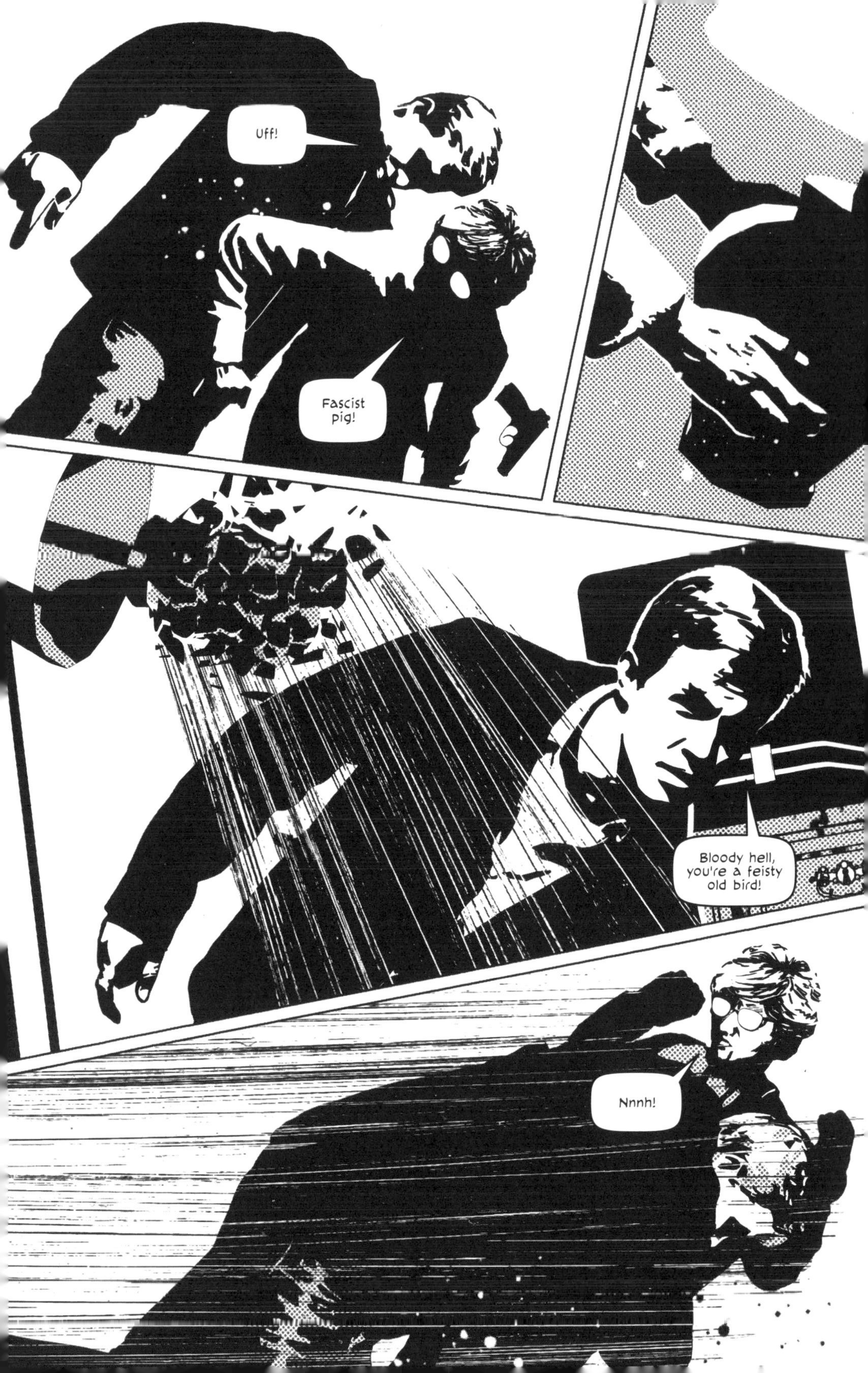
Uff!
Fascist pig!
Bloody hell, you're a feisty old bird!
Nnnh!

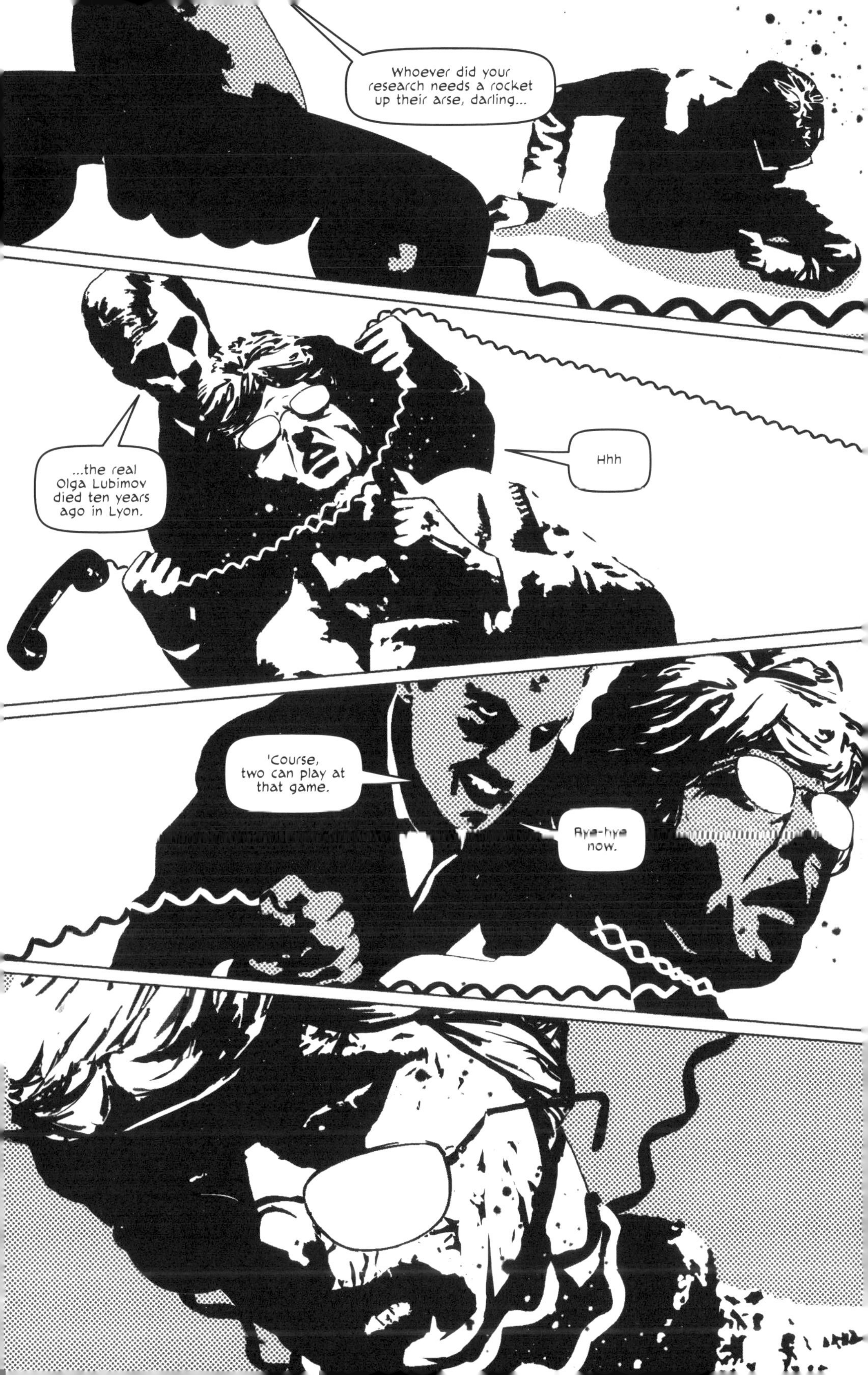
Whoever did your research needs a rocket up their arse, darling...
...the real Olga Lubimov died ten years ago in Lyon.
Hhh
'Course, two can play at that game.
Bye-bye now.

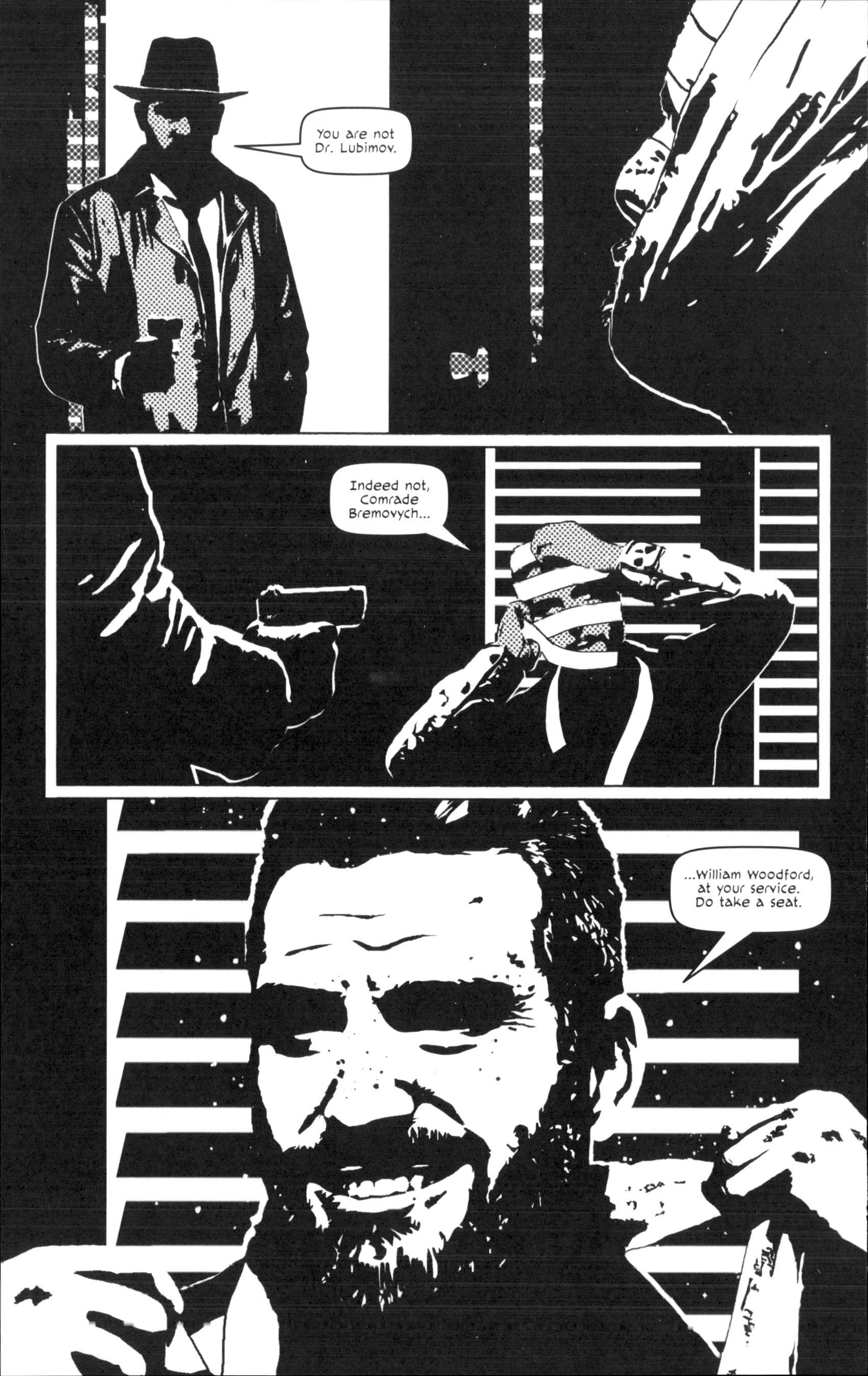
You are not Dr. Lubimov.
Indeed not, Comrade Bremovych...
...William Woodford, at your service. Do take a seat.

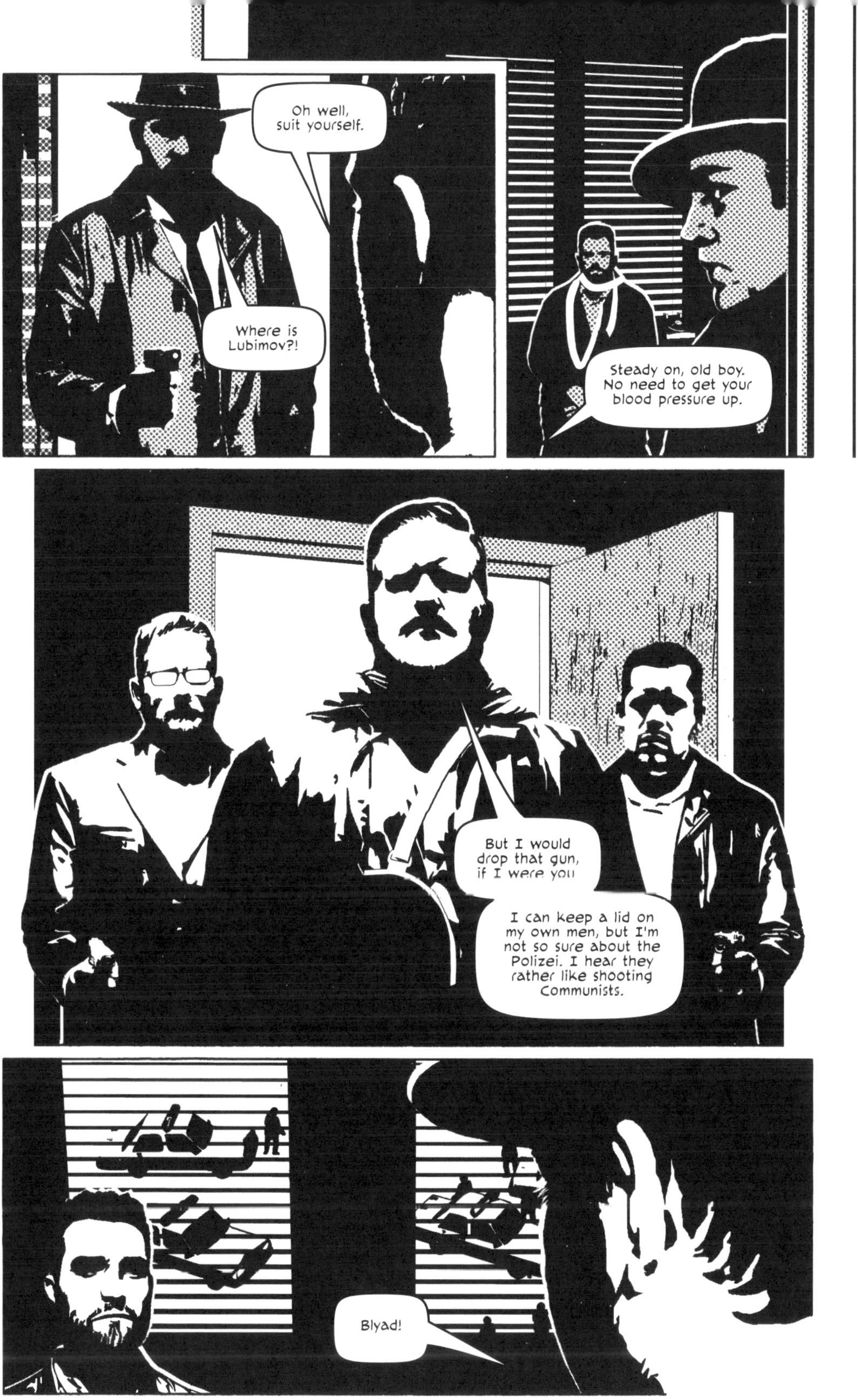
Oh well,
suit yourself.
Where is
Lubimov?!
Steady on, old boy.
No need to get your
blood pressure up.
But I would
drop that gun,
if I were you
I can keep a lid on
my own men, but I'm
not so sure about the
Polizei. I hear they
rather like shooting
Communists.
Blyad!

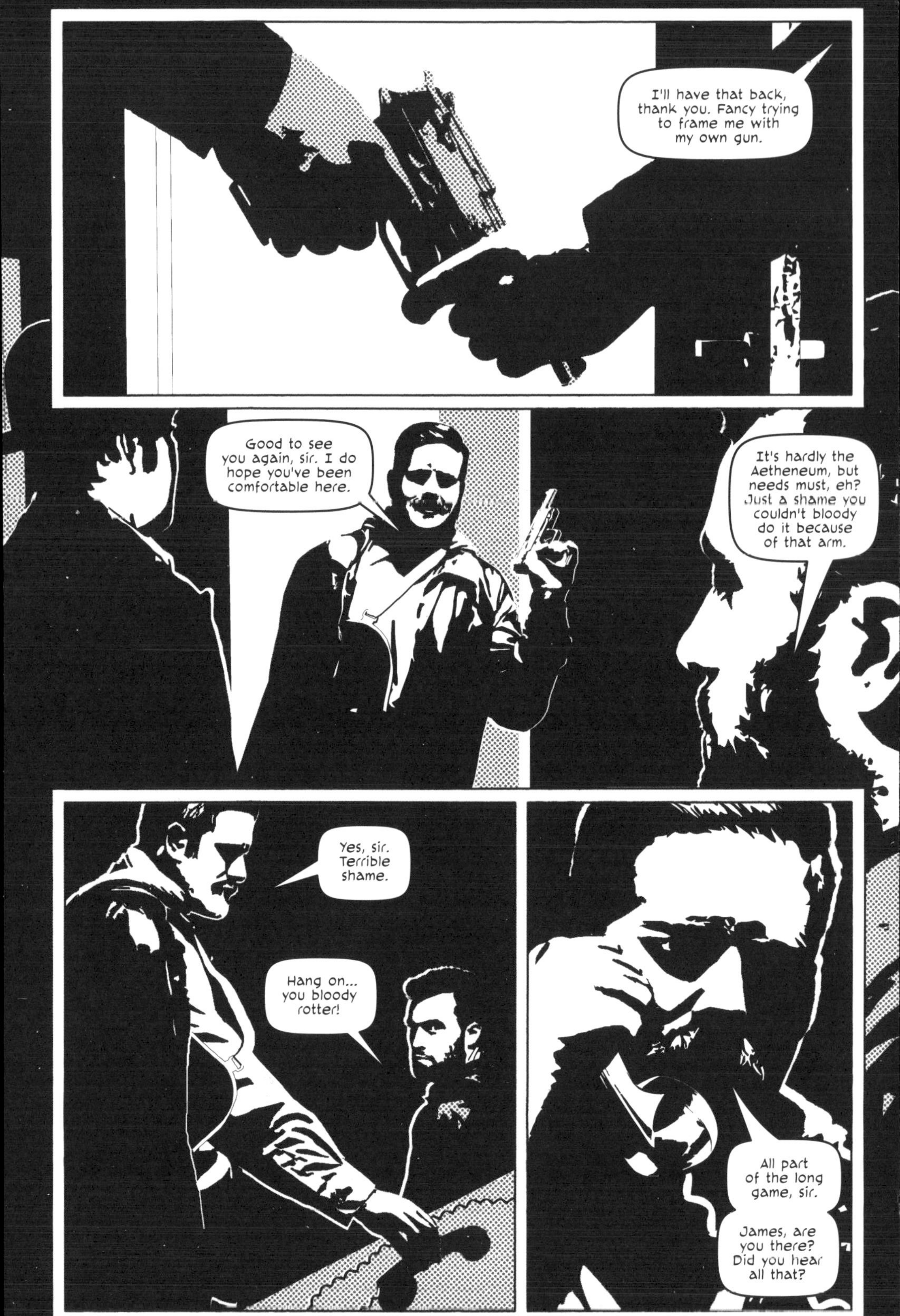
I'll have that back, thank you. Fancy trying to frame me with my own gun.
Good to see you again, sir. I do hope you've been comfortable here.
It's hardly the Aetheneum, but needs must, eh? Just a shame you couldn't bloody do it because of that arm.
Yes, sir. Terrible shame.
Hang on... you bloody rotter!
All part of the long game, sir.
James, are you there? Did you hear all that?

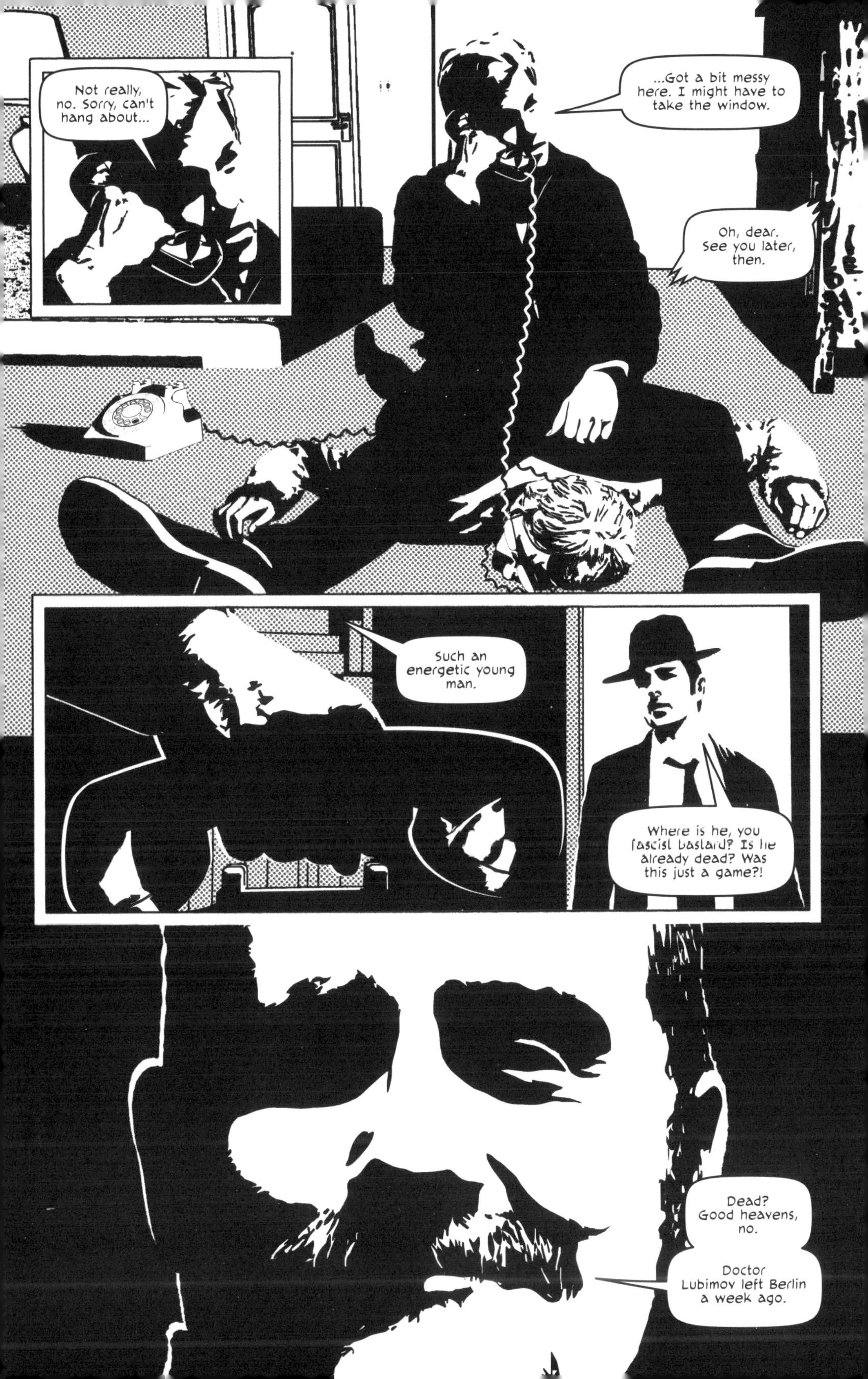
Not really, no. Sorry, can't hang about...
...Got a bit messy here. I might have to take the window.
Oh, dear. See you later, then.
Such an energetic young man.
Where is he, you fascist bastard? Is he already dead? Was this just a game?!
Dead? Good heavens, no.
Doctor Lubimov left Berlin a week ago.

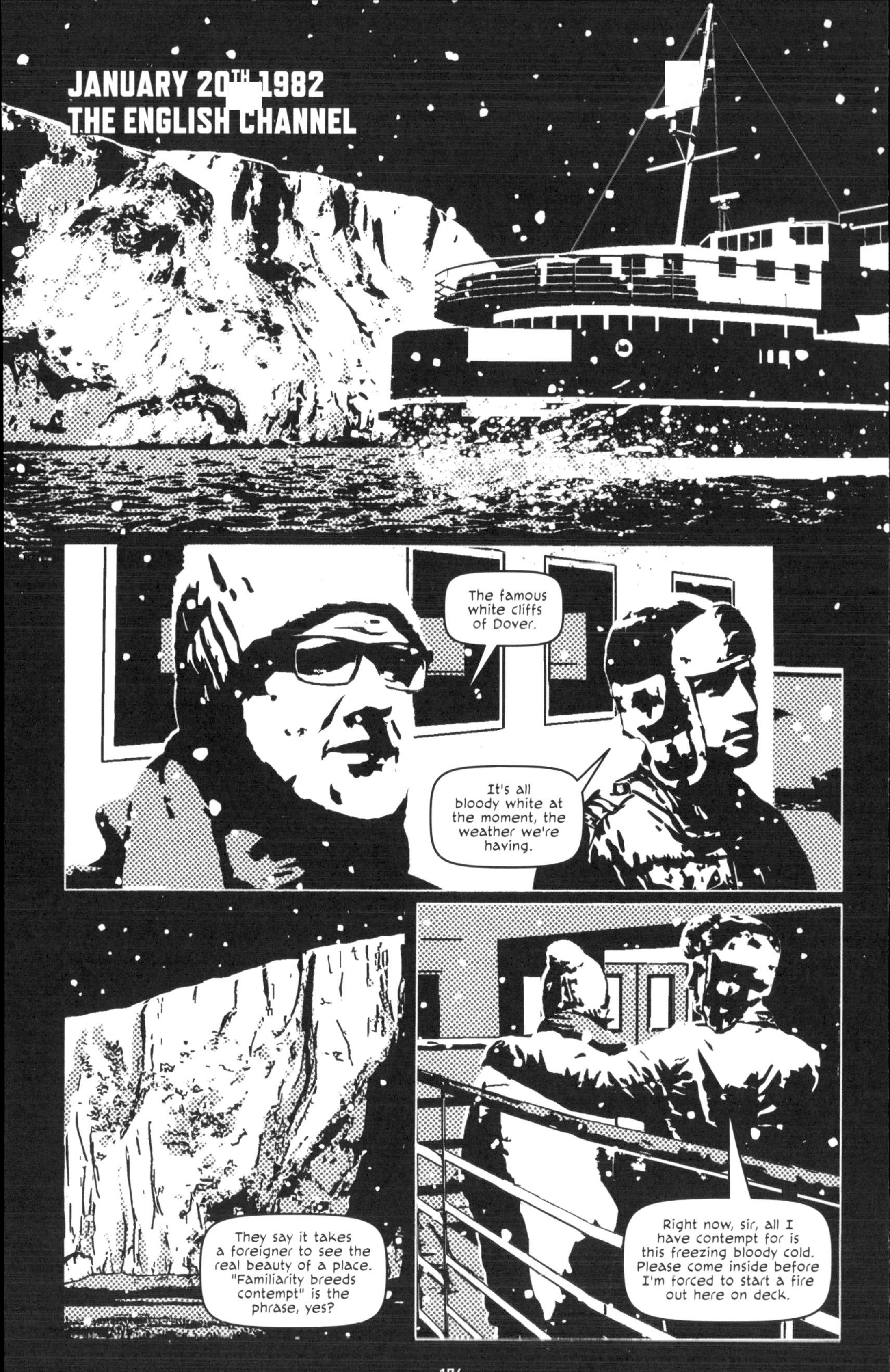
JANUARY 20TH 1982
THE ENGLISH CHANNEL
The famous white cliffs of Dover.
It's all bloody white at the moment, the weather we're having.
They say it takes a foreigner to see the real beauty of a place. "Familiarity breeds contempt" is the phrase, yes?
Right now, sir, all I have contempt for is this freezing bloody cold. Please come inside before I'm forced to start a fire out here on deck.

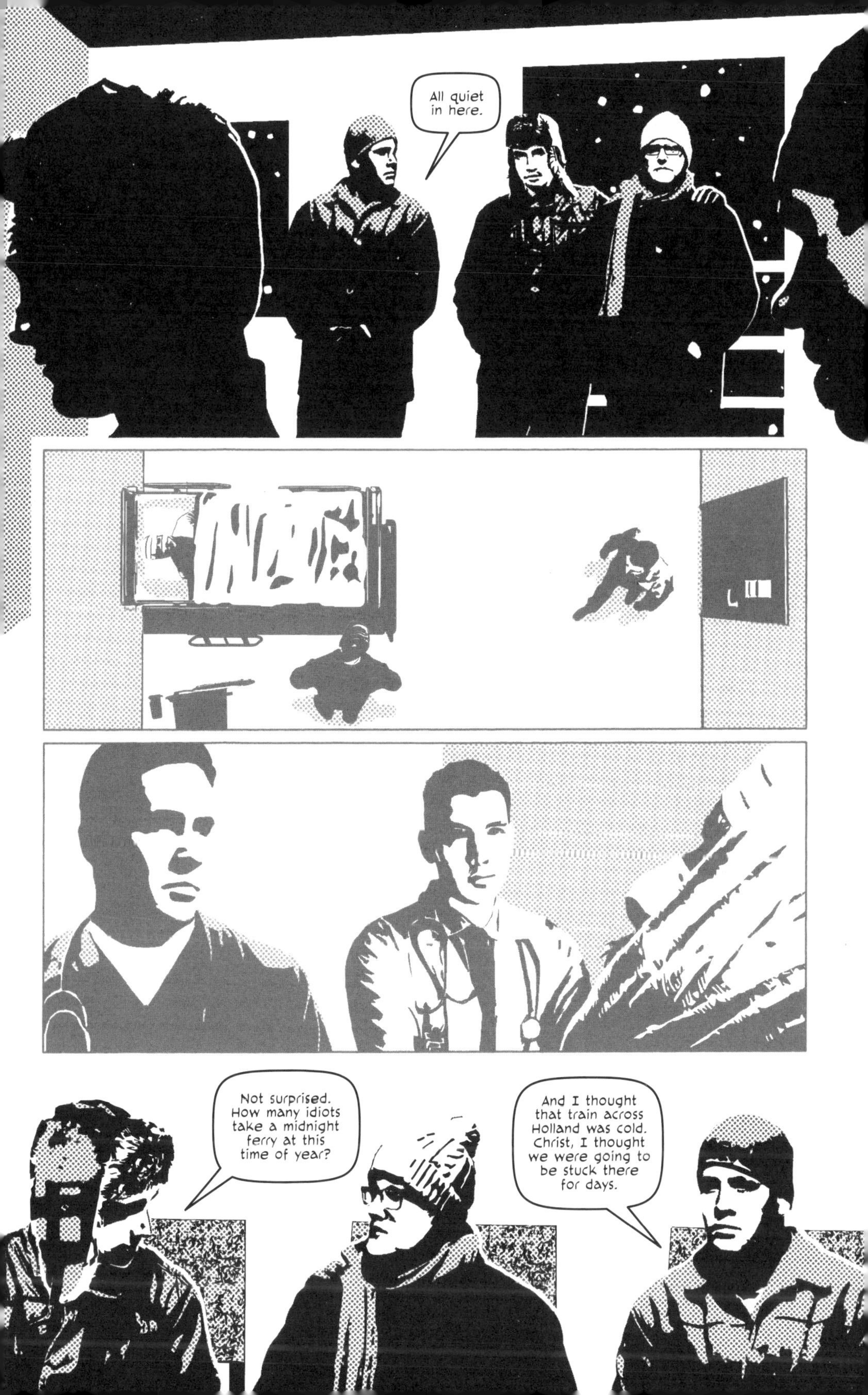
All quiet in here.
Not surprised. How many idiots take a midnight ferry at this time of year?
And I thought that train across Holland was cold. Christ, I thought we were going to be stuck there for days.

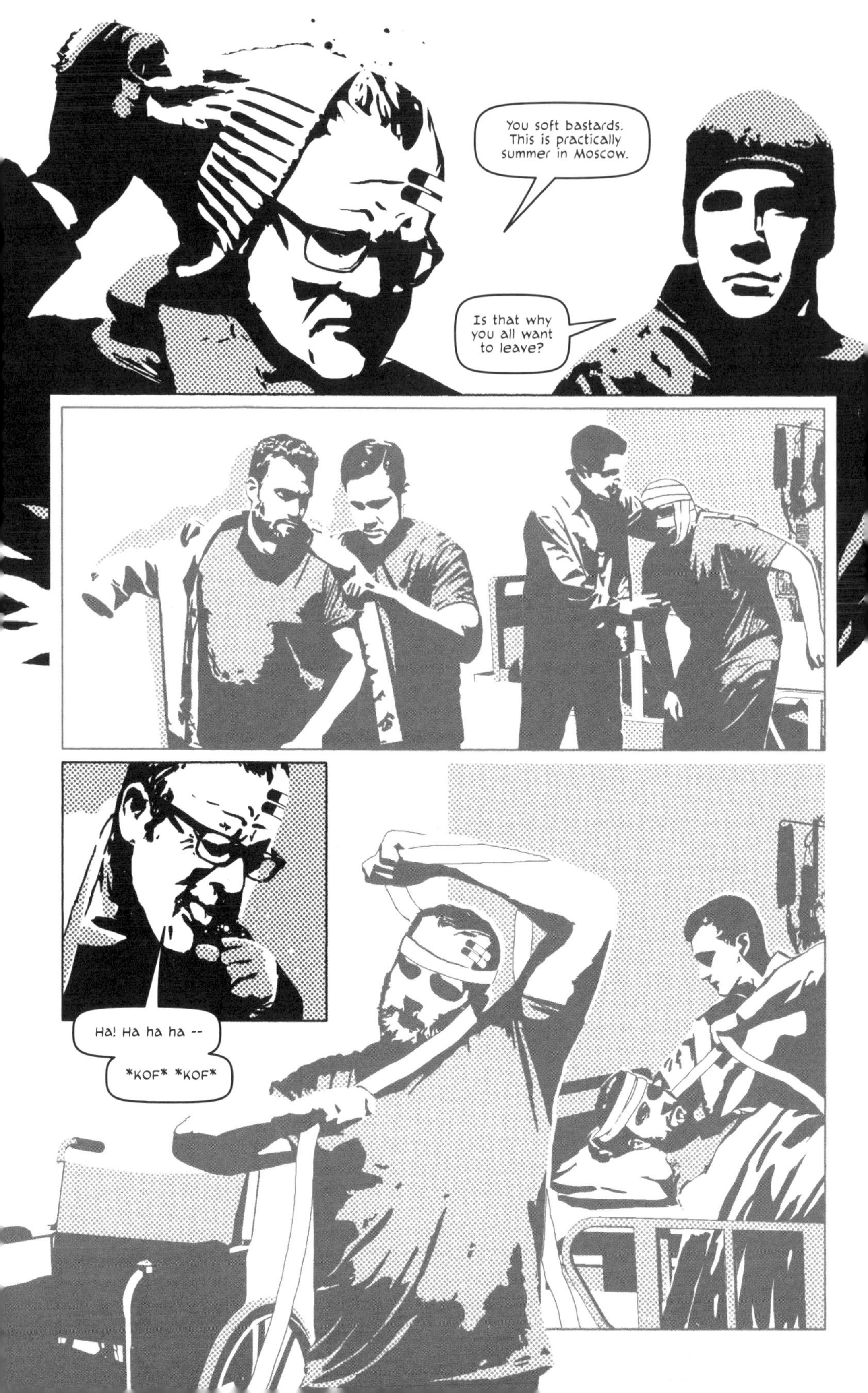
You soft bastards. This is practically summer in Moscow.
Is that why you all want to leave?
Ha! Ha ha ha --
KOF *KOF*

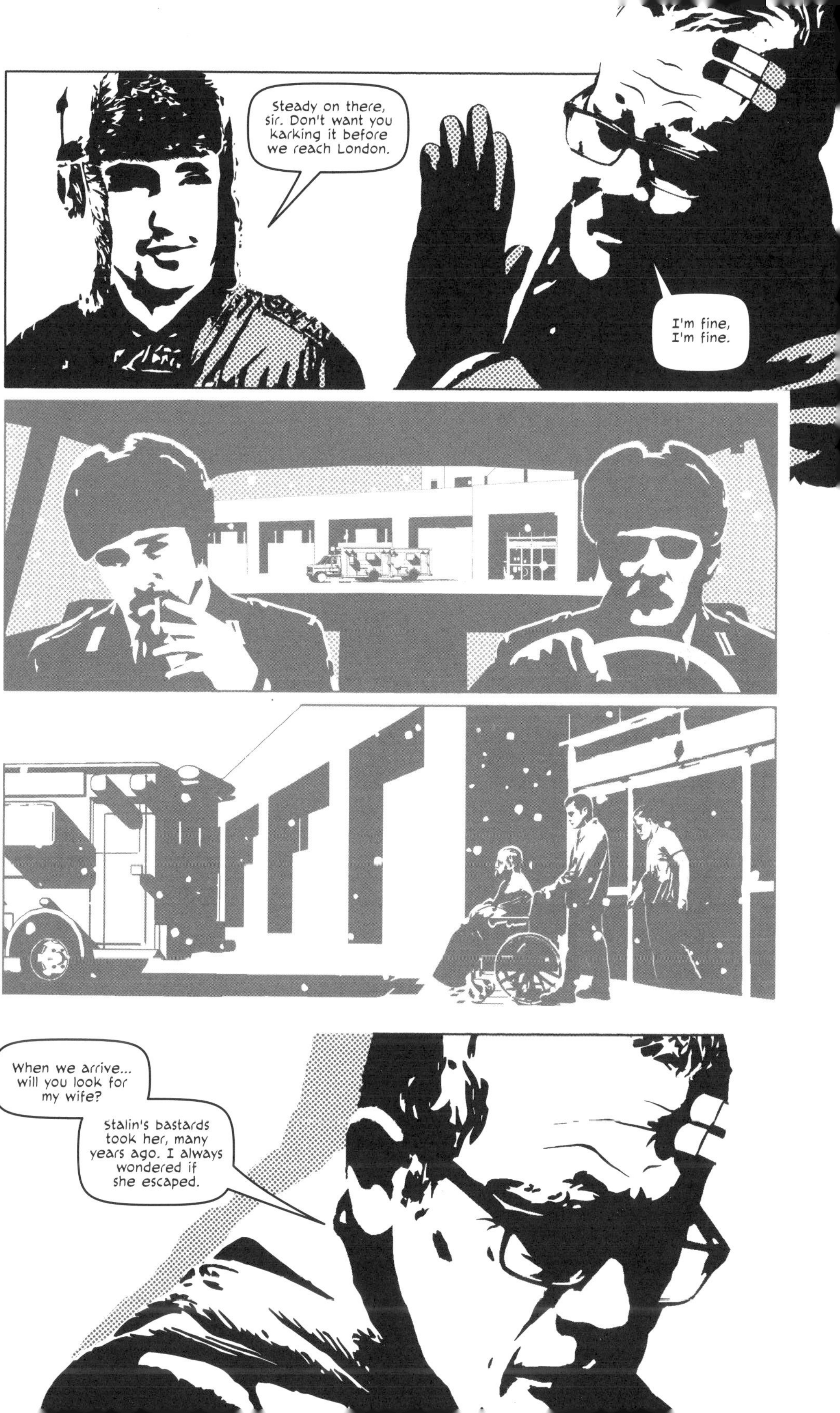
Steady on there, sir. Don't want you karking it before we reach London.
I'm fine, I'm fine.
When we arrive... will you look for my wife?
Stalin's bastards took her, many years ago. I always wondered if she escaped.

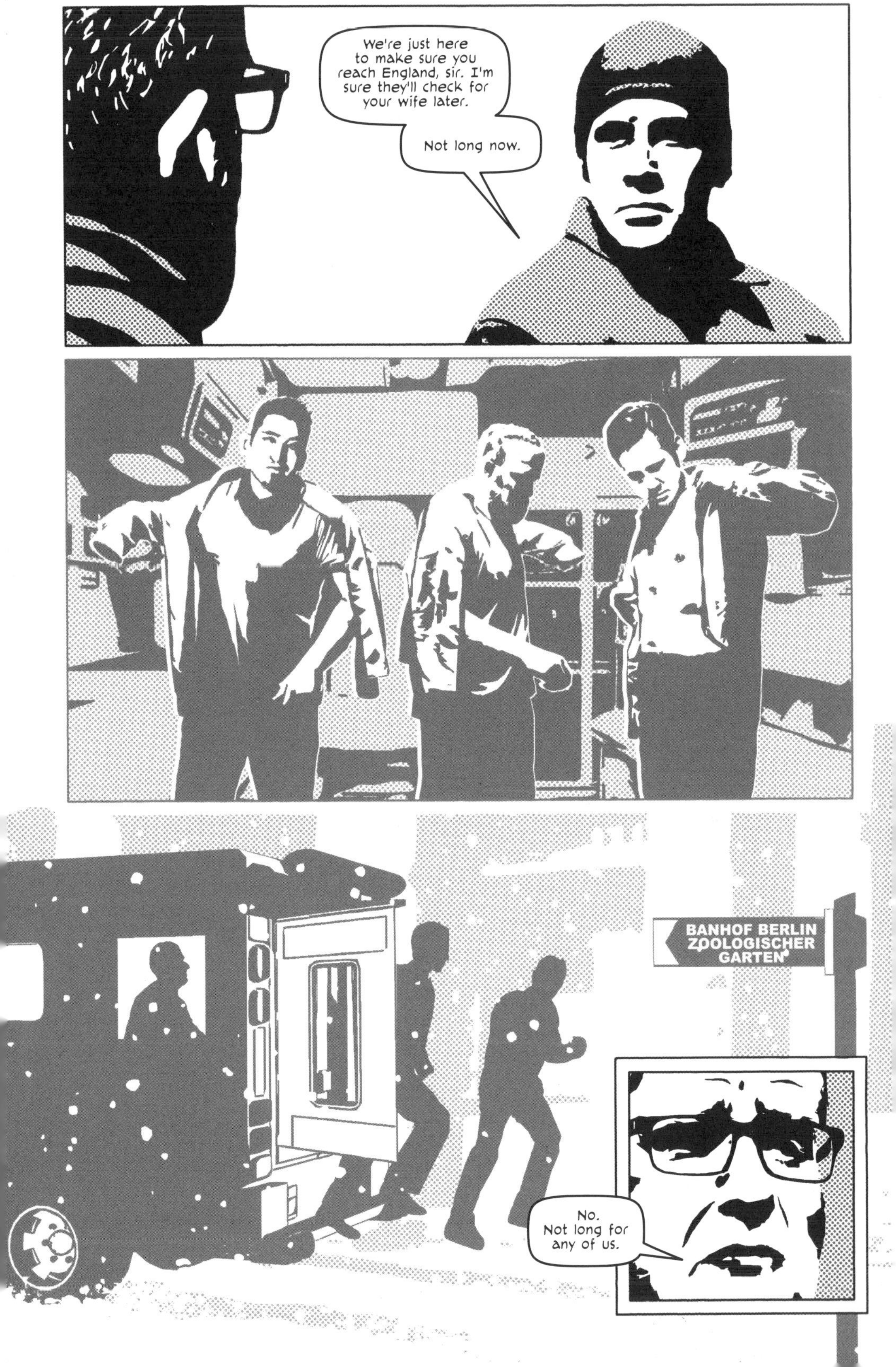

We're just here to make sure you reach England, sir. I'm sure they'll check for your wife later.
Not long now.
BANHOF BERLIN ZOOLOGISCHER GARTEN
No. Not long for any of us.

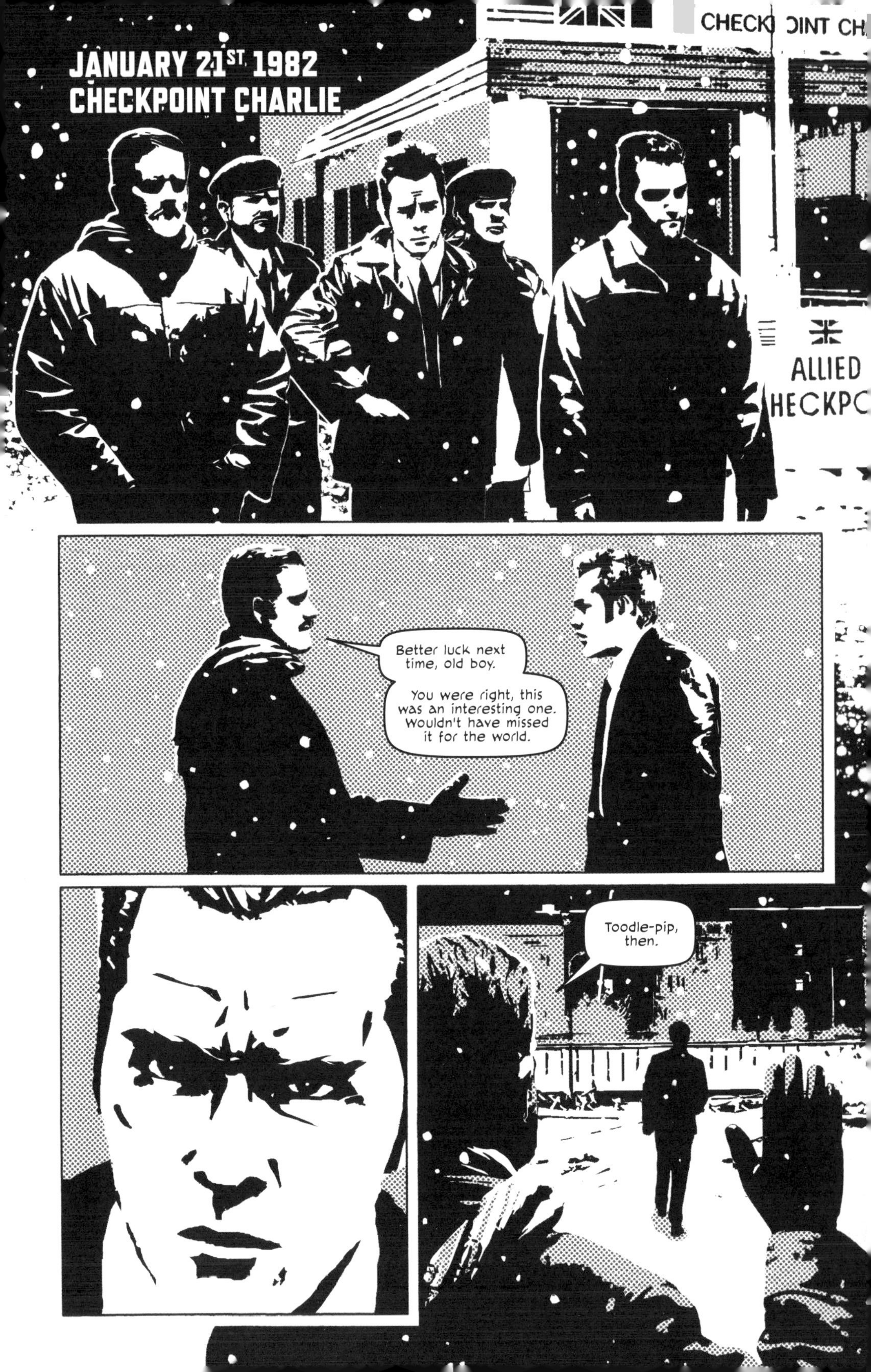

JANUARY 21ST, 1982
CHECKPOINT CHARLIE
CHECK OINT CH
ALLIED
HECKPO
Better luck next time, old boy.
You were right, this was an interesting one. Wouldn't have missed it for the world.
Toodle-pip, then.

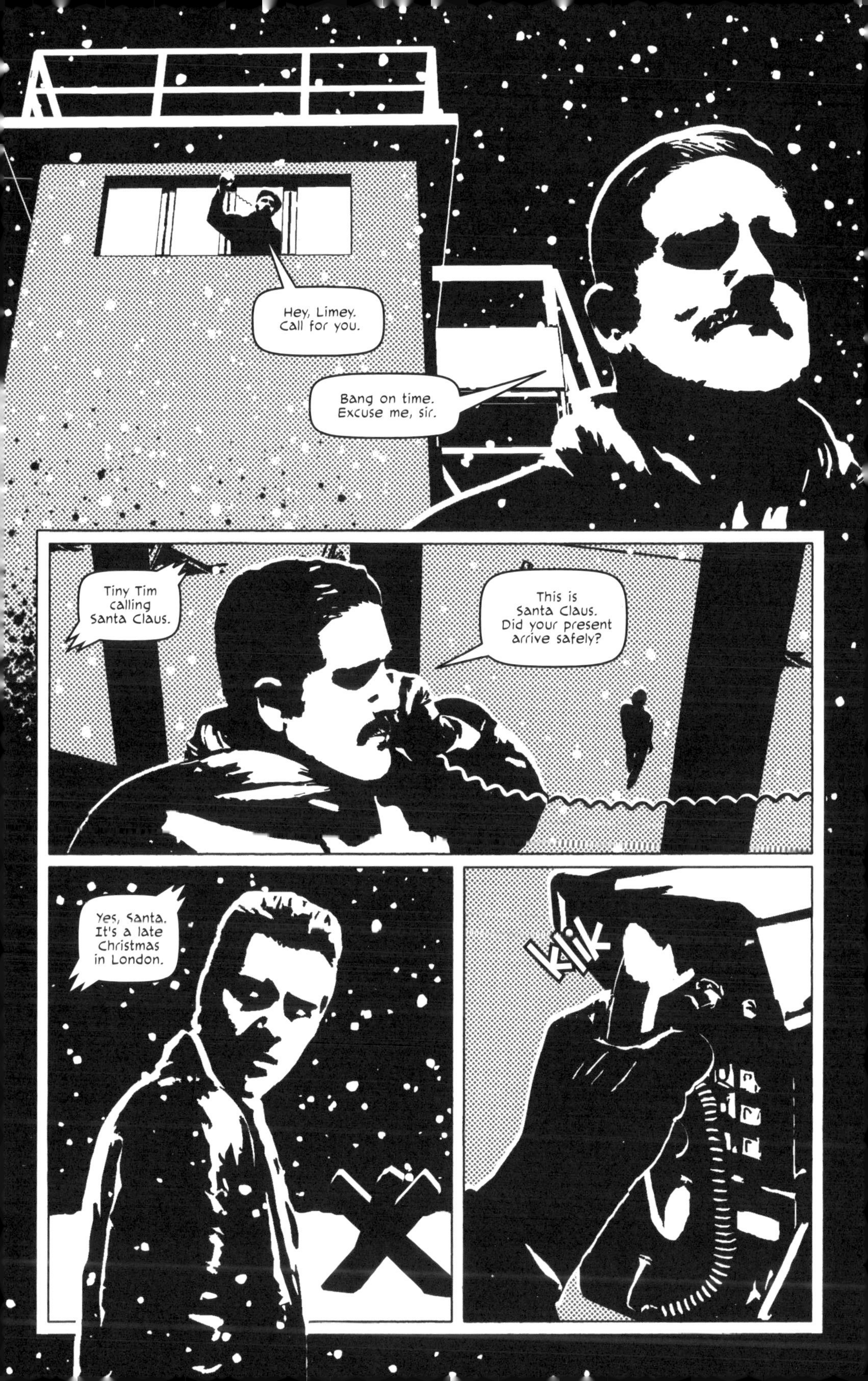
Hey, Limey.
Call for you.
Bang on time.
Excuse me, sir.
Tiny Tim
calling
Santa Claus.
This is
Santa Claus.
Did your present
arrive safely?
Yes, Santa.
It's a late
Christmas
in London.
KLIK

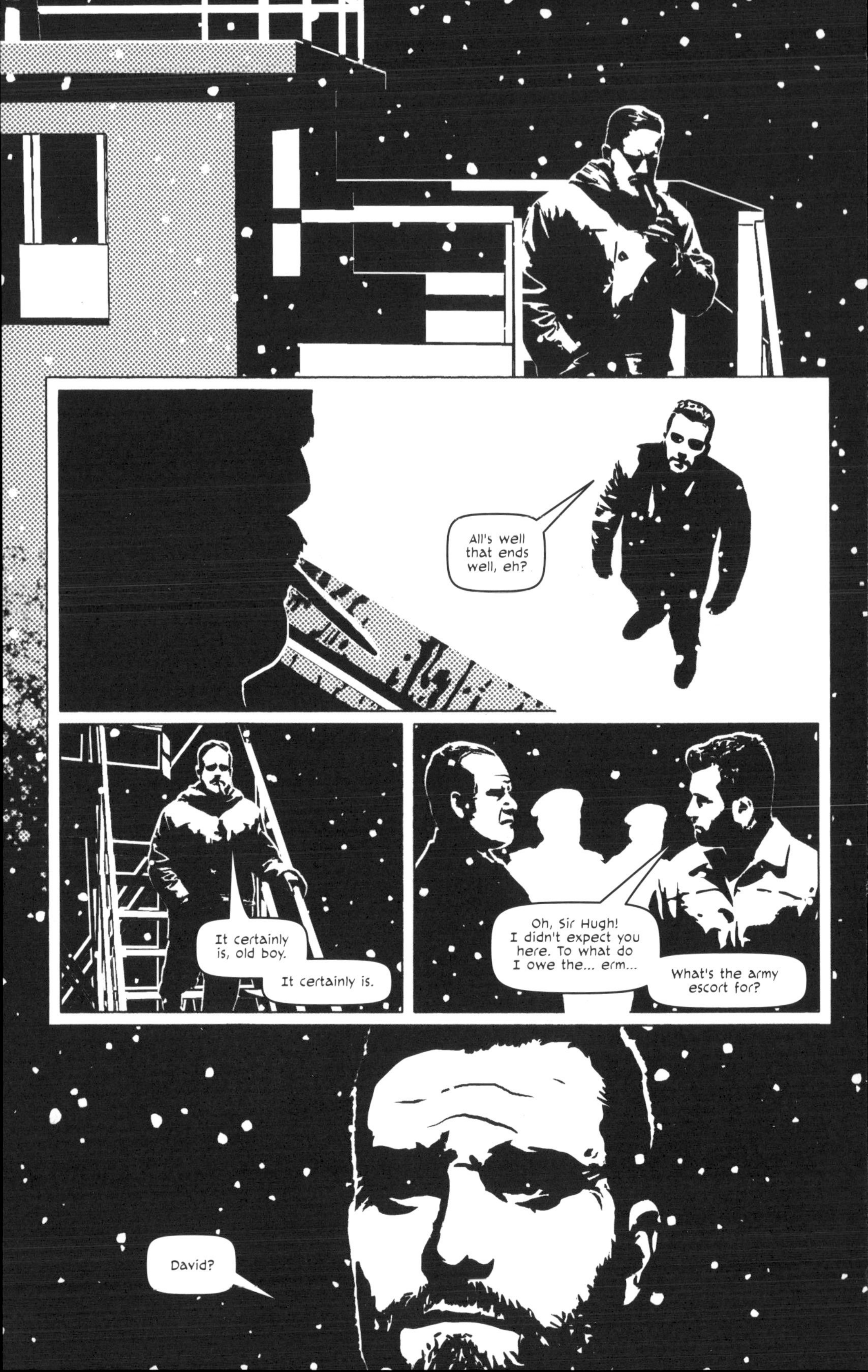
All's well that ends well, eh?
It certainly is, old boy.
It certainly is.
Oh, Sir Hugh! I didn't expect you here. To what do I owe the... erm...
What's the army escort for?
David?

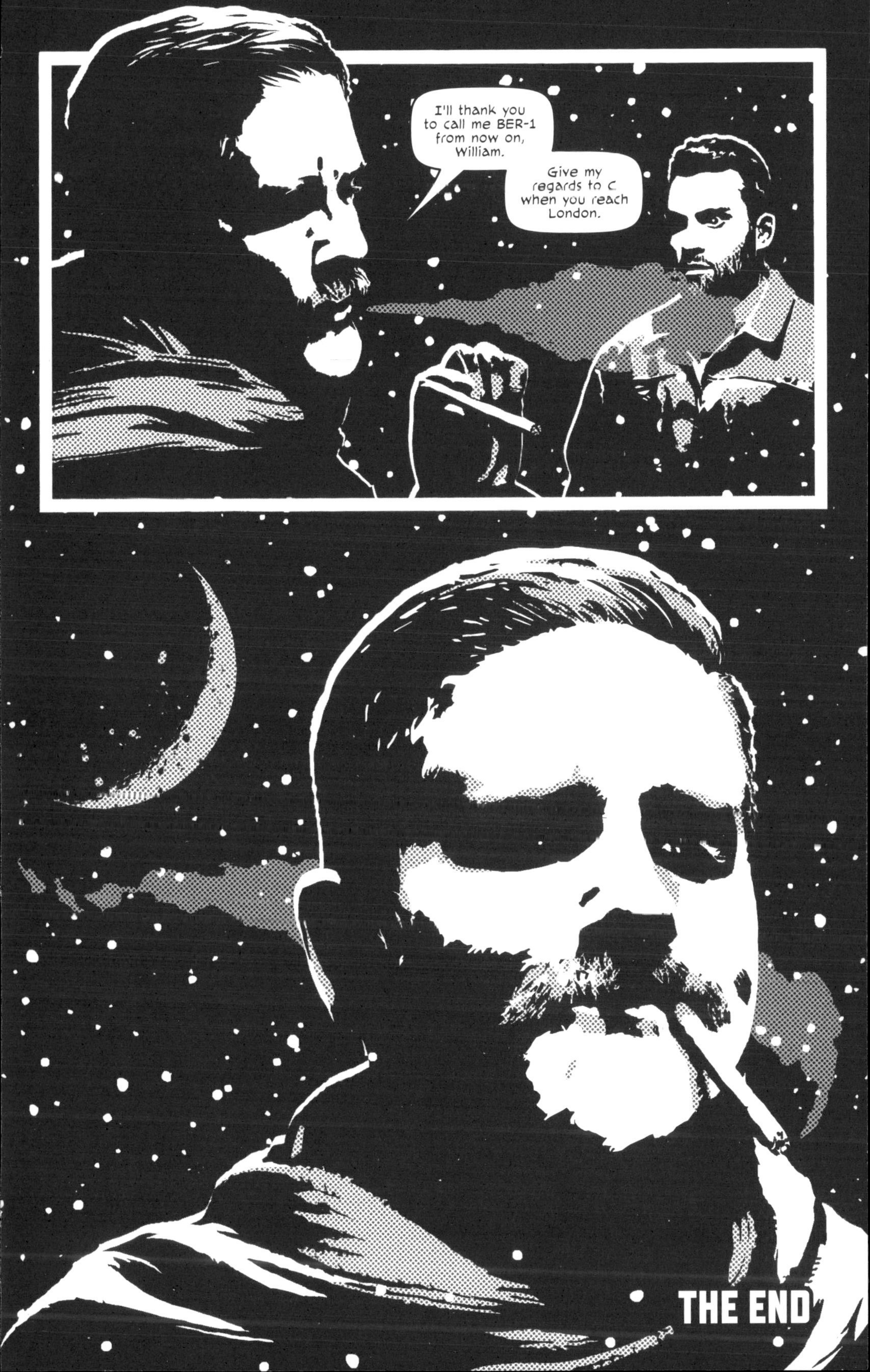
I'll thank you to call me BER-1 from now on, William.
Give my regards to C when you reach London.
THE END

WRITTEN BY

ANTONY JOHNSTON

ILLUSTRATED AND LETTERED BY

STEVEN PERKINS

THE
COLDEST
WINTER

DESIGN BY

KEITH WOOD

EDITED BY

CHARLIE CHU

THE COLDEST WINTER

BY **ANTONY JOHNSTON** & **STEVEN PERKINS**

Published by Oni Press, Inc.

PUBLISHER **JOE NOZEMACK** · EDITOR IN CHIEF **JAMES LUCAS JONES**

V.P. OF MARKETING & SALES **ANDREW MCINTIRE** · SALES MANAGER **DAVID DISSANAYAKE**

PUBLICITY COORDINATOR **RACHEL REED** · DIRECTOR OF DESIGN & PRODUCTION **TROY LOOK**

GRAPHIC DESIGNER **HILARY THOMPSON** · DIGITAL ART TECHNICIAN **JARED JONES**

MANAGING EDITOR **ARI YARWOOD** · SENIOR EDITOR **CHARLIE CHU**

EDITOR **ROBIN HERRERA** · EDITORIAL ASSISTANT **BESS PALLARES**

DIRECTOR OF LOGISTICS **BRAD ROOKS** · LOGISTICS ASSOCIATE **JUNG LEE**

ONI PRESS, INC.
1305 SE Martin Luther King Jr. Blvd.
Suite A
Portland, OR 97214
USA

onipress.com · facebook.com/onipress · twitter.com/onipress
onipress.tumblr.com · instagram.com/onipress
antonyjohnston.com · @AntonyJohnston · stevenperkinsart.com · @SPerkinsArtist

First edition: December 2016

ISBN: 978-1-62010-369-2 · eISBN: 978-1-62010-060-8
Library of Congress Control Number: 2016943123

1 3 5 7 9 10 8 6 4 2

THE COLDEST WINTER, December 2016. Published by Oni Press, Inc. 1305 SE Martin Luther King Jr. Blvd., Suite A, Portland, OR 97214. THE COLDEST WINTER is ™ & © 2016 Antony Johnston. Unless otherwise specified, all other material © 2016 Oni Press, Inc. Oni Press logo and icon are ™ & © 2016 Oni Press, Inc. All rights reserved. Oni Press logo and icon artwork created by Keith A. Wood. The events, institutions, and characters presented in this book are fictional. Any resemblance to actual persons, living or dead, is purely coincidental. No portion of this publication may be reproduced, by any means, without the express written permission of the copyright holders.

PRINTED IN CHINA

ANTONY JOHNSTON

Antony Johnston is an award-winning, *New York Times* best-selling author of graphic novels, video games and books, with titles including *The Coldest City* (now a film starring Charlize Theron), the epic series *Wasteland*, Marvel's superhero *Daredevil*, and the seminal video game *Dead Space*. He has also adapted books by bestselling novelist Anthony Horowitz, collaborated with comics legend Alan Moore, and his titles have been translated throughout the world. He lives and works in England.

antonyjohnston.com

STEVEN PERKINS

Steven Perkins has been a professional comic book artist and writer since 2001. In that time, he's worked on projects such as *Silent Hill*, *Max Payne*, *CSI: Crime Scene Investigation*, *Se7en*, and *Credence*, as well as his original graphic novel, *Pacity*. Steven currently resides in Los Angeles, not far from the beach.

You can see more of his work at *StevenPerkinsArt.com*.

NOVEMBER 1989.

MI6 spy Lorraine Broughton was sent to Berlin to investigate the death of another agent, and the disappearance of a list revealing every spy working there. She found a powderkeg of mistrust, assassinations and bad defections that ended with the murder of MI6's top officer, as the Berlin Wall was torn down.

Now Lorraine has returned from the Cold War's coldest city, to tell her story.

And nothing is what it seems.

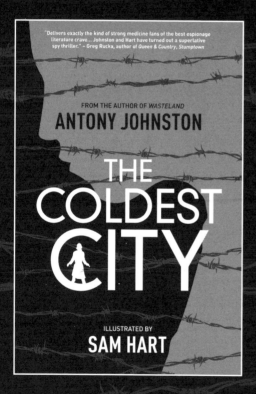

"Delivers exactly the kind of strong medicine fans of the best espionage literature crave... Johnston and Hart have turned out a superlative spy thriller." – Greg Rucka, author of *Queen & Country*, *Stumptown*

FROM THE AUTHOR OF *WASTELAND*

ANTONY JOHNSTON

THE COLDEST CITY

ILLUSTRATED BY

SAM HART

176 PAGES
HARDCOVER, BLACK AND WHITE
ISBN 978-1-934964-53-8
$19.99 US

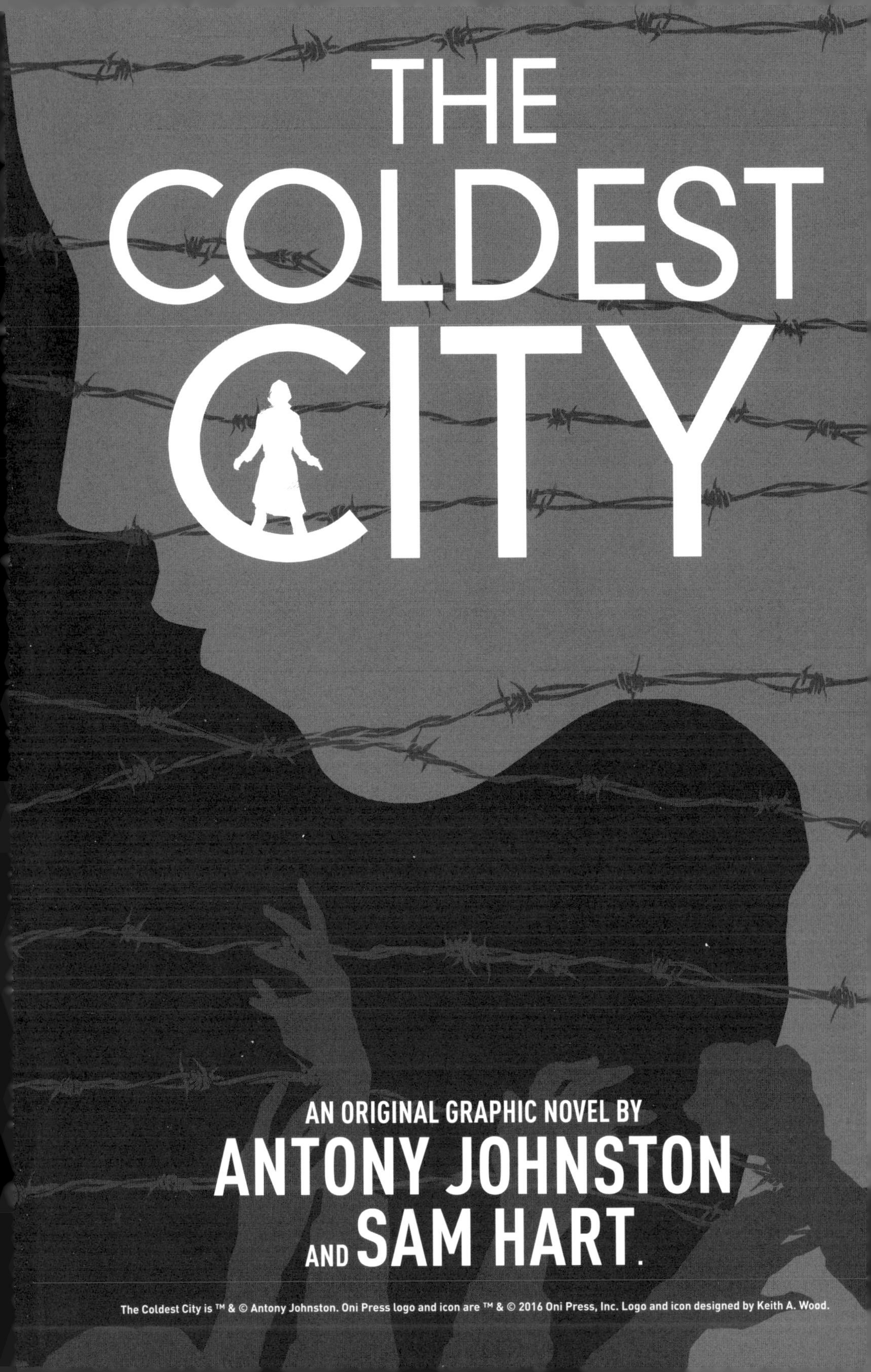
THE COLDEST CITY
AN ORIGINAL GRAPHIC NOVEL BY
ANTONY JOHNSTON
AND SAM HART.

OTHER BOOKS BY ONI PRESS!

HEARTTHROB
VOLUME 1: NEVER GOING BACK AGAIN
By Christopher Sebela, Robert Wilson IV, and Nick Filardi
136 pages · softcover · color
$9.99 US · ISBN 978-1-62010-338-8

QUEEN & COUNTRY
DEFINITIVE EDITION, VOLUME 1
By Greg Rucka, Steve Rolston, Brian Hurtt &
Leandro Fernandez
376 pages · sofcover · black and white
$19.99 US · ISBN 978-1-932664-87-4

PETROGRAD
By Philip Gelatt & Tyler Crook
264 pages · hardcover · 2 color
$29.99 US · ISBN 978-1-934964-44-6

GUERILLAS
VOLUME 1
By Brahm Revel
168 pages · sofcover · black and white
$14.99 US · ISBN 978-1-934964-43-9

For more information on these and other fine Oni Press comic books and graphic novels, visit www.onipress.com.

To find a comic specialty store in your area, call 1-888-COMICBOOK or visit www.comicshops.us.